The Romantic Generation

Based on the Charles Eliot Norton Lectures

The Romantic Generation

CHARLES
ROSEN

Harvard University Press
Cambridge, Massachusetts

Publication of this book has been supported
through the generous provisions of the
Maurice and Lula Bradley Smith Memorial Fund

First Harvard University Press paperback edition, 1998

Designed by Gwen Frankfeldt

Library of Congress Cataloging-in-Publication Data

Rosen, Charles, 1927–
The romantic generation / Charles Rosen.
p.   cm.
"Based on the Charles Eliot Norton Lectures"—Half title.
Includes index.
ISBN 0-674-77933-9 (cloth)
ISBN 0-674-77934-7 (pbk.)
1. Romanticism in music.
2. Music—19th century—History and criticism.
I. Title.
ML 196.R67   1995
780′.9′034—dc20   94-46239
CIP
MN

To Henri Zerner

Contents

Preface

It is equally fatal to have a system and not to
have a system. One must try to combine them.

—Friedrich Schlegel, *Athenaeum Fragments*

The death of Beethoven in 1827 must have given a sense of freedom to the composers born almost two decades earlier: Chopin and Schumann in 1810, Mendelssohn the year before, Liszt the year after. Perhaps only Chopin was not intimidated by the commanding figure of authority that Beethoven represented for generations to come. I think it is probable that Beethoven's death hastened the rapid development of new stylistic tendencies which had already made themselves felt and which, indeed, even influenced his own music.

The death of Chopin in 1849 was not so signal an event for the world of music, but it, too, marked the end of an age. Schumann was to die only a few years later, after entering an insane asylum; in the 1850s Liszt renounced much of his adventurous early manner, pruned his youthful works of their excesses, and developed new directions of style, many of which would be realized only after his death by musicians who took no account of his experiments. In 1850 the young Brahms arrived upon the scene, and it was clear that there was a new and more conservative musical philosophy in the air.

In these writings on music from the death of Beethoven to the death of Chopin, I have limited myself to those composers whose characteristic styles were defined in the late 1820s and early 1830s, a compact group in spite of widely differing musical ideals and the evident mutual hostility frequently met with among them. Slightly older than the composers born around 1810, Berlioz nevertheless belongs essentially with them. In addition, a consideration of Bellini and (more briefly) Meyerbeer is inescapable for an understanding of the period.

On the other hand, Verdi and Wagner are absent, as their stylistic individuality was fully shaped only in the 1840s; their greatest achievements belong with the next generation. A minor figure like Alkan is omitted for the same reason; he became interesting essentially after 1850 by his extension of the Liszt tradition and the way he opened up piano music to the operatic effects of Meyerbeer. Hummel continued to write in the early 1830s, and Rossini for several decades beyond, but they were both, along with Beethoven, the immediate musical ancestors of the composers born around 1810.

This book originated as the Charles Eliot Norton lectures, given in 1980–81, and has been expanded at the request of Harvard University Press—although both the Press and I were somewhat taken aback at the magnitude of the expansion. I found it harder than I had expected to make some of the points both clear and convincing, and I apologize if I have tried the reader's patience. The position of Chopin, in particular, has been traditionally surrounded with prejudice and misunderstanding which are only beginning to be cleared up in our time. I do not try to provide a complete picture of the period from 1827 to 1850, but only of those aspects of the music that most interested me—or, rather, about which I thought I had something interesting to say—and the project was more complex than I had at first envisaged. It was not so much that, as William Empson has somewhere remarked, the boring thing about criticism is that you have to put in all the obvious things or people will think "He didn't even see *that*"; rather that the music of the 1830s was explicitly entangled with art, literature, politics, and personal life in ways that were less straightforward, more ambivalent than the music of the decades just preceding. The claim of artistic autonomy that was made for music, rightly or wrongly, by the late eighteenth century, was neither really upheld nor abandoned by the following generations: rather, an attempt was made to incorporate some of the artist's own life and experience into the claim of autonomy, to transform part of the artist's world into an independent aesthetic object.

In Chapters 2 and 3 I have tried to give an account of the place of music within two important literary traditions: the fragment as an artistic form, and the new feeling for Nature and landscape. The development of "characteristic" music and of the Romantic *Lied,* among the most remarkable creations of the period, are bound up with the poetry and the scientific literature of the time and of the immediately preceding age. I have presented what amounts to a selected anthology of texts to illustrate the discussion, and hope that they will be of more help for an understanding than any more extensive explanation— and more entertaining. It will be obvious that, even if the relevance of the texts to the subject was my main concern, I have above all chosen ones that I enjoyed, and of course I hope the reader will enjoy them as well.

In the fourth chapter, two of the most basic technical changes in the musical language of the time are discussed briefly but with enough illustrations to allow us to see how they functioned: the use of mediant relationships, and the four-bar phrase. Most of these illustrations, as well as those in the rest of the book, I enjoy playing, listening to, and thinking about. I am more concerned here to explain the continued survival of some of the music of the time than to resurrect those works which can be performed today only as historical curiosities. If I have written nothing about figures like Stephen Heller, Sigismond Thalberg, Ignaz Moscheles, and others, that is not beause I do not sometimes enjoy hearing their works but because I have nothing to say about them that has not been better said by others. This is also true about more ponderable figures like Donizetti, Auber, and Marschner. Nevertheless, resurrection is an important aspect of historical criticism, and only works if the revival is a practical success. It should be obvious, however, that very little of Chopin is in urgent need of revival; and with Schumann, Liszt, and Berlioz, an esoteric concentration on the less frequently performed pieces is actually a disservice to them. There are, however, many little-known works for which I should like to be a passionate advocate: Liszt's *Die Lorelei,* Bellini's *Beatrice di Tenda,* and Schumann's Canons for Pedal Piano, to name only a few.

There is no attempt here to revive those few women composers whose work remained almost completely repressed during this time. To do so would be, I think, a distortion of the real tragedy of the creative female musician in the nineteenth century. It is misleading to emphasize the claim that there were women composers whose considerable achievements were pushed aside and went unrecognized; the fate of the greater talents—Clara Schumann, for example—was even more cruel: they were never, in fact, allowed to develop to the point where they could have taken a justified pride in work that was unheard, invisible—even that was denied them. They were harshly excluded from history, and attempting to bring them uncritically and naively back into it neither does them posthumous justice nor acknowledges the difficult reality of their lives.

The music of Schumann, Chopin, and Liszt is still the center of almost every pianist's activity, and a listing of all the books I have read on these composers and their world and all the conversations I have had about them would be impossible, and not very useful to anybody even if I could remember—although I should cite André Monglond's *Le Préromantisme* (Paris, 1930) as an important source for some of the literature discussed in Chapter 3. Some parts of these lectures date back many years: the one on the Romantic Fragment, for example, was given, in somewhat similar form, at Wesleyan University more than thirty years ago, and many of the ideas appeared in talks that I gave at the Gauss Seminars at Princeton, and in the Messenger Lectures at Cornell. I have not tried to incorporate any of the interesting research and criticism on the period that have come out since the lectures were given and to make this book even longer by further discussion. I hope to have paid my major debts by acknowledging help received, but I have preferred to avoid polemic and not always indicated whatever disagreements I might have had with other critics.

The manuscript of this book was substantially in its final form by February of 1991, and the only major revision has been to expand the section on Bellini and to add a more decisive conclusion to the final chapter. In the past few years, however, Chopin scholarship has taken a turn for the better with Nicholas Temperley's article in *The New Grove* and the work of Jim Samson and Jeffrey Kallberg. The latter's essays on the genres of the Prelude and the Nocturne concerned what I had written so closely that I have been forced to add a few pages that take account of the important considerations that he raised, but I have not tried to bring my own text up-to-date in any other important respect. I should like, however, to mention here the excellent volume of 1992 edited by Jim Samson, in which Kallberg's essay appeared and in which the essay by Simon Finlow, "The Twenty-Seven Etudes and Their Antecedents," manages to give Chopin's originality its due while pointing out his debt to previous work; John Rink's essay, too, on tonal architecture in Chopin's early music gives the best study of an aspect of Chopin that needed consideration. In addition, in *Nineteenth-Century Piano Music,* edited by R. Larry Todd (New York, 1990), I have recently come across a brilliant discussion of Schumann's piano music with the most cogent account of the late period by Anthony Newcomb, which, to my regret, I read too late to use here. I am sure that I have been influenced by the admirable writings of Edward T. Cone on Berlioz and other composers, some of which I read many years ago, but I can no longer remember what I have taken from him and what I thought up on my own, just as it would be pointless to try and disentangle my own thinking from my debts to Hermann Abert, Donald Francis Tovey, and Heinrich Schenker. Any plagiarism has been inadvertent; in any case I have always been flattered on the rare occasions when someone has taken something from me without acknowledgment: plagiarism is the sincerest form of flattery.

I owe a great deal to the help of friends and colleagues. Philip Gossett's counsel on Italian opera was invaluable, and Jeffrey Kallberg saved me from several mistakes concerning Chopin; I am deeply grateful for their generosity in reading long parts of my manuscript. Kristina Muxfeldt and David Gable were also generous with aid on both general and specific problems. Richard Cohn was very helpful indeed with Chapter 4. Reinhold Brinkmann kindly made available some fascinating research on Schumann's *Lieder.* Joseph Kerman gave me excellent advice and encouragement many years ago at Oxford on the subject of the fragment as Romantic form. The idiosyncrasy of Chopin's ornamentation in the early B Major Nocturne was shown to me some years ago by Pierre Boulez, and when I was sixteen years old Moriz Rosenthal pointed out that the first tonic chord in root position in the Schumann C Major Phantasie is found on the last page of the first movement just before the quotation from Beethoven's *An die ferne Geliebte* (for this reason I have paid no attention to recent speculation that Hermann Abert was the first to notice the quotation, as Rosenthal learned of it from Liszt—it would have been astonishing if Liszt had not remarked on it).

Piero Weiss and Bruno Lassuto have generously made available their copies of original editions of Schumann, and Marta Gràbòcz helped me to obtain a photograph of the manuscript of Schumann's Phantasie from the library at Budapest. (It contains the original ending of the last movement discovered by Alan Walker.) Walter Frisch made it possible for me get a photograph of the London edition of Chopin's Sonata in B flat Minor, and discussing the subject of this book with him was very helpful; I am grateful to the library of Columbia University for the possibility of reproducing some pages of this edition. The staff of the rare book room at the Regenstein Library of the University of Chicago was wonderfully helpful in allowing me to use their superb collection of Chopin first editions, and I have reproduced many pages here for the illustrations. I want to thank Richard Blocker for preparing the example of the opening of the love music from Berlioz's *Roméo et Juliette*. I should like to be able to give a more detailed account of all the help I have received from many friends and colleagues over the years, and the conversations and advice that have contributed to this book. Finally, I must express my appreciation of the kindness and patience of Kate Schmit and Margaretta Fulton of Harvard University Press.

Note on the musical illustrations

For Chopin and Schumann, I have used with few exceptions the editions published during their lifetimes (I have not been able to find reproducible copies of the original editions of Chopin's second scherzo and of two or three of the mazurkas, and have reproduced a few pages from the Breitkopf & Härtel nineteenth-century critical edition). The original editions are not entirely accurate, of course, but at least the mistakes are due to the inadvertence and incompetence of the engravers and the carelessness of the proofreaders (including the composers) rather than to the systematic interference of editors.

For many composers—Mozart, Beethoven, Brahms—satisfactory editions are available for modern performers. For Schumann and Chopin, however, almost all twentieth-century editions are badly flawed. Chopin had most of his works published simultaneously in Paris, Leipzig, and London; in some cases slightly different versions were sent to each publishing house. The principle that the last decision of the composer is the definitive one is not helpful here: the variations of phrasing, pedal indications, dynamics, and even notes show that the text was something much more fluid for Chopin than for Beethoven. The old nineteenth-century critical edition has some volumes well edited by Brahms (the Sonatas, Mazurkas, and Ballades), largely representing the text printed in Leipzig and the manuscripts sent to Germany. The various editions of Chopin's students, like Mikuli, however, may be an invaluable testimony to contemporary interpretation, but they deliberately introduce articulations of phrasing that Chopin went to great pains to eliminate, leave out accents and other dynamic indications that the editors felt to be troublesome, and freely alter pedal indications and even the pitches. In the twentieth century, the most important publication was the so-called Paderewski edition, and its deficiencies and inaccuracies were an international scandal: it also contained a good deal of textual information in the bibliographical notes, not all of it trustworthy. A new and much better edition was started in Poland under the direction of Jan Ekier, but very few volumes have so far been issued: a promise of a translation of the textual notes was made, but so far these have appeared only in Polish. The volumes published by Henle are still governed by the illusion that there is a definitive version of a work by Chopin and that all the variants can be consigned to the textual notes. Perhaps impatient with the slowness of his new Polish critical edition, Ekier has published a few excellent volumes for Universal, above all the Nocturnes. Relations among the various editions published by Chopin himself are very complex and are rendered even more difficult by the annotations that Chopin made for his pupils, many of these representing important and valuable changes. I do not myself command any great understanding of the full details of these relations, and have chosen my illustrations for their readability and availability, confident only that the original copies would supply a relative degree of authenticity. (I have given indications of provenance only when these were pertinent to my argument. I do not claim that the illustrations are absolutely authoritative, and providing all the bibliographical information would have been interesting only to a very few scholars: I apologize to them, but they will have to go back to the original copies anyway for any further study.)

The editing of Schumann, particularly the piano music, is both better and worse: most of it was written before the composer was twenty-nine, and he himself revised several of the early works twelve or more years later, when he was clearly out of sympathy with his youthful audacity. The superiority of the earlier versions is often at least tacitly acknowledged: the first phrase of the *Davidsbündlertänze,* for example, is so much worse in the second edition that I have never heard any pianist except Walter Gieseking play it in that form. Clara Schumann edited the first complete edition of her husband's works and sometimes printed successive versions separately. Unfortunately, in many cases she did not follow the advice given her by Johannes Brahms and reproduce the original versions with no change; in the second piece of the *Kreisleriana,* for example, she printed the second version with the dynamic indications of the first. Nevertheless, her edition is still the best one generally available, and her changes are an important witness to contemporary performance and have, naturally, a certain authority as well. The selection of the piano music edited by Wolfgang Boetticher for Henle gives important information and corrects many minor points but is one of the worst editions: Boetticher systematically prefers the later and inferior versions and incompletely and inaccurately gives the variants of the early ones (there is no point, for example, in telling pianists that there is a ritenuto in one bar with no further precision when there are eight slow beats to the bar and the ritenuto is on the seventh beat). For these reasons, the original editions, even with the occasional misprint, remain the most satisfactory sources. When I have not been able to find a good copy, I have used Clara Schumann's edition, particularly for the Impromptus on her own theme, where she has edited the early and late versions separately.

The most important piano works of Franz Liszt were edited with great fidelity to the original notation early in this century by the so-called Liszt-Stiftung edition, supervised by Ferruccio Busoni and printed by Breitkopf & Härtel. Although incomplete, this edition reproduces Liszt's text with less interference than the new critical edition now being produced in Budapest. Unfortunately, the Liszt-Stiftung ceased publication before the opera fantasies and Liszt's arrangements of songs by Schubert, Chopin, and himself appeared, and I have had to use other sources for the illustrations of these works. The *Réminiscences de Don Juan* was scrupulously edited by Busoni, who placed his considerably rewritten version in larger print underneath Liszt's original (I compared it with the two autograph manuscripts at the New York Public Library, and found it accurate).

Quotations from the "Scéne d'amour" in Berlioz's *Roméo et Juliette* come from the piano score authorized by the composer.

Preparatory versions of some of the following pages were printed in *Nineteenth-Century Music* (Summer, 1990); in *The Piano,* edited by Dominic Gill (Oxford, 1983); and in book reviews in *The New York Review of Books* (12 August, 1983; 12 April, 1984; 26 April, 1984; 6 November, 1986; and 28 May, 1987). All have been considerably altered and revised.

The Romantic Generation

CHAPTER ONE

Music and Sound

Imagining the sound

Inaudible music may seem an odd notion, even a foolishly Romantic one—although it is partly the Romantic prejudice in favor of sensuous experience that makes it seem odd. Still, there are details of music which cannot be heard but only imagined, and even certain aspects of musical form which cannot be realized in sound even by the imagination.

We put our aural imagination to work as a matter of course every time we listen to music. We purify the music by subtracting what is irrelevant from the undigested mass of sound that reaches our ears—the creaking chairs of the concert hall, the occasional cough, the traffic noise from outside; we instinctively correct the tuning, substitute the right pitches for the wrong ones, and erase from our musical perception the scratchy sound of the violin bow; we learn in just a few minutes to filter out some of the obtrusive resonance of the cathedral which interferes with the clarity of the voice leading. Listening to music, like understanding language, is not a passive state but an everyday act of creative imagination so commonplace that its mechanism is taken for granted. We separate the music from the sound.

We also add to the sound whatever is necessary for musical significance. During every performance we continually delude ourselves into thinking we have heard things which cannot have reached our ears. At the climax of the final movement of the Sonata in C Minor, op. 111, by Beethoven, most pianists take (correctly, I think) so slow a tempo that the culminating B♭ has died away long before it is resolved, but that makes no difference—we all hear the B♭ as continuing to sound and take no note of its actual disappearance:

On one of Beethoven's pianos the B♭ decays very quickly, and even on a modern concert grand it has diminished to inaudibility before its resolution to an A♮. There are, in fact, no dampers on a piano for notes in so high a register, and holding the key down will not allow the sound to last any longer. It would make no difference on either an early nineteenth-century piano or a modern one if the B♭ were written and played as a short sixteenth note with rests instead of the tied long notes that Beethoven wrote:

but this notation, which corresponds to the physical and acoustical facts, would make no musical sense. We hear the B♭ as lasting for two reasons: it is the end of a series of long notes, most of them sustained by trills—the third beat of each bar, indeed, sustained twice as long as the others; more important, the F in the bass turns the B♭ into a dissonance which requires the resolution into the A♮, and we (not the instrument) make the link between the notes and sustain the B♭ until the release of tension. We create the necessary continuity that does not actually take place—or, rather, the expressive force of the music causes us to imagine as actually existing what is only implied.

To a certain extent, this hearing of the inaudible is a part of the more general phenomenon of listening to the piano: we ignore the decay of sound except when it is exploited by the composer. On the piano a note decays immediately after the impact of the hammer on the string, reaches a lower plateau of sound, and then starts a second and slower decay. No true legato is therefore possible on a piano, but this is not a fact of any importance in eighteenth- or nineteenth-century music: the playing of a melody on the piano aspires to the condition of a perfect vocal legato, and the audience accepts the ideal as a reality when it is approached closely enough by the performer. The decibel needle on a recording machine may jump quickly to the right and then back at once to the left as each successive note is struck on the piano, but our perception of the music knows nothing of that. We are, indeed, aware of both the initial and secondary decays of sound in a work like Boulez's *Constellation* because they provide the basic rhythmic structure of the piece, but Beethoven never exploits the decay structurally—although he sometimes does so atmospherically—and we hear the sounds in a Beethoven piano sonata as if they were sustained by string instruments or voices.[1]

Nevertheless, this climactic moment of opus 111 is exceptional in that the listener not only disregards the diminishing of sonority characteristic of the instrument, but supplies in his imagination a sound which has actually ceased to exist. At the point of greatest intensity, Beethoven opposes the most distant registers of the keyboard—the weakest and the strongest—and implies from each register an equal power which no instrument is capable of giving and which must therefore be created by the listener. More than any composer before him, Beethoven understood the pathos of the gap between idea and realization, and the sense of strain put on the listener's imagination is essential here. The best argument for using the pianos of Beethoven's time in place of the modern grand piano is not the aptness of the old instruments but their greater inadequacy for realizing such an effect, and consequently the more dramatic effort required of the listener. The modern piano, however, is sufficiently inadequate to convey Beethoven's intentions.

As I have said, a passage like this is not isolated in music: in less extreme ways, the listener must constantly alter, purify, and supplement what he hears in the interests of musical intelligibility and expressiveness, taking his cue from what is implied by the performer. That is why the choreographic gyrations of the virtuoso conductor are so important to the audience's comprehension, if not to the orchestra's: an accent accompanied by an outflung arm seems literally to become louder and more intense. This aspect of music is inaudible only in the physical sense: it is heard in the imagination, very much as the composer hears as he writes, or the musician as he silently reads a score.

Inaudible music has a more radical form, however: the musical concept unrealizable as sound, even in the imagination. Carl Philipp Emanuel Bach had remarked that not everything in music can be heard (the idea is probably much older), and we take an example of the absolutely inaudible—as opposed to the practically inaudible—from the work of his father: the six-voice ricercar of the *Musical Offering*. At one point of this masterly fugue, there is a false entrance in the bass followed by a real entrance in the baritone—that is, an incomplete statement of the theme (only the first three notes here) followed by a full statement:

---

1. It is the pianist, rather than the composer, who reckons with the decay of sound in order to achieve clarity and to give the impression of continuity. (We may dismiss here as absurd the recent contention that the indication *fp* in Beethoven—at the opening of the Sonata Pathétique, for example—calls for the fast decay of the instruments of his time. If the decay was inevitable, there was no point in asking for it. In piano music, as in every other kind, *fp* meant a loud accent in an otherwise soft passage.)

The last note of the false statement and the first of the real are the same note, and the overlap makes it impossible to hear that there are two different voices and two different successive statements, partial and full. What one hears is:

After the fact, one can perceive that there are two voices, as the last note of the false statement is prolonged into the full statement. The passage, however, is preceded by a sequence of similarly overlapping false statements, in which the passing of one voice into another is in no way perceptible. Only if the two voices were played on different instruments could we distinguish one from the other, and, in spite of its being engraved and published in score, the six-voice ricercar is a work for keyboard. The beautiful exchange from voice to voice is, therefore, perceptible only through the eye and not even potentially audible in performance: it exists in the mind of the performer.

There has been some misunderstanding about this fugue, due partly to the original publication in full score, which gave rise in the twentieth century to the erroneous belief that it was for some unspecified combination of instruments. Nevertheless, the ricercar is for keyboard alone. Both Carl Philipp Emanuel Bach (who was with his father when King Frederick the Great gave him the theme for the fugue) and Forkel, the first biographer of Bach, are decisive on this point: the six-voice ricercar is "for two hands without pedal" (that is, without the pedal keyboard found on organs and on several harpsichords and clavichords of the time). The manuscript is on two staves, and the passage I have quoted was originally notated:

The gap between the notation and the effect for the ear is the point of this passage: to make a single voice out of two, and to form one long continuous line out of two separate statements, one false and one real. The publication in full score was not simply for clarity: it also demonstrated the independence of the voices, elucidated the contrapuntal movement, and set into relief those aspects of the music that cannot be realized for the ear.

The art of Johann Sebastian Bach at its most learned—as in this ricercar—is based on a relation between the audible and the inaudible. The independence of the voices in a fugue of this kind is absolute, but it can only be partially heard. The junction of two voices in a unison, wonderfully employed in the six-voice ricercar but a frequent effect in all contrapuntal writing, marks an extreme: the independence of the voices here passes over from the intermittently perceptible to the absolutely inaudible. The highest art of the composer is to make the counterpoint blend together into a continuum out of which the individual voices rise and are set into relief. The purpose of Baroque counterpoint is not the opposition of different voices but the creation of harmonic unity out of independent parts. Bach's way of setting one part after another in relief on the surface of the mass of sound was crucial to the Romantics, Chopin and Schumann in particular.

A constant aural perception of six individual parts is neither a reasonable nor a desirable goal. An understanding of the achievement of this fugue and of the fugue in "antique style" in general—one of the limit points of Baroque style—depends on the knowledge that behind what one hears—the mass of sound and the intermittent prominence of the individual voices—lies a perfect musical structure of six voices, each beautiful in isolation as well as in combination, a structure that can never be completely realized in sound. An awareness of the relation between sound and structure can be experienced with full intensity by the performer alone, who not only sees the score (as a friend looking over his shoulder might also do), but also senses the total independence of the voices through his fingers while he hears the way they blend into a mass. The absolute independence and the combination of voices is revealed by the score, but it is not, properly speaking, visual; neither can it be fully grasped aurally. The harmonic movement of the mass of sound, which proceeds as if guided by a figured bass, is a witness to the complex harmonic relationships among the voices; the intermittent isolation of individual voices is a witness to their independence. The imperfect realization in sound of a perfect structure is the foundation of this private art.

Until now, we have been considering the question of music and sound as if it were a general one, the answers valid for all time: with the concept of a private art, we enter into history, above all because an art whose full understanding is restricted to composer and performer has become somewhat distasteful to us. It was already almost unintelligible a quarter of a century after Bach's death; by then, it was no longer conceivable that an aspect of musical structure should be unrealizable in sound even by the imagination. Mozart wrote that fugues should always be played moderately slowly so that the entrances of the theme can be heard—and, as we have seen, Bach sometimes deliberately arranged his entrances so that they were imperceptible to the ear. The idea of music had changed radically since the death of Bach. That music should be completely audible was as obvious to Mozart as it was irrelevant for Bach. Further, Mozart arranged many of the fugues from the *Well-Tempered Keyboard* and the *Art of Fugue* for small string ensembles to make them public, or at least semipublic for the salon of Baron von Swieten. The history of transcribing the keyboard fugues of Johann Sebastian Bach begins, therefore, about thirty years after his death. Publication of the *Well-Tempered Keyboard*—in the literal sense of making public—was under way long before the first printing of the work in 1800. Not that all of Bach's fugues were private: the great organ fugues and those in the cantatas and Passions were intended to be heard in public (and in these the entrances of the theme are clearly set in relief). But the majority of his keyboard fugues were for private pleasure and instruction: the *Well-Tempered Keyboard,* the *Art of Fugue* and the *Musical Offering.* In particular, the learned fugue in "stile antico"—that is, in *alla breve* time with sophisticated stretto entrances, generally serious and even grave in manner—was for either keyboard or chorus. Fugues for instrumental ensemble had always another character, with concertolike openings and developments, and with brilliant and light textures. A performance by several instruments of any of the fugues from the *Art of Fugue* or of the ricercars from the *Musical Offering* would have been unthinkable during J. S. Bach's lifetime.

It is, no doubt, a good idea today; the Webern transcription of the six-voice ricercar has extended to a large audience a greater if still imperfect knowledge of Bach's achievement. By illuminating the interchange of voices through instrumentation, by emphasizing the independence and opposition of voices through tone color and phrasing, it has made the art of Bach more accessible—unless one reflects that this art depends upon a delicate balance between the simple beauty of what one hears and the more complex but never obtrusively audible technique which makes it possible. The keyboard fugues of Bach rarely exploit tone color, except in the most abstract terms of, for example, thickness against thinness of texture, fast-moving rhythms contrasted with sustained long values. Sonority does not often play an important role in Bach's contrapuntal art, in spite of a few wonderful exceptions. The *Well-Tempered Keyboard,* for example, has been performed to equally great effect on instruments of sonorous qualities as different as harpsichord, clavichord, organ, and early eighteenth-century pianoforte. That is why the beauty of the keyboard music of Bach is almost impervious to all of the various realizations in sound to which it has been subject, from the transcriptions of Mozart and Liszt to those of Busoni, Webern, and the Moog synthesizer. The music is only partially conceived in terms of what can be heard: it resists a complete translation into the audible.

It is fitting that a discourse on Romantic music should commence with a meditation on the art of Bach. The Bach revival is still sometimes considered an early nineteenth-century phenomenon, although this is hardly tenable: in the 1780s Mozart was deeply affected by Bach, and at the same time Beethoven was being brought up on the *Well-Tempered Keyboard.* Bach was well known to European musicians as a composer of keyboard music through manuscript copies of this work long before systematic publication began in 1800. The "revival" of Bach in the Romantic period was basically a rediscovery of his choral works and a new evaluation of his technique: his art was no longer simply a model for the fugue, as it had been in the eyes of Mozart, but for the art of music as a whole. The new approach to Bach and to Baroque music in general, however, did not extend to the sound of that music on the original instruments. Few musicians in the 1820s and '30s had the slightest interest in the sonority of old harpsichords or Baroque organs (Ignaz Moscheles was an engaging exception). What they saw, and needed to see, in Bach was the achievement of an ideal. Bach's music is not typically Baroque; it is an extreme form of the stylistic possibilities. It goes further than any other since the work of Palestrina in attaining the purity of counterpoint: an ideal set of independent voices on paper combining into a beautiful mass of expressive sound that only intermittently suggests the theoretical foundation.

Romantic paradoxes: the absent melody

The absolutely inaudible is rejected from music during the period of Viennese Classicism in which every musical line is potentially or imaginatively audible, but it makes a dramatic reappearance in the music of Schumann. The most striking of many examples is one of the episodes in the *Humoresk,* the last of the great piano works of Schumann's early years:

There are three staves: the uppermost for the right hand; the lowest for the left; the middle, which contains the melody, is not to be played. Note that the melody is no more to be imagined as a specific sound than it is to be played: nothing tells us that the melody is to be heard as vocal or instrumental. This melody, however, is embodied in the upper and lower parts as a kind of after-resonance—out of phase, delicate, and shadowy. What one hears is the echo of an unperformed melody, the accompaniment of a song. The middle part is marked *innere Stimme,* and it is both interior and inward, a double sense calculated by the composer: a voice between soprano and bass, it is also an inner voice that is never exteriorized. It has its being within the mind and its existence only through its echo.

At one point the paradox is stretched still further. This page has three phrases, each eight measures long, and the first and third phrases are almost identical— only the inaudible "inner voice" is changed. (The very last note in the left hand is different, and two accents are added, but these are minor alterations to give the return of the opening phrase a new sense of conclusion.) When the first phrase begins again at bar 17, the "inner voice" is momentarily blank—it reappears only with the second bar of the melody. For one bar a voice which was not present before is *not,* now, *not present*—but with a kind of Romantic logic, the two negatives do not make a positive. As far as can be heard, bars 1 and 17 are identical; it makes no difference to the ear whether or not the "inner voice" is void. No doubt a sensitive performer will play the following bar 18 with the slightly greater fullness that would accompany and acknowledge the reentry of a solo voice, and this kind of delayed reentry has sufficient precedence in vocal music, opera and *Lieder,* before Schumann. Nevertheless, the empty bar is a poetic joke, a reminder of the impossibility of conceiving the nature of the unspecified sonority of which the music we hear is an echo.

Later, Schumann magically exploits this quality of echo, and when this mysterious page returns, it seems to come from a long distance:

This is only the remote resonance of the original appearance, an echo of an echo. It would be more precise to say here that the melody has disappeared, and we are left only with the reduced echo of the harmonies. At the end, however, the inaudible makes itself heard, and the last five notes of the melody reveal themselves clearly in the lower octave of the right hand (the arpeggios in bars 25 and 29 call attention to the lower voice). This is the only place where the "inner voice" turns outward.

These pages of Schumann may contain a secret, but they do not hide one: on the contrary, they insist openly on the presence of a secret, with their strange sonority that both dispenses with a fully developed melody and continually suggests one, and with the even more extraordinary resonance of the return. The inaudible in Schumann's music is not conceived, as in Bach, as a theoretical structure which can only be imperfectly realized in sound, but as a structure of sound which implies what is absent. The actual heard sound is primary, a sound here of improvising an echo, an accompaniment to a melody which exists only in its reflection; a performance which does not bring out this shadowy quality and the flickering uncertainty of the rhythm is a betrayal of the score. In Bach the notation implies something beyond the reach of every realization, but in Schumann the music is a realization which implies something beyond itself.

This is even more striking in Schumann's opus 1, and it may seem, at this point in the composer's career, to be a kind of manifesto:

Here, in the last pages of the "Abegg" Variations, Schumann plays the motto theme A–B–E–G–G (B in German notation is the English B♭) not by sounding the last four notes but by taking them away, one by one, from the chord of B♭–E–G. This is the first time in history that a melody is signified not by the attack but by the release of a series of notes. The motto, however, ends with a repeated final G. If the motto is played by releasing each successive note, we are faced with a paradox: when the G is released once on the piano, it is no longer there to be released again—the motto is not only unplayable as conceived but unimaginable. Schumann signifies as much by another paradox: he adds accents to the sustained notes.

On the piano an accent in the middle of a sustained note is a contradiction in terms. That has not prevented the composer from trying to contrive a way to realize it. The most humorous suggestion in the score is to put down the damper pedal at the point of the accent: the extra resonance may not be audible beyond six inches from the instrument, but the delicate thump of the pianist's foot may be interpreted as a musical event. Any attempt to realize this paradox in sound, however, is a misunderstanding. Schumann's accent is an impossibility even in the imagination, since it indicates an impossible release. It is, therefore, unlike Beethoven's notation of a swell on a sustained note in the Sonata for Piano in E Minor, op. 90:

Here one can imagine a crescendo and diminuendo after the attack (and an electronic treatment of taped piano sound could, in fact, produce just that): more important, however, Beethoven's indication suggests the kind of expressive touch the passage demands, a delicate vibration that dies away surprisingly into its resolution. Schumann's capricious notion, however, of an accented note on the piano without an attack is a true paradox, a fantastic joke.

Schumann's humor is rarely either witty or light: the unrealizable musical structure, the musical motto hidden and partly inaudible, must have stirred his musical fantasy. We would be wrong, however, to think of this paradox as in any way a revival of the interaction between abstract structure and sensuous realization that is found in Bach, in spite of the fundamental importance of Bach for Schumann's generation. In the passage from the "Abegg" Variations, it is not the abstract form but the sensuous conception that leads to the paradox. It is because Schumann is thinking of the motto in terms of almost pure sound, in terms of release and attack as well as of pitch and rhythm, that the impossibility arises: a note can be attacked twice, but a double release without a second attack is nonsense on the piano. The unprecedented outlining of the melody through the release of the notes of a chord brought Schumann to the edge of the absurd. He had no hesitation in stepping over this frontier in his first published work.

It is an essentially Romantic paradox that the primacy of sound in Romantic music should be accompanied, and even announced, by a sonority that is not only unrealizable but unimaginable. How the released notes communicate the motto to the listener, force it on his attention, gives us the measure of Schumann's sensibility to sound. Normally the release of a note would not be heard this way, would convey no intelligible motif to the listener, but here the presence of the motif is inescapable. It is clear that the pianist must bring out the first two notes, A and B♭, with the thumb of his right hand, but the rest of the work is done for him by Schumann. Releasing the B♭ sets the E into relief: it is now the bass instead of a less important inner voice; releasing the E in turn isolates the G, as all other sound has disappeared. The motto has been played often enough for the repetition of the G to be supplied by the listener—

or, rather, for the listener to feel deprived by the impossibility of realizing the repetition in terms of the radical sonority invented by the composer. In this passage of Schumann's opus 1, sonority plays a structural role as important as pitch and rhythm. It is only a brief moment, but it announces a long and revolutionary process of change in our conception of music. Before Schumann and Liszt, sonority was only the dress of pitch and rhythm: no matter what the genius of the composer for instrumentation, from Giovanni Gabrieli to François Couperin and to Mozart, tone color had never been a determining element of form.

The new role of tone color in Schumann's music may be seen in "Eusebius" from *Carnaval*. The melodic form is one of great simplicity. The thirty-two bars are made up of only two four-bar phrases repeated in the following order, *AA, BA, BA, BA:*

The melody, rhythm, and harmony of these two four-bar phrases remain relatively invariant throughout, but the repetitions are overridden by the form imposed through tone color—pedalling, dynamics, texture, register, and octave doubling. What we hear is not *AA, BA, BA, BA* but a simple ternary or *ABA* structure, which cannot be said to coincide with the melodic form although it is in phase with it. As far as melody and harmony go, there is no very significant difference between the outer and the central sections, but for the listener's experience of the form of "Eusebius," pitch and rhythm are secondary and tone color is preeminent. In the large ternary structure a quiet opening in three-part polyphony is succeeded by an increasingly expansive and elaborate middle section, and then a very simple, almost exact return. In the outer parts, the inner voice is slightly varied: the important change is made in the central section—the register is changed, the dynamic level raised, the texture thickened, and the pedal added.

For the full effect of "Eusebius," it is necessary to obey Schumann's directions strictly and to play the beginning and end absolutely without pedal: the middle section, by contrast, is evidently intended to swim in pedal (there is no other way to sustain the bass notes as long as the harmony demands). This contrast of sonorities, which determines the form of the piece, also carries its meaning within *Carnaval*. "Eusebius" is the first part of a double self-portrait, and represents the introverted, repressed side of Schumann. The dry, soft sound of the piano without pedal is private, withdrawn into itself: in the middle, the passionate nature of the music breaks through into the full vibration of the piano, only to withdraw once again at the end.

Classical and Romantic pedal

Schumann's use of the pedal is personal here, but it springs from a new sense of the role of sonority in music. There are few better ways to understand the revolution in style accomplished in the nineteenth century than by examining the way composers required the sustaining pedal to be used. It is, in fact, as much by the pedal as by the possibility of gradations of touch that the piano is distinguished from all other instruments. By means of the pedal the pianist is able to control the decay of sound in various ways—gradual release, half-pedal (allowing the dampers just to touch the strings without fully damping the sound), pedalling before or after the attack of the note.

The wrong question to start with is: What did it sound like when the dampers were lifted, and the strings left free to vibrate, on an instrument contemporary with the composer? That is an interesting subject, but a secondary one. It cannot be evaded, but to start there is to forget the wide range of sonorities that different instruments of the same era could provide, to ignore the delicate balance between touch and pedalling, and to assume arbitrarily that a composer's inspiration is always tied to the specific sounds of the instruments available to him. The first question, in time as well as importance, is: Why did the composer indicate the pedal? Or, more precisely: What is the function of the pedal in a given passage?

The pedal has two different basic functions (as well as some subsidiary ones): it sustains struck notes, and it allows those which are not struck to vibrate in sympathy. Until this distinction is clear, no sensible observation can be made about the notations for pedalling on late eighteenth- and early nineteenth-century instruments.

Haydn's indications of pedal are rare; two late ones are a good point of departure: they occur in the last sonata he wrote, the C Major (H.50), published in England in 1791. The first is found at the center of the development section of the first movement, and the second occurs in the same movement in the recapitulation in a secondary development. Both these places involve the main theme, and to understand the kind of effect demanded by Haydn, we must look back at the way the theme was presented before. The opening Allegro of the sonata is extraordinarily dry, remaining *staccato* for two bars and attenuating the dryness only minimally as it continues:

As the work progresses this dryness is gradually overcome. The process can be illustrated by the three appearances of the main theme in the development section, which opens with the notes of the main theme now unified by a counterpoint in another voice, and with a heavier touch indicated after the first three notes:

A little later, even the opening three-note motif has become much weightier:

Finally, we arrive at the first of Haydn's indications of "open pedal," and all dryness has been removed from the theme:

This clearly makes such an extraordinary blur even on the pianos available to Haydn that H. T. Robbins-Landon was moved to conjecture that "open pedal" meant a soft pedal, either a muffling device or *una corda*. An interesting article by Richard Kramer has shown, by a comparison with Clementi's and Dussek's notation in English publications of the 1790s, that Haydn's "open pedal" literally means raising the dampers and sustaining everything that follows. Kramer remarks that, in this passage from the development, the harmony reaches the most remote point within the structure of the movement, and Haydn emphasizes this moment with "the ghostly echo of the principal theme in A-flat."[2]

We should also stress the thematic transformation imposed by the blurred pedal and the *pianissimo,* above all in relation to the second indication of "open pedal" after the beginning of the recapitulation:

2. Richard Kramer, "On the Dating of Two Aspects in Beethoven's Notation for Piano," Beitrage '76–'78 Beethoven Kolloquium 1977, ed. R. Klein (Kassel, 1978), pp. 160–173.

Here the main theme is in the left hand; now not only all sense of dryness has been destroyed but also all rhythmic definition: the contour of the theme has been softened almost beyond recognition against the syncopated right-hand line, both lines blurred softly like the sound of a music box.

These successive appearances of the principal theme show a progression from the sharpest possible articulation to one in which all the notes blend together indistinctly. The two indications of pedal are only the final points of this transformation. The pedal is used here as a form of reorchestration which sets the thematic process in relief, to give a different sonority to the different forms of the theme. If this is to make sense, the modern habit of adding a delicate wash of pedal throughout a performance, of allowing the whole instrument to vibrate constantly with the music, has no place in a performance of Haydn. It is evident that the dry sound without pedal is the normal one for Haydn, although he exaggerates the dryness in this work with the bare *staccato* texture of the opening. The pedalled sonority, on the other hand, is the more exotic sound, a special effect. Here, too, Haydn surpasses his contemporaries by forcing this effect beyond the limits to which they were generally prepared to go.

Beethoven equals Haydn in audacity. It has been said by his contemporaries that he used the pedal much more extensively than the indications in his scores lead us to believe, but we must not take that to mean that he pedalled in modern style, continuously but tactfully. For him, as for Haydn, the pedal was a special effect, and a study of the places where he insisted upon it may help us to add it at other points where he gave no directions. We may turn now to the notorious indications for the main theme of the rondo-finale of the *Waldstein* Sonata, op. 53:

Played thoughtlessly on the modern piano, this makes a terrible smudge: Beethoven asks the performer to hold the pedal down steadily through many changes of harmony, releasing it only in bars 8, 12, and 23. Major and minor modes, tonic and dominant harmonies would all seem to be fused together almost impossibly by this instruction. Beethoven is, however, very firm about holding the pedal down; later in the work he writes:

So intent is he on having the pedal held throughout bar 101 that he writes *three eighth-note rests* in place of the more usual and convenient one eighth note, one quarter. He wants the pedal held almost to the end of the bar, released only with the last eighth-note rest—and we can see from the autograph that, in order to make this absolutely clear, he has actually scratched out the quarter rests he originally wrote, substituting in each case two eighth-note rests in their place. (Why does he write the last note of the phrase as an eighth note if it is going to be sustained anyway by the pedal?—in order to avoid an accent. The first note of the phrase, on the other hand, is written as an eighth note in order to *imply* an accent, to indicate an attack. Such are the vagaries of notation when it comes to delicate matters like phrasing. The short notes and the rests here reinforce one traditional Classical phrase pattern of an accented opening downbeat and a feminine ending.) Note that the opening bars of the movement performed on an early nineteenth-century piano of the kinds available to Beethoven would also make a disagreeable blur unless played with considerable care. In this passage the primary function of the pedal for Beethoven may be partly coloristic, but it is above all *motivic*.

The theme of the rondo begins with the low C bass note, and not with the repeated treble G's: the bass note is always an essential and integral part of the theme. The function of the pedal here is to sustain every appearance of this note. In order to get this motivic pedal point, Beethoven was evidently willing to countenance a certain amount of light blurring. If the right hand is played as softly as possible (Beethoven marks *sempre pianissimo*), so that the notes just speak without resounding, a delicacy and clarity can be achieved even on the modern concert piano. (An alternative solution would be to sustain the bass notes with the concert piano's middle pedal, but this is less satisfactory, and could compromise the secondary but important coloristic effect intended.) It should be emphasized that Beethoven's directions for pedal in this passage can, with a little care, be fully carried out on the modern concert piano with wonderful effect.

The sustaining of the opening bass notes is absolutely essential to the thematic conception of this rondo. If the opening page is pedalled correctly, the development section takes on a new meaning:

This passage, which continues at great length, is not an arpeggio over a left-hand accompaniment but a right-hand decoration of a left-hand theme, the opening fragment of the main theme. This movement, therefore, is one of the first in the history of the pianoforte in which the motivic structure of the music rests upon the technical capacities of the pedal. It must be emphasized again, however, that an understanding of the music and an interpretation of it depend on our first asking, not what it *sounded* like, but what the purpose of the notation was. The primary purpose of the pedal here is to sustain the low note: the vibrancy of the open pedal is both a bonus and a liability, a beautiful cloud of sound that threatens to engulf the music. Like Haydn, Beethoven did not object to a certain blurring and sometimes indicates pedal in the only register where it would have made a blur on his own piano:

The function of the equally notorious pedal indications at the opening of the slow movement of Beethoven's Piano Concerto no. 3 in C Minor lies at the opposite pole: it is not the sustaining of the bass that is essential but the richness of the sonority. (On ancient as well as modern pianos, an insensitive performance will result in a smudge, although the problem can be solved even on the twentieth-century concert grand, if not, in this case, with ease.) What is significant in this passage is not where the pedal is to be held down, but where it is to be released:

The chord in bar 4 is to be played without pedal, as are bars 7 and 8. There is to be a change of pedal at the end of bar 10, but the rest of the passage was evidently intended to swim in pedal. It is, however, less the sustaining power of the pedal that counts in this passage than the way it makes the piano vibrate and contrast with the unpedalled sound.

The withholding of this vibrancy in bar 4 gives this chord a strange effect of distance, after the rich sonority of the opening bars: the sound suddenly withdraws, and the movement towards C sharp minor (in bar 2) becomes graver with the contrast in tone color. The *senza pedale* of bars 7 and 8 has a similar effect, but here even more deeply expressive. The sound is suddenly more delicate, the texture thin: all the concentration is focused horizontally on the upper line instead of on the harmony. The return of vibrancy marks the surprising move to G major and the release of the pedal the turn back to E—although this brief change of pedal must be made almost as much for clarity as for expression.

We must note here the essentially Classical nature of this procedure. The pedal is used here as an extension of dynamics, as a means of characterizing the different succeeding functional and emotional significances of the phrases— bringing out the inward sentiment of bars 7–8 by withholding the pedal, adding the pedal to set in relief the dramatic change to a G major chord in bar 9. The sound effects of the pedal work precisely like accents or contrasts of dynamic levels. They can be properly reproduced on a modern concert instrument by what is called half-pedal, that is, raising the dampers just slightly so that they still remain in contact with the strings, but not enough to cut off all the resonance when the keys are released. This achieves a very delicate blur at the change of harmony, which quickly dies away as the new chord is held. It is an effect difficult to achieve, however, and must be practiced carefully on each individual instrument. The essential point, in any case, of Beethoven's indications at the opening of the slow movement is the opposition of pedalled and unpedalled sonorities, and the modern pianist must seek to find an equivalent.

In sum, Beethoven uses the pedal either for sustaining important structural notes or as a form of dynamic contrast. In an early work like the *Moonlight* Sonata, he can also require the pedal as a form of orchestration. Playing the first movement of the *Moonlight* as Beethoven directed, very delicately *(delicatissimamente)* with full pedal throughout *(senza sordini,* "without dampers") on an early nineteenth-century instrument with little sustaining power, produces a lovely sonority difficult to reproduce with a modern keyboard. But none of these procedures—orchestration, dynamic emphasis or contrast, the sustaining of important notes—is essentially at odds with late eighteenth-century style. They are merely expansions of standard procedures of the previous generations: they extend to the pedal what had previously been achieved by phrasing, dynamics, and instrumentation.

The opposition between pedalled and unpedalled sonority is difficult to realize today for both psychological and acoustical reasons. We find it hard to swallow the idea that, although Haydn and Mozart had the so-called loud pedal at their command, they did not use it, in the modern fashion, to give a continuous sympathetic vibration. This has nothing to do with the difference between early pianos and the nine-foot monster now used for concerts: the dry sound can be as enchanting on modern instruments as on the older ones. But it is an intimate sound, unsuited to the large concert hall: it does not carry as well; the instrument does not appear to sing out, to command attention. It is, indeed, for this quality of intimacy that Schumann demanded dryness of sound at the beginning and end of "Eusebius," his "Self-Portrait as Introspective Artist." In playing Mozart and Beethoven today in large halls on instruments new or antique, a compromise is always necessary: a continuously dry sound in a large concert auditorium is as much a distortion of the music as the more usual absolute disregard of Beethoven's indications. These indications need to be translated for modern acoustics as much as for modern pianos.

The change to continuous pedalling seems to occur in the 1820s, perhaps in response to the growing importance of public concerts. A new style of pianism was created which affected even the most intimate works. Pedal markings are excessively rare in Schubert, for example. The Sonata for Piano in G Major, D.894, has only one, in the tenth bar of the first movement, also marked *ppp*. This suggests that Schubert adheres to the Classical system, in which the dry sound is the norm and the pedalled sound is a special effect. But the marking in the slow movement of the Sonata in B flat Major, D.960,

imposes a modern sonority. It must not be interpreted with tact, as some editors have suggested: the left-hand notes are notated as short only in order to indicate that they are to be played delicately and let the melody in the right sing through. What is strikingly advanced about this passage is precisely the quality of sound: the rhythmic pattern in the left hand touches the octave overtones of C♯, and the pedal allows them gently to vibrate. Here, more than anywhere else in his work, Schubert anticipates the style of the next decades.

The revolution in style effected by the generation of Chopin, Schumann, and Liszt, born around the year 1810, is intimately linked to new pedal techniques. We may start with the most normal use and progress to the most eccentric. The opening of Chopin's Nocturne in E flat Major, op. 9, no. 2, gives us a standard:

Here the function of the pedal is both to sustain and to induce sympathetic vibration. The pedal sustains the bass line, which would otherwise be lost; but, above all, it allows the piano to sing.

The first beat of this Nocturne is instructive: by means of both the pedal and the spacing of the chord, it exploits, as few works had done before, the sympathetic overtones of the piano. The G in the right hand sings because of the E♭ four octaves below it, and the two quavers that follow the low E♭ continue to reinforce the vibrations of both the E♭ and the G, bass and melody. Throughout this passage the spacing is conceived in terms of the vibration of the piano, a vibration made possible by the pedal, which sustains the main notes while others arrive and reactivate their harmonics. Note that the overtones of this passage, like those of all nineteenth-century piano music, are conceived in terms of equal temperament. In just intonation the minor seventh is an important overtone, and therefore an important component of the sonority, while the major seventh is a very distant harmonic and of little weight; in equal temperament this arrangement is reversed. In the first bar the Ds in the inner voices of the second beat vibrate against the E♭ below them, held by the pedal. On the third and fourth beats, it is the pedal that makes the extraordinary dissonance of the parallel ninths between upper and lower voice sound so mellifluously, heard as they are in terms of the vibration created through the inner parts.

Other composers, notably Mozart, had tried by means of spacing to exploit the piano's capacity to make one note sing sympathetically against another. But although Mozart's pianos had pedal mechanisms, he never wrote music which required them for this purpose. (There are no pedal indications in any of Mozart's works for piano.) The new style of Chopin and the extraordinary sonority he created for the first time depend above all on a novel and original use of the pedal.

Even Chopin's radically new conceptions of polyphony and phrasing depend on the pedal, as an interesting problem in the Ballade no. 3 in A flat Major demonstrates. It is reproduced incorrectly in most editions, and the manuscript is instructive (see next page, and also page 312, bars 99–117). At the second bar of the second system, Chopin started to write a pedal indication and then crossed it out, placing the pedal only in the second half of the bar. Four bars later, when the phrase is repeated, the same indication occurs, now left blank without hesitation: the first half of the bar is again to be played "dry" and the pedal introduced only later.

This twice breaks the phrase in two. Notice first that the pedal is systematically placed with the bass line in a way that few pianists pedal today. What is most significant, however, is the insistence on leaving half a bar without pedal—an idea that occurs to Chopin only as he writes, as we can see. This is not how he indicated the pedal for the same theme when it occurred two pages back; and at a later appearance of the theme he again places a break, but at a different point. Not only the phrase is shaped by the pedal; the polyphonic

movement in this passage is blended and moves in blocks as the pedal sustains and articulates the harmony.

This shaping of the phrase and articulation of the harmony by means of the pedal are carried further in Ballade no. 1 in G Minor. A horn call introduces a second theme:

Here the pedal articulates the rhythm in bars 73 and 74: the hemiola of the melody in these bars creates a momentary triple time, and the pedal continues to impose the duple time of the opening measures. Unless Chopin's indications are strictly observed, this effect goes for nothing. In bars 76 and 78, with great subtlety, Chopin carries out exactly the contrary effect: the melody has returned to duple time, but the pedal, which changes to catch the bass note on the third quarter note of both bars, makes a counteraccent at this place. From bars 72 to 74, the pedal reveals the descending inner line C–B♭–A♭–G. Changing the pedal on the E♭ and the D—the way it is generally performed—creates a false bass and distorts the line. If we compare bars 76 and 78 to bars 68 and 70, which they repeat (literally, in the case of 70 and 78), we see a remarkable difference. No suggestion of triple rhythm is found in 68 and 70: 68 is divided neatly in two parts by the pedal; 70, in a higher register with no danger of blurring, is unified by a single pedal mark, which brings a much fuller sonority. These two examples from Ballades 3 and 1 show how the pedal can be used to create a polyphonic rhythm, bringing out a counterpoint that would otherwise remain hidden within the texture.

In the piano writing of the Romantic generation of the 1830s, in fact, a fully pedalled sonority becomes the norm: the piano is expected to vibrate fairly constantly, and an unpedalled sonority is an exception, almost a special effect. Furthermore, the phrase is now shaped at least partially by changes in this full vibration. The change of pedal is crucial to the conception of rhythmic movement and to the sustaining of the melodic line over the bass.

At this point we have come fairly close to the modern conception of pedalling. Still to be developed was what might be called "syncopated" pedalling—that is, depressing the pedal before or after the attack of a note. Moriz Rosenthal believed that this was a development of the later nineteenth century, and that earlier pianists had always pedalled on or with the note. There are still pianists today who "beat time" with their right foot; but in general, syncopated pedalling is now so inbred that doing it any other way would seem as unnatural to most pianists as playing without vibrato would seem to the modern violinist. (The consistently vibrant sound of the piano required by Romantic style is, of course, the equivalent of the continuous and unremitting vibrato of modern string playing.)

Schumann's use of the pedal is very much more adventurous than Chopin's. The indications are, indeed, sometimes vague. "With pedal" is generally placed at the beginning of most pieces—and its absence is more interesting than its inclusion (an omission often demands at least a consideration of the possibility of oversight). But at other times Schumann's pedalling is both precise and remarkable. Since Schumann, as we have seen, invented the idea of playing a melody by *withdrawing* notes from a chord—a melody by absence—it is fitting that his most famous pedal effect should be a withdrawal of sound. It occurs in *Carnaval* at the end of "Paganini":

After playing the four resounding thirds with full pedal, the pianist depresses the keys of the next chord without allowing the hammers to strike, and then changes the pedal. All the strings of the piano have been ringing with the previous *fortissimo,* and the change of pedal withdraws all the sympathetic vibrations except those in the notes silently held down. As the other sounds die away, there is an extraordinary auditory illusion: the notes of the chord appear with what seems like a crescendo. This is probably the first use of piano harmonics by themselves in the history of music—and a device rarely to be used again until the opus 11 of Schoenberg, although after that it was to have a busy future. (Did Schumann appreciate the irony of creating the most specifically pianistic effect in his portrait of a violinist?) It would be misleading to describe this passage as a modulation from F minor to A flat major realized by overtones: the emergence of the overtones of V^7 of A flat from the chord of F minor is as fundamental as the harmonic structure.

This is an extreme effect in Schumann, but it shows that for him a musical conception was not merely "realized" in sound but was identical with the sound: the musical idea *is* the pedal effect. Similarly, the seventeenth piece of Schumann's *Davidsbündlertänze,* op. 6, is labelled "As if from a distance," but the words describe the music rather than the other way around:

The echo of the melody in the bass register melts into both the inner ostinato on F♯ and the pedal point on B. The passage must swim in pedal, so that the bass and treble notes are sustained against the inner ostinato. This is not merely a price to be paid for a pretty effect but the whole point of the music: a soft, widely spaced texture blurring tonic and dominant harmony together in a single mist.

A few bars later the distant resonance includes full chromatic harmonies (bars 17–18). We do not need to be told how to play the pedal in this passage. To sustain the bass, the dampers must remain raised throughout. On paper this seems impossibly daring, yet in performance the effect is miraculous: no composer could have written such a passage who had not discovered it for himself while improvising at the keyboard. The sonority of the piano has now become a primary element of musical composition, as important as pitch or duration.

Conception and realization

It may be difficult for us today to comprehend the novelty of this development: we take it for granted that a composer writes down what he hears in his imagination. In the most naive terms, of course, we recognize that this is absurd. Beethoven did not listen to a noise in his head, say to himself, "That sounds like a D minor triad in 6/4 position with an added B flat," and proceed to write the opening of the last movement of the Ninth Symphony. However, we believe with some justification not only that a composer hears what he writes as he composes, but also that the ideal performance is the one that most closely approximates what the composer had in mind. This appears to be a self-evident truth (the hardest sort of truth to discover, as someone has re-marked), but it will not stand up to close examination.

For some performances of *Messiah*, Handel wrote out the ornamentation of two of the arias for singers evidently incapable of doing it for themselves. These are rare documents: for once we are correct in saying that Handel expected to hear what he had written. At all other times he would have been disagreeably surprised if a singer had adhered faithfully to the text and performed the aria without ornament. It is true that decoration in the early eighteenth century—as in almost all periods—was largely a conventional affair; but there was always a range of possibilities, a repertoire of expressive formulas, and it would have been impossible to predict with any certainty, even at final cadences, exactly what the singer would choose. Even if Handel himself imagined a specific type of ornamentation while writing down the simpler, undecorated version, that would be interesting psychologically but irrelevant as far as considerations of style and performance are concerned. The art of composition in such cases is the creation of a structure that will support, and even inspire, a wide range of realizations—and it should be remembered that much of the expressive force of High Baroque music depends on the improvised decoration.

For the same period, certain aspects of texture necessary to the realization were also left to be decided at the pleasure of the performer. A figured bass leaves the spacing, the thickness of the harmony, and the voice leading free, although this freedom must not be exaggerated: the range of choice was much smaller than in the case of decoration, and an obtrusive performance of the continuo part is a vice of modern harpsichordists and must have been rare in the eighteenth century, even if we take into account J. S. Bach's expressed preference for a full four-voice realization. Furthermore, it is not clear whether the size of the forces available for performance had much influence on the actual composition. Indeed, a recent controversy about the execution of Bach's choral music centered on whether the works were written in terms of the very limited forces that Bach was generally able to command at the Thomaskirche in Leipzig or in terms of the forces that he explicitly said he would like to have. To a certain extent this is a false problem: every composer is influenced by his knowledge of what the piece will actually sound like from poignant past experience of the conditions of performance, but no interesting composer resists the repeated temptation to transcend these conditions.

Perhaps because of these limitations, however, Bach chose to notate the decoration of his vocal and keyboard works with a fullness that disconcerted many of his contemporaries—his supporters claimed that one should be grateful to have a model of realization for keyboard players (with a few exceptions only the keyboard works were published), and this educational ideal was as central to Bach's purpose as it must have been to the project of François Couperin, who also fully notated the ornamentation of his *Ordres* for harpsichord. As for the vocal works (essentially the cantatas and Passions), Bach was writing for the provincial small town that was Leipzig in the eighteenth century; he did not have at his command the international stars of Handel's opera company, but only the very much less glamorous local talents. Handel's prima donnas were famous for their improvised ornaments—brilliant in one case, expressive in the other: they would have been outraged if Handel had attempted to circumscribe this freedom. If the gap between composition and realization often seems greater in Handel than it does in Bach, that is because Bach has already taken upon himself some of the work of realization. With only slight exaggeration we might say that composition in the early eighteenth century was the creation of abstract patterns of pitch and rhythm, which were subsequently realized—by composer or performer, the distinction was not quite so firmly drawn at the time—in instrumental tone color, texture, and ornament.

If we are to continue to maintain that the composer always heard in his imagination what he was creating, we must often fall back on the more modest claim that he heard an abstract structure of pitch and rhythm that was to be filled out later. For periods earlier than the Baroque, we often have to retreat even from this. I am not thinking only of those sixteenth-century works that can have both a diatonic and a chromatic realization, because these are extreme cases (although I do not think that one can understand the more normal cases without comprehending the extremes). Nevertheless, slight chromatic alterations of the composer's text were generally expected from performers, and it is an anachronism to attempt to define, say, a sharpened leading tone as a precise pitch, as if all musicians were using equal temperament, or even a genuinely systematic alternative system of tuning.[3] It is interesting to reflect that the slight chromatic alteration that one actually heard in performance in

3. This imprecision of pitch concerns register as well: it was only after 1750 that a note as well defined as middle C had a meaning in actual performance practice that did not vary by as much as a third or more.

the sixteenth century and earlier was called *musica ficta:* the real, nonfictive music was the inaudible structure that conformed theoretically to the mode.

The faith in the existence of a single correct realization of the *musica ficta* for each piece has now largely been abandoned, but it did not die easily. The belief that the composer heard in his head at least the exact pitches that he wrote made it at first impossible to comprehend that some aspects of the pitch content of a work, even before ornamentation, were left to the discretion of the performers for several centuries. We can all accept slight expressive alterations of pitch, like vibrato, as being part of a realization, but deviations of a half step strain our credulity, and systematic alterations which radically affect the harmonic character of some pieces are harder to swallow. Nor do we like the idea that a theoretical structure can take precedence over a practical realization. Yet musical structures, conceived and notated but as yet unrealized, can have a particular beauty that is only partially related to any imagined performance—an irreducibly inaudible beauty, so to speak.

Conception and realization begin to draw more closely together in the late eighteenth century. Dynamics are specified in greater detail. Ornamentation improvised by the performer is no longer a musical necessity but a luxury—or, at worst, a form of self-indulgence; it hangs on in slow movements (those marked *Adagio,* in particular) and above all in opera, where its role is severely limited only in the nineteenth century, largely owing to the efforts of composers like Rossini. The *obbligato* accompaniment replaces the improvised accompaniment. Continuo playing dwindles from a necessary filling out of the harmony into a simple means of keeping a large ensemble together, and finally dies out altogether in the first decades of the new century. We cannot yet speak of an identity of conception and realization: it does not seem possible to reorchestrate Mozart, but occasionally Mozart himself did it with some success. The Wind Sextet, K.384ª, is a convincing work in its transformation into a string quintet, but it does become less colorful and somewhat less striking. Alan Tyson has shown that the Concerto for Piano in A Major, K.488, was begun with oboes and not clarinets in mind: by the time Mozart was able to finish it, he had clarinets in his orchestra, and he altered the opening of the score accordingly. Mozart seems to have preferred clarinets to oboes. The two versions of the Symphony in G Minor, K.550, are not genuine alternates: the instrumentation without clarinets surely came into being only to make the work available to more orchestras; clarinetists were less common than oboists at that time.

Tovey has remarked somewhere that when Mozart gives a melody to, say, the oboe, we find it a wonderful inspiration, but that when Beethoven does it, the effect is less striking only because it does not occur to us that any other instrument would be possible. This suggests that Beethoven has reached the ideal fusion of conception and realization. Indeed, Beethoven's transcriptions of his own works for other instruments have, without exception, no artistic interest; they testify only to the conditions of making money in the world of music around 1800. Both the violin concerto transcribed for piano (except for its interesting cadenza accompanied by four kettledrums) and the Grosse Fuge arranged for four hands at one keyboard are absurd.

Nevertheless, I think that with Beethoven one must continue to speak of the priority of conception over realization, a priority which is both temporal and logical. This conception, however, is so adapted that there is a unique realization. The opening bars of the *Hammerklavier* demonstrate the relation between musical idea and instrumental color:

The material here is the motif that saturates the first movement:

This motif is projected in the first bar over the low, middle, and high registers, encompassing the greater part of the audible range. In order to function, this projection requires a single tone color in all three registers, preferably a neutral color such as only the piano can give. That is why an attempt, like Weingartner's, to orchestrate this opening is so disastrous: the orchestra needs many instruments and a variety of tone colors to achieve the single, unified gesture of the pianist. Yet it would be a mistake to think of the sound of the piano, even of Beethoven's own, as either the inspiration or the material of the musical idea: the working out of the motif takes precedence over tone color.

For Beethoven, music was still shape, realized and inflected by instrumental sonority: other realizations may be as absurd as arrangements of the *Hammerklavier*, for example, always are, but the musical conception takes precedence over its realization in sound. The sonority serves the music. For Schumann, however, as for Chopin and Liszt, the conception was worked out directly within the sonority as a sculptor works directly in clay or marble. The instrumental sound is shaped into music.

Schumann's use of tone color as an integral part of the initial conception does not reveal itself only in the creation of original sounds or in flashy effects like the emergence of harmonics from the vibrant *fortissimo* at the end of "Paganini." Many of his most unassuming pages also start from an exploitation of texture or sonority. The *Waldscenen,* Schumann's only large-scale piano work to be written towards the end of his career, begins with an elegant play of sonorities:

The horn call unobtrusively suggested in the left hand is the traditional Romantic evocation of the forest, the distant echoing sound that stands for memory: these forest scenes are filled with sentimental nostalgia. As the first bar opens, the melody is in the left hand, while the right hand plays an accompaniment figure which echoes it. Almost without our being aware of it, this accompaniment becomes the melody in the first half of the second bar. The transition is ambiguous, since melody and accompaniment are really the same, slightly out of phase, but there is a shift of register accomplished delicately and with the utmost discretion. The left-hand register in bar 2, now become subordinate, actually retains all the melody notes; it seems to lack the D at the end of the second beat of bar 2, but this note appears in the right hand as an octave doubling. A later passage shows that the performer is not meant to emphasize the lower note of the octave D in bar 19, or to bring out a continuity in the lower register:

The shift of register is even more obvious here. The melody starts in the left hand and is echoed in the right: then the principal voice is displaced to the echo, and the melody appears delayed after the beat. Most subtly, the notes of the melody on the beat begin to seem anticipations of the "real" melody in the right hand. Exactly where the shift takes place depends on the performer, who can push it forward to the last beat of the first bar; it is also possible to return the melodic emphasis to the lower register in bar 2 (and in bar 19) with the half note on the third beat.

This complex interplay of texture depends on the fact that the upper register is privileged to our ears: we expect the melody to be there. This is the natural result of a system which makes a sharp hierarchical distinction between melody and accompaniment: placing the melody below the accompanying voices seems

to go against the grain in order to achieve an interesting but special effect.[4]
Eighteenth- and nineteenth-century composers delighted in the effect. One of
the most useful devices for exploiting the relation between principal voice and
accompaniment was the heterophonic accompaniment, which we see in this
passage, and which was largely developed during the 1830s: an accompaniment which repeats the melody in the principal voice, but with an altered
rhythm—a shadow, an echo, or a prefiguration. Schumann uses it here with
supreme skill. Crucial to the oscillation between the registers and between
melody and accompaniment in this piece is the unified sonority of the piano.
This is not used, as in Beethoven or Haydn, to produce a uniquely adequate
realization of motivic development: the interplay of registers exists in Schumann for its own sake—or, better, for the discontinuous, indefinite resonance
that softens the contour of the melody. It may even be said that the melody
which realizes this interchange of registers is never once played correctly, with
register and beat well defined: both are left uncertain, and it is this precisely
calculated indefiniteness that helps to create the poetic atmosphere.

In the last piece of the *Waldscenen,* "Abschied," there is a similar shift of
register from tenor to soprano:

Melody and accompaniment are parallel here, too. The right hand starts as a
decorated form of the tenor's opening leap from C to B♭, and principal melody
and accompaniment draw together into a unison in bar 14. The shift to the
soprano is found at the opening of bar 16: the sudden move into the upper

---

4. In the fifteenth, and most of the sixteenth, centuries, the tenor was privileged, not the
soprano, but this depended on a polyphony of independent voices in which the relation of melody
to accompaniment was the exception. Today not only do we notate the tenor part in the G clef,
an octave above its real sound, but we actually hear a solo tenor paradoxically as above the higher
notes in an orchestra or accompanying piano, as if he were in a different and higher space. When
a solo tenor is given music which is a fifth below the accompaniment, this interval can sound
oddly like a fourth, as we tend to take the lower note in the accompaniment as the fundamental
bass note.

octave gives a surprising passion to the phrase, which continues with even greater expressive force. The upper line in bar 17 divides in two, both heard as a continuation of the first two beats. This ambiguity of voice leading is a typically pianistic effect, very difficult to realize with the orchestra.

The loveliest of Schumann's pieces from the *Fantasiestücke*, op. 12, "Des Abends," exploits a different kind of ambiguity of register. The music here springs so directly from piano sound that one must count as part of the material of the work not only motifs, harmony, and texture, but also certain aspects of piano technique, above all the way the thumbs can be placed on the keyboard:

To cross one thumb over the other is a simple and natural position: one finds it easily while improvising, and there is no risk of tangling the two hands, as there is when one places the fingers of one hand within those of the other. Schumann directs that this piece be played with crossed thumbs almost throughout, although all of the notes can be simply executed without using this position. The layout of the hands can give us a clue to the way he and his contemporaries revolutionized sound, and permanently altered the relation of composition to realization.

Principal voice and accompaniment are here opposed rhythmically as 3/8 and 6/16. The accompaniment rhythm is the basic one, and the melody is to be heard as syncopated against it: in order to emphasize the syncopation, the time signature is actually 2/8, with the sixteenth notes written as triplets. This was a technique that Schumann could have learned from earlier composers, Schubert above all, but his use here is deeply personal.

The sonority of the accompaniment is exquisite. The simplicity of surface hides an extraordinary subtlety. The lower note of the right hand belongs to the accompanying texture, but it is in the triple rhythm of the melody, and the repetition of this note by the thumb adds a delicate counterrhythm that reinforces the syncopation; it serves to blend the two opposing rhythmic systems. The spacing of the left-hand figuration gives a soft bell-like resonance, as the D♭ of the bass in the first six bars is followed immediately by its second overtone, A♭, played quietly by the thumb. The fingering induces almost unconsciously the softest of accents on the A♭, which is implied as well by the contour of the figuration in the lower stave. This nuance, almost imperceptible when sensitively played, is essential to the structure. The A♭ is the note on which principal voice and the accompanying vibration come together on a unison, immediately after the melody crosses for one note into the register of the harmonic underpinning. This happens in bar 3, and it causes a slight alteration of the rhythm: the figuration of the left is very briefly delayed so that its A♭ can become a melody note, a rubato that changes the significance of this inner voice.

The stillness of the music depends on the way the sound is conceived for the hands. Crossing the thumbs allows the lower part of the right hand to remain anchored with almost no movement, and this would be spoiled if the layout were rearranged. The left hand's motion, too, is unchanged for six bars. Only bar 3, where figuration and melody intertwine, disturbs the absolute tranquility of the surface on which the melody moves. At first this melody seems modest, a simple, commonplace falling and rising scale: however, the beginning and end of both descent and ascent are dissonant to the harmony. Even more expressive is the way upward and downward motion are converted into each other: the resolution of the final dissonance of each is delayed—the B♭ in bar 2 is not resolved immediately into an A♭, the E♭ in bar 4 must wait to be resolved into the F.

The surface is further disturbed by the simple ornament in bar 6 as the music proceeds. The growing intensity is created as much by sonority as by harmony. In bar 7, not only does the principal voice descend into the register of the accompaniment, but the accompaniment rises, and the B♭ in the left hand echoes the B♭ of the melody in the previous bar, and in bar 8 echoes the melody immediately: the close repetition of B♭ makes the note ring, and the resonance sets the rhythm into relief. Until bar 12 the two thumbs are always a third or fourth apart, but in bar 11 the right-hand thumb rises out of the accompaniment and starts to follow the melody at the lower octave. This corrupts the integrity of the voice leading and creates the most telling of dissonances in bar 12, the minor second that inflects the climax of the melody: there is no more beautiful nuance in all of Schumann. The melody has risen, but its doubling at the octave is still heard below part of the accompaniment. The thumbs remain crossed even here. The next four bars, while they carry the melody to its highest point, are essentially a resolution onto the dominant A♭, and they enrich the bass pedal on E♭ with the diminished seventh chords outlined by the inner voices.

These effects arise from the spacing of the chords, inspired by the configuration of the hand. The echoes, the soft bell-like resonance, the subtle syncopation, the crossing of registers so that melody and subordinate voices blend together with the tranquillity of the evening hour that Schumann wishes to recall—all this depends on the possibility of placing one thumb over the other. Melody is integrated into the general texture, accompaniment becomes intensely expressive. The inner voices (the thumbs above all) give life to the piece. From the inner parts come the expressive dissonance between G♭ and F in the first bar, and the delicate chromaticism that enters in bar 3.

In bars 21 to 24 an inner voice not only becomes the principal one while still remaining below part of the left-hand figuration (the simple ornament in bar 22 reminds us of the former supremacy of the soprano line), but on the last note of bar 24, for one extraordinary moment the inner part turned principal part becomes the harmonic bass on the C♭: the *ritenuto* allows us to savor this briefly before the "true" bass reasserts itself on the following beat. The ambiguity of register and the interplay of sonority reach their culmination here and are rounded off a few bars later when the soprano part descends into the low register, and then the bass takes over the solo line.

Nothing demonstrates better than the four bars 21 to 24 how certain aspects of performance have been integrated into structure. They are an example of what eighteenth- and nineteenth-century musicians called *rubato,* which was an expressive form of ornamentation, a delaying of the melody note until after the bass has been played. This Classical rubato never died out, and indeed was abused early in the twentieth century by pianists like Paderewski, who at times seemed unable to get their hands to play together. It is essentially a central European and French form of ornamentation (it was sometimes called *temps dérobé*), and was less common in Italy at the end of the eighteenth century: the young Mozart reported that the Italians were very astonished when they heard him use rubato. Mozart wrote out an example of how to play the Classical rubato when he filled out the decoration in the slow movement of the Sonata for Piano in C Minor, K.457. Here is the theme of the Adagio as it first appears:

and here is the more heavily ornamented later appearance with a rubato in the third bar:

All forms of decoration can be made structural, either by using them as motifs or to give increased animation to the surface of the music. When the melody is systematically delayed until after the beat, the effect is not only one of increased expression but of a steady syncopation which can make the rhythm appear twice as fast. This can be seen from the slow movement of the Sonata in A flat Major, H.46, by Haydn,

and also in the slow movement (rubato, like all forms of decoration, is most at home in slow movements) of Mozart's Sonata for Piano and Violin in A Major, K.526:

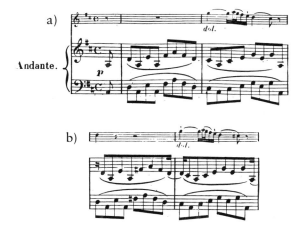

Schumann's written-out rubato in bars 21 to 24 of "Des Abends" is structural in a more profound sense, so that it is not clear whether rubato is the right term for the procedure (although the derivation from the classical technique and its expressive effect are obvious enough). The inner voice, alto or tenor (it is impossible to decide, as it is always the right hand that plays it, but it is almost always below the upper voice of the left-hand figure), which becomes the principal voice here, has already been established from the beginning as coming after the beat. In its insistent repetition it provided a pattern that was syncopated with respect both to the accompaniment in duple time and to the melody in triple. It moved briefly in parallel with the upper voice and confirmed the climax harmonically. It has been an essential part of the structure before it becomes in bar 21 the principal melodic line played rubato—and (in contrast to the examples from Haydn and Mozart) when it becomes a rubato, its rhythm has not changed one jot. The ambiguity of the voice leading at the precise moment when it turns from accompaniment to melody on the G♭ at the opening of bar 21 is increased by the preparation. The G♭ has been sounding for four bars in a row in the voice (tenor?) represented by the left-hand thumb, and at bar 21 the two voices coincide for the first time—the resonance, in fact, implies briefly that the melody voice is coming out of the left-hand figure, but the triple rhythm reasserts the priority of the right-hand voice, and the ornament in the upper voice at bar 22 confirms the beat even more powerfully than the bass note and makes us hear the expressive delay with greater conviction. Schumann's uncanny ability to erode the abstract structure of voice leading which he had learned as a student, and to create ambiguities of resonance, gives "Des Abends" its atmosphere of reverie.

Tone color and structure

I have spoken of the Romantic innovations in texture, tone color, and resonance as if they were somehow less abstract than structures of pitch and rhythm, more directly accessible to experience, and this is in some measure misleading. The sound of an oboe, clarinet, or piano is no less abstract a conception than the sound of a B♭ of unspecified tone color: a thick texture is no more sensuous than a dotted quarter note. It would also be absurd to think that Liszt and Berlioz were any more responsive to instrumental sonority than Giovanni Gabrieli or Domenico Scarlatti. It is not that the music of the 1830s was more aptly conceived for the instruments specified than the works of Frescobaldi or Couperin. On the contrary, there are passages in Chopin (the final three pages of the Polonaise-Fantaisie, for example) which are exceptionally unpianistic. The sensitivity to tone color of Handel and Mozart may have been equalled, but it was not surpassed in the nineteenth century.

In one sense, however, the music of the Romantic generation is more intimately bound up with aural experience than that of the previous ages. The composers of the late eighteenth century had already integrated dynamics into composition in a new way: dynamics were no longer used only for simple contrast or for their expressive value; the accents of a Haydn theme often have a clear motivic significance. Beethoven carried this even farther: his music uses the dynamics of a theme or motif for large-scale development and transformation. In the decades that followed, what Haydn and Beethoven had done for dynamics was applied to other aspects of musical experience—resonance, pedalling, tone color—by the contemporaries of Schumann and Liszt.

The revolutionary nature of the achievement may be seen at once if we look at transcriptions. Before the work of the generation that came to maturity in the 1830s, no transcription sought to capture and retain the instrumental qualities of the original. Beethoven's arrangement of the Violin Concerto for the piano did not try to make the piano sound like a violin. The original series of pitches has merely been transferred to another instrument. J. S. Bach arranged his Concerto for Harpsichord in D Minor (itself an arrangement of a work for violin) as a cantata for chorus and solo organ: in the successive transformations the instrumental qualities of the original are almost indifferent. In one respect harpsichord and organ are diametrically opposed: the long sustained notes are most prominent on the organ, the faster-moving lines on the harpsichord. Each instrument realizes different aspects of the same structure, which remains invariant while tone color changes. Here is the rescoring for harpsichord of Bach's C Major Sonata for Solo Violin (an arrangement once thought to be by Johann Sebastian Bach himself, but now believed to have been done somewhat later, perhaps by Wilhelm Friedemann Bach):

Not even a suggestion of the original instrumental color is conveyed. Similarly, Mozart's arrangement of Bach fugues for string quartet and trio retain nothing of their keyboard character. Much the same may be said of Handel, in his time the most brilliant master of instrumental color: in none of the hundreds of readaptations of his own and other composers' music does the sound of the original play any role. Arrangements of vocal music for instruments have existed since the fourteenth century, and they became very common in the sixteenth, but no transcription of a motet for the lute, for example, gives us any sense of vocal style. It is not until the 1830s and the transcriptions of Liszt that the reproduction of the original sonority on the new instrument becomes a major preoccupation. Liszt invents wonderful pianistic illusions of orchestral instruments and of the interplay between voices and instruments: even his most extravagant versions retain at their heart a certain fidelity to the original sound.

Delight in instrumental color for its own sake is not new with Liszt: it is found even in a period like the seventeenth century, when instrumental music takes a very inferior second place to vocal style, and the exploitation of instrumental sonority is displayed by composers as different as Monteverdi and Buxtehude. Nevertheless, orchestral color is not one of the fundamentals of form before the Romantic generation; tone color was applied like a veneer to form, but did not create or shape it. There were a few cracks in this solid view which confined the basic material of music to the neutral elements of pitch and rhythm: among the interesting exceptions are those moments of pure play of sound in Scarlatti's sonatas, where the keyboard instrument mimics trumpets, drums, oboes, and guitars. Most significant of all are the "free" forms, the preludes of the French harpsichordists, the organ toccatas of the Germans, above all those of Buxtehude and Bach. Since there is no pretension to strict composition here, the composer is liberated from traditional procedures and can use instrumental color to bring new forms into being. The toccata displays the instrument and tests it. It aims not at composition, but at an illusion of improvisation.

In improvising, conception and realization are theoretically one and the same. Practically, of course, there is generally a basic model that guides the improvising performer, but the listener is intended to believe that the creation is truly spontaneous. The relation to the instrument, its mechanics as well as its sound, is all-important here: the improviser often feels as if the instrument itself is creating the music. This delight in tone color and in the physical contact with the instrument must, we suppose, have existed from the primitive beginnings of music, but it was the Romantic generation that introduced it directly into the initial stages of strict composition. The change was not thoroughgoing, of course: composers would long continue to erect neutral structures of pitch and rhythm, and then clothe them in instrumental dress. From Schumann and Liszt to Mahler and Debussy and to our own decades, however, it is evident that timbre, register, and spacing play a greater and more determining part in the conception of the most interesting and significant works. The Romantics cannot be said to have enlarged musical experience except insofar as all original composers have done so, but they altered the relationship between the delight in sound and the delight in structure; they gave a new importance to aspects of musical experience considered until then of secondary interest or relegated entirely to the performer. They permanently enlarged the role of sound in the composition of music.

Fragments

Renewal

The first song of Schumann's *Dichterliebe* begins in the middle, and ends as it began—an emblem of unsatisfied desire, of longing eternally renewed. The introduction returns not only before the second stanza but at the end as well. It starts as if continuing a process already in motion, and ends unresolved on a dissonance (see next page).

The vocal line also remains unresolved, as if the music springs not so much from the return of May in the opening verse as from the last words: "my desire and longing." The direct inspiration is, of course, Heine's poem; the musical representation, nevertheless, is dependent on a radical evolution in style. Not until Schumann's generation was it possible to end with a dissonance—unless one excepts Mozart's sextet "A Musical Joke," where each player ends crashingly in the wrong key (no doubt Mozart enjoyed the effect, but the real innovator, obviously, is the composer who took seriously what everyone before him had thought nonsensically funny). The last chord of Schumann's song is the dominant seventh of F sharp minor: more than any other chord in the classical vocabulary, a dominant seventh demands an unequivocal resolution, and the proper resolving chord is the most fundamental one, the tonic. There is, in fact, no F sharp minor chord anywhere in the song—and some doubt whether F sharp minor is really the key of the song. With an introduction that does not fix the tonality but seems to take a previously settled harmony and rhythmic motion for granted, and with an ending that prolongs the dissonance of the opening phrase, "Im wunderschönen Monat Mai" is a brilliant and famous example of the open form which was one of the ideals of the period.

This way of putting it, however, does imperfect justice to Schumann's art. Vocal line and piano part may, separately, be unresolved in themselves, but they successively resolve each other. The first bars of the singer dissolve all the

painful tensions of the introduction into an A major cadence. In turn, the last notes of the singer move naturally into the E♯ that follows in the piano:

die   Lie - be auf - ge - gan - gen.

Although the harmony at the end of the vocal line is consonant (a D major triad), it is the line itself that is dissonant, that demands resolution. In the context of the song, indeed, even the harmony calls out for the resolution brought by the piano:

The extraordinary craft of the song lies in the relation between voice and piano, the sense of the different musical spaces occupied by each, and the way resolution finally arrives only outside the space in which the tension was principally defined. The harmony of the final bar remains, naturally, unresolved—but we have already heard it resolved twice, in bars 4 to 6 and 15 to 17:

The form is circular: the opening of each section in turn resolves the previous one and ends, itself unresolved—only a dissonant close is possible. The form goes around only twice, but logically there is no reason for it not to continue indefinitely, and it is part of the wonderful effect that we feel the infinite possibility of return. In this sense the dominant seventh chord is only the apparent close of a form that has no end, of a *da capo senza fine;* the form is closed on itself, although open in all imaginable realizations. In insisting upon the implicit resolution, I do not want to minimize the magical effect of the final chord which suspends motion without completing it.

It is significant that at the moment when the piano resolves the vocal line, piano and voice clash most strikingly. The G♮ in bar 12, which is the climax of the singer's melody, is followed a second later by the G♯ above it in the piano:

voice　　piano

The most important opposition in the score is here, and it creates a dissonance of great emotional power in the principal line as it passes from voice to piano; it immediately and appropriately follows the words "die Liebe aufgegangen" (love arose), and then, in the second stanza, "mein Sehnen und Verlangen" (my desire and longing). The harmony implied by the vocal melody is momentarily frustrated, annulled by the instrumental sound (the dissonance would be far less striking if it were wholly outlined within either voice or piano). The effect is reinforced by the phrase rhythm: until this point the phrases have been a simple succession of four-bar units, and this is broken just here as the piano starts a new phrase in the last bar of the singer's phrase, and the introduction returns before the singer has quite finished.

"Introduction" is the wrong word: the melody is seamless—some of the notes have words put to them. The overlapping between voice and piano results in an unbroken line:

From this it should be clear that the singer's melody grows directly out of the piano's—it is the same shape inverted:

Even more significantly, the piano interlude in turn, when it comes back, appears to grow out of the vocal line. At the end of the first stanza we realize that the second playing of the opening bars outlines the same shape as the second part of the vocal melody, "Then love rose in my heart":

As this proceeds, its full contour is anticipated in the piano by

and the return of the opening sums it up, intensifies it, and resolves it:

In short, the piano seems to derive from the voice by diminution, just as the vocal melody came from the piano motif by inversion. It would be simpler to think of the whole song as the continuous development of a single motif.

The ambiguous relation of voice to instrument is crucial to Schumann's technique. When the voice enters, it is almost perfectly doubled by the piano—almost, as the voice begins by repeating one note that the piano ties, and anticipates the next note (B), a sixteenth note before the piano (bars 4 to 5). This kind of small deviation from exact doubling is common practice long before Schumann, a device essential to the use of an accompaniment that doubles a solo voice or instrument: it was found in the previous century in opera and in chamber music as well as in songs, and Schubert employed it to great effect. No one, however, exploited it as radically and obsessively as Schumann, as we can see even in the small space of this short song: as it proceeds, voice and piano move gradually farther apart without ever completely separating.

The two versions, vocal and instrumental, of the same melody appear to pull at each other in bars 5 to 12 as one moves ahead or drags behind, creating dissonances between successive notes of the melody, many of which remain unresolved or only partially resolved—resolutions which come too late to be completely convincing or to muffle the gradually increasing tension. In bars 9 to 12 the piano doubles most of the notes of the melody, but plays them too late and holds them too long:

The C♯ in the piano at the end of bar 9 is never, in fact, resolved. Schumann plays with our sense that resolution in another register or in another space is incomplete as voice and piano move out of phase, and the dissonances enrich the harmony in a way totally unacceptable to classical counterpoint (the resolving D appears in the piano too late—only in bar 11, when the harmony has changed).

At the end of the phrase, we might consider the voice and piano to have split apart as the piano's G♯ attacks the previous G♮ in the voice, except that the melodic line remains essentially unbroken.

The subtle interplay between solo melody and accompaniment occasionally found in earlier composers is transcended here. The piano is no longer an accompanying instrument, and the complete melody is contained only within

its part. Every note of the melody appears in the piano and is notated as a
melody note in a principal voice, except for bars 10 and 12: we accept the fact
that the necessary resolving D cannot be found in the upper line of the piano
in bar 10, and is delayed until bar 11 (where it still doubles the voice); we
accept the transformation of G♮ to G♯. Our acceptance of these tensions is
essential to Schumann's purpose. The blurring of accompaniment and solo part
is mirrored in the voice leading within the piano, as accompanying voices fuse
with the principal voice. We are meant to hear the first bar as one single
expressive line:

although it is notated—and also understood—as four-voice harmony. This
technique is sustained throughout.

These ambiguities—the keyboard part as four-voice texture and yet as single
line, voice and instrument as opposed and yet as one unified melody—are
further extended on a larger scale to the harmony. The piano, when alone,
appears to be in F sharp minor; the voice enters with a clear A major cadence.
The controversy about the real key of the song seems to me largely misguided,
although Schenkerians, who insist on A major, have the obvious advantage,
since only the A major of bars 5 to 8 give one the traditional sense of rest and
of release of harmonic tension. It should also be obvious that the contrast of
F sharp minor and A major is only a surface opposition: like Chopin (in the
Scherzo no. 2 and the Fantasy, op. 49), Schumann treats the relative minor
here and elsewhere as a variant form of the tonic, using it rather for a change
of mode and not of tonality. The controversy, however, reveals a genuine
ambiguity on which the emotional power of the song rests. The dominant
seventh of F sharp minor is paradoxically the most stable chord in the song,
and we return to it over and over again. The A major that enters with Heine's
poetry is, in fact, a surprise, and line 3 of the stanza immediately initiates a
turning back towards F sharp minor, a movement that is never completed. It
may be reasonable to claim that A major is the basic key, but to insist too
much upon it is to obscure the fact that Schumann has elaborated a form in
which the tonic is itself unstable. (The second song will both resolve and
intensify these contradictions.) The revolving structure wonderfully makes the
A major cadence less convincing the second time than the first since we now
know that it will have such a transitory effect, and the most unstable chord,
the dominant seventh, becomes the stable pivot around which everything turns.

Without for a moment challenging the system of tonality, Schumann here
stands basic tonal structure on its head. The standard tonal procedure (with
the exception of forms like toccatas and fantasies, which are intended to act

as free improvisation) is to define a point of rest, a central triad, move away from it, and return to it one or more times. Schumann's song, however, starts with a traditionally unstable chord, moves to a point of rest, a stable cadence, and returns to the unstable chord as its goal. It is crucial for the conception that the return be identical with the opening so that the form is infinitely repeatable. The structure is finished in conception, although both beginning and end are open in sound. The closure is defined not by the points of rest but by a potentially infinite oscillation, adequately revealed by two stanzas. Completely balanced and yet unstable, it is a perfect Romantic fragment: complete in itself, a fragmentary image of the infinite, the return of springtime, the renewal of desire.

The Fragment as Romantic form

The Romantic Fragment—at once complete and torn away from a larger whole—had a distinguished literary history by the time Schumann wrote *Dichterliebe*. It came into being with the early Romantic movement in Germany, the circle of young artists, philosophers, scientists, and poets in Jena during the very last years of the eighteenth century, and was for a brief time their principal form of expression: it characterized the movement. One might say that the creator of the Fragment was Friedrich Schlegel, who offered this definition of the form (the definition is itself one of the series of 451 "Fragments" printed in 1798 in the *Athenaeum*, a literary review published by Schlegel and his brother August Wilhelm from 1798 to 1800):

A fragment should be like a little work of art, complete in itself and separated from the rest of the universe like a hedgehog.

Ein Fragment muss gleich einem kleinen Kunstwerke von der umgebenden Welt ganz abgesondert und in sich selbst vollendet sein wie ein Igel.

The hedgehog (unlike the porcupine, which shoots its quills) is an amiable creature which rolls itself into a ball when alarmed. Its form is well defined and yet blurred at the edges. This spherical shape, organic and ideally geometrical, suited Romantic thought: above all, the image projects beyond itself in a provocative way. The Romantic Fragment draws blood only from those critics who handle it unthinkingly. Like its definition, the Romantic Fragment is complete (this oxymoron was intended to disturb, as the hedgehog's quills make its enemies uncomfortable): separate from the rest of the universe, the Fragment nevertheless suggests distant perspectives. Its separation, indeed, is aggressive: it projects into the universe precisely by the way it cuts itself off.

The literary form is generally aphoristic, and derives ultimately from the French maxims of the seventeenth century, perfected by La Rochefoucauld and

La Bruyère. The most direct source, however, was the late eighteenth-century polemicist Chamfort, whose *Maxims and Characters* showed that the form could be given a more provocative and cynical twist. This is clear enough in his most famous sentence: "Love in society is often only the exchange of two fantasies and the rubbing together of two epidermises."

The classical aphorism not only expressed its thought with precision; it also narrowed the sense of the words, focussed their meaning. La Rochefoucauld was a master of this kind of focus:

Women can master their coquetry less easily than their passion.

When our merit declines, our taste declines as well.

The only thing that should surprise us is that we are still able to be surprised.

Les femmes peuvent moins surmonter leur coquetterie que leur passion. (no. 334)

Quand notre mérite baisse, notre goût baisse aussi. (no. 379)

On ne devrait s'étonner que de pouvoir encore s'étonner. (no. 384)

The words become more precise here, and they lose some of the agreeable fuzziness that they acquire in everyday speech. We move towards a kernel of meaning: the force is centripetal. This is even true of the more poetical of La Rochefoucauld's maxims:

Neither the sun nor death can be looked at steadily.

Magnanimity despises everything in order to have everything.

Le soleil ni la mort ne se peuvent regarder fixement. (no. 26)

La magnanimité méprise tout, pour avoir tout. (no. 248)

The precision does not destroy the poetic resonance but intensifies it.

With Chamfort, however, the words often lose their definition as the thought gains in precision:

Everything I learned, I have forgotten: the little I remember, I guessed.

Tout ce que j'ai appris, je l'ai oublié: le peu ce dont je me rappelle, je l'ai deviné.

The words in this observation begin to expand as if with some kind of inward pressure: the direction is centrifugal. As we puzzle out the thought, the individual words—"learn," "forget," "guess"—begin to move to the margins of their meaning, to connote more than they denote. This expansive movement attains its greatest power with the Romantic Fragment, and it entailed a renunciation of classical focus.

The fashion for publishing fragments began several decades before the fragments of Friedrich Schlegel, and works of considerable distinction were so presented. The important theories of Lavater, for example, appeared as *Fragments on Physiognomy* (1775–1778), and the most celebrated work of German literature, Goethe's *Faust,* was first made public as a fragment in 1790. These fragments acknowledged and proclaimed their unfinished form, although Lavater took an important step towards the more paradoxical Romantic conception when he affirmed that not merely the form but the very conception of his thought was necessarily fragmentary. Schlegel gave the genre a firmer basis when he implied that the fragmentary state was not a necessary evil but a positive virtue. It was above all a modern virtue: "Many works of the ancients have become fragments: many works of the moderns are already conceived as fragments" *(Viele Werke der Alten sind Fragmente geworden. Viele Werke der Neuern sind es gleich bei der Entstehung).* Starting as a student of Greek literature, Schlegel felt that the perfection of the classical work was unattainable in his own day; in place of classical beauty, modern art had to be satisfied with the "interesting." Clearly, the "interesting," a more dynamic concept than the "beautiful," is necessarily imperfect, and Schlegel's aesthetics of the fragment justified a new and progressive sense of art.

The Romantic Fragment, imperfect and yet complete, was typical of the age in its effort to have its cake and eat it too. Each Fragment is, or should be, a finished form: it is the content that is incomplete—or, rather, that develops further with each reading. Schlegel's *Fragments* carry the seeds of their own development, and even the seeds of their own criticism:

> The Germans, they say, are the greatest people in the world in respect to the elevation of their sense of art and their scientific thought. Indeed: only there are very few Germans.

> *Die Deutschen, sagt man, sind, was Höhe des Kunstsinns und des wissenschaftlichen Geistes betrifft, das erste Volk in der Welt. Gewiss: nur gibt es sehr wenige Deutschen.*

This both affirms and undermines the patriot's pride. If the affirmation still stands after the undermining has done its work, that is because the work begun is not finished: the fragment sets in motion a process to which the end is not in sight. When Schlegel claims that every man has one novel in him, and it doesn't matter if he writes it or not, the relation of literature to life, novel to biography, is made permanently ambiguous; and the ambiguity is not static but constantly shifting as one seeks to apply the thought. The more one ponders this fragment, the more difficult it becomes to fix the concept of "novel," which changes as it goes from art to life. Starting from the invention of the maxim in classical times, it is evident that all maxims were, ideally, presented for meditation, for continuous interpretation; but the Romantic Fragment implicitly shows the act of interpretation already in motion.

The Romantic Fragment is, therefore, a closed structure, but its closure is a formality: it may be separated from the rest of the universe, but it implies the existence of what is outside itself not by reference but by its instability. The form is not fixed but is torn apart or exploded by paradox, by ambiguity, just as the opening song of *Dichterliebe* is a closed, circular form in which beginning and end are unstable—implying a past before the song begins and a future after its final chord.

After the *Athenaeum* fragments, literary Europe was inundated by little collections of observations, maxims, and aphorisms by major and minor figures. Schlegel had already included fragments by the theologian Schleiermacher, by Novalis, and by his brother August Wilhelm Schlegel in his own collection. A separate set of Novalis, called *Pollen Dust,* was printed in the first issue of the *Athenaeum,* and Schlegel later added a new series, *Ideas.* Many of these "fragments," particularly those of lesser writers, were ordinary observations, run-of-the-mill maxims, and Novalis had already objected that many fragments by Schlegel himself were not true "Fragments" at all. An aesthetics of the fragment was gradually diffused throughout literature, with a considerable influence in the other arts. In music Schumann was the greatest representative of this aesthetic. This may have been in part because his favorite reading came from the German authors of the first decades of the nineteenth century, Jean-Paul and E. T. A. Hoffmann. It was probably Hoffmann who had the greatest effect on Schumann, and Hoffmann was closest in practice to early Romantic theory: he stands midway between the members of the Jena circle and the next generation of writers, including Heine.

Open and closed

A song that ends on a dominant seventh chord is an example of the Fragment so obvious and so limited that it may lead us to overlook how the aesthetic works throughout much of Schumann's music, and in the music of his contemporaries as well. The second song of *Dichterliebe,* "Aus meinen Tränen," will carry us a step further. It has a final cadence on the tonic, and almost no ambiguity in defining its tonality, but in an important sense it has even less of a beginning or an end than the first song:

It has become the fashion, when performing *Dichterliebe,* to go from the first to the second song without pause. A short pause of two or three seconds would, I think, bring out the way that the opening song is both complete in itself and inconclusive, but in any case the second song begins by appearing to clarify the ambiguities of what precedes. The ambiguity of F sharp minor versus A major is resolved halfway through the first bar in favor of F sharp minor— and then shifts immediately and unequivocally to A Major! The opening bar takes off, in fact, from the ambiguity, plays with it; the effect depends on the previous song.

Schumann's setting of "Aus meinen Tränen" is, on the surface, even simpler than Heine's poem: the eight verses in two stanzas are reduced by the composer to four phrases in one stanza, and the vocal lines of the first, second, and fourth phrases are almost identical. The resulting primitive form *AABA,* however, is inflected subtly at the opening of the fourth phrase. Bar 3 has more notes than the corresponding bars 7 and 15, but this is only because Heine gives eight syllables to the line while the other verses have only five, and Schumann makes the minimum alteration in the melody's rhythmic contour to accommodate the poem. By contrast, the extra syllables in the fourth phrase in bars 12 to 14 (nine, as opposed to seven in bars 1–3 and 4–6) are exploited by Schumann to create a more intense expression. It is, however, the rewriting of the accompaniment in bars 12 to 14 that transforms the already twice-heard phrase into something new, that creates the climax and makes it clear that this is the end of the song.

Except, of course, that the singer does not end—and that the final notes in the piano are absolutely perfunctory. Here, Schumann exploits with even greater effect the ambiguity of the location of the principal melodic line in voice or piano that we perceived in the first song. The voice doubles every note of the melody in the piano, with one exception—the last note of the repeated phrase I have labelled *A*. This phrase appears three times, and three times the singer stops with a pause just before the end. It is the instrument that rounds off the penultimate harmony each time, and each time with an unobtrusive *pianissimo*. I think it is evident that the pianist should always play the cadence in tempo after the fermata, even the final one—the *ritardando* applies only until the fermata, rounding off the vocal line rhythmically while leaving it incomplete harmonically. The last chord satisfies the formal requirement of resolving the dominant seventh chord that the first song withholds, but the poem and the song are clearly over with the fermata.

"Flowers grew from my tears and my sighs became a choir of nightingales. If you love me, my child, I shall send thee all the flowers, and the song of the nightingale will sound before your window." Schumann's setting emphasizes, not the movement from despair to hope, but the sense that the hope is not yet fulfilled. The singer ends each phrase as a question; the piano concludes without concluding. The second song prolongs the unsatisfied desire of the first, and the note on which the singer pauses three times and leaves suspended at the end is, in fact, a B, the last note of the first song left suspended in the piano. The resolution comes always too late, and it never comes to the singer.

The use of repetition is remarkable: three times the penultimate harmony is left suspended, and after the first two fermatas the pianist's cadence is so delayed as to be an upbeat to the next phrase. The reshaping of the final phrase leads us to expect a more elaborate cadence: the harmony gains in intensity with a new chromatic alto part that descends from G♮ through F♯ and F♮ to E, the texture is richer; and the dynamics, now opening *pianissimo,* not *piano,* shape the phrase with an expressive swell and diminuendo; above all, Schumann adds a pedal indication, which implies, with no doubt whatever, that the pedal should have been used sparingly or not at all until this bar, which should vibrate with a fullness of emotion. After all this reworking, the second half of the phrase reappears absolutely unaltered, except that the pause before the cadence is now more than twice as long. Schumann was a master at constructing a cadence which still leaves one of the polyphonic elements unresolved, but he never used the device more powerfully or more expressively than at this point. By playing off the voice against the piano, he shows amazingly that a dominant seventh can be followed by its tonic without reaching a truly satisfying resolution, and provides an extraordinary musical image of his text with the simplest means.

"Aus meinen Tränen" is complete and perfectly shaped, but without a satisfactory beginning or end. Its opening makes independent sense on paper, but in performance it seems above all to prolong the first song, "Im wunderschönen Monat Mai"—not merely to complement it, and fit with it the way the adagio of a sonata or symphony is related to the opening movement. The harmonic sense of the first bar of the second song depends absolutely on the previous song. Further, the A major cadence at the end of the first two phrases, which was so perfunctory after the fermata as to appear like an upbeat to the following phrase, is equally perfunctory after the even longer final pause, and now seems a simple upbeat on the dominant to the D Major of the third song. This compromises the end as well as the beginning. The song fulfills the apparently contradictory aesthetic of the Fragment: it appears to be a separate, closed traditional structure that satisfies all the formal requirements, with a well-defined melody and V^7/I cadence, and yet it makes no sense in independent performance.

This inner contradiction distinguishes the Fragment in music from pieces like the slow movements of Beethoven's *Waldstein* and *Appassionata* Sonatas which cannot be played independently (they act as introductions, and move without pause or cadence into what follows), or from works which could be performed independently, like the adagio variations of Beethoven's Sonata, op. 111, but which attain their full meaning only within the context of the whole work. "Aus meinen Tränen," like "Im wunderschönen Monat Mai," is both an independent form and nonsense if executed on its own—not merely poorer in meaning and disappointing in effect, but puzzling and even inexplicable.

From this principle Schumann was able to create a song cycle that is structurally an advance in technique, if not in value, over those by Beethoven and Schubert. In Beethoven's *An die ferne Geliebte,* the songs all run together without pause as a continuous series; by contrast, the individual songs of Schubert's cycles can be sung out of context, although their significance is deeper and fuller when they are performed as part of the cycle. Schumann combines both systems: *Dichterliebe* and *Frauenliebe und Leben* are made up of apparently independent songs which cannot be independently performed. Among the songs are some exceptions: "Ich grolle nicht," for example, from *Dichterliebe,* used to be popular in Lieder recitals (and, for all I know, still is). Several of the songs from *Frauenliebe und Leben* can be performed separately: the last song, however, is impossible on its own; the third, "Ich kann's nicht fassen," demands to be heard as a dramatic C minor trio between two songs in E flat major; and the little wedding march as a postlude to the fifth would sound strange outside the cycle, particularly as the inconclusive end on a bare sixth suggests that it will be followed at once by the succeeding piece.

It is facile to conceive of the Romantic Fragment only in terms of its ending; the idea behind it is considerably richer. The eleventh song of *Dichterliebe* (or thirteenth, if we retain the manuscript songs that Schumann cut on publication), "Ein Jüngling liebt ein Mädchen" (see next page), shows this more complex status:

> A young man loved a girl
> Who had chosen another man:
> The other man loved another girl
> And married her.
>
> The girl took out of spite
> The first good man
> Who came along;
> The young man was in a bad way.
>
> It's an old story
> But it remains always new
> And to whomever it happens
> It breaks his heart in two.

Taken by itself, this opens with a jolly swing to it, but only the first two bars have the character of a folk song, while the rest has a coarse air which is, like the poem, at once infectious and repellent. The tune is not only undistinguished, it is ostentatiously commonplace, with several deliberately awkward moments, like the end of the first stanza (bars 11 and 12); in the last stanza

the repeated notes of the final bars of the vocal part (bars 29–31) are, moreover, positively ugly. Even if one puts a higher value on this song as an independent piece of music than I think justified, it is clear that for Schumann it could not exist outside the cycle. It is, in its angular and banal insistence, a deliberately bad song, but magnificent in its place. Its coarseness makes Heine's facetiousness more profound as well as more dramatic. Taken by itself it might be a comic parody: in the cycle, its comedy is not humorous but deeply moving, above all because it makes no concessions to grace or charm.

Schumann is perhaps the first composer to transform a musical joke into a tragic effect, to use the banal or the awkward not merely for comic relief but seriously—this presupposes an ability to discover a genuine musical interest in the banal, or the ungainly, and we clearly have something of that here. It is a new kind of musical irony, far removed from the elegant Mozartean irony of *Così fan tutte,* or the bitter aristocratic irony Liszt found in Chopin. It may, in fact, have been Schumann's comprehension of the seductive possibilities of the banal phrase which made him so repulsive to Chopin, but which makes him so modern, so much a precursor of Mahler, Berg, and Stravinsky. If "Ein Jungling liebt ein Mädchen" were more distinguished musically, it would not have so powerful an effect in its place in the cycle. This was a revolutionary achievement: the inspiration here is drawn directly from the words "It's an old story, but remains ever new," but the musical use of the commonplace has a force to which the words do not aspire. In any case, it was not Heine who taught Schumann the use of irony: he had already developed it in his piano music several years before, and it was in the great keyboard sets that he learned the technique of creating a cycle of fragments.

Words and music

The influence of Heine was, however, already a possibility in these earlier keyboard works. Before Schumann published any songs, he had been planning a series of *Lieder* without voice—poems of Heine's for the pianoforte. It may even be that some of the melodies for this project appear in the piano sets or in the song cycles that succeeded them. In any case, the metamorphosis of speech into music—and, indeed, music into speech—implied by the unfulfilled project finds an equally subtle realization in the technique of Schumann's songwriting, where voice and instrument—sometimes doubling each other, sometimes out of phase or with the melody passing from one to the other— realize a single unified line. Schumann is carrying out in musical form the relationship of music and language as it was conceived in the circle of Schlegel in Jena. The doctrine was presented in the *Fragmente aus dem Nachlasse eines jungen Physiker, ein Taschenbuch für Freunde der Natur* (Fragments from the Posthumous Papers of a Young Physicist, a Pocket Book for Friends of Nature), published in 1810 by Johann Wilhelm Ritter. The ideas on music in this odd and extraordinary esoteric work were, as we shall see, known to Schumann.

Born in 1776, Ritter lived to the age of thirty-four. His last years were romantically dissolute, and he died of tuberculosis in a manner more suited to the popular idea of a poet than a scientist. His thought centered to some extent on that mystical and shallow Romantic philosophy of science called *Naturphilosophie,* but some of his scientific work was genuinely important, in particular the discovery of ultraviolet rays and the use of the battery (recently invented by Volta) to separate water into hydrogen and oxygen: like many physicists of the time, he was fascinated by the phemonenon of animal magnetism. He was admired by Goethe as well as by Novalis and Schlegel, and his portraits of some of the members of the Jena circle in the introduction to his book are a precious witness to the character of that early avant-garde group.

The pages on music are found in the appendix to Ritter's *Fragments,* and they identify music not only with speech but with consciousness itself:

The existence and the activity of man is tone, is language. Music is also language, general language, the first of mankind. The extant languages are individualizations of music—not individualized music but relating to music as the separate organs relate to the organic whole . . . Music decomposes into languages. This is why each language can in addition serve music as its accompaniment; it is the representation of the particular in the general; song is language in a double sense, the general and the particular at once. Here the particular word is raised to general intelligibility—above all to the singer himself. The folk of all languages understand music, all languages are understood by music itself and translated into the general. Nevertheless, man himself is the translator. It is to be remarked that his general language does not come from him; but it is itself given with his consciousness, and to this degree comes forward itself. For only in expressing himself is man conscious. This takes place invariably in general speech first; the particular follows. Thus every one of our spoken words is a secret song, for music from within continuously accompanies it. In audible song, the inner voice is raised as well. Song is praise of the creator, it completely expresses the moment of existence.

Des Menschen Wesen und Wirken ist Ton, ist Sprache. Musik ist gleichfalls Sprache, allgemeine, die erste des Menschen. Die vorhandenen Sprachen sind Individualisierungen der Musik; nicht individualisierte Musik, sondern, die zur Musik sich verhalten wie die einzelnen Organe zum organisch Ganzen. Die Musik zerfiel in Sprachen. Deshalb kann noch jede Sprache sich der Musik zu ihrer Begleiterin bedienen; es ist die Darstellung des Besonderen am Allgemeinen; Gesang ist doppelte Sprache, allgemeine und besondere zugleich. Hier wird das besondere Wort zur allgemeinen Ver-

*ständlichkeit erhoben—zunächst dem Sänger selbst. Die Völker aller Spra-
chen verstehen die Musik, alle (Sprachen) werden von der Musik selbst
verstanden und von ihr in die allgemeine übersetzt. Und doch bleibt der
Mensch selbst der Übersetzer. Merkwürdig, dass ihm jene allgemeine
Sprache nicht ausgeht. Aber ist sie mit seinem Bewusstsein selbst gegeben
und tritt mit diesem Grade selbst hervor. Denn nur ausgesprochen ist der
Mensch sich bewusst; dieses geschieht allemal zunächst in der allgemeinen
Sprache, und die besondere folgt. So ist jedes von uns gesprochene Wort
ein geheimer Gesang, denn die Musik im Innern begleitet ihn beständig.
Im lauten Gesange erhebt die innere Stimme sich bloss mit. Gesang wird
Schöpferlob, er spricht den Moment des Daseins ganz aus.*

The idea that music is the first speech of mankind was almost a commonplace by the time Ritter wrote. A radical version of this dates back as far as
Giambattista Vico's *Scienza nuova* of 1725: the most primitive form of speech
is music and dance. Part of the impetus for the idea came from a recognition
that the oldest witnesses to language are in verse, not prose; even for a writer
as skeptical as Voltaire, prose is the later and more sophisticated form, verse
the more ancient. For Johann Georg Hamann, the philosopher who inspired
Goethe and the *Sturm und Drang,* poetry is older than prose just as gardening
is older than agriculture. We may understand this by remarking that the
aesthetic sense is the first condition of language as it implies the sense of order,
the desire to arrange sounds into patterns, essential to the structure of speech.
In the *Metakritik* of 1781, Hamann's attack on Kant's *Critique of Pure Reason,*
his expression is even more extravagant: he resolves Kant's paradoxes of space
and time by incorporating space and time as preconditions of expression—or,
as he writes, space is painting, time is music. In short, a temporal ordering is
the initial musical structure, and a perception is not a passive event but an
active expression. Awareness implies a representation to oneself. Perception of
the world in time is already language, and music is its most general form.
Hamann only carries the tendencies of his era to a surprising extreme, but he
does not stand apart from the general line of thought, in which music was
increasingly understood as a basic model of expression. Ritter's claim that
music is given with consciousness is not far from Hamann.

What Ritter adds to this speculation is the conception of music as general
speech, and of French, German, and so forth as individualizations of music.
The separate languages are fragments of music, which, as he puts it, splits or
decomposes into "different tongues." The idea of music as general language
is picked up and developed by E. T. A. Hoffmann in his *Kreisleriana,* and was
therefore certainly known to Schumann. Hoffmann paraphrases Ritter without
naming him; he calls him only "an ingenious physicist" *(ein geistreicher
Physiker).* The relation of music to language as the general to the individual
is particularly apt as a description of Schumann's technique of songwriting, in
which the general musical line is individualized only intermittently into words:

the full line is either in the piano or passed from piano to voice. This technique would become the basis of the Wagnerian music drama, in which a general musical line is also intermittently individualized into words, but transcends both orchestra and voice; the technique of the complete phrase only incompletely realized by either voice or accompaniment is, however, largely developed by Schumann. The originality of this approach is that it radically transforms the traditional relationship of song to accompaniment.

In the simplest forms of this relationship, the piano provided either a harmonic underpinning of the melody or else—even more primitive in effect, although a somewhat later development—a mere doubling of the vocal part with added harmonies. Indeed, often in the late eighteenth century only the instrumental part of the song had to be printed, and the singer simply executed the top line of the piano. This excessively naive form came with the imitation of folk style and with the effort, in the last decades of the century, to achieve a purely natural, unsophisticated melodic style. A more complex form was also practiced, which borrowed opening and closing instrumental sections from the aria (sometimes, indeed, these instrumental passages appeared to punctuate the inner part of the stanza, and this, once again, finds its model in the aria and the concerto). The piano may echo the close of the vocal melody, repeat the cadence; it may introduce the song with a tune of its own which can reappear like a refrain. It does not, however, invade the vocal melody or take over its functions. The principle in all of these types is the independence of the vocal melody, which is a coherent and satisfying whole in itself even when the prelude, postludes, and echoes are elaborate. The greatest innovation of Schumann is not so much (as is sometimes thought) the lengthy instrumental endings that we find in so many of his songs, but the incomplete destruction of the independence of the vocal form. The vocal melody can no longer stand on its own as an intelligible structure—at the same time, the melody is not fully represented by the instrumental part. The independence is not totally suppressed; Schumann is able to play with the ambiguity, sometimes to oppose voice and instrument, to identify them at other moments, and finally to have them realize the same musical line, but out of phase with each other.

This erosion of the traditional relation had already been initiated by Schubert, but less radically and far less systematically. There are, however, several of his songs where it is set out, beginning with an early setting (dated 27 February 1815) of Goethe's "Ich denke dein":

The voice springs out of the introductory bars and completes them, carries forward the instrumental line, which, indeed, seems to illustrate the sunrise of the opening verse. The effect has its analogue in some of the accompanied recitatives of early nineteenth-century opera or oratorio, and it cannot, in fact, be repeated by Schubert in successive stanzas, which begin simply with the entrance of the voice. Much more clearly a development of pure song technique is the late "Im Frühling"; and this is, as well, closer to Schumann's ambiguous play with structure, as the instrumental introduction appears initially to be independent, and is then integrated into the vocal line. The first stanza will show the mastery with which Schubert controls the shift of function:

It is not my purpose here to consider the way the sudden eruption of memory induces the exquisite change to the remote harmony of A major, and how the return of consciousness of the present brings back, with the pathetic change of mode to A minor, the simple return to the tonic, although these matters will concern us later. At this point I want only to emphasize the compromised independence of the four-bar introduction: the singer at first appears to ignore it, and strikes out on a new melody of his own; the introduction returns, however, with the singer's first tonic cadence (in bar 10) as if it were an instrumental refrain—this time, however, it is not ignored by the singer but interrupted and carried forward to a different development. What is significant is not the reappearance of the introductory melody in the vocal part—that was already a commonplace device—but the interruption of the instrumental line in the middle of a phrase by the voice, an interruption that expands a two-bar phrase into three bars. We must not underestimate the effect of this interruption: the voice sounds as if it were initiating a new phrase as well as finishing an earlier one. As a result, the vocal phrase in itself appears rhythmically complete (bar 11 is an antecedent to bar 12) while harmonically and even melodically incomplete (bar 11 is a consequent to bar 10). Voice and instrument still remain in their separate musical spaces: the two musical lines are only partially fused.

This incomplete fusion often becomes, with Schumann, not a passing effect but a basic principle of construction. In "Der Nussbaum" the first two bars—as in Schubert—appear to be an introduction:

When the opening reappears in bars 5 and 6, it seems like an answer to the half phrase in the voice: it completes the vocal line, and yet has the character of an instrumental refrain. Its rhythmical weight is dubious, half a consequent of what precedes, half initiation of a new phrase. The transposed reappearance in bars 9 and 10 now clarifies the new status: it completes the vocal melody, and has become "individualized" into words, to use Ritter's terms. Most remarkable, however, is the shift in bars 31 to 40:

The opening motif, now given a new harmonic direction and played *ritenuto,* is the beginning of a phrase, and the repetition in bars 33 and 34 in the voice is the answer. This is a reversal of the original musical sense, and the expressive power depends on the double meaning: the instrumental phrase is heard both as a separate unit and as either a completion or an antecedent of a vocal phrase. The ambiguity is drawn out further: bars 39 and 40 are at one and the same time an intensified echo of the previous phrase (a technique derived from Schubert) and the beginning of a move back to the tonic that is completed instrumentally. Schumann juggles throughout with two-bar and four-bar phrase structures that depend partly on a relation of vocal melody to instrumental interjection. The vocal line is neither completely intelligible alone nor completely integrated without ambiguity into the general line: the song is a true Fragment.

In a passage that is a clear extension of Ritter's essay on music and language, E. T. A. Hoffmann wrote:

> But how often in the soul of the musician does the music sound at the same moment as the words of the poet, and, above all, the poet's language in the general language of music?—From time to time the musician is clearly conscious of having thought of the melody without any relation to the words, and it springs forth with a reading of the poem as if awakened by a magic touch.

> *Aber wie oft erklingt mit den Worten des Dichters im Innern des Musikers zugleich die Musik, und überhaupt des Dichters Sprache in die allgemeine Sprache der Musik?—Zuweilen ist sich der Musiker deutlich bewusst, schon früher die Melodie gedacht zu haben, ohne Beziehung auf Worte, und sie springt jetzt beim Lesen des Gedichts, wie durch ein Zauberschlag geweckt, hervor.*

This was the most modern aesthetic stance of that age: it is not the words that are embellished and imitated by music—the proper ideal was now music becoming language, music as the precondition of speech that becomes individualized into words. As the novelist Wilhelm Heinse had already written in the 1780s: "it is not the music which is the dress of words, but words which are the dress of music" (*Die Sprache ist das Kleid der Musik, und nicht die Musik das Kleid der Sprache*),[1] a surprising statement for the time, but far more banal later. It would be unjust to interpret this as a simple claim for the primacy of music. The goal was a fusion of words and music, but for this to be realized, the music must take precedence but not dominate: it had to appear to need no justification from the poetry, to establish an independent claim to existence. The fusion of music and poetry was supposed to result from a coincidence of meaning of two independent forms of expression. In practice, of course, this ideal fusion is attainable only intermittently, and either poetry or music must step down and be made to serve the other. This is the source of Schumann's constant play of ambiguity, where predominance is shifted back and forth between voice and piano. It is a form of irony, an attempt to express obliquely what cannot be acceptably stated in a more direct fashion.

1. Wilhelm Heinse, *Sämtliche Schriften* (Leipzig, 1903–1910), Book 8, II (Tagebuch), p. 298.

The simplest version of this irony is the frequent out-of-phase doubling, where both voice and piano present the same melody but with slightly different rhythms: the vocal line given the inflections of speech, the instrumental line obeying other promptings, dragging behind or anticipating (as we have seen at the opening of the *Dichterliebe*). There are, however, more profound examples of such irony. One of the most striking is the coda to the third song of *Frauenliebe und Leben*, "Ich kann's nicht fassen, nicht glauben":

The poem has ended, and the singer only returns in bar 76 to repeat the first verse of the song with new music. It is part of the extraordinary pathos of this coda that the singer cannot execute the climax in bar 79: she must leave it to the piano. The sequence clearly demands that the ascent from F (bar 71) to A♭ (bar 75) will rise ultimately to C (bar 79), but this is too high for the singer. (A successful execution of the high C by the singer would create an obtrusive operatic virtuosity completely out of style.) Even the pianist must strain to realize the sequence—or appear artistically to strain—as the arpeggiated grace notes in bar 79 give a sense of stretching to encompass what no normal hand can reach. We have here an absolute coincidence of words and music, but a coincidence reached by a paradox: "I cannot grasp it, cannot believe it" is translated into music by the impossibility of realizing the conception vocally, although the singer returns as if to take over the principal line from the piano. But this line remains in the piano, and the singer has to fall back at the climax to a subsidiary and dissonant counterpoint. (If the song were transposed down to allow the singer to double the piano melody at the end with ease, all pathos would be lost.) When piano and voice move together again, it is only to realize the painful dissonance of A♭ against G in the piano part at bar 81, and this, too, is set in relief by Schumann in bar 82 where the piano and voice create emphatic parallel fifths. This is not the only place in Schumann where the significance arises from the impossibility of musical realization—but the effect is, we must affirm, essentially musical, enriched by the words but not totally dependent on them. It is part of the irony that the singer unnecessarily and imperfectly interrupts a pure instrumental coda: Schumann creates a literary effect entirely by musical means.

The emancipation of musical language

The new relation of music and language found in Schumann's *Lieder*, and already implicit in some of Schubert, needed two long parallel developments to come into being, one in linguistics and one in music. Language was gradually reconceived not simply as the fundamental means of communication but as an independent system, a world of its own, as Wilhelm von Humboldt said,[2] separate from the exterior world of reality and from the subjective world of consciousness; only through the world of language are we able to realize that the subjective and objective worlds were the same. In a way, like Schlegel's hedgehog, language itself was a work of art independent of the reality that surrounded it, and which yet paradoxically implied that outer reality from within itself. Music in turn was also reconceived as a separate world of its own, not simply as the expression of words spoken or unspoken. These two developments need to be sketched if we are to understand how music could become an abstract model for language, and how the relation of text and music was profoundly reformulated in early nineteenth-century song.

The seventeenth and eighteenth centuries were a period of considerable speculation on the origin of language. Almost every philosopher had something to say: Locke, Rousseau, Condillac, Helvetius, Hamann, Herder, Fichte—all either tried to reconstruct the way language could have arisen in a primitive state or suggested that it was given, divinely or naturally, with human nature itself. There were, in fact, so many monographs on this subject that by the beginning of the nineteenth century the Academy of Sciences at Berlin announced that it would no longer accept papers treating of the origin of language.

2. *Hellas und Latium* (written in 1806, unpublished until 1896).

The discussion had two aspects. The first was the replacement of the account in Genesis (in which God made a gift of language to Adam, who named the animals) by one more suited to the secularization of thought, an account that would seem both rational and probable. The other aspect is more complex: it has been remarked that a search for origins is a hidden request for a definition, an attempt to describe the nature of something, projected—however fictionally—in time as a narrative. The question of the origin of language is not properly answered by a place (Mesopotamia, say, or China) and a date, however remote. What was wanted was a decision on what point in the scale of sounds and signs made throughout the animal kingdom could one speak properly of language, from the buzzing of insects, the song of birds and their flashes of plumage, the barking of dogs and the wagging of their tails, to the wailing of human babies. How much structure is needed for any of these to be language? What exactly is the function of language: the representation of truth, the expression of beliefs and feelings, the communication of needs and commands, a means of enforcing social behavior and of ordering relations within the family and the tribe? Philosophers invented interesting stories about man in the state of nature to convey their answers to such questions. Fichte, for example, imagined one primitive man, frightened by a lion, returning to his fellows and roaring at them to convey the presence of danger. This sort of fable implied that language worked by naming objects, and that its function was social and practical. If, however, the original form of language was music and dance, as Vico had claimed, the function of language was aesthetic and expressive.

The appearance of Sir William Jones's Sanskrit dictionary sent a shock into all linguistic speculation: it called attention to the relations among the Hindu, Germanic, Greek, and Romance tongues, implied their kinship. Sanskrit was quickly judged—mistakenly, of course—as the root of all these languages, the Ur-tongue from which they sprang. It is significant that, for the German Romantics, Sanskrit became a metaphor for natural language, uncorrupted by social pressures, undeformed by false ideals. "The true Sanskrit," wrote Novalis, "would speak for the sake of speaking, because speaking is its desire and its being" (*Die echte Sanskrit spräche, um zu sprechen, weil Sprechen ihre Lust und ihre Wesen sei*).[3] The rapid development of comparative linguistics drew attention away from the vocabulary and towards the phonetic and grammatical structure of different languages: this may seem paradoxical at first, but the study of the transfer of words from one language to another only emphasized the different systems into which they were integrated. Wilhelm von Humboldt, the first of the great comparative linguists, claimed it was foolish to search for the origin of language because a single word of a language implied the entire structure of which it was a part.

---

3. Novalis, *Die Lehrlinge zu Sais,* third paragraph.

Humboldt, too, like Novalis, insisted on the independence of language; it has a life of its own, and cannot be completely controlled by the will of the speaker. Friedrich Schlegel's observation "Words often understand each other better than the people who use them"[4] is only a witty version of something like the same truth. And this is the model for Ritter, who begins his discussion of music by observing, "Tones are beings who understand each other, as we understand tone. Every chord may already be a mutual tone-understanding, and come to us as an already created unity."[5] In this view, music, like language, is an ordered system which precedes its many and various manifestations; and, as we have seen, for Ritter and later for E. T. A. Hoffmann, the basis of language is a musical order.

By the late eighteenth century, music, like language, had become understood more and more as an independent, self-sufficient system, less as an imitative art. The orthodox classical view for which all the arts were imitations of nature was only too simply applicable to painting and sculpture, but had always run into difficulties with music. The standard solution to the problem was to recognize music as the imitation of sentiment. So basic is this position that in painting, the use of colors as a mimesis of sentiment was called the musical theory of color. (In a letter of Poussin, when one of his patrons complained that the colors of his painting of the *Seven Sacraments* were less appealing than those of *Moses Found in the Waters of the Nile,* he explained that different sentiments required different hues, like different modes in music.)[6] The orthodox theory of imitation created little trouble during the Baroque era, when even a fugue could be unified and characterized through a single affect or sentiment. The inadequacy began to be felt during the latter half of the eighteenth century. It is not that imitation of sentiment is irrelevant to, say, a Haydn symphony, but that it had come to seem an inadequate way of approaching even the nontechnical aspects of such a work, its generation of increasing excitement and its final spacious resolution, its resemblance to a dramatic form. By 1755 Adam Smith, occupied for the moment with aesthetics rather than economics, could write that music was essentially not an imitative art at all, except in superficial ways in its simulation of cuckoos and babbling streams, and that a work of pure instrumental music gave "a very high intellectual pleasure not unlike the contemplation of a great system in any other science."[7]

This implicit and flattering comparison of music to Newtonian physics was made possible by the recent triumphs of the pure instrumental style. Great works of pure instrumental music had existed before, from the lute composi-

4. Friedrich Schlegel, *Über die Unverständlichkeit,* third paragraph.

5. Johann Wilhelm Ritter, *Fragmente aus dem Nachlasse eines jungen Physikers,* Anhang. (Heidelberg, 1810), p. 233.

6. Letter to Chantelou, 24 November 1647.

7. *The Early Writings of Adam Smith,* ed. J. Ralph Lindgren (New York, 1967), p. 168.

tions of the sixteenth century, the organ toccatas of Frescobaldi in the seventeenth to the suites of Couperin and the compilations of Bach in the first half of the eighteenth. Nevertheless, these were in most important respects unpretentious masterpieces: pure instrumental music ranked low—just above songs—in the hierarchy of musical genres, at the top of which were religious compositions and opera, occupying a position comparable to historical and religious pictures within the genres of painting. Keyboard music, for example, was either dance music, like the suites of Couperin and Bach (and dance music was a genre considered so low that when in the 1780s a musicians' union was formed in Vienna, it expressly refused to admit dance musicians), or educational music: even works as ambitious as Bach's *Goldberg* Variations were published as keyboard exercises, as were the most spectacularly virtuosic of Scarlatti's sonatas. The equally spectacular organ toccatas of Bach existed only as a peripheral accompaniment to religious ceremonies.

It was the gradual spread of the public concert that emancipated music from its dependence on court and church and made pure instrumental music the explicit vehicle of the sublime. (By public concert I mean only those for which admission was charged, free open-air band concerts being, for example, a very different kind of function.) The true money-maker at public concerts throughout the eighteenth century was the oratorio, particularly those by Handel, but pure instrumental works gradually filled an increasingly large place on the programs. This development was accompanied by a change in aesthetics, the new conception of a work of art as an independent object with no function except that of inducing contemplation or delight. The insistence on the independence of the work of art that one finds in Kant, and then in Schiller, became a commonplace in the nineteenth century. It was peculiarly suited to instrumental music, which was considered for a time an ideal model for the other arts, a kind of ultimate or absolute to which painting and poetry could only strive in vain.

No doubt the emancipation from court and church created only the illusion of independence. The public concert and the sale of sheet music made demands as constraining as the ceremonies of court and church. There was, however, an important difference. It had never been a reproach to a composer that he correctly tailored his religious music to fit the demands of the Church, that his art was subservient to his devotion: on the contrary, towards the end of his life, Haydn was widely criticized by his contemporaries, who complained that his masses were insufficiently religious and contained passages of trivial music. The moral status of court art was slightly more ambiguous: poets, for example, were expected to provide gross flattery, painters to embellish their aristocratic sitters. It was not clear, however, that no shame was attached to this: when Ronsard, in 1564, dedicated his new volume of poems to a friend (the historian Pierre Paschal) rather than to an aristocratic patron, he boasted of the moral superiority of his action. Nevertheless, composers of music had never been accused of unnatural glorification of those in power (although, in point of fact, many court cantatas—even when we consider only the music and not the text—are certainly as base a form of flattery as any Renaissance dedication or preface). Fulfilling the economic demands of the public concert, however, was a different matter. For the late eighteenth-century mind, religious music should express devotion and piety, court music pomp and elegance; but the new symphonies and concertos written for public performance with paid admissions were not intended to express making money—or even to represent too evident a striving for popular success. Courting popularity has always been thought even more demeaning than courting private favor, and works of art created specifically to make money are considered more shameful than those produced only for self-expression.

The sincerity of the artist now becomes a criterion of artistic value. This is a natural result of the work conceived as an independent aesthetic object. The work has its own law, its own reason for existing: it is produced by the artist not for a purpose but because he must—"out of an inner necessity" would be the catchphrase. For the Romantic artist, self-expression is not self-serving or even personal; it often, indeed, entails a sacrifice of the self. This gives us the impetus behind avant-garde ideology, which arose in fact at the very end of the eighteenth century. When the work of art is initially rejected by the public, this provides its moral credentials; it demonstrates that the work was not created for popularity or for money, and justifies its success with posterity. The difficulties in this position were immediately evident: Wordsworth, for example, was inspired to claim that the original work is forced to create its own audience. No one has ever been completely comfortable with the contradictions that this view entails, but two centuries have not provided a better answer.

Instrumental music was the ideal representative of this illusion of art as divorced both from social function and from established religion. The imitative weakness of music became its trump card: music has significance, makes sense as language does, but its powers of reference are feeble. It refers only with difficulty beyond itself, and seems to create an independent world of its own, divorced from reality but richly meaningful. This independent world of instrumental music was the marvel and the envy of the other arts, and it gave music a prestige it had probably not had since the time of Plato. The new prestige is decisively expressed in 1799 by Friedrich Schlegel in fragment 444 of the *Athenaeum:*

It generally strikes many people as strange and ridiculous if musicians talk about the ideas [= themes] in their compositions; and often it may even happen that we perceive that they have more ideas in their music than about it. Whoever has a feeling, however, for the wonderful affinity of all the arts and sciences will at least not consider the matter from the superficial and so-called natural point of view, according to which music should be nothing more than the language of sentiment, and he will find a certain tendency of all pure instrumental music to philosophy not inherently impossible. Must not pure instrumental music itself create its own text? And is not the theme in it developed, confirmed, varied, and contrasted in the same way as the object of meditation in a philosophical series of ideas?

Es pflegt manchem seltsam und lächerlich aufzufallen, wenn die Musiker von den Gedanken in ihren Kompositionen reden; und oft mag es auch so geschehen, dass man wahrnimmt, sie haben mehr Gedanken in ihrer Musik als über dieselbe. Wer aber Sinn für die wunderbaren Affinitäten aller Künste und Wissenschaften hat, wird die Sache wenigstens nicht aus dem platten Gesichtspunkt der sogenannten Natürlichkeit betrachten, nach welcher die Musik nur die Sprache der Empfindung sein soll, und eine gewisse Tendenz aller reinen Instrumentalmusik zur Philosophie an sich nicht unmöglich finden. Muss die reine Instrumentalmusik sich nicht selbst einen Text erschaffen? und wird das Thema in ihr nicht so entwickelt, bestätigt, variiert und kontrastiert wie der Gegenstand der Meditation in einer philosophischen Ideenreihe?

Earlier in the eighteenth century, with Mozart, for example, the technical German word for "theme" was *Gedanke* ("idea"), and Schlegel ennobles the art of music by taking this literally rather than metaphorically. In the final sentence, however, he uses the less ambiguous word *Thema,* and gives it a new intellectual resonance.

This makes music an abstract model for thought, a structure that underlies logic and language, a form of pure reason that precedes language, if such a thing may be said to exist. Schlegel's observation is directly inspired by late eighteenth-century sonata style, and by that element which is most evident to the listeners at a public concert: the treatment of the theme. The terms "entwickelt, bestätigt, variiert und kontrastiert" variously mingle the functions of development, recapitulation, and exposition, and we can see how sonata form came eventually to seem so fundamental a pattern, as if it contained the basic elements of reason—in the 1830s A. B. Marx's original term for sonata form was the "form of free development."

The high prestige of music was not confined to German Romantic thought. Coleridge goes farther than Schlegel and makes instrumental music the model for historical process, or, rather, a model for the representation of history:

Certainly there is one excellence in good music, to which, without mysticism, we may find or make an analogy in the records of History. I allude to that sense of *recognition,* which accompanies our sense of novelty in the most original passages of a great Composer. If we listen to a simphony

of Cimarosa the present strain still seems not only to recall, but almost
to *renew,* some past movement, another and yet the same! Each present
movement bringing back as it were, and embodying the Spirit of some
melody that had gone before, anticipates and seems trying to overtake
something that is to come: and the Musician has reached the summit of
his art, when having thus modified the Present by the Past, he at the same
time weds the Past *in* the present to some prepared and corresponsive
future. The Auditor's thoughts and feelings move under the same
influence: retrospection blends with anticipation, and Hope and Memory,
a female Janus, become one Power with a double Aspect. A similar effect
the Reader may produce for himself in the pages of History, if he will be
content to substitute an intellectual complacency for pleasurable sensation. The Events and Characters of one Age, like the Strains in Music,
recall those of another, and the variety by which each is individualized,
not only gives a charm and poignancy to the resemblance, but likewise
renders the whole more intelligible.

This, from *The Friend* of 1809, is almost as remarkable for its ignorance as
for its brilliance: Cimarosa is certainly the wrong composer, as he does not
seem to have written many symphonies—and even if we consider the opera
overtures under that head, they would not represent an important or typical
achievement. It suggests that Coleridge's observation about music comes to
him secondhand rather than from immediate experience, that he is partly
repeating what he has been told about music by informed amateurs, and
chooses Cimarosa for an unfortunate illustration because of his contemporary
fame. In fact, this makes the passage doubly valuable as it represents not so
much Coleridge's personal reaction but informed contemporary opinion, and
reveals the way a cultivated public listened to a symphony and how much they
were aware of the inner relationships of a work. For this awareness the radical
developments of late eighteenth-century style were responsible and had created
a heightened consciousness of listening. I must emphasize that for Coleridge it
is not the conventional aspects of a piece that recall other moments but "the
most original passages of a great composer"—and here he is clearly reflecting
the most enlightened musical opinion, as we can see from the articles on
Beethoven by E. T. A. Hoffmann a few years later. The application to history,
however, must be Coleridge's own property: it is typical of his invention. A
few years later, historiographer J. G. Droysen realized that the writing of
history was a formal procedure, not a simple setting down of fact or reflection
of reality; a history of the Reformation, for example, was like a novel by Sir
Walter Scott, with a clear beginning, middle, and end, although a moment's
thought will make us aware that the causes of the Reformation reach endlessly
back in time and that, insofar as it has existed as a definable entity, it has never

ended. Coleridge had anticipated this historiographic position and, indeed, gone beyond: history for him was a formally independent aesthetic structure like a work of music, a way of ordering experience artistically. The most original passages in Haydn and Beethoven, for example, are shocking and yet logical, unexpected and yet prepared: the historian must similarly find a way to preserve the sense of the unexpected event, and then show how it arose and how it will project into the future. It was pure instrumental music that made Coleridge's insight possible, and he conceived this view of music not as a mystical sense but as a generally available public experience. The abstract forms of music had come to seem very grand.

It was the meaninglessness of music which had become essential to its grandeur; it accounts for its unique prestige. When Constable's pictures were first exhibited abroad at the Paris Salon of 1824, he wrote to his friend Archdeacon Fisher:

> My wife is now translating for me some of their [the French critics'] criticisms. They are very amusing and acute—but very shallow and feeble. Thus one—after saying "it is but justice to admire the *truth*—the *color*— and *general vivacity* and richness"—yet they want the objects more formed defined, &c., and say that they are like the rich preludes in musick, and the full harmonious warblings of the Aeolian lyre, which *mean* nothing, and they call them orations—and harangues—and highflown conversation affecting a careless ease—&c., &c., &c.—Is not some of this *blame* the highest *praise*—what is poetry? What is Coleridge's Ancient Mariner (the very best modern poem) but something like this? However, certain it is that they have made a decided stir and have set all the students landscaping thinking—they say on going to begin a landscape, Oh! this shall be—*a la Constable*!!![8]

"Which *mean* nothing"! The reproach of the French critics was Constable's title to glory. In the attempt to make landscape painting speak for itself, create its own world with no reference to history or picturesque narrative, the recent example of instrumental music served to many artists as a stimulus, a promise of success.

By the earliest years of the nineteenth century, music had become the most prestigious of the arts. Even before Hegel asserted that music was the archetypal Romantic art, J. W. Ritter had made a similar claim: in 1806, towards the end of the strangest of his publications, an essay called "Physics as an Art," addressed to the Munich Academy of Sciences, he wrote that music "seems to be for recent times or for the future what architecture once was for older times

8. *John Constable's Correspondence*, vol. 6, ed. R. B. Beckett (Ipswich, 1968), p. 186.

or for the past," and could not decide whether music had already reached its highest point or whether that was still to come. It was pure instrumental music that was the source of the greatest admiration and became the model for literature and the plastic. This is evident enough in the proposal of Novalis for a new kind of literature:

> Tales, without logic, nevertheless with associations, like *dreams*. Poems— simply *sounding well* and filled with beautiful words—but also without any sense or logic—at most single stanzas intelligible—they must be like mere broken pieces of the most varied things. At best, true poetry can have an *allegorical* sense on the whole, and an indirect effect like music, etc.

> *Erzählungen, ohne Zusammenhang, jedoch mit Association, wie* Träume. *Gedichte—bloss* wohlklingend *und voll schöner Worte—aber auch ohne allen Sinn und Zusammenhang—höchstens einzelne Strofen ver- ständlich—sie müssen, wie lauter Bruchstücke aus den verschiedenartigen Dingen seyn. Höchstens kann wahre Poësie einen* allegorischen *Sinn im Grossen haben und eine indirecte Wirkung wie Musik etc.*

This is, much in advance, the surrealist program for poetry. The technique of the fragment ("mere broken pieces"!) allowed the artist a partial detachment of his work from reality, made a much more freely conceived relationship possible. What the poets and painters envied was the freedom of music to manipulate its own forms and symbols, apparently without reference to a reality outside itself.

The attempt to extend that freedom to the other arts produced some strange forms. The musical inspiration is most tangible in a work like *Die Verkehrte Welt* (The Upside-Down World) by Ludwig Tieck, which starts with a "Symphony" in prose, a rhapsodic representation in words of a musical work opening with an "Andante in D Major" and including a verbal "Pizzicato with Violin Accompaniment." This is more than mere stylistic virtuosity: it is a genuine homage to the art of music. The curtain first goes up on the "Epilogue" ("Now, gentlemen, how did you like the play"), and we can see the Romantic poet trying to liberate the elements of his art from external reference and to acquire the same power over them that the musician had over his notes. The elements even assert their own freedom: in the opening scene, Scaramouche refuses to continue his comic personage and will not listen to the poet, who protests, "But the play—" Scaramouche interrupts: "What play! I am also a play, and I also have the right to speak along with it" (*"Was Stück! Ich bin auch ein Stück, und ich habe auch das Recht, mit zu sprechen"*). *Stück*, however, is "piece" as well as "play," and Tieck's play on words here intro- duces the aesthetic of the fragment.

This aesthetic does not completely destroy the relation of part to whole, of art to reality, but disturbs it and puts it into question. To make sense of Coleridge's fragment *Kubla Khan,* we must first accept it as sublime nonsense. Hazlitt wrote of it: "It is not a poem but a musical composition. We could repeat the opening lines to ourselves not the less often for not knowing the meaning of them."[9] Charles Lamb, too, said in a letter to Wordsworth (April 26, 1816) that Coleridge read *Kubla Khan* aloud "so enchantingly that it irradiates & brings heavan & Elysian bowers into my parlour while he sings or says it, but there is an observation Never tell thy dreams, and I am almost afraid that Kubla Khan is an owl that wont bear day light, I fear lest it should be discovered by the lantern & clear reducting to letters, no better than nonsense or no sense." *Kubla Khan* is not only the most famous English example of the Romantic fragment but an ideal specimen: it seems complete to most readers in spite of—or because of—the prose introduction about the man on business from Porlock who prevented Coleridge from finishing it. The man from Porlock, however, is forever part of the poem, and helps to justify the eccentricity of form as well as contribute to it.

The attempt partially to detach the elements of an art from their representation of a reality, however fictive, runs through the period and across frontiers. The initial literary model was perhaps the experiments of Sterne's *Tristram Shandy,* where the narrative even incorporates the marbled endpapers of the novel. Sterne was followed with admiration by Diderot, who interrupts an anecdote of his hero in *Jacques le fataliste* after only a page to claim that, as the author, he could make the reader wait for the rest of the story for a year or even two or three years. Clemens Brentano went still further in his novel *Godwi,* which he wrote in 1801 as the youngest member of the Schlegel circle in Jena. In the second volume, the hero on a walk with the narrator remarks, "There is the pond I fell in on page 146 of the first volume." When the narrator dies, the characters finish the book and write memorial poems for him. These paradoxical self-references—examples can be found in many other literary works of the period—are like the surprising moments of recollection that Coleridge judged so profound in pure instrumental music, but they are even more a parallel to the wonderful play with structure and function that characterizes the music of Haydn and Mozart. The same effect of satisfying paradox is found, for example, in Haydn's Quartet in D Major, op. 50, no. 6, which begins with a final cadence as its opening theme.

This kind of displacement of function is essential to late eighteenth-century musical style: shifting a theme from tonic to dominant, the most common device of the period, is an alteration of the sense on which the entire structure may depend. The use of these effects in literature, however, enforces a dislo-

9. Review of Christabel [etc.] in the *Examiner,* June 2, 1816, p. 349, printed in Donald Reiman, *The Romantics Reviewed* (New York, 1972), p. 531.

cation of reference which seems to tear the work, at least momentarily, away from any possible outside reality: it becomes a fragment, a complete form ripped from a larger context. Unlike music, language always appears to have a reference outside itself. The musical inspiration of much Romantic literature is betrayed by the terminology of the period: in 1811 E. T. A. Hoffmann asserted that the first Romantic composers were Haydn and Mozart. This is a reasonable claim when we remember that one of the ideals of Romantic art was the creation of a coherent world which does not depend on reality or simply reflect it, but runs parallel to it: the independence of a work of art, music, or literature may be legitimately thought of as a form of Romantic alienation. Yet for most of the important works of what is generally considered Romantic style today, the independence of the work is never clear-cut but always ambiguous, even compromised.

Tieck's *Puss-in-Boots (Der gestiefelte Kater)* of 1797, for example, incorporates what are apparently members of the public into the play, and when one of them remarks, "The play itself seems to be a play within a play," we may reflect that what we see is a play within a play within a play, like a set of Chinese boxes. "Tell me," the King says to Prince Nathaenael von Malinski, "How do you speak our language so fluently, since you live so far away?" The prince replies, "Be quiet, or the audience will notice that there is something unnatural." These tricks are derived from the Baroque drama, above all the works of Jonson and of Beaumont and Fletcher (acknowledged by Tieck as models), where the allusions to the stage are as frequent as they are in Shakespeare and Calderón. In his *Ursprung des deutschen Trauerspiels,* however, Walter Benjamin observed that the Romantic revival of these deliberate destructions of stage illusion have a new purpose: in the Baroque they served to show that life is an illusion, like a play; in the Romantic period they attempt to give a new status to the work, to persuade us that art is real life. This is a pretension to which no previous age aspired, but it is revealed by even the smallest details of the most original works. "More in my next letter" *(Nächstens mehr)* are the last words of Friedrich Hölderlin's novel *Hyperion,* and we conclude that the book is to continue indefinitely into a reality beyond the last page, as the first song of the *Dichterliebe* extends into an undefined future.

Experimental endings and cyclical forms

The extraordinary stylistic changes of late eighteenth-century music may have provided much of the inspiration for the literature of the turn of the century, but the literary forms that resulted were deeply eccentric. It was these works—paradoxical, anticlassical, often with startlingly unbalanced proportions—which in turn influenced the music of the generation of composers that followed. The most clearly affected by literature and art were Schumann,

Berlioz, and Liszt, but neither Mendelssohn nor Chopin remained untouched by literary developments, like the revival of Celtic and medieval poetry, as the overtures of Mendelssohn and the Ballades of Chopin explicitly demonstrate. With Chopin, however, we must not look for a specific literary work as a narrative model but for a new tone, a new atmosphere and new structures: the literary influence does not result in a program; the music does not refer beyond itself. Just as poets and painters had attempted to recreate with words and paint the freedom and the abstract power of music, so the generation of musicians born around 1810 tried to capture the originality of form and the exotic atmosphere of the literature and art they had grown up with. The appearance of the Fragment in its most obvious form—a piece that begins in the middle or does not have a proper grammatical end—is only the simplest example of the new spirit of experiment, and the way it breaks down the established conceptions of what a work of music ought to be relates it to the major stylistic developments of the time.

The opening song of the *Dichterliebe* is not the only example of an independent piece that ends with the most naive form of the Fragment, a simple dissonance like a dominant seventh chord. One of the independent sections of Berlioz's *Lélio* is rounded off in the same way. Liszt's setting of Victor Hugo's "S'il est un charmant gazon," composed in 1844, has a lovely inconclusive ending with a dominant seventh chord over a tonic pedal. When Liszt published it in 1860, he added another optional two-bar cadence for the pianists frightened by the fragment:

Another song written a year earlier, "Ich möchte hingehen" on a poem by Georg Herwegh, ends with a tonic chord, indeed, but approaches it with little sense of cadence and undercuts the final chord by removing the fundamental bass note and leaving an emphatic 6/4 chord:

This fragment has great power, and the conclusion is justified by the final verse, "The poor heart of man must break in pieces."

The beautiful early version of *Harmonies poétiques et religieuses* of 1834 ends with Liszt's favorite diminished seventh chord:

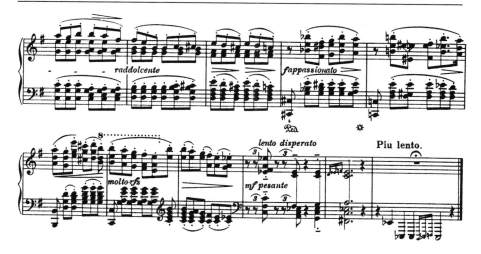

and there is a similar ending to the austere last version published in 1883 for baritone of Petrarch's sonnet no. 104.[10] Liszt was, however, unusual in remaining faithful throughout his life to the early Romantic forms and to their spirit.

It would be simplistic to limit a discussion of the Fragment to pieces with inconclusive final chords. The concept was capable of broader interpretation, and even the final cadence could be a tonic triad and still convey a sense of subtly opening up the ending. The Nocturne in B Major, op. 32, no. 1, by Chopin begins unpretentiously with a lovely two-bar phrase, repeated at once and prettily decorated:

10. Renumbered sonnet 90.

This does not allow one to suspect the final page:

The increased passion is only a partial preparation for the astonishing operatic recitative that follows, which seems both unprovoked and satisfying, as it completes without resolving. Chopin often placed the climax near the end, but here the climax takes place after the nocturne is strictly over. Previously Schubert had also experimented with minor endings to pieces in the major mode (although in this nocturne the final chord is not exactly minor, as the triad is removed to leave only an octave tonic still sounding).

The literary prestige of the Fragment accounts for the popularity of sets of musical miniatures in the early nineteenth century, but it remained for Chopin and Schumann to exploit the full possibilities of the miniature. Schumann's piano cycles, like *Carnaval* and the *Davidsbündlertänze,* are based on the recurrence of the same motifs throughout the work. The precursors of this technique are the Baroque suites of dances and of characteristic pieces (the suites of Handel and the *Ordres* of Couperin, for example), where successive dances often begin with the same motif. Schumann was also clearly influenced by the eighteenth-century variation set, in which a progressive complexity of texture often determines the treatment of the theme (sometimes with a less complex section at the center, as in Bach's Passacaglia and Fugue in C Minor for Organ). The *Impromptus on a Theme of Clara Wieck*, op. 5, with its free treatment of Clara's theme, prepares the piano cycles to come. In Schumann, however, the order of the pieces is never a simple progression: caprice and imagination play determining roles.

Chopin's Preludes, op. 28, seen from the outside as a simple collection of disparate short pieces, is the most impressive example of a set of tiny Fragments. It is often considered a "cycle"; it achieves unity apparently through the simple addition of one piece to another. It is clear that a complete performance of opus 28 was not thinkable during Chopin's lifetime, either in the salon or in the concert hall; nor is there any evidence that Chopin played the whole set privately for a friend or pupil, as Bach is said to have played the entire first book of the *Well-Tempered Keyboard* for a student. Jeffrey Kallberg has argued eloquently that only individual preludes or small groups of preludes were intended by Chopin as the effective presentation,[11] and this was, indeed, the way that Chopin himself actually performed them. Today's fashion of playing them as an entire set does not allow us fully to appreciate the extraordinary individuality of the single numbers.

Nevertheless, the aesthetics of the fragment would suggest that the opposing demands of the opus as a whole and of each individual prelude are intended to coexist without being resolved. The conception of a unity that transcends any possible mode of presentation is not one that was foreign to the Romantic period—or, indeed, to the Baroque of the early eighteenth century, as (among many other examples) the third part of Bach's *Klavierübung* can attest. The series of chorale-preludes arranged in the order of the text of the ordinary of the mass, preceded by the *St. Anne's* Prelude and followed by the *St. Anne's* Fugue as a frame, is a wonderfully satisfying intellectual form that can have had no relevance for performance at the time, whatever audiences of today might be prepared to accept.

The Preludes of Chopin are modelled on those of the *Well-Tempered Keyboard* in many ways, above all by their purely systematic ordering. Chopin's scheme is as simple as Bach's rising chromatic scale: all the major keys ascending the circle of fifths, each one accompanied by its relative minor mode (that is, C major, A minor, G major, E minor, D major, etc.). Like Bach's first prelude, Chopin's will always be understood as an opening piece. However, unlike Bach's final Prelude and Fugue in B Minor, Chopin's final Prelude in D Minor is conceivable only as an ending—remarkably so, since its last bars

11. Jeffrey Kallberg, "Small 'Forms': In Defence of the Prelude," in *The Cambridge Companion to Chopin,* ed. Jim Samson (Cambridge, 1992).

present a sonority that is not fully a closure but seems to project beyond the work:

In addition, the tonal sequence chosen by Chopin is much more satisfactory in terms of successive listening than Bach's chromatic scale. Each prelude is harmonically related to the previous one, and Chopin often exploits this relationship strikingly when he begins a prelude with the last melodic note of the preceding one.

He appears to proclaim this as a kind of manifesto at the very opening of the set, as the second prelude is intelligible above all as a modulation from the final E of the opening prelude to its own A minor cadence:

This affecting, mysterious Fragment consists of four almost symmetrical four-bar melodic phrases, each one framed by interruptions of the accompaniment as in the *Lieder* of Chopin's contemporaries, and this gives an extraordinary flexibility to the rhythm (see chapter 4). Although the opening note of the second phrase is slightly shortened, and that of the third phrase lengthened, the melody is regular, while the interludes of accompaniment give a new rhythmic form which does not affect the melody, seemingly independent. This builds into the prelude the rhythmic freedom generally left to the performer and demonstrates the new identity of composition and realization.

The piece opens with the final E of the first prelude. Much ink has been spilt over the question in which key the second prelude begins: Heinrich Schenker's answer of G major is the most cogent, as that is certainly the first complete cadence, and also the dominant of the preceding C major Prelude. Nevertheless, to Chopin, here as elsewhere, line is more basic than harmony, and he arrives at A minor above all through the two lines of treble and bass, which are partially identical (the parallel octaves are impressive) and partially out of phase:

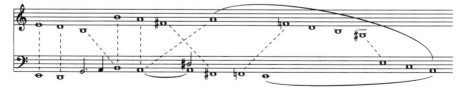

Both treble and bass by the ninth bar descend to the A, which will become the tonic, and the bass remains there briefly instead of going to the expected D, while the melody, in a perfect echo of the first phrase, moves down to F♯. The expressive inner voices remain steady, creating this chord

which remains basically unaltered as treble and bass exchange their notes:

The bass then descends chromatically to the dominant, and the melody impels its motif downward in thirds to the tonic cadence:

Both melody and bass descend essentially from E to E, and transform the meaning of this note from the third of C major to the dominant of A minor; the process is the occasion for the most mysterious poetry, grave and moving. Perhaps the principal element of expression is the exquisite inner-part writing which holds everything together at the crucial moment of transformation:

In passages where the texture and harmony appear most radical and most ambiguous, Chopin's counterpoint (which, as he remarked to Delacroix, was the "logic" of music) is the controlling agent.

Chopin expended great subtlety to ensure a convincing movement from one prelude to the next. It is a technique that he had recently worked out in the Etudes, above all opus 25 (although already in opus 10, the third Etude, in E major, was originally marked to be followed *attacca* by the fourth, in C sharp minor). In the Preludes there is a wonderfully nuanced play of contrast of character and sentiment; two pieces of the same tempo and type never follow each other immediately. A few of the Preludes, certainly, make little sense played as single works: the C sharp Minor Prelude, half mazurka, half improvisation, is too slight, and the F Minor too unaccountably violent played out of context. Others sustain an independent performance with great effect. I think that we must accept that the Preludes are conceived only paradoxically as a whole, and yet that modern performances of the entire set bring out aspects of the work certainly present in, and even integral to, its conception, but which Chopin did not consider essential to its realization in sound.

To the extent to which the Preludes are a cycle—that is, a work in which the significance as well as the effectiveness of the individual numbers depends on their place within a larger order—they are the most radical of all the Romantic examples. The unity does not depend upon thematic relationships; there are, in fact, motivic parallels between one prelude and another, but the musical power never depends in any important way upon even a semiconscious awareness of these recurrences (what significance they might have lies largely in defining Chopin's melodic style). There is no harmonic closure to the Preludes; the scheme that ties them together is purely additive, and the last prelude is only affectively, and not tonally, an ending to the whole set of twenty-four. In the sets of short piano pieces by Schumann—the *Papillons,* the *Davidsbündlertänze,* the *Humoresk*—there is, not a specific narrative program, but the suggestion of a program, an implied narrative that cannot be spelled out but that carries the music along and helps to hold the work together. The Preludes, however, imply nothing of the sort; throughout his life, Chopin's outmoded sense of musical decorum always resisted any attempt to impose an explicit nonmusical sense on any of his works.

The Preludes have been compared to the short modulations that pianists of the time used to improvise in order to introduce the tonality of the next piece, but they do not modulate or resemble in any way the improvisations that, when I was a child, I heard Josef Hofmann and Moriz Rosenthal employ in their recitals. In fact, in the strict sense, Chopin's Preludes are not preludes at all: they may certainly be used as brief prefaces to more substantial works, but they are not primarily intended to function that way. The title "prelude," puzzling to some, both acknowledges the debt to Bach—Chopin knew the only way he could rival Bach's famous twenty-four—and asserts the original character of each of Chopin's own twenty-four, at once provisional and beautifully complete. The provisional character of each prelude does not appear well when the piece is used to introduce a different and longer work, but does when it is played on its own or introduces the next prelude of the set. Although inspired by the preludes of Bach, they are more concentrated, more intense, laconic. Like a fragment of Schlegel, each one is a miniature—separate, individual, and complete in itself—that implies and acknowledges a world outside.

Before Chopin and Schumann others had composed miniatures, notably Beethoven and Schubert—although Schubert's are comparatively long-winded: the *Moments musicaux* constitute a beautiful set, but the individual numbers are not strikingly enriched by their context. Several of Beethoven's Bagatelles make little sense or little effect played separately, above all opus 119, no. 10, in A major and no. 2 in C major: their fragmentary quality is a comic effect. Chopin, on the other hand, has wit and irony but little humor, and his Preludes, even the grotesque ones, are never funny; when modest, they are elegant and graceful, and the most eccentric ones are deeply serious.

The comic fragments of Beethoven have the same relation to the poetic fragments of the next decades that Mozart's use of the whole-tone scale in *A Musical Joke* bears to Debussy's works:

Mozart may have enjoyed the whole-tone scale, but he certainly thought it was funny and out of tune. Those Bagatelles of Beethoven's that are serious, such as opus 119, no. 11, in B flat major, may be played as separate pieces without loss of significance. The last set of his Bagatelles, opus 126, is a true cycle, but the individual pieces are no longer miniatures.

"Cyclical form" is an ambiguous as well as a vague term: it has another meaning in addition to that of a set of apparently independent pieces that must be understood and performed as a whole. Traditionally it also signifies a large work in which an earlier movement reappears as part of a later one. The return of part of the scherzo of Beethoven's Symphony no. 5, in the middle of the finale, is perhaps the most famous example, but it is not the first essay of its kind: that would probably be Haydn's Symphony no. 46 in B Major, where a few phrases of the minuet come back towards the end of the finale. In spite of the examples in Beethoven and Schubert, fewer than a dozen, this remained a relatively infrequent form until the late 1820s, when it became common practice with Mendelssohn and Schumann, and inspired the later attempts by Brahms and Tchaikovsky.

In this sense, cyclical form is not a form at all but the disturbance of an established form. A return is not cyclical if it is required by tradition—if it is expected, in short; a cyclical return must be a surprise. When the accepted form demands a return, then we have a sonata reprise, or a *da capo* aria, or a minuet with trio, or a replaying of the theme at the end of a set of variations. A cyclical form makes an earlier movement intrude on the domain of a later one. It is this dislocation of an accepted form which had such an appeal to the

Romantic composer: it enabled him to use a traditional form but give it a more personal urgency. In a cyclical form the return may be unjustified by traditional formal requirements, but it must nevertheless be justified by the context and by the musical material: it must appear to be not rhetorical but organic. This double aspect—a disruption of a standard form which seems to grow out of the music, to be necessary more for reasons of sensibility and inner development than of tradition—had a natural aptness for an aesthetic of the fragment: the return is both an intruder from outside the new movement and a necessary part of its inner logic.

This is already clear with the earliest examples: it is not the beginning of the minuet that returns in the finale of Haydn's Symphony no. 46 but the second phrase—which closely resembles the main theme of the finale,[12] and indicates a kinship between the two movements. Haydn delivers to us the secret of cyclical form with wit and good humor and with none of the poetic and pretentious seriousness it was later to have: the interruption breaks down the individual movement, but by so doing draws attention to a larger unity.

The same forces are at work in the scherzo's eccentric return in the finale of Beethoven's Symphony no. 5: once again it is not the opening bars of the scherzo that return but the second theme—and it is this theme which clearly recalls to every listener the opening of the first movement. The interruption slightly dislocates the structure of the finale and brings out the relationship between first, third, and fourth movements. Moreover, the return occurs not at the end of the movement but just before the recapitulation. This fulfills an important convention of finales, due most notably to Mozart rather than Haydn, and followed by Beethoven: the use of rondo form, or else the introduction of the characteristics of rondo form into a binary sonata form—in particular, the appearance of a new theme at the subdominant in the central section with the development. The tonic minor, being in the flat direction, can serve as a substitute for the subdominant: the return of the scherzo creates a larger unity, fulfills a traditional structural need, and yet breaks down the individual form unexpectedly, both by the use of material from another movement and by the sudden shift of tempo and meter. It also prepares the recapitulation in the finale in a way that parallels the opening of the movement, as the scherzo was joined to the finale without pause, and the introduction to the finale is repeated at this point.

These "cyclical" interruptions undergo a radical transformation at the hands of the Romantic composer: in the most significant cases they no longer occur after a fermata, bringing the movement to a momentary halt, but are integrated seamlessly into the texture. They are still surprising, as we unexpectedly come upon music from an earlier movement, but the point of junction is cleverly

---

12. For an analysis of this relationship, see my book, *The Classical Style: Haydn, Mozart, Beethoven*, p. 148.

concealed. This is already clear with Schubert, above all in the Trio for Piano and Strings in E flat Major, op. 100, but the supreme model was provided by the sixteen-year-old Mendelssohn in his octet. The opening theme of the scherzo,

reappears in the finale, but we find ourselves back in the scherzo almost without being able to put our finger on the exact point that it returns. The finale is marked *presto,* and it is clear that the tempo must be exactly double the tempo of the scherzo—in fact, it is really the same tempo, as we should take the basic eighth-note texture as equivalent to the sixteenth notes of the scherzo:

It is a later theme that will be the essential vehicle of the return:

This theme has the same underlying structure as the main theme of the scherzo, and Mendelssohn is able to go from one to the other in the development section of the finale without altering the texture. In addition, the harmony of the opening theme of the scherzo is identical to the first theme of the finale:

and Mendelssohn can combine both principal themes of the finale with the scherzo:

What is astonishing is the complete ease with which a synthesis accomplished. The integration into the new movement is now total, although, at the same time, the earlier movement is still heard as a quotation.

The sense of the cyclical return as both inside and outside the finale relates it directly to the Fragment. Perceived both as a quotation from an earlier movement and as a theme derived from its new context, the cyclical return simultaneously attacks and reaffirms the integrity of the individual musical structure: it displays the double nature of the fragment. This early masterpiece by Mendelssohn remained the model for most of the later experiments in cyclical form, but only rarely was a similarly convincing simplicity achieved.

Ruins

The development of the fragment is clearly influenced by the contemporary taste for ruins. Already present in Renaissance and Baroque times, this taste had undergone a significant transformation over the centuries. During the Renaissance, the ruin was appreciated both for its moral significance and for its eccentricity, as well as for its bearing witness to a sacred past. The most beautiful and picturesque ruins in fifteenth-century painting, Italian as well as Flemish, are found in representations of the Nativity: the ruins are a sign for the synagogue, the Old Law, partially destroyed and left incomplete by the new Revelation. The picturesque quality of ruins gradually tended to outweigh the moral and historical significance, and in the sixteenth and seventeenth centuries, architecture began to introduce the more dramatic effects of ruins into new construction: dropped keystones in the work of Giulio Romano, broken pediments with Francesco Borromini. These techniques are like the heavy rustication on the Italian palaces of the Renaissance, ways of directly incorporating Nature into Art. The artists appear to rejoice in the momentary destruction of an established figure: the broken edge has the charm of novelty; reality intrudes and is domesticated by artifice.

The fashion for the picturesque ruin in the eighteenth century, however, brings a different note: the fragment is no longer the introduction of Nature into Art but the return of Art, of the artificial, to a natural state. In the ruins of Piranesi and of Hubert Robert, architecture begins to recede into landscape, to merge with the process of growth. Piranesi exaggerates the heroic proportions of his ruins: they induce a tragic sense of resignation, of melancholy. They dwarf the little human figures that wander about them, and they often sink under the weight of the vegetation that begins to cover them. To induce this melancholy, contemporary gardeners began to construct ruins in their landscapes, just as the eighteenth-century English garden banished symmetry and attempted by artificial means to appear even more natural than Nature.

The final stage arrived in the last decade of the eighteenth century, when it became clear that the ruin of the work of art, including works of literature, was not only inevitable and natural but welcome—at least to some degree. A new style permanently alters, and even partially destroys, the value and significance of preceding ages: after Beethoven, the music of Mozart would never sound quite the same again. Attempts to recapture the initial contemporary effect will always remain an important critical activity, but they can never completely succeed. It is not clear that we need to deplore this. The works of our own time will eventually be subject to similar misinterpretation. It should be understood that literature is designed to function that way. In 1794 Schiller wrote in a review of Friedrich Matthisson's landscape poetry: "The real and express content that the poet puts in his work remains always finite; the possible content that he allows us to contribute is an infinite quantity" *(Der wirkliche und ausdrückliche Gehalt, den des Dichter hineinlegt, bleibt stets eine endliche; der mögliche Gehalt, den er uns hineinzulegen überlässt, ist eine unendliche Grösse)*. Schiller acknowledges here that the artist cannot completely control public understanding; he can at best guide the directions in which it is to go. The most responsible artist, in short, creates the work in terms of its inevitable ruin. It might be said that the ruin is now no longer an unhappy fatality but the ultimate goal of the work. When Sir John Soane designed the Bank of England early in the nineteenth century, he presented the governors of the bank with three oil sketches so that they could see what they were paying for (bankers are not naturally adept at reading architectural plans): the first sketch showed the Bank brand-new, shiny and bright; the second portrayed the structure after it had mellowed for some years, developed an attractive patina and some ivy; the final sketch imagined the Bank in a thousand years as a noble ruin. The governors were being urged to build this ruin for posterity. (It has, in fact, been ruined in a very different sense by the meddling of later architects.)

Earlier writers, Montaigne most strikingly, were intermittently conscious that posterity would read into their works meanings that they had never intended and that they could not even imagine, but they saw this as something odd, as a curious weakness and limitation of the human mind. Montaigne observed:

But fortune shows us indeed even more clearly the part that she has in these works [of literature and painting] by the graces and beauties that are found in them not only without the intention but even without the consciousness of the workman. An apt reader often discovers, in the writing of somone else, perfections other than those that the author had put in and perceived himself, and lends to the work richer meanings and appearances.

Mais la fortune montre bien encores plus evidemment la part qu'elle a en tous ces ouvrages, par les graces et beautez qui s'y treuvent, non seulement sans l'intention, mais sans la cognoissance mesme de l'ouvrier. Un suffisant lecteur descouvre souvant ès escrits d'autruy des perfections autres que celles que l'autheur y a mises et apperceues, et y preste des sens et des visages plus riches.[13]

Montaigne welcomes these happy misinterpretations as gifts of fortune, wonderful but arbitrary accidents. For Schiller and for the first generation of Romantic authors, however, it was a natural process, and they tried to exploit it. Since the ruin of the work was inevitable, the artist could capitalize on this by building into the writing the principles of its own destruction. Many of the literary forms of this period are provisional—not only experimental but impossible to repeat, above all in the creations of Tieck, Novalis, and Hölderlin, as well as those of Byron, Coleridge, and Wordsworth. These works often seem to proclaim the difficulty of maintaining their artistic integrity, and they hint to the reader of the ways they may be eroded. Novalis, in the last of the Fragments published under the title *Pollen Dust,* remarked:

The art of writing books is not yet invented. It is, however, on the point of being invented. Fragments of this kind are literary seeds. There may indeed be many a barren grain among them: nevertheless, if only a few were to sprout!

Die Kunst Bücher zu schreiben ist noch nicht erfunden. Sie ist aber auf dem Punkt erfunden zu werden. Fragmente dieser Arte sind literarische Sämereier. Es mag freilich manches taube Körnchen darunter sein: indessen, wenn nur einiges aufgeht!

This fragment itself is not only provisional, tentative, but glories in its refusal to reach the definitive; and it is given to us with a premonition of its own death, imminent or deferred, with the prospect of its ruin.

13. Montaigne, *Essais,* Book I, chap. 24.

Disorders

The Romantic fragment and the forms it inspired enabled the artist to face the chaos or the disorder of experience, not by reflecting it, but by leaving a place for it to make a momentary but suggestive appearance within the work. The sense of chaos, its creative role, was seen by some of the early Romantics as essential to modern art. Many of Friedrich Schlegel's notes from the years 1797 to 1802 are speculative fragments (they remained unpublished until recently)[14] on the relation of art and chaos, concerned above all with the most characteristic of modern Romantic forms, the novel *(Roman)*. One statement of 1798 is decisive:

Form of the novel a refined artistic chaos.

Roman in der Form ein gebildetes künstliches Chaos.

Somewhat later in 1802, this is extended in summary fashion to contemporary style in general, and relates the sense of chaos to a representation of the organic:

Vegetable = chaotic is the character of the Modern.

Vegetabilisch = chaotisch ist der Charakter der Modernen.

Chaos has become a metaphor for the biological disorder of a nonmechanistic universe, the disorder of everyday experience. It is above all a signal of the problem of representing such a universe within an artistically ordered form.

The chaotic was not the fragmentary (since the Romantic fragment was "complete in itself and separate from the rest of the universe"): Schlegel in fact explicitly opposed them. The opposition was not a perfect one, however, as two notes of 1798 on style betray:

Rhyme must be chaotic, and yet as chaotic with symmetry as possible. From this can be inferred the system of Romantic meter.

Der Reim muss so chaotisch und doch mit Symmetrie chaotisch sein als möglich. Darin liegt die Deduction des romantischen Sylbenmaasse.

In other words, a rhyme must appear to be a happy accident, not a forced imposition of the poet: yet it imposes a symmetrical order. The combination of chaos and symmetry seemed to grant the Romantic critic of poetry his usual

---

14. In *Kritische Friedrich-Schlegel Ausgabe,* vol. 16 (Paderborn, 1981).

pleasure of having his cake and eating it too. Schlegel extended this combination to prose as well:

> The principle of Romantic prose exactly like that of verse—*symmetry* and
> *chaos,* quite according to the old rhetoric; in Boccaccio both are very
> clearly in synthesis.
>
> *Das Princip der romantischen Prosa ganz wie das der Verse*—Symmetrie
> *und* Chaos, *ganz nach der alten Rhetorik; im Boccaz diese beiden in
> Synthese sehr deutlich.*

The most successful Fragments preserve the clearly defined symmetry and the
balance of the traditional forms but allow suggestively for the possibility of
chaos, for the eruption of the disorder of life. This prevision acts like the quills
of the hedgehog, which both sharpen and blur the perfect definition of the
animal's shape.

As Schlegel wrote in the *Athenaeum:*

> You can only become a philosopher, not be one. As soon as you think
> you are one, you stop becoming one.
>
> *Man kann nur Philosoph werden, nicht es sein. Sobald man es zu sein
> glaubt, hört man auf, es zu werden.*

Apparently simple, this Fragment is symmetrical, well balanced, and closed in
expression—but it invites and even forces the reader to crack it open by
speculation and interpretation. Its outward balance demands to be transformed
into a more fruitful disorder. The form is closed and rhetorically conventional
but the awakened resonance is open.

The technique of the Fragment was, for a brief time, an unstable but
successful solution to the problem of introducing the disorder of life into art
without compromising the independence and integrity of the work. In music,
the Romantic Fragment similarly leaves a place—ambiguous and disconcerting—for an unresolved detail which undermines the symmetry and the conventions of the form without ever quite destroying them. The most famous of
Chopin's Fragments is the Prelude in F Major, from opus 28, with its poetic
ending on a dominant seventh chord:

It may seem astonishing that the accented E♭ at the end does not weaken the tonic chord. On the contrary, the four-times repeated V/I cadence made the last bars absolutely final: the E♭ only makes it mysterious—an extraordinary achievement as there is nothing mysterious about the common dominant seventh chord. This is not merely an effect of sonority, although the accent on the E♭ makes it ring like a bell: the dissonant note serves to prolong the final chord beyond the confines of the little form.

It could be maintained that in this prelude the ending on a dominant seventh chord does not arrive unprepared. There is a surprisingly heavy frequence of dominant seventh chords in this short prelude (in bars 2, 3, 6, 7, 8, 10, 11, 12, 14, 16, 18, 19, 20, and 21), and the way the last note in the left hand delicately alters the sonority in bars 8 and 12 makes them very similar to the final bars. It is true, therefore, that the final chord is prepared, but it is in no way palliated or excused. One might even speak of a shock value unaffected by the passage of a century and a half if the effect were not so lovely and so delicate. But if the E♭ does not weaken the final tonic, it does serve to expose that tonic as an artificial symmetry, an arbitrary convention, to suggest a different world of musical experience outside the formal traditions that Chopin's contemporaries knew and that we still largely recognize today. The E♭ is clearly an intrusion that enlarges the significance of the form and makes the final tonic chord uncanny. It is an ideal example of the alienation that was the defining characteristic of Romantic style for Novalis: "to make the familiar strange, and the strange familiar."

Quotations and memories

Schumann was even more attached than Chopin to the effect of a note, a phrase, or even a section that seems at first hearing to arrive from outside the form. With "Florestan," the second part of his double self-portrait in *Carnaval*, he made it a part of his signature. Florestan was the extrovert, violent, and capricious side of Schumann's personality, and his portrait is interrupted after the first phrase by a reminiscence of one of Schumann's earliest published works:

COQUETTE.

What is revolutionary here is not the introduction of a quotation from another work but the way it is made to sound like a quotation. If Schumann's directions are faithfully carried out, the phrase will appear to be an intruder from somewhere else, even to those who have never heard another work by Schumann. The quotation, marked *Adagio* and *leggiero*, is isolated by the radical changes of both tempo and sonority. It is also an intruder that breaks up the normal four-bar period. On its first appearance (bars 9 to 10) it is so brief as to seem inexplicable, not a significant independent phrase but just a simple scale. The second appearance (bars 19 to 22) changes everything: the scale is revealed as the beginning of a well-defined melody, a slow, expressive waltz. Both appearances interrupt a much faster waltz, passionate and raging, and both interruptions are fragments, the first so fragmentary as to be not quite intelligible.

It is the puzzling too-short first quotation that gives sense to the second. Initially the quotation is an imperfectly understood phrase, only half remembered. Then the memory becomes clearer, so much so that Schumann can now identify it as "(Papillon?)"—but with a question mark. The sudden changes to a slow tempo and light soft touch make the phrase come in a sort of half light and as if from a distance: the question mark is not so much a cryptic note by the composer as a direction to the pianist, telling him how to play the phrase. This page is one of Schumann's finest experiments in representing musically the sensation of memory; a few years later he was to put this to good account on a larger scale in the song cycles.

Composers before Schumann had exploited contrasts of tempo and character within a single movement (the first page of Beethoven's Sonata for Piano in E Major, op. 109, is a famous example). Schumann's genius was to make the contrast puzzling, tentative, only gradually intelligible. As "Florestan" continues, in fact, the contrast is progressively eliminated. Only the first appearance of the memory breaks the four-bar period, which is then preserved through the rest of the piece. As it proceeds, Schumann integrates the rising and falling scale of the memory with the more characteristic shape of the opening motif. The two voices in the right hand of bars 31 and 32 suggest the opening of the "Papillon?" and incorporate it into the initial turbulent texture, and the identity is made even more evident by bars 42 and 43. The memory is completely absorbed into the present, and the piece ends *fortissimo* on a dominant ninth chord as a simple fragment in an access of passion. Afterwards, the first four bars of "Coquette" provide a cadence.

The triumph of the musical Fragment is the first movement of Schumann's Phantasie in C Major, op. 17, originally titled "Ruins" in manuscript. Schumann himself felt that this movement was the most powerful manifestation of his genius. It is certainly his most successful and most original essay in a large form. While the song cycles, along with the *Davidsbündlertänze, Kreisleriana,* and *Carnaval,* are equally impressive achievements, they are collections of Fragments. The first movement of the Phantasie reveals the aesthetic of the single Fragment magnified, with a sweep and energy that occurs nowhere else.

Like "Florestan," this movement is based on the quotation of a phrase from outside the work but absorbed into it; as in "Florestan" the full quotation is delayed. Both the absorption and the delay are spectacular in the Phantasie in

C Major. Most of the themes in the first movement are based on the quotation, but we must wait to hear this until the final page of the movement. Once again, Schumann's ability to create an effect of quotation marks in music is astonishing. When the phrase finally arrives, we recognize it as the source of so much of the material already heard, but it appears as a new theme in a new slow tempo—and with the first satisfying resolution to a tonic chord in root position that we find in the movement. The quotation is therefore the point of rest and the center of gravity.

Like the quotation in "Florestan," this last page of the first movement of the Phantasie is a reminiscence—but this time of a melody by another composer. It is the beginning of the last song of Beethoven's *An die ferne Geliebte.* Most of Schumann's contemporaries with a knowledge of recent music would have recognized the source—certainly Liszt, to whom the Phantasie was dedicated and who had transcribed *An die ferne Geliebte* for piano. In any case, Schumann alerts his public to the presence of a secret by the epigraph to the Phantasie published in the first edition, four lines of verse by Friedrich Schlegel:

> Through all the sounds that sound
> In the many-colored dream of earth
> A soft sound comes forth
> For the one who listens in secret.
>
> *Durch alle Töne tönet*
> *Im bunten Erdentraum*
> *Ein leiser Ton gezogen*
> *Für den der heimlich lauschet.*

The "secret tone" is the phrase of Beethoven, and the Phantasie was, in fact, written to raise money for a monument to Beethoven at Bonn. Schumann wrote to his distant beloved, Clara Wieck, from whom he was still separated by order of her father: "For hours I have been playing over and over again a melody from the last movement of my Phantasie . . . Are you not the secret tone that runs through the work? I almost think you are." This was a very proper and suitable thing for an artistic young man to write to his fiancée. Intrepid biographical critics pay no attention to the "almost." Too firm an identification of an element in a work with an aspect of the artist's life does not further understanding but block it. The work is not intended to convey the artist's experience as directly as a telegram, or to substitute his memory for ours: it is made to be filled with our experience, as a vehicle for the feelings of all who perceive it. Nothing shows this more clearly than Schumann's letter to Clara: as a listener to his own music, not as a composer, he has understood how his love for Clara can be poured into the mold of his work. The melody from the

last movement about which he writes to Clara must be this one, marked
"Etwas bewegter":

It is the only one that could conceivably be played over and over again for
hours. It, too, is more cryptically a quotation from Beethoven; the source, as
we know from Schumann himself, is the Seventh Symphony, and it probably
comes from the following passages in the first and above all second movements
(quoted here from Liszt's transcription for the piano):

It is typical of Schumann's musical thinking to construct this complex network of references outside his music—to quote Beethoven, and then to have Beethoven's distant beloved refer to Clara. But this should give a clue to the nature of Schumann's achievement. It is not Schumann's music that refers to Clara but Beethoven's melody, the "secret tone." Above all, at the end of Schumann's first movement, the quotation from Beethoven appears not as a reminiscence of another composer, but as at once the source and the solution of everything in the music—up to that final page. The reference becomes self-reference: the phrase from Beethoven seems as much to derive from what has preceded as to be the source. In fact, one cannot take the full measure of Schumann's accomplishment in this work without observing that the quotation from *An die ferne Geliebte* sounds as if Schumann had written it. This is only in part because Beethoven has, in his wonderful song cycle, anticipated many aspects of Schumann's style, or because Schumann had recognized himself in Beethoven's work, but above all because the entire movement of Schumann is a preparation for, and development of, the concluding phrase. That explains why the phrase will appear as something remembered even to those who have never heard the Beethoven cycle: it is played in its original form only at the end, but recalls, now resolved and stabilized, all the excitement and tension that has gone before.

Only the first two bars of Beethoven's melody are quoted by Schumann:

It is easy to hear that in Schumann's opening melody

the motif

comes from Beethoven's

But Schumann's opening is even more clearly derived from the fourth bar of Beethoven's original melody

which Schumann does not quote at the end of the movement. In the Phantasie, the quotation functions as the point of rest, the final moment of stability, the arrival at the tonic. Schumann's purpose is not the revelation or the acknowledgment of a source outside the work but the integration of the source into the work. This entails the familiar contradiction—the Fragment is complete in itself—but the puzzle is only one of logic, not of sensibility.

The melody of Beethoven's unquoted bars 3 and 4 outlines the triad of D minor, the supertonic minor (ii) of C major, and determines at the very opening the large-scale structure of the movement. The harmonic structure is, in fact, so idiosyncratic that it is worth describing briefly; it will help to explain both Schumann's extraordinary success and why it was so difficult to repeat. The D minor chord over a dominant pedal opens the work (Theme I), and C major is defined only by implication:

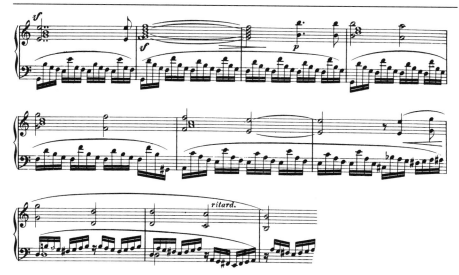

After a single *sforzando* on the dominant G, the D minor chord is blurred in the accompaniment *(piano)*, but clearly outlined by the melody *(fortissimo!)*. After a new theme (II), a lyrical version of the main theme (Iᵃ) closer to the original Beethoven melody appears in D minor, and this harmony is now established in its own right with the dominant pedal on G removed:

Still another version (I^b), even closer to the Beethoven song, continues the D minor:

This leads to a second playing of the lyrical versions I^a and I^b now in the subdominant major, F, the relative major of D minor:

As a secondary tonality of an exposition, the subdominant is very rare and absolutely unclassical. It is, however, established directly out of the harmony of the opening bass, and it leads directly to the chord of its own supertonic (G minor) and back to D minor in a series of broken phrases. We return to C major and the opening theme by a simple sequence of rising subdominants: D minor, G minor, C minor.

As I have observed, the chord of the tonic major in root position is evaded by
Schumann until the end of the piece. After a short stretto in faster tempo, the
opening theme reappears on a tonic pedal, but still unresolved, with the
dissonant harmony of D minor insistently present; and it is rounded off with
a half cadence and a fermata, which serve to prolong the tension of the
"exposition":

This is the extreme point of contradiction: the harmony of this cadence is
both tonic C major and dominant G major and neither. It is a dominant
seventh chord on G with the tonic C underneath it as a bass—and then an
expressive C minor scale places the G in the bass, but with a B♭ which attempts
to nullify the dominant seventh chord, and achieves this with the G minor "in
the style of a legend" for four bars—only to return to the tonic minor. This
extraordinary cadence is the culmination of Schumann's earlier play with
dissonance, weakening both tonic and dominant with supertonic minor and
subdominant.

The ambiguous cadence explains the succeeding pages. A sonata exposition,
which the Phantasie mimics (and it was originally to be called a grand sonata),
generally leads to a full cadence on the dominant, and is followed by a
development section: the first part of a ternary form on the other hand,
generally ends with a tonic cadence, and is followed by a contrasting central
section. "Im Legendton" is both a contrasting section, in slower tempo almost
entirely concentrated in the tonic minor, and a development section which
works principally with themes II and Iᵃ.

The "recapitulation" is no more orthodox. It begins at bar 129, and after
a few phrases the rest of the "exposition" is played transposed down a whole
step: the supertonic D minor becomes the tonic minor, and everything in F
major reappears in E flat major. The opening theme returns at the end, and is
now resolved—for the first time—by the quotation from Beethoven's *An die
ferne Geliebte*.

This kind of analysis in the style of a railway timetable ("We arrive at the
tonic pedal at 119 and depart at 129") is generally neither interesting nor
enlightening. It serves here, however, to demonstrate unusual emphasis on the
subdominant or flat area—F major, D minor and C minor—and the way these
harmonies are derived from the character of the opening theme and the
Beethoven song. In Classical technique the subdominant area is used to reduce
tension, to prepare resolution: Schumann paradoxically employs it with
astonishing mastery to increase and prolong tension. He can do this because

the tonic C major has been fully established but never affirmed by its triad in root position. Resolution in this movement is almost always into a dominant pedal, into the minor mode, or into a tonic pedal in which an intrusive dissonance prevents the C major triad from asserting itself before the end.

In spite of the apparent acceptance of Classical sonata proportions and structure, the Phantasie does not work like a Classical or even a post-Classical sonata. It does not contrast themes of different character; it does not oppose tonic and dominant (or tonic and mediant) and intensify and resolve the opposition; it does not start at a point of rest, move dramatically to a greater intensity and return to a state of equilibrium. It begins with great tension, descends towards resolution and is frustrated, moves to a point of greater tension, and initiates the process over and over again. The structure is like a series of waves, starting with the climax, losing momentum each time, and then beginning again. Except in the slower middle section, the music does not build to a climax; on the contrary, it continually threatens to collapse, to split into pieces—and does in fact break down gradually starting at bar 70, into a series of fragments:

In eleven bars there are four indications of *ritenuto*, two *ritardandi*, *adagio* twice, and three fermatas. Further, in the original edition, bars 81 and 82 are isolated by double bars on either side. It is only with difficulty that the movement recovers its life in the extraordinary syncopations that follow and that destroy the clarity of the beat (quoted p. 107).

We may think of this moment of breakdown here as a destruction of form—but only a momentary one. This is the maximum perturbation of structure allowed to the Romantic Fragment: a brief intrusion of chaos is still controlled by the conventional symmetry. It alters the significance of the total work, however, and illuminates the originality of the large conception. Schumann's radical innovation was a new large sense of rhythm conceived as a series of waves of energy, crucial to later composers like Wagner and Strauss.

This innovation justifies the original title "Ruins." To encompass this form, however, it was necessary to reveal the basic material only at the very end when all tension has evaporated. The combination of this new feeling for rhythm with an idiosyncratic version of Classical form can clearly be accomplished only once; it was not a conception which could be either developed or repeated. It is the acceptance of the Fragment that enables Schumann in this one large movement to achieve a new sense of musical continuity.

At first Schumann intended to bring back the phrase from *An die ferne Geliebte* at the end of the last movement of the Phantasie, turning this even more persuasively into a Fragment: the melody is now an intruder from another movement as well as from another composer. In this original ending the quotation reappears with a change of harmony in bar 145 that introduces the chord

which had played such a crucial role:

The accented A's and the fermata at the end of the arpeggios lead directly into the A which initiates the quotation from Beethoven. When these arpeggios appeared at the opening of the movement, this A was the climax and the first note to be sustained:

Schumann's original ending turned this brief moment of melody into a complete theme, and one that was familiar to us from the opening movement. Before publication he opted for prudence, struck out this poetic final page, and added three bars of perfunctory arpeggios in its place:

If an editor had made this change, we would call him a vandal. The Fragment was always a difficult concept to maintain, hovering between compromise and provocation.

A quotation is, of course, a memory made public, but the phrase by Beethoven in Schumann's Phantasie acts within a complex hierarchy of memories. As it originally appeared in Beethoven's song cycle it was already a memory, a final song that reminded us so much of the opening song that it became the opening song almost without our realizing that a transformation had taken place. In the first movement of Schumann's Phantasie, it is now a memory both of the Beethoven cycle and of all the themes of Schumann's movement derived from it and resolved by it. As it stands in the manuscript version of the last page of the final movement, it is a memory both of the Beethoven song and of Schumann's first movement, and it is subtly reharmonized to recall the first movement more persuasively. The manuscript ending of the finale, in spite of the careful way it is prepared by the very opening bars, creates a momentary break in the form of the last movement, only to imply the greater unity of the work as a whole.

There is nothing novel about quotations in music, or in the use of another composer's tune as the basis of a composition. What is radically new here is the mode of integration, the way Schumann makes Beethoven's melody sound as if it were derived from its new context, as if Schumann's music could expand organically to produce a scrap of Beethoven. The Romantic Fragment acknowledges what is alien to it and incorporates it. The phrase of Beethoven is made to seem like an involuntary memory, not consciously recalled but inevitably produced by the music we have just heard. A memory becomes a fragment when it is felt as both alien and intimate, when we are aware that it is as much a sign of the present as of the past.

Absence: the melody suppressed

An imperfect, incomplete memory is doubly a fragment. Schumann's *Frauen-liebe und Leben* ends with a memory—but one that has been mutilated at the moment of greatest pathos. After the death of her husband, the woman sings:

> I withdraw silently into my inwardness,
>   The curtain falls
> There I have you and my lost happiness
>   You are my world

> *Ich zieh' mich in mein Innres still zurück,*
>   *Der Schleier fällt*
> *Da hab' ich dich und mein verlornes Glück*
>   *Du meine Welt*

and the piano alone replays the first song quietly, the memory of the woman's first sight of the man she would marry:

It is, however, not quite the first song but only the accompaniment, and, significantly, no distinction is made here between the piano's initial bar of introduction in the opening song and the beginning of the sung melody.

The accompaniment of an entire stanza is played without any alteration. In the opening song the piano doubled most of the singer's notes—until the climax, when the piano drew back and left the melody entirely to the voice:

When the accompaniment is played by itself, the melody appears to retreat into an inner voice in bars 11 and 12 and to disappear entirely in bar 12, to return again only at the end of 13.

The disappearance is not quite perfect: the melody continues to exist as a memory. I do not think any auditor forgets the wonderfully expressive phrase

having heard it twice in the first song. *"Taucht aus tiefstem Dunkel"* are the words here—"rises from deepest darkness"—and the motif actually rises in the listener's mind out of the void left by the piano in the postlude. The accompaniment, it is true, offers a stimulus, the notes

are hidden within it as

It must be emphasized, nevertheless, that in the postlude this bar does not reach to the level of intelligible melody; there is a gap here that must be filled by the listener. The postlude is a memory, and part of the memory is missing: it has to be recalled, willed to return—as it inevitably is. Schumann has forced the listener to acknowledge the eternal imperfection of memory and to complete the song. The end of the cycle is not a return but the ghost of a return, a fragment or shadow of the original. The voice no longer exists, and with it has died part of the melody. It was an extraordinary inspiration in the opening song to withdraw the piano's doubling of the melody at the climax, leaving the woman's voice isolated. In the postlude, to make this moment of the greatest pathos in the opening song disappear is a stroke of genius. It is at once the least and the most important moment: least important, because most easily recalled and supplied by the listener; most important, because its absence is deeply frustrating. In the end, the unexpected void is more affecting than the original melody.

Mountains and Song Cycles

Horn calls

Horn calls and the sound of wind through leaves open "Der Lindenbaum" (The Lime Tree), the fifth song of Schubert's song cycle *Winterreise* (Winter's Journey):

The horn calls may at first appear curious: there are no horns in Wilhelm Müller's poem. These are traditional hunting-horn formulas, associated, certainly, with forests, but there are no forests in Müller's poem: the lime tree is an urban tree at the city gate.

The rustling of the leaves has a certain ambiguity as well. It is now winter, and there are no leaves; the poem speaks only of the rustling of the twigs. It is clear, however, that the triplets of the opening do not represent the sound of twigs. Our identification of the triplets with wind is indeed confirmed later in the song, but that will be the present wind of winter which blows off the traveller's hat. The wind of the introduction is not a winter wind but the wind of summer, the rustling is a symbol of memory.

The horn calls, too, are symbols of memory—or, more exactly, of distance, absence and regret. A similar horn call opens Beethoven's *Les Adieux* (The Farewell):

and it continues to resound throughout the rest of his first movement, with a wonderful series of blurred echoes on the last page:

"Le son du cor au fond des bois," the sound of the horn in the depths of the woods is one of the few pieces of romantic iconography to find a firm foothold in music.

Horn calls and the wind are combined elsewhere by Schubert, in "Suleika 1," for example (Brahms thought this the greatest of his songs):

This is the East wind which stirs up the dust and the leaves, but it later brings news of the distant beloved, and with the words of absence and separation appear the horn sonorities in the inner voices:

The motion that we associated with the wind at the opening of the song never stops, and the horn calls steal in with unsurpassed subtlety as if from afar.

"The Lime Tree" goes further: it is saturated in horn sounds. The opening stanza is scored as if for a quartet of horns:

manches liebe Wort;   es zog in Freud'und Lei_de   zu   ihm_mich immer fort.

> At the spring before the city gate
> There stands a lime tree
> I dreamt in its shade
> So many sweet dreams

The traditional sign for absence is essential: the lime tree is, in fact, not visually present in the song. The traveller wishes it to remain invisible, to keep only the memory:

> I had even today to go
> By it in the deepest night
> There have I, still in darkness,
> Closed my eyes.
>
> *Ich musst auch heute wandern*
> *Vorbei in tiefer Nacht,*
> *Da hab ich noch im Dunkel*
> *Die Augen zugemacht.*

The tree, in whose bark the traveller had carved his words of love, is not seen, only heard, as the scraping of the twigs calls the lover to his death:

> And its twigs rustled
> As if they called to me:
> Come here to me, companion
> Here will you find your peace.
>
> *Und seine Zweige rauschten*
> *Als riefen sie mir zu:*
> *Komm her zu mir, Geselle,*
> *Hier findst du deine Ruh.*

This is the first song in *Winter's Journey* to speak of the longing for death, which will become the main burden of the cycle. *Winter's Journey* moves towards death, and the peace that the rustling twigs promise the young man is the peace of death. "The Lime Tree" is also the first song in a low register after four in a relatively high one. (When the cycle is performed, as it so often is, by a baritone, this relation is missed; the first four songs are then transposed downward, but "Der Lindenbaum" is generally left in the original key, as it sits well for baritones, and indeed lies too low to be transposed like the others. The cycle makes its proper effect only when sung by a tenor.) The preceding songs all end a fourth to a ninth higher than "The Lime Tree," and the graver, more somber register of this song introduces a new sound; in context, the simple lyric resignation is even more serious than the despair, ironic and passionate, of the opening songs.

The wind unites past and present in "The Lime Tree," and it determines the structure of the song. Three times the melody is sung, the first two preceded by the introduction with its rustling leaves and distant horn calls (on its second appearance the introduction is shortened to four bars). Before the melody comes for the third and last time, however, voice and piano unite to describe the winter wind:

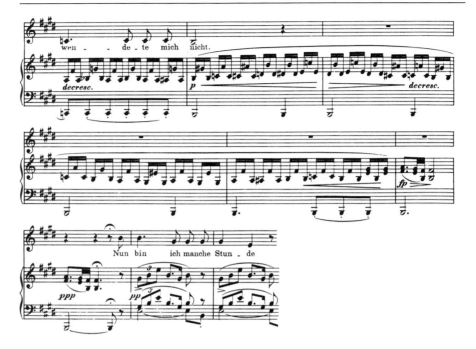

The cold wind blew
Straight into my face.
The hat flew off my head.
I did not turn.

The poet does not turn because he does not wish to see what must remain a
memory: he tries to imprison the tree in the past. The wind forces the present
on him, as it changes without warning from summer breeze to the blast of
winter. In this stanza the motif of the wind is transformed from a remembrance
into an evocation of what is actually happening, a phenomenological description of the experience of remembering and of being attacked by reality at the
same time.

We may say that the introduction actually appears three times, twice instrumentally to represent the past, and the third time integrated with the vocal
line, to bring the present before us—or, in fact, to confound memory and
immediate perception. This third appearance, transformed, is the only place in
the song where the motif of the wind is combined with the vocal part, where,
in fact, the introduction invades the song proper. It is the dramatic climax, and
it breaks the symmetry of the music. It also breaks the symmetry of the verse:
there are six stanzas in Müller's poem, and Schubert's melody spans two

stanzas. He uses one stanza, however, for the winter wind—for the fusion of remembered time with actual time—and the third appearance of the melody has the words of only one stanza left and must repeat them in order to reach its full length.

Memory is the central theme of early nineteenth-century lyric poetry. It was Schubert's genius to find a way to represent both past and present with the same motif. The opening song of *Winter's Journey* is a walking song, as are many of the successive ones. From the first bars of "Good Night," the sense of walking combines with the anguish of memory:

A stranger I came
A stranger once more I depart.

Fremd bin ich eingezogen,
Fremd zieh' ich wieder aus.

The opening of the vocal line is at once painful and casual: the first note is an awkwardly difficult high F, but it is there unaccented, almost in passing. The steady walking rhythm takes precedence. The sense of grief and regret is in the harmonies, in the way the melody opens by expressively outlining a ninth, and above all in the accents that break up the even surface, disturb the regular movement without impeding it.

Landscape and music

The double time scale, the representation of the past through the immediate sensation of the present, made possible one of the greatest achievements of Romantic style: the elevation of the song from a minor genre to the vehicle of the sublime. The great polyphonic song writing of the Renaissance was a long-dead tradition: only the accompanied song lived on. Throughout the eighteenth century, however, the accompanied song was a despised form, unfit for truly serious consideration. No important composer of the period wasted much of his time on writing songs; those of Bach, Handel, the two Scarlattis, Rameau, Hasse, Jomelli, Gluck, Mozart, and Haydn are a negligible part of their output, although some of them, Gluck in particular, wrote interesting ones. Mozart, for example, occasionally produced a modest song in his spare time, as a relief from more important matters. The most imposing of these, "Abendempfindung" (Evening Sentiment), has been called a precursor of the

Romantic *Lied,* but it is nothing of the kind: in *arioso* style—half aria, half accompanied recitative—it is a miniature operatic *scena,* and has little in common with later developments. As a setting of landscape poetry it is, however, significant. It was the lyric poetry of landscape that was the chief inspiration in the development of the *Lied,* and gave vocal music the grandeur that had until then been reserved for opera and oratorio. The first great successes of Schubert may somewhat obscure this: two songs from Goethe, "The Erl-King," a ballad; and "Gretchen at the Spinning Wheel," a scene from *Faust.* Unlike Mozart's "Abendempfindung," "Gretchen" has nothing operatic about its style, and owes little to theatrical tradition. "The Erl-King" derives to some extent from operatic formulas: the ballad, however, remained a separate enclave in the domain of the *Lied,* and had little influence on the concurrent developments that were to lead to *Winterreise.* The direction that Schubert's genius was to take was not revealed in the setting of dramatic texts or of narratives but in his engagement with short lyric poems, most often sentimental descriptions of nature—his early settings of Ludwig Hölty give the truest indications of his later power: brief exquisite evocations of nightingales, harvest time, and mournfully frustrated passion.

It is above all through landscape that music joins Romantic art and literature. The first song cycle is a series of landscapes, Beethoven's *An die ferne Geliebte* (To the Distant Beloved). Other candidates are sometime brought forward for this path-breaking role (including a set of songs by Carl Maria von Weber), but none of them has the unity, cohesion, or power of Beethoven's and, later, of Schubert's cycles: they are only loosely related groups of songs that do not even pretend to a more impressive status. It is, in fact, the pretensions of the song cycle that make it such an extraordinary phenomenon. With it, a modest genre, intended largely for the unambitious amateur, becomes a major endeavor that in weight and seriousness rivals grand opera, the Baroque oratorio, or the Classical symphony. The triumph of these pretensions is doubly remarkable: first, in that the basis is still the simple lyric song; and second, that the triumph remained unchallenged—the song cycles of Beethoven, Schubert, and Schumann have never needed apology or resuscitation, unlike the operas of Schubert, the chamber music of Schumann, and the oratorios of Liszt. The prestige of the great song cycles is a testimony to the central role they played in the history of Romantic art. They realized one of the ideals of the period: to give the lyrical expression of Nature an epic status, a genuine monumentality, without losing the apparent simplicity of a personal expression.

The creation of the song cycle is a parallel to the replacement of epic poetry by landscape poetry and the elevation of landscape painting to the commanding position previously held by historical and religious painting—more than a parallel, indeed, as these achievements supported each other, and were all part of one cohesive development.

The elevation of a minor genre to the level of the sublime was a conscious and deliberate movement in literature and painting. How conscious it was in music I am not sure, although I can hardly imagine that Schubert would have composed two enormous song cycles without thinking that he was giving greater dignity and importance to the art of the *Lied* in which he was then acknowledged to be preeminent. For literature and painting, the goal of making pure landscape without historical or religious figures into a major form that would acknowledge no superior was explicitly set out in a number of texts of the late eighteenth and early nineteenth centuries. Perhaps the most interesting of these is Schiller's 1794 review of Friedrich Matthisson's poems (another passage already cited above, p. 93), as it attacks the problem head on. Schiller is the most influential figure in late eighteenth-century European aesthetics, but this review has been generally overlooked. I quote at length as it presents some of the basic doctrines of Romantic art, and the extraordinary roles played by both landscape and music in the Romantic movement:

> It is something quite different whether one takes pure nature with no living creature simply as the *locale of an action* in a picture and, where it is necessary, uses it to color the representation of the action, as the history painter and the epic poet often do, or whether one does exactly the inverse like the landscape painter, and makes pure Nature the heroine of the picture with people only as figurants [the extras in a stage production]. The first method has countless examples in Homer, and who could equal the great painter of Nature in the truth, individuality and vivacity with which he realizes the locale of his dramatic pictures? But it lay with the moderns (to which the contemporaries of Pliny belong in part) to make this part of Nature the object of its own representation in landscape paintings and poems, and so enriched the domain of art, which the ancients seem to have restricted to humanity and that which resembles humanity, with this new province.

> *Es ist nämlich etwas ganz anderes, ob man die unbeseelte Natur bloss als Lokal einer Handlung in eine Schilderung mit aufnimmt und, wo es etwa nötig ist, von ihr die Farben zur Darstellung der beseelten entlehnt, wie der Historienmaler und der epische Dichter häufig tun, oder ob man es gerade umgekehrt, wie der Landschaftmaler, die unbeseelte Natur für sich selbst zur Heldin der Schilderung und den Menschen bloss zum Figuranten in derselben macht. Von dem ersten findet man unzählige Proben im Homer, und wer möchte den grossen Maler der Natur in der Wahrheit, Indivualität und Lebendigkeit erreichen, womit er uns das Lokal seiner dramatischen Gemälde versinnlicht? Aber den Neuern (worunter zum Teil schon die Zeitgenossen des Plinius gehören) war es aufbehalten, in Landschaftsgemälden und Landschaftspoesien diesen Teil der Natur für*

sich selbst zum Gegenstand einer eigenen Darstellung zu machen und so das Gebiet der Kunst, welches die Alten bloss auf Menschheit und Menschenähnlichkeit scheinen eingeschränkt zu haben, mit dieser neuen Provinz zu bereichern.

Among the moderns Schiller counts the ancient Romans, but this should not mislead us: the independence of landscape was a controversial issue above all for the contemporaries of Schiller. Was landscape one of the fine arts, Schiller goes on to ask, or merely one of the decorative arts *(angenehme Künste)?*—and he then proceeds to lay down the principles which will admit pure landscape to the highest rank. To achieve this triumph landscape must both liberate our power of imagination and work directly upon us with a specific effect. The decorative arts free our imagination, allowing it an unbounded play of agreeable associations, but they do not work directly upon our hearts. Landscape must become a symbol of the human if it is to rise to the level of drama, history, and epic. Schiller reaches the center of his theme, the art of music as a model for the other arts:

There are two ways that Nature without living creatures can become a symbol of the human: either as representation of feelings or as representation of ideas.

Feelings, indeed, cannot be represented *by their content* [*Inhalt*], but only by *their form,* and there exists a generally beloved and effective art which has no other object than this form of feelings. This art is *music,* and insofar as landscape painting or landscape poetry works musically, it is a representation of the power of feeling, and consequently an imitation of human nature. In fact, we consider each painterly and poetic composition as a kind of musical work, and we subject them in part to the same laws. Even from colors we require harmony and tone and even modulation, so to speak. We distinguish in every poem the unity of thought from the unity of feeling, the musical progression from the logical—in short, we demand that every poetic composition, along with the expression of its contents, be also an imitation and expression of feeling and act upon us like music. From the landscape painter and landscape poet we demand this in still higher degree and with a clearer consciousness, because with both of them we must abandon some of the rest of our demands from the products of the fine arts.

Now, the entire effect of music (as a fine art and not simply as a decorative one) consists in accompanying and making perceptible the inner movements of the spirit analogously through outer ones . . . If the composer and the landscape painter penetrate the secret of the laws which rule the inner movements of the human heart, and study the analogy which exists between these movements of the spirit and certain outer movements, they will be transformed from ordinary image makers into true soul painters.

Es gibt zweierlei Wege, auf denen die unbeseelte Natur ein Symbol der menschlichen werden kann: entweder als Darstellung von Empfindungen, oder als Darstellung von Ideen.

Zwar sind Empfindungen, ihrem Inhalte *nach, keiner Darstellung fähig; aber* ihrer Form *nach sind sie es allerdings, und es existiert wirklich eine allgemein beliebte und wirksame Kunst, die kein anderes Objekt hat als eben diese Form der Empfindungen. Diese Kunst ist die* Musik, *und insofern also die Landschaftmalerei oder Landschaftpoesie musikalisch wirkt, ist sie Darstellung des Empfindungsvermögens, mithin Nachahmung menschlicher Natur. In der Tat betrachten wir auch jede malerische und poetische Komposition als eine Art von musikalischem Werk und unterwerfen sie zum Teil denselben Gesetzen. Wir fordern auch von Farben eine Harmonie und einen Ton und gewissermassen auch eine Modulation. Wir unterscheiden in jeder Dichtung die Gedankeneinheit von der Empfindungseinheit, die musikalische Haltung von der logischen, kurz wir verlangen, dass jede poetische Komposition neben dem, was ihr Inhalt ausdrückt, zugleich durch ihre Form Nachahmung und Ausdruck von Empfindungen sei, und als Musik auf uns wirke. Von dem Landschaftsmaler und Landschaftsdichter verlangen wir dies in noch höherem Grade und mit deutlicherem Bewusstsein, weil wir von unsern übrigen Anforderungen an Produkte der schönen Kunst bei beiden etwas herunter lassen müssen.*

Nun besteht der ganze Effekt der Musik (als schöner und nicht bloss angenehmer Kunst) darin, die innere Bewegungen des Gemüts durch analogische äussere zu begleiten und zu versinnlichen . . . Dringt nun der Tonsetzer und der Landschaftmaler in das Geheimnis jener Gesetze ein, welche über die innern Bewegungen des Menschlichen Herzens walten, und studiert er die Analogie, welche zwischen diesen Gemütsbewegungen und gewissen äusseren Erscheinungen statt finden, so wird er aus einem Bildner gemeiner Natur zum wahrhaften Seelenmaler.

Much of this is traditional, even old hat, in particular the idea that music is an imitation of nature insofar as it is a representation of feeling. That music works as an analogy to the sentiments is basic to classical aesthetics. Nevertheless, Schiller hedges: music as an imitation of nature had already caused considerable uneasiness by the late eighteenth century (as we have seen). For Schiller, music is not an imitation of the content of feelings but only of their form. This is an attempt to acknowledge the abstraction of music and then to transfer it to landscape painting and poetry. Schiller is concerned to leave the content of feeling to the listener and remove it from the work of music itself in order to allow the listener's power of imagination full play.

What follows in Schiller's review, however, is considerably less traditional, and it both represents the aspirations of contemporary artists and forecasts some of the concepts of the Jena circle, the avant-garde group of German Romantic artists and philosophers that was to be formed only four years later:

> But landscape Nature can, *secondly,* be drawn into the circle of humanity if it is made into the expression of Ideas. We do not mean here in any way that awakening of ideas which is dependent on chance association; for this is arbitrary and unworthy of art; but that which follows by necessity from the laws of the symbolizing power of imagination. In active spirits awakened to the feeling of their moral worth, reason never idly observes the play of imaginative power, but is ceaselessly forced to make the play of chance coincide with its own procedures. If now, among these appearances, one comes forth which can be treated according to the (practical) rules of reason itself, this appearance appears to reason as an emblem of its own activity; the dead letter of Nature becomes a living language of the spirit; and the outer and inner eyes read the same writing of appearances in completely different ways.

> *Aber die landschaftliche Natur kann auch* zweitens *noch dadurch in den Kreis der Menschheit gezogen werden, dass man sie zu einem Ausdruck von Ideen macht. Wir meinen hier aber keinesweges diejenige Erweckung von Ideen, die von dem Zufall der Assoziation abhängig ist; denn diese ist willkürlich und der Kunst gar nicht würdig; sondern diejenige, die nach Gesetzen der symbolisierenden Einbildungskraft notwendig erfolgt. In tätigen und zum Gefühl ihrer moralischen Würde erwachten Gemütern sieht die Vernunft dem Spiele der Einbildungskraft niemals müssig zu; unaufhörlich ist sie bestrebt, dieses zufällige Spiel mit ihrem eigenen Verfahren übereinstimmend zu machen. Bietet sich ihr nun unter diesen Erscheinungen eine dar, welche nach ihren eigenen (praktischen) Regeln behandelt werden kann, so ist ihr diese Erscheinung ein Sinnbild ihrer eigenen Handlungen, der tote Buchstabe der Natur wird zu einer lebendigen Geistersprache, und das äussere und innre Auge lesen dieselbe Schrift der Erscheinungen auf ganz verschiedene Weise.*

What Schiller has to say goes to the heart of the new Romantic elevation of landscape and its ties to music. The charms of landscape painting and poetry are no longer simply the evocation of the beauties and the delights of a pastoral existence, nor the virtuosity of the artist's imitation of the objects of Nature. What Schiller demands is that the poet and the artist show us the correspondence between the sensuous experience of Nature and the spiritual and intellectual workings of the mind. Only this can give landscape the dignity of epic poetry and religious and historical painting. It is striking that Schiller is careful to ask not for particular moral content from either poem or picture but for an identity of sensuous and intellectual forms, and this justifies his evocation of music. It was not the ability of music to call up emotions or sentiments by some conventional code that interested Schiller and his contemporaries, but the capacity of music to create meaning without referring to a world beyond music itself, so that sensuous form and significance seemed to be inseparable. This does not, however, make for an abstract art of pure form without content. On the contrary, as Schiller goes on to affirm, it liberates the arts of poetry and painting from a narrow dependence on a fixed content and allows free range to the possibilities of meaning:

> Every lovely harmony of forms, tone, and light which delights the aesthetic sense, equally satisfies the moral one; every continuity with which lines in space and tones in time join together is a natural symbol of the inner concordance of the spirit with itself and of the inner coherence of action and feeling; and in the beautiful aspect [*Haltung*] of a pictorial image or musical composition is painted the still more beautiful one of a morally regulated soul.
>
> The composer and the landscape painter achieve this simply through the form of their representation, and simply dispose the spirit to a certain kind of feeling and to the reception of certain ideas; as for the content of these ideas and feelings, they leave that to be found by listener and spectator. The poet, however, has one advantage here: he can put a text to each feeling, can support the symbol of imaginative power by the content and give it a specific direction. But he must not forget that his interference in these affairs has its limits. He may indicate these ideas, allude to these feelings, but he must not spell them out himself, must not intrude on the imaginative powers of his readers. Every closer definition will be felt here as a burdensome limitation, for the attraction of such *aesthetic ideas* lies precisely in the fact that we look into the content itself as into a bottomless depth.[1]

Jene liebliche Harmonie der Gestalten, der Töne und des Lichts, die den ästhetischen Sinn entzücket, befriedigt jetzt zugleich den moralischen; jene Stetigkeit, mit der sich die Linien im Raum oder die Töne in der Zeit aneinander fügen, ist ein natürliches Symbol der innern Übereinstimmung des Gemüts mit sich selbst und des sittlichen Zusammenhangs der Handlungen und Gefühle, und in der schönen Haltung eines pittoresken oder musikalischen Stücks malt sich die noch schönere einer sittlich gestimmten Seele.

Der Tonsetzer und der Landschaftmaler bewirken dieses bloss durch die Form ihrer Darstellung und stimmen bloss das Gemüt zu einer gewissen Empfindungsart und zur Aufnahme gewisser Ideen; aber einen Inhalt dazu

---

1. This passage then ends with the passage quoted above, p. 93.

zu finden, überlassen sie der Einbildungskraft des Zuhörers und Be-
trachters. Der Dichter hingegen hat noch einen Vorteil mehr: er kann jenen
Empfindungen einen Text unterlegen, er kann jene Symbolik der Ein-
bildungskraft zugleich durch den Inhalt unterstützen und ihr eine be-
stimmtere Richtung geben. Aber er vergesse nicht, dass seine Einmischung
in dieses Geschäft ihre Grenzen hat. Andeuten mag er jene Ideen, anspielen
jene Empfindungen; doch ausführen soll er sie nicht selbst, nicht der
Einbildungskraft seines Lesers vorgreifen. Jede nähere Bestimmung wird
hier als eine lästige Schranke empfunden, denn eben darin liegt das Anzie-
hende solcher ästhetischen Ideen, *dass wir in den Inhalt derselben wie in*
eine grundlose Tiefe blicken.

Schiller recommends to landscape painting the abstractness of music, the
inability to define its own "content" which creates the "bottomless depth" of
meaning; and he warns that the poet must strive to allow the reader some of
the same freedom of interpretation that the painter and musician are forced to
grant spectator and listener. (By "content" [*Inhalt*] Schiller meant more or less
what the nineteenth century was to call "subject.") The landscape painter of
the late eighteenth century was trying to break down the classical tradition of
heroic landscape that dominated the French seventeenth century, in which each
landscape illustrated a mythical, biblical, or historical event, like *Moses Found
in the Bullrushes,* or *The Birth of Dionysus.* These old-fashioned subjects were
doomed to disappear, although the academic artists hung on to them for
many decades. The advanced landscape painters—Richard Wilson, Gainsbor-
ough, John Robert Cozzens, and a few years later Constable, Caspar David
Friedrich, Corot, and the main nineteenth-century tradition—continued the
pure landscape of the Dutch seventeenth century, but often now with the heroic
grandeur of the French classical school, to which the Dutch aspired more rarely.
The idealized landscape was replaced by the "portrait" landscape, a representation of a specific recognizable site. In the terminology of the time, these
portrait-landscapes had no subject—they conveyed feelings and ideas like
music, without reference to history or myth, merely by the arrangement of the
elements of nature on canvas.
When we move from music as a representation of feeling to music as an
expression of ideas—and the ideas expressed are, strangely and explicitly for
Schiller, divorced from content—we part company with an imitative art and
find one that is a model for the logic of the imaginative power. This view of
music was dependent on the stylistic developments of late eighteenth-century
music, in which dramatic change and transformations of harmony and motifs
replace unity of sentiment as central concerns. As a result, the relation of music
to literature and painting is paradoxical. The triumph of landscape poetry in
England and Germany, and of prose description in France, is accomplished
between 1795 and 1805: Wordsworth, Coleridge, Hölderlin, Goethe, Bren-

tano, Chateaubriand, and Sénancour are the great representative figures. The similar triumph of pure landscape painting, which attains the sublime without recourse to the historical subject, is more diffuse and extends from the middle of the eighteenth century until the 1830s, from Loutherbourg to late Constable. Music seems to lag considerably behind. The *Pastoral* Symphony by Beethoven of 1808 is still idealized landscape, a form of Classical pastoral; it does not describe a particular site; its stream, peasant dance, and thunderstorm are generalized; the sentiments portrayed are still within the tradition of Haydn's *Seasons*. The *Pastoral* Symphony does not aspire to the personal tone and the individual particularity of the contemporary lyric description or the topographical picture. For this we must wait until Beethoven's *An die ferne Geliebte* of 1816, Schubert's *Winterreise* of 1828, Liszt's *Album d'un Voyageur* of 1835, and Schumann's *Liederkreis* of 1840 on poems of Eichendorff, in which landscape in music reaches its transcendental level. The composer of songs, here, necessarily comes later than the poet: he must wait for verses to set. However, the tardiness of the art of music is an illusion: as we see from Schiller, it is music that inspires the triumph of landscape painting and poetry by demonstrating the possibility of creating an art that achieves the grandest effects apparently without referring outside itself.

The traditional weakness of music had now become its strength for Schiller and his contemporaries. Considered as a form of speech, music is deeply imperfect: it does not rise to the level of even the simplest forms of communication; it cannot convey a proposition. By music alone we are not able to tell our friends that we are leaving tomorrow or give them a recipe for soup. Even its classical and much-vaunted supremacy in the representation of sentiment was challenged by theorists in the later eighteenth century, above all by Adam Smith, Denis Diderot, and Michel Chabanon. Music represents sentiment only ambiguously, vaguely, and uncertainly. Music does not communicate emotions or even, properly speaking, express them. What it does is inspire and stimulate emotion. It acts directly on our nervous system and bypasses all conventions or codes of meaning. The significance of music was not, theorists came to believe, based on an arbitrary system like that of language, where words mean what they do simply because the dictionary and the culture it represents say so. Music worked in a more physical, even animal, fashion.

It is true that, in the earlier eighteenth century, theorists had tried to constrain music within a system of rhetoric, to develop an almost emblematic code for the representation of sentiment. The effect of this system on the actual composition of music has no doubt been exaggerated, but its diffusion had some effect. Above all, the tendency of a late Baroque piece to confine itself to the working out of a single texture, or at most to a contrast of two textures, made it easy to accept each work as the unified representation of a single sentiment, or *Affekt*. The instrumental music of the later eighteenth century, with its more dramatically organized forms, made such a conception impossible, and music became the model of an art supposedly free of conventional symbolism.

The sense of the direct physical action of music became acute after the middle of the eighteenth century. It is strikingly exposed in an interesting play published in 1777 by Louis Ramond de Carbonnières, a figure to whom we must return; he was to become one of the greatest masters of landscape description. The play, written in imitation of Goethe's *Werther,* was Ramond's first work, with the elaborate title *The Last Adventures of the Young D'Olban: Fragments of Alsatian Loves.*[2] As in *Werther,* a young man commits suicide out of frustrated love, but Ramond revealed his later interest in mountains by having his hero climb to the top of a high rocky hill in order to shoot himself. The opening scene is a piano lesson given to a young lady, and the teacher (no doubt intended to be somewhat comic, as he is called Solfa) presents a view of music more than half serious in its enthusiasm:

Solfa: Play this passage again. Do you really feel everything it expresses?
Lali: (With a sigh) It's sad.
Solfa: Is that all? *(He plays it.)* What sounds . . . what harmonies! . . . this suspension, that uncertainty which calls for a resolution . . . which expects it . . . promises it . . . Do you not feel at heart an anxiety, a sadness mingled with hope, a ray of consolation? . . . *(He replays the passage.)* Here is the cadence, the final which satisfies all.
Lali: (Smiling) How many things you find in a few notes!
Solfa: Ah, what can we not find? . . . continue, miss, continue . . . there is not a sound which does not find, not awaken a sympathetic chord in one of our nerves. Music moves, nourishes the soul, gives it new ideas, recalls, extends old ones. A good musician, a true musician . . . not one who just follows the notes mechanically without understanding the meaning . . . Play this sharp! . . . do you not feel the way it stretches the soul, and prepares it for the emotion that follows . . . A good musician, a true musician must be the most sensitive man, the most in tune with himself and others, the most compassionate . . . in a word, the most virtuous . . . Only wait, just wait for me to show you the secret magic of harmony: each chord will bring you new sensations; each leading tone will augment your love for the general order . . . ah! a beautiful piece of music, properly understood, is the finest moral treatise. [Ellipses in the original.]

Solfa: *Répétez, répétez ce passage là . . . sentez vous bien tout ce qu'il exprime?*
Lali: *Il est triste.*
Solfa: *N'est-il que cela? . . . (il le joue) quels tons . . . quelle harmonie! . . .*

2. *Les derniers aventures du Jeune d'Olban; fragement des amours alsaciennes* (Yverdon, 1777).

*cette suspension, cette incertitude qui demande un repos . . . qui l'attend
. . . le promet.—Ne sentez vous pas dans le coeur une inquiétude, une tristesse mélée de'espérance, d'un rayon de consolation?—(il rejoue le passage)
voilà la chute, la finale qui satisfait à tout.*
Lali: (Souriant) *Que de choses vous trouvez dans quelques notes!*
Solfa: *Eh! que n'y trouve-t-on pas?—continuez, mademoiselle, continuez—il
n'y a pas un son qui ne trouve, qui ne réveille un accord simpatique dans
quelqu'un de nos nerfs. La musique émeut, nourrit l'áme, lui donne de nouvelles idées,rappelle, étend les anciennes . . . Un bon musicien, un vrai musicien—et ce n'est pas celui qui ne sait que suivre machinalement les notes,
sans en comprendre le sens.—Faites donc ce dièze! . . . ne sentez vous pas
qu'il tend l'âme, and la prépare à l'émotion de ce qui suit? . . . Un bon musicien, un vrai musician doit etre l'homme le plus sensible, le plus d'accord
avec lui-même et avec les autres, le plus compatissant . . . en un mot, le
plus vertueux.—Attendez seulement, attendez que je vous découvre la magie
secrète de l'harmonie: chaque accord vous amènera de nouvelles sensations;
chaque degré de sensibilité augmentera votre amour pour l'ordre général;
. . . ah! un beau morceau de musique, bien compris, bien senti, est le
meilleur traité de morale.*

This is perhaps the only document that gives us an insight into the ideas
about music current among the group of university students in Strassburg that
formed the nucleus of the original group of the *Sturm und Drang*. Born in
Strassburg in 1755, Ramond went to the university there when Goethe was
also a student. His early play, from which I have quoted the piano lesson, was
dedicated to Jakob Michael Reinhold Lenz, the finest dramatist of the *Sturm
und Drang* after Goethe, and one of Goethe's closest friends. It was with Lenz
that Ramond went to the Swiss Alps, a voyage that inspired the first of the
writings on mountains that were to make him famous throughout Europe. The
strong influence of German thought on French Romanticism begins much
earlier than usually dated, and it is already pronounced in the work of Ramond. The slightly comic air of his professor of music assures us that the ideas
he is expressing must have been fashionable ones at the time.

In Ramond's piano lesson the expressive force of music appears to be
concentrated in its grammar and syntax rather than its vocabulary: it is not
the melodies or the rhythmic character that interest Solfa but the harmonies
and the cadences, the chromatic alterations ("sharps") and the chords. The
interest and the power of music is seen by Solfa as centered in its structure. It
is above all the relation of dissonance to consonance which influences his
imagination—the suspensions and resolutions. By these means music does not
so much express as stimulate the creation of new ideas, and it does so by acting
not on the mind but directly on the nerves. This makes it evident that music
can never be reduced to a code of meaning or to a simple set of conventions

that prescribed different forms of expression, and it gave the musician a freedom and power greater than that of poet and painter, who were bound not only by the demands of the traditions of classical rhetoric and iconography but also by the constraints of imitation and the rules of decorum that accompanied them. Displacing the weight of expression from motif and melody to structure is one of the achievements of the music of the late 1760s and 1770s, and it was the source of the new expressive freedom, a freedom from convention. Such freedom was not as great as it seemed then, but it dazzled contemporary painters and poets. Landscape could, it was felt, offer the same freedom, a liberation.

Schubert's and Beethoven's horn calls give us an exceptional example of early nineteenth-century musical iconography as opposed to simple tone painting of bells, babbling streams, and cuckoos, but such examples are rare, and this one has a peculiar character. It was clearly not seen as imposed arbitrarily: its bare fifths softly played seem to come from far away, and the sense of distance stands as a natural metaphor for absence. How much of its effect is due to its individual sonority and how much to its associations with the poetry of the time we can only speculate (and its frequent appearance in verse must have been due to the sonority of the hunting horns as well as to the experience of hearing them from a distance in the forest). In Romantic music these horn calls come from landscape; they appear in Schubert and Beethoven with a novel aura of the sublime and the melancholy derived from the new ambitions of landscape painters and poets. In the extraordinary triumph of landscape, we can see both painter and poet using elements of Nature—foliage, rocks, mountains, and above all the unifying power of light—the way a musician uses harmonies and motifs.

Landscape and the double time scale

It is only apparently a paradox that the newfound freedom of imagination was revealed most strikingly not in composed, idealized landscapes but in the exact reproduction of the appearance of particular sites. It is in the topographical picture, the portrait-landscape, that the poetic quality is at its most concentrated, most intense. Artists were able to profit from the example of music because a new way of experiencing and scrutinizing Nature had developed during the last decades of the eighteenth century.

The change in sensibility could be the occasion of a certain amount of elitist pride:

> It is well known what a wonderful effect is made by contrasts in a work of art, and they have a magic force in the spectacles of nature. But in the latter (and one could perhaps say the same of the former) there are contrasts of a kind not made for all eyes. They are born of subtle grada-

tions, of fugitive correspondences, of masses and colors that one might almost call modest, since they do not manifest all their respective differences, all their clandestine mixtures, at first sight. To recognize them, to discern them, one must have an eye considerably accustomed to the beauty of the countryside. The banks of the Rhine teem with such contrasts.

È notissimo di che mirabile effetto sieno i contrasti nelle opere dell'arte; ed hanno una magica forza negli spettacoli della natura. Ma in questi (e potrà forse dirsi lo stesso di quello) v'hanno alcuni contrasti di una specie che non è fatta per tutti gli occhi. Nascono da sottili gradazioni, da fuggevoli corrispondenze, da masse, da colori, direi quasi, modesti, perocchè non esternano a bella prima tutte le rispettive lor differenze, tutte le lor furtive mistioni. A ben ravvisarle, a discernerle, conviene aver l'occhio alquanto accostumato al bello campestre. Le rive Renane sovrabbondano di siffatti contrasti.

This total aestheticizing of landscape comes from the tenth letter of a once famous book by the abbot Aurelio di Giorgio Bertòla, *Picturesque and Sentimental Voyage on the Rhine (Viaggio pittorico e sentimentale sul Reno)* of 1795.[3] It is typical of this elegant pre-Romantic poet, who wrote happily of "the sounds of painting and the colors of music," and described each successive view of the river in exquisitely pictorial terms. "What is most to be observed," he insisted, "is the whole that each [prospect] composed, and the links that each preserved with the other." It is precisely these links that are—one of the novelties of the late eighteenth-century approach to landscape—the sense of movement and change in the experience of Nature. The different scenes are described as they had been perceived in time, and we are made aware how scenes past change our sense of present views.

Neither "objective" nor "subjective" would adequately characterize the new modes of representing Nature. The landscape is described objectively in terms of immediate sensation; even the role of memory is portrayed directly as part of the present. These excerpts from the ninth letter, "Da Magonza a Eibingen," resume many of Bertòla's preoccupations:

Now behind a plain thickly dense with plants of different foliage, the gray or the blue of mountains near or far; now beautiful groups of trees in various little islands, above all towards the village of Mombach lying on the left, and near which a small river enters the Rhine, which after a little space takes the form of a regular canal; here new slopes of mountains and, on the peaks of one or another, old fortresses awakened by their position and structure a hundred ghosts of knightly romance. The villages appeared and disappeared before our eyes like so many floating islands . . .

3. New edition, Florence, 1942.

I turned back: the series of hills seen, so to speak, in profile, their tops jutting out in another direction, the clumps of trees in other proportions, the villages half hidden or visible in a spaciousness that they had not had before, left me only with difficulty to reconstruct the landscape in the middle of which I had just passed a moment ago with my eyes open and greedy: and this was indeed a source of pleasure; nor could I believe that uncertainty could give birth to so great a pleasure.

Both the bank and the view of the river become nevertheless reanimated, thanks to the town of Winkel which stands out on the right, and the village of Weinheim on the opposite edge; the river Selz, born in the lower Palatinate, gathers in a short space many streams and torrents in order to be worthy of flowing into so great a river. Not far from there a little valley in the east, enamelled with various greenery and on the open side adorned by the village of Geisenheim, interrupts the heights; the Rhine, wanting to imitate the form of the land, becomes like a lake. Thence the village of Eubingen divided by a torrent, and a little island opposite, and melancholy plantations on the border of an enormous cleft of a pyramidal rock that one at first sight would take to be great mausoleum, and its browner masses cut away and hanging, and supple stripes tending here towards the cerulean, there to blood red, compose another model that says imperiously: "Look at me, paint me, explore me."

Ora dietro un piano foltissimo di piante di diversa verdura il grigio o l'azzurro di monti meno e più lontani; ora begli aggruppamenti di alberi in varie isolette soprattutto verso il villaggio di Monback, che siede a sinistra, e presso cui un fiumicello si esce col Reno, il quale prende indi a non molto la forma di regolar canale; quivi nuove degradazioni di monti, e in cima all'uno o all'altro di essi antiche rocche risvegliatrici per la loro posizione e struttura di cento fantasmi di romanzesca cavalleria. I villagi comparivano e scomparivano a'nostri occhi quasi tante isolette nuotanti . . .

Mi rivolsi indietro: la serie delle colline veduta, dirò così, di profilo, le lor punte sporgenti in altra direzione, sotto altra proporzione i gruppi degli alberi, mezzo nascosti i villaggi o apparenti in un'ampiezza che non avevano prima, mi lasciavano a stento raffigurare quel paese, in mezzo a cui con occhi sì aperti e sì cupidi io era passato un momento innanzi: lo che pure era sorgente di diletto; nè io avrei mai creduto che la dubbiezza potesse partorirne di così grandi.

E la riva e il prospetto del fiume vengonsi tuttavia rianimando mercè il borgo di Winkel che spicca a destra, e il villaggio di Weinheim sul margine opposto, e il Selz che, nato nel Palatinato inferiore, per farsi degno di metter foce in così gran fiume, vien raccogliendo in poco spazio assai rivi e torrenti. Non lungi di là una valletta a levante smaltata di varia verdura, e nel lato più arioso adorna del villaggio di Geisenheim, interrompe le eminenze; il Reno volendo ivi imitare la forma delle terra, lagheggia

*alquanto. Indi il villaggio di Eibingen tramezzato da un torrente, e
un'isoletta per contro, e malinconiche piantagioni sull'orlo delle enormi
fenditure di rupe piramidale, che uno a bella prima non altro guidi-
cherebbe essere che un gran mausoleo, e al suo piè bruni massi ritagliati
e pendenti, e strisce flessuose che qua danno nel ceruleo, là nel sanguigno,
compongono altro modello che dice imperiosamente: Guardami, dip-
ingimi, indagami.*

Visual delight, sentiment, and exploration become one in the new appreciation of landscape and Nature. In Bertòla's fourteenth letter, we can see that
many decades of scientific speculation about the geological history of the earth
lie behind the feeling for Nature at this time:

One of the most singular and pleasing things for a traveller on the Rhine
is the view of the way he has just taken: I have not failed to indicate this.
From time to time these views are so new that you would swear that they
were not those of a land that you had already seen. The frequent and
enormous bends of the mountains, the ample river basins closed and
surrounded by the mountains themselves, are the main creators of this
very agreeable deception: finding ourselves in the middle of these basins,
we could not see how we had entered, nor comprehend where we would
have to go out; and more than once disdaining geography we wondered
doubtfully if this was a lake in which the Rhine was to finish; these doubts,
successively reborn and destroyed, formed a mass of sensations which
gripped the mind in a joyous tumult. Often turning around to look, we
were so entranced by what stood ahead and yet still enamored of what
we had at our backs that we did not know where to fix our eyes. This
frequently happened when we sailed in these surroundings.

   Further, the idea came to me more than once of the primal, terrifying
force of this water against the manifold embankments of one mountain
or another, and imagination rejoiced in ranging freely through the vortices
of centuries, speculating on the wondrous voyages and the gigantic labors
of this river. It seemed to me at times that I heard through the tortuous
apertures the frightening voice, so to speak, of its youthful anger; and
sometimes I seemed to see it move, split, hollow out, open up, and crush
the hard, pertinacious rocks upon which it made war, reinforced by the
forces of the alluvial mountains . . .

*Una delle più singolari e più aggradevoli cose per chi vada pel Reno, si è
il prospetto della via già trascors: nè io ho tralasciato d'indicarlo una
volta. Tratto tratto sono essi prospetti sì nuovi che si giurerebbe non esser
quello il paese che si è già veduto. Le frequenti ed enormi piegature
de'monti, e le ampie vasche del fiume chiuse e contornate dai monti*

medesimi, formano principalmente questo gratissimo ignanno: trovandoci in mezzo ad esse vasche noi non vedevamo per dove vi fossimo entrati, nè intendevamo per dove dovessimo uscirne; e più d'una volta calpestando la geografia, volevamo dubitare esser quello un lago ove il Reno andasse a finire: da questi dubbj successivamenti rinascenti e distrutti fomasi un cumulo di sensazioni, da cui è stretta l'anima in un giocondo tumulto. Sovente rivoltici indietro, eravamo così rapiti di quel che ne stava dinanzi, e così ancora innamorati di quel che avevamo allora alle spalle che non sapevamo ove più fermare lo sguardo. El tanto ne avvenne mentre navigavamo in questi contorni.

A me andava ancora più d'una volta per l'animo l'idea de'primi terribili sforzi di queste acque contro il moltiplice argine di tali e tanti monti: e l'immaginazione godea di spaziare nel vortice de'secoli, conghietturano i mirabili viaggi e i giganteschi lavori de questo fiume. Mi parea talvolta di udire fra quelle tortuose aperture la spaventevole voce, dirò così, de'giovanili suoi sdegni; e talvolta mi parea di vedere scostarsi, fendersi, incavarsi, aprirsi, deprimersi le ardue e pertinaci rocce, cui esso movea guerra, rinforzato dagl'impeti delle montane alluvioni . . .

Not only the recent past is integrated here with the immediate sensation, but even the millennial past, the geological history of the landscape; time is experienced at the macrocosmic level. This double scale—long-range time and the fleeting sensation of the moment—becomes an essential part of the new mode of representation in the late eighteenth century, and it gives the description of landscape in this age its peculiarly original power. It is found in all those writers of landscape who aspired to the new sense of the sublime, and who gave to pure landscape its novel supremacy. The same complex juggling with time scales which lends a new eloquence to natural description can be seen at the opening of Georg Forster's *Ansichten vom Niederrhein* (Views of the Lower Rhine) of 1790. The most astute of the German supporters of the French Revolution, Forster began his writing career astonishingly at the age of nineteen by recounting in English his experiences on one of Captain Cook's trips around the world. His essays on literature and politics had a strong influence on the early Romantic group of writers in Jena, above all Friedrich Schlegel. This is the beginning of his trip down the Rhine:

Once upon a time we must have been fated to find today otherwise than we expected. In place of yesterday's splendid sunshine, which we flattered ourselves would continue, we had a gray day, whose less brilliant qualities—as we have learned from novels and educational literature—were compensated by the useful. For since the magic of a beautiful light was lacking and the familiar scene could provide no novelty, that left us many hours for our occupations. On the trip through the Rheingau, I read the account of a voyage to Borneo—may the national pride of my compatriots forgive me—and my imagination was warmed and refreshed by the glowing colors and the powerful vegetable growth of which our present wintry surroundings could give us nothing. Viticulture, because of the crippled form of the vines, produces a somewhat shabby landscape; the thin stalks, now denuded of foliage and always ordered stiffly in rows and files, form a thorny surface, whose prosaic regularity does not please the eye. Here and there nonetheless we saw a little almond or peach tree, and many early cherry trees covered with snow blossoms, red and white; indeed, in even the narrow part of the course of the Rhine, between the mountain crevices, on the bare cliff walls and terraces unadorned by vine stalks, hung such a child of springtime, awakening in us the beautiful hopes of the future.

Not, therefore, that we continued to dream ourselves in the eternal summer of the palm trees. We sat hourlong on the deck and gazed into the green, now, at low water, the refreshing green of the waves of the Rhine: we feasted our eyes on the rich wine coast, studded with towns that hung together, to the buildings beckoning from afar of the Johannisberg deanery, to the sight of the romantic Mouse Tower and, hanging on the opposite cliff, the Observatory. The mountains of Niederwald threw a deep shadow upon the even, mirror-clear river basin, and in this shadow stood forth Hatto's Tower, white, lit by a chance sunbeam; and the cliffs, under which the stream rushed, made it picturesquely beautiful. The Nahe, with its steep bridge and the city on its bank, flowed quietly down from the walls of Bingen, and the mightier waters of the Rhine plunged into its embrace.

Wonderfully had the Rhine forced a way for itself between the narrow valleys. At first sight one could hardly comprehend why it pressed itself between the cliff walls of Schiefer instead of flowing into the more level region around Kreuznach. But one soon realized after a closer examination that in this direction the whole surface rises and is a true mountain declivity. If it is permissible for the searcher of nature to conclude from the present reality about the possible past, it appears conceivable that at one time the expanse of water of the Rhine before Bingen, brought up short and contained by the mountain walls, was forced initially to rise, flood the entire plain, swell over the level of the cliffs of the Bingen cavity, and then rush irresistibly over this in the direction that the river still takes. Gradually the water burrowed deep into the cliff bed, and the surrounding plane appeared once again. If this is granted, the Rheingau, a part of the Pfalz and the district around Mainz up to Oppenheim and Darmstadt, was once an inland lake until the barrier of the Bingen rocky valley was overcome and the torrent could flow out.

Es war einmal Verhängniss, dass es uns heute anders gehen sollte, als wir erwartet hatten. Statt des herrlichen gestrigen Sonnenscheins, mit dessen Fortdauer wir uns schmeichelten, behielten wir einen grauen Tag, dessen minder glänzende Eigenschaften aber, genau wie man in Romanen und Erziehungsschriften lehrt, das Nützliche ersetzte. Denn weil der Zauber einer schönen Beleuchtung wegfiel und der bekannten Gegend keine Neuheit verleihen konnte, so blieb uns manche Stunde zur Beschäftigung übrig. Auf der Fahrt durch das Rheingau hab' ich, verzeih es mir der Nationalstolz meiner Landsleute! eine Reise nach Borneo gelesen und meine Phantasie an jenen glühenden Farben und jenem gewaltigen Pflanzenwuchs des heissen Erdstrichs, wovon die winterliche Gegend hier nichts hatte, gewärmt und gelabt. Der Weinbau giebt wegen der krüppelhaften Figur der Reben einer jeden Landschaft etwas Kleinliches; die dürren Stöcke, die jetzt von Laub entblösst, und immer steif in Reih' und Glied geordnet sind bilden eine stachlichte Oberfläche, deren nüchterne Regelmässigkeit dem Auge nicht wohl thut. Hier und dort sahen wir indess doch ein Mandel- und ein Pfirsichbäumchen und manchen Frühkirschenstamm mit Blüthenschnee weiss oder röthlich überschüttet; ja selbst in dem engeren Theile des Rheinlaufs, zwischen den Bergklüften, hing oft an den kahlen, durch die Rebenstöcke verunzierten Felswänden und Terrassen ein solches Kind des Frühlings, das schöne Hofnungen auf die Zukunft in uns weckte.

Nicht immer also träumten wir uns in den ewigen Sommer der Palmenländer. Wir sassen stundenlang auf dem Verdeck, und blickten in die grüne, jetzt bei dem niedrigen Wasser wirklich erquickend grüne, Welle des Rheins; wir weideten uns an dem reichen mit aneinander hangenden Städten besäeten Rebengestade, an dem aus der Ferne her einladenden Gebäude der Probstei Johannisberg, an dem Anblick des romantischen Mäusethurms und der am Felsen ihm gegenüber hangenden Warte. Die Berge des Niederwalds warfen einen tiefen Schatten auf das ebene, spiegelhelle Becken des Flusses, und in diesem Schatten ragte, durch einen zufälligen Sonnenblick erleuchtet, Hatto's Thurm weiss hervor, und die Klippen, an denen der Strom hinunterrauscht, brachen ihn malerisch schön. Die Nahe, mit ihrer kühnen Brücke und der Burg an ihrem Ufer, glitt sanft an den Mauern von Bingen hinab, und die mächtigeren Fluthen des Rheins stürzten ihrer Umarmung entgegen.

Wunderbar hat sich der Rhein zwischen den engen Thälern einen Weg gebahnt. Kaum begreift man auf den ersten Blick, warum er hier (bei Bingen) lieber zwischen die Felswände von Schiefer sich drängte, als sich in die flachere Gegend nach Kreuznach hin ergoss. Allein bald wird man bei genauerer Untersuchung inne, dass in dieser Richtung die ganze Fläche allmälig steigt, und wahrer Abhang eines Berges ist. Wenn es demnach

überhaupt dem Naturforscher ziemt, aus dem vorhandenen Wirklichen
auf das vergangene Mögliche zu schliessen; so scheint es denkbar, dass
einst die Gewässer des Rheins vor Bingen, durch die Gebirgswände
gestaucht und aufgehalten, erst hoch anschwellen, die ganze flache Gegend
überschwemmen, bis über das niveau *der Felsen des Bingerlochs anwach-*
sen und dann unaufhaltsam in der Richtung, die der Fluss noch jetzt
nimmt, sich nordwärts darüber hinstürzen mussten. Allmälig wühlte sich
das Wasser tiefer in das Felsenbett, und die flachere Gegend trat wieder
aus demselben hervor. Dies vorausgesetzt, war vielleicht das Rheingau, ein
Theil der Pfalz, und der Bezirk um Mainz bis nach Oppenheim und
Darmstadt einst ein Landsee, bis jener Damm des Binger Felsenthals
überwältigt ward und der Strom einen Abfluss hatte.

Forster's literary dreams of Borneo unite with his impressions of the Rhine
as he brings together two distant spaces. He then forces together two different
times: the prehistoric Rhine as it slowly molded the landscape, and the gray
light of a modern winter's day. What is significant, above all, is that neither
prehistoric time nor the present moment is described as a static picture, but as
continuously changing actions. Both are understood by Forster as process. The
Romantic landscape at its most striking is in perpetual movement, and this
movement encompasses both past and present and allows them to interpenetrate each other. The initial triumphs of the new mode of description were
chiefly the mountains seen as organic, living creatures, and the principal stimulus was the study of mountains and their formation.

Mountains as ruins

Mountains had a privileged role in the development of modern sensibility. The
new taste of the eighteenth century for Gothic horror and the fashionable
craving for strong emotions fostered a novel desire to be terrified by landscape.
The dizzying heights and fearful abysses of Alpine Nature were no longer
objects of disgust. Travellers now delighted in seeking out sensations of acro-
phobia. The terror of high altitudes was often accompanied by a light-headed
feeling of liberation.

Mountains forced a new sense of time on European naturalists—and on
tourists and connoisseurs of landscape. The discovery of marine fossils at high
altitudes made a great impression: Was the entire earth, mountains and all,
once covered by the ocean, which then receded, or did the mountains rise above
the sea by volcanic eruption? Some seventeenth-century skeptics (followed,
oddly, by Voltaire) preferred to believe that the fossil seashells were either
chance images of Nature that merely happened to look like seashells, or else
crustaceans thrown away in the Alps by pilgrims who had eaten them on the

way to Rome—not fossils at all. For most scientists, however, the evidence was only too clear,[4] and the realization that the present earth was radically different from that of the past gradually entered into the experience of landscape.

Most writers traced the origin of mountains to some cataclysmic event: a universal deluge, volcanic eruption, or even, in Thomas Burnet's beautiful and notorious *Sacred Theory of the Earth* (published from 1680 to 1691)—a collapse of the earth's crust towards a fiery and watery center. For Burnet the mountains we see are ruins, fragments of a more primitive and perfect world.

> The greatest objects of Nature are, methinks, the most pleasing to behold; and next to the great Concave of the Heavens, and those boundless Regions where the Stars inhabit, there is nothing I look upon with more pleasure than the wide Sea and the Mountains of the Earth . . . And yet these Mountains we are speaking of, to confess the truth, are nothing but great ruins; but such as show a certain magnificence in Nature; as from old Temples and broken Amphitheaters of the *Romans* we collect the greatness of that people . . .
>
> There is nothing doth more awaken our thoughts or excite our minds to enquire into the causes of such things, than the actual view of them; as I have had experience my self when it was my fortune to cross the *Alps* and *Appennine* Mountains; for the sight of those wild, vast and indigested heaps of Stones and Earth, did so deeply strike my fancy, that I was not easie till I could give my self some tolerable account how that confusion came in Nature.[5]

Burnet moves unconsciously towards the Romantic delight in Alpine scenery, but still remains explicitly with the traditional, Classical distaste for mountains seen close up. He writes:

> Look upon those great ranges of Mountains in *Europe* or in *Asia*, whereof we have given a short survey, in what confusion do they lie? They have neither form nor beauty, nor shape, nor order, no more than the clouds in the Air. Then how barren, how desolate, how naked are they?

His description, however, makes them curiously attractive to a modern taste, and clearly, in an odd, unacknowledged way, to his own. As bad as they look now, he remarks, they must have appeared even worse at their cataclysmic formation:

---

4. For a brilliant account of the controversy, see Paolo Rossi, *I Segni del tempo: storia della terra e storia delle nazioni da Hooke a Vico* (Milano 1979).

5. Thomas Burnet, *The Sacred Theory of the Earth,* new ed. (Carbondale, 1965), pp. 109–110.

'Tis true, they cannot look so ill now as they did at first; a ruine that is fresh looks much worse than afterwards, when the Earth grew discolour'd and skin'd over. But I fancy if we had seen the Mountains when they were new-born and raw, when the Earth was freshly broken, and the waters of the Deluge newly retir'd, the fractions and confusions of them would have appear'd very gastly and frightful.

Burnet does not like fragments (or "fractions") unless improved by the patina of antiquity.[6]

Almost exactly a century later, in a notebook of the 1790s, Ramond de Carbonnières was to take a very different approach to the antiquity of mountains in his description of the granite peaks of the Pyrenees, and he senses the order of the mountain debris and the slow action of time:

The blocks of granite with which the soil is formed, covered, and strewn present a reddish hue caused by the decomposition of mica. The granite still in place seems less colored. It is a white-gray which cannot fail to draw the least attentive eye, struck by the ferruginous color of the rocks in all the neighboring valleys. Everything is different here from what we have seen elsewhere. Granite mountains have more regular pyramidal forms, spiky summits, more uniform slopes. The region that I traversed was only a mass of large and small peaks, all more or less similar. An identical color which was diffused over all the rocks augmented the severe and somber tranquillity of the landscape. Some groups of knotty and bizarre pines ornamented the least elevated pyramids with a verdure that sympathized with them; and the snow covering its high summits served to cut them off in a more trenchant manner from the deep blue of the sky. The calm of which this region gave me the idea came from something other than the absence of living beings, the silence and the distance of habitations. It came from the form itself of these rocks, which hold themselves on their bases and affect none of those inclined, contracted, menacing positions presented by the stretches of schist mountains; they have an air of repose and attest the antiquity of the times that saw them born. Even their destruction had nothing disquieting. It seems regular and tranquil. Their ruins announce no catastrophes. They appear to be there only to prove that nothing here below is immortal . . .
    It is here that one should observe granite, the pyramidal forms of the rocks, the regular crystallization of its masses. These are the summits one traverses, climbs, and investigates, and this is how they appear to the naturalist. Great commotions, irregular accidents, disastrous events have not scattered, drawn, or mutilated their debris. Time alone has acted with

6. Ibid., pp. 110, 112.

its powerful but light hand. It has insensibly pushed apart these surfaces which adhered only by the intimacy of contact, and separated these crystals of which even the most piercing eye could not discern the elements. It was during the winter that the frozen water, acting secretly under the cloak of a prolonged snow, enlarged the fissures, holding together what it divided until the spring came. The link then becomes liquid, the water flows out, and the rock falls apart. You see these proud pyramids, like the developing bud, like the pinecone which sows its pine nuts, open their hard scales, seized upon at once by vegetation. It seems as if it were in order to give birth to the pine tree, the juniper, the bearberry, that these rocks have just opened out and flowered. But the roots finish the work of water, and soon the rock is nothing more than a mass of regular pieces of debris, fallen softly to the ground they dominated, where the observer will recognize the constant shapes, measure the unvarying angles, contemplate in its rudiments the simple and learned work of Nature.

Les quartiers de granit dont le sol est formé, couvert & jonché présentent une teinte rougâtre düe à la décomposition du mica. Le granit en place en semble moins coloré. Il est d'un gris blanc qui ne peut manquer d'attirer les regards les moins attentifs, frappés dans toutes les vallées voisines de la couleur férragineuse des roches. Tout icy est diférent de ce que l'on a vu ailleurs. Les montagnes de granit ont des formes pyramidales plus régulières, des cimes hérissées, des pentes plus uniformes. La région que je parcourais n'était qu'un amas de pics grands & petits, tous plus on moins semblables. Une meme couleur répandüe sur tous ces rochers augmentait la sévère et sombre tranquillité du païsage. Quelques groupes des pins noueux & bizarres ornaient les pyramides les moins élevées d'une verdure qui sympathisait avec elles; & la neige répandue sur les hauts sommets servait à les découper d'une manière plus tranchante dans l'azur foncé du ciel. Le calme dont cette région me donnait l'idée tient à autre chose qu'à l'absence des etres animés, au silence, à l'éloignement des habitations. Il tient à la forme même des rochers qui se tiennent assis sur leurs bases & n'affectent aucume de ces positions inclinées, contractées, menaçantes que présentent les bandes des montagnes schisteuses, ont l'air du repos & attestent l'antiquité des tems qui les ont vû naitre. Leur destruction meme n'a rien d'inquiétant. Elle semble régulière et tranquille. Leurs ruines n'annoncent point de catastrophes. Elles paraissent n'etre là que pour prouver que rien icy bas n'est immortel . . .[7]

C'est icy qu'il faut obsérver le granit, les formes pyramidales de ses rochers, la cristallisation régulière de ses masses. ce sont des sommets que l'on parcourt, que l'on gravit, que l'on foule. Et comme ils se montrent

---

7. *Carnets Pyreneens*, Tome II (Lourdes, 1931), pp. 32–33.

au naturaliste! De grandes commotions, des accidens irréguliers, des évènemens désastreux n'ont point éparpillé, entrainé, mutilé leure débris. Le tems seul a tout fait de sa main puissante mais légère. Il a insensiblement écarté ces surfaces qui n'adhéraient que par l'intimité du contact, & séparé ces cristaux que la conformité de leurs angles avait réuni en masses dont l'oeil le plus perçant n'aurait pas discerné les élémens. C'est pendent l'hyver que l'eau glacée, agissant secrétement sous un manteau de neige prolonge, élargit les fissures. alors elle soutient ce qu'elle divise. mais le printemps arrive. Le soutien se liquéfie, l'eau fuit & la roche est désunie. Vous verriés ces orgueilleuses pyramides, comme le bourgeon qui se développe, comme la pomme du pin qui seme ses pignons, ouvrir leurs dures écailles dont aussitot la végétation s'empare. Il semble que c'est pour enfanter le pin, le génévrier, la Busserolle, que ces roches viennent de s'épanouïr. mais les racines vont achever le travail des eaux, & bientot le rocher n'est plus qu'un morceau de débris réguliers doucement tombés sur le sol qu'ils dominaient, et où l'observateur reconnaitra des figures constantes, mesurera des angles qui ne varient point, contemplera dans ses rudimens le simple et savant ouvrage de la nature.[8]

The poetic sentiment, even the unobjectionably trite moral observation, come from Ramond's sense of time and long-range movement. For the Romantic philosopher, granite had a special significance: it was believed to be the oldest building block of the earth. The "air of repose" attests to that antiquity, a witness to the thousands of years of erosion that made the granite shapes so much more regular than those of the ranges of schist mountains. The belief in the latent expressiveness of forms was an essential part of late eighteenth-century aesthetics, but it unites here with geological speculation.

Between Burnet and Ramond there had appeared in 1749 the *Theory of the Earth* of Buffon and his equally influential *Epochs of Nature* of 1778. In place of catastrophic change, Buffon emphasized the slow, imperceptible alterations of time. With more eloquence than any previous writer, he replaced the hypothetical convulsions of cosmological speculation with the daily repeated action of the course of nature which we see happening before our eyes. The mountains were produced by the flow of sea currents, which deposited the shells that were fossilized.[9] The 6,000 years of the history of the world allowed by the Bible were increased by Buffon to 75,000 in his published work. Privately he estimated 600,000, and then 10 million years, but was fearful of disclosing these more radical conclusions, afraid that few would follow him. These and similar speculations profoundly altered the relation of history to landscape: it is no longer the single event—battle, flood, or mythical action—which dignifies a

8. Ibid., pp. 41–42.
9. See Rossi, *I Segni del tempo*, chaps. 13 and 15.

landscape with an aura of antiquity, but the long-term processes that reach from an inconceivably distant past into the visible present.

Human history would naturally seem petty measured by geological and cosmological time. The replacement of "historical" landscape by "pure" land-scape in the work of antiestablishment painters like Constable and Friedrich was not surprising: "pure" landscape in paint—or in verse or prose—now attempted to render the sense of natural, not human, history, the visible evidence of past time in the personal sensation. As "historical" landscape lost its once unchallenged prestige, "pure" or "genre" landscape was, so to speak, historicized, endowed with a complex sense of time that had only been incipient or, at best, intermittent in the great Dutch landscapes of the seventeenth century. The picturesque landscape with ruins of the eighteenth century was replaced by landscape as itself a progressive ruin—the process of corruption and renewal in Nature. At the turn of the century, the multiplicity of time found its most poignant expression in Sénancour's *Reveries on the Primitive Nature of Man* of 1800,[10] with its picture of the solitary observer of nature:

It is in the wild places that the solitary man receives an easy energy even from the inanimate; behold him on that bank in the valleys' shadow. Seated on the mossy trunk of the uprooted fir, he considers that mag-nificent stalk that the years have nourished and that the years have sterilized; and those numerous plants choked under its vast ruin, and the vain power of its branches buried under the tranquil waters that they protected with their proud foliage for three centuries. He hears the moun-tain wind that goes down to be swallowed up in the dark forest and strives intermittently to agitate its depths. He follows the fall of the leaf that detaches itself from the beech; an invisible breath carries it on the agitated wave: it is the unexpected moment when the animated multitude, for which the leaf was both nourishment and homeland, must end its ephem-eral destinies in the watery abyss. He observes this immobile rock of which twenty centuries have begun the irresistible destruction. The waters have tired its base with their perpetual undulations; the action of the air has dried its ruined front: into its imperceptible cracks lichen and moss have entered in order to devour it in silence; and the twisted roots of a yew, still weak and already old, work steadily to separate its half-opened parts. Can you imagine this solitary man? Imagine all he experiences in the womb of movement and silence, of vegetation and ruins? Can you imagine him as he advances with the waves, bends with the branches, trembles with the fugitive bird? Can you feel him when the leaf falls, when the eagle screams, when the rock cracks? . . .

10. Eighth Revery, end of last paragraph.

C'est dans les lieux sauvages que le solitaire reçoit de l'inanimé même une
facile énergie; vois-le sur cette rive dans l'ombre des vallées. Assis sur le
tronc mousseux du sapin renversé, il considère cette tige superbe que les
ans ont nourrie, et que les ans ont stérilisée; et ces plantes nombreuses
étouffées sous sa vaste ruine, et la vaine puissance de ses branches en-
sevelies sous les eaux tranquilles qu'elles protégèrent trois siècles de leur
orgueilleux ombrage. Il écoute le vent de la montagne qui descend s'en-
gouffrer dans la forêt ténébreuse, et s'efforce par intervalle de l'agiter dans
sa profondeur. Il suit dans sa chûte la feuille qui se détache des hêtres; un
souffle invisible la porte sur l'onde agitée: c'est l'instant imprévu oú la
multitude animée, dont elle étoit l'aliment et la patrie, doit finir dans
l'abîme des eaux ses destinées éphémères. Il observe ce roc immobile dont
vingt siècles ont commencé l'irrésistible destruction. Les eaux ont fatigué
sa base de leurs perpétuelles ondulations; l'effort de l'air a desséché son
front ruineux: dans ses fentes imperceptibles le lichen et la mousse se sont
introduits pour le dévorer en silence; et les racines tortueuses d'un yf
encore foible et déjà vieux, travaillent constamment à séparer ses parties
entr'ouvertes. Le conçois-tu bien ce solitaire? conçois-tu tout ce qu'il
éprouve au sein du mouvement et du silence, de la végétation et des ruines?
le vois-tu s'avancer avec les ondes, se courber avec les branches, frémir
avec l'oiseau fugitif? le sens-tu quand la feuille tombe, quand l'aigle crie,
quand le roc se fend? . . .

The ingenious confusion of momentary, seasonal, and millennial time gives
one the illusion of grasping the processes of nature from microscopic to
macroscopic level, of comprehending the reciprocal movement between erosion
and creation. Sénancour combines recent popular notions of biology, geology,
and psychology into an impressive new form of poetry. What is represented
with great power is different rates of change, the multiple tempi of nature.

The portrayal of change, the representation of a reality that is fluid, ever in
motion, is generally acknowledged as typical of Romantic style, and it is indeed
no less powerful in music and painting than in literature. Nevertheless, the
fluidity of style is a manifestation of a more profound change in the way the
world was perceived. Instability became a source of inspiration as well as of
anxiety. The world of politics was not understood as a simple conflict of
opposing states or a clash of interests; political systems seemed to be breaking
up from within. The idea that society could be remade became a general
conviction, and not just the speculation of a few eccentric utopian thinkers.
Philosophers reconceived the ego as a process, rather than a stable essence: for
Fichte, the ego came into existence only as an act of defining itself. The simple
opposition of mind and body, spirit and matter, begins to collapse. The concept
of matter as force and energy takes shape, and physics starts to assume some
of the characteristics of a historical science.

In this fusion of science and poetry, no figure is more significant than Louis Ramond de Carbonnières: he prepared the masterpieces of landscape description of the turn of the century. In 1782 he translated William Coxe's letters on Switzerland, and added a considerable number of observations of his own. These became the principal literary inspiration for Wordsworth's first published work, the *Descriptive Sketches* of 1793: sixteen lines are acknowledged by Wordsworth as a direct translation from Ramond's prose observations, and much of the rest of the poem depends on them as well. In his *Voyage to America*, Chateaubriand declared his intention of imitating Ramond; and the greatest Romantic master of landscape prose, Sénancour, singled out Ramond as a model in an article in the *Mercure de France* (September 1811), "Style in Descriptions," where Buffon, Chateaubriand, and even Rousseau are not found to be without reproach—Rousseau, interestingly because his famous descriptions of the Valais in Switzerland in *La Nouvelle Héloise,* unlike those of Ramond, are not sufficiently exact to enable one to identify the site with any precision.

Ramond was important in developing the new way of describing natural phenomena at the end of the eighteenth century. He does not so much describe the landscape as the act of seeing it: at the same time—and here lies the most striking originality of Romantic description—the immediate visual sensation brings an awareness of the landscape's history, geological, botanical, or sentimental. Ramond was interested above all in the origin of glaciers. In his *Observations faites dans les Pyrénées* of 1789[11] he recounts his discovery of a mass of ice, which was not a glacier, however, but a cavern created by the snowfalls of successive years, which only partially melt during the summer and then freeze again, to be packed down by the next year's falls:

I was, then, buried under forty feet of snow, and I distinguished all the layers. I saw the great winters, separated by many years, distant by several inches. I recognized the scorching summers by the thinnest and most transparent bands; the mild years by the more porous layers. I observed above all, in the entire mass, the insensible transition from the light hexagonal snow to the heavy globulous snow; from this to opaque half-ice, crumbly and reducible to spherical particles; then from this opaque ice to a harder, more transparent ice, whose broken edge, however, was furrowed by a network of crossed striations, which displayed the soldering together of its different parts; and finally from this ice, as yet hardly coherent, to a band of ice completely hard and of such transparency that I distinguished the smallest objects perfectly across fragments four inches thick. This ice, however, still enclosed air bubbles; it was still light, and the break did not present absolutely plane surfaces. This layer, besides,

11. Published in Paris (1789), pp. 108–109.

was very thin; it carpeted only the lower surface of the snows, and the vault of its caverns.

J'étois donc enseveli sous quarante pieds de neige, et j'en distinguois toutes les couches. J'y voyois les hivers fameux, que séparent bien des années, distans de quelques pouces. Je reconnoissois les étés brulans, aux bandes les plus minces et les plus transparentes; les années douces, à des couches plus poreuses. Je remarquois sur-tout, dans la masse entière, le passage insensible de la neige légere, hexagone, à la neige globuleuse et lourde; de celle-ci, à la demi glace opaque, friable, et réducible en parcelles sphériques; ensuite de cette glace opaque, à une glace plus transparente et plus dure, dont cependant la cassure étoit sillonnée de stries croisées en rézeau, qui montroient la soudure de ses différentes parties; et enfin, de cette glace, encore peu cohérente, à une bande de glace tout-à-fait dure et d'une telle transparence, que je distinguois parfaitement les plus petits objets, à travers des fragmens de quatre pouces d'épaisseur. Cette glace, cependent, renfermoit encore des bulles d'air; elle étoit encore légere, et ne présentoit pas, dans sa cassure, des surfaces absolument planes. Le couche, d'ailleurs, en étoit très mince; elle tapissoit uniquement la surface inférieure des neiges, et la voute de ses cavernes.

Every detail brings a sense of its history, but the significance of the past appears almost paradoxically as immediate sensation. "I saw the great winters . . . I recognized the scorching summers." Time is revealed by the immediate perception of space: "Separated by many years, distant by several inches." The oldest ice has become transparent and hard. The two time scales of immediate vision and the slow passage of years and decades merge.

Landscape and memory

Neither the precise observation of nature nor the sense of long-range development is new. Many writers since the Renaissance have found ways of expressing an intensely penetrating experience of things seen (one famous sixteenth-century example is Roger Ascham's description in his book on archery of wind patterns revealed in falling snow).

What is new is the combination of immediate perception with a sense of immensely slow natural development. The interaction of two time scales (or even multiple ones) found its most striking expression in topographical description, in the portrait-landscape—the image not of an ideal landscape but of a real place, made instantly recognizable by the terms of the description. The beauty of the portrait-landscape was indistinguishable from its exactness and its precision. One passage in Ramond remained famous long after his books had ceased to be printed, and it was included in anthologies for French high school students until very late in the nineteenth century. We are reminded of its date of 1789 by the sentimental patriotism of the final sentence.[12] It describes Ramond's descent from the glacier above the circus of Gavarnie on the border between France and Spain (already one of the more important tourist sites in the eighteenth century because of the spectacular scenery) into the valley of Gedro, with its swift mountain stream. These pages reveal the Romantic sense of the complexity of time in landscape at its most extraordinary. The specific moment is early evening, when the atmosphere becomes momentarily heavy and the sense of smell becomes keen:

From the height of the rock of Gavarnie, I had passed from winter to spring; from Gavarnie to Gedro, I passed from spring to summer. Here, I experienced a soft and calm warmth. The newly mown hay exhaled its rustic smell; the plants gave out the fragrance that the rays of the sun had developed, and that its presence no longer dissipated. The lime trees, all in flower, perfumed the atmosphere. I entered the house from which one sees the hidden falls of the torrent of Héas. At the end of the courtyard, there is a rock which overlooks them, and I went to seat myself there. Night was falling, and the stars, successively and in order of magnitude, pierced through the darkened sky. I quitted the torrent and the crash of its waves to go breathe the air of the valley and its delicious perfume. I reascended slowly the road I had come down, and I sought to account for the contribution of my soul to the sweet and voluptuous sensation that I felt. There is something mysterious in odors which powerfully awaken the remembrance of the past. Nothing recalls to this extent places that one has loved, situations that one regrets, minutes whose passage leaves traces all the more profound in the heart that they leave so little in the memory. The odor of a violet restores to the soul the pleasures of many springtimes. I do not know what sweeter instants of my life the flowering lime tree witnessed, but I felt keenly that it stirred fibers that had long been tranquil, that it stimulated reminiscences linked to happy days; I found, between my heart and my thought, a veil that would have been sweet, perhaps . . . sad, perhaps . . . for me to raise; I took pleasure in this vague reverie so near to sadness, aroused by the images of the past; I extended on to Nature the illusion that she had caused to be born, by uniting with her, in an involuntary movement, the times and the events of which she had stirred up the memory; I ceased to be isolated in these wild places; a secret and indefinable intelligence established itself between them and me; and alone, on the banks of the torrent of Gedro, alone but under that sky which saw all the ages flow away and which emcompasses all the climates, I aban-

12. Ibid., pp. 87–89.

doned myself with emotion to a security so sweet, to this profound sentiment of coexistence inspired by the fields of one's own country.

Du haut du rocher à Gavarnie, j'avois passé de l'hyver au printems; de Gavarnie à Gedro, je passai du printems à l'été. Ici j'éprouvois une chaleur douce & calme. Les foins nouvellement fauchés, exhaloient leur odeur champêtre; les plantes répandoient ce parfum que les rayons du soleil avoient développé, & que sa préfence ne dissipoit plus. Les tilleuls, tout en fleurs, embaumoient l'atmosphére. J'entrai dans cette maison où l'on voit les cataractes cachées du Gave de Héas. Au fond de la cour, il y a un rocher qui les domine, & j'allai m'y asseoir. La nuit tomboit, & les étoiles perçoient successivement & par ordre de grandeur, le ciel obscurci. Je quittai le torrent & le fracas de ses flots, pour aller respirer encore l'air de la vallée, & son parfum délicieux. Je remontois lentement le chemin que j'avois descendu, & je cherchois à me rendre compte de la part que mon ame avoit dans la sensation douce & voluptueuse que j'éprouvois. Il y a je ne sais quoi dans les parfums, qui réveille puissamment le souvenir du passé. Rien ne rappelle à ce point, des lieux chéris, des situations regrettées, de ces minutes dont le passage laisse d'aussi profondes traces dans le coeur, qu'elles en laissent peu dans la mémoire. L'odeur d'une violette rend à l'ame les jouissances de plusieurs printems. Je ne sais de quels instans plus doux de ma víe le tilleul en fleur fut témoin, mais je sentois vivement qu'il ébranloit des fibres depuis long-temps tranquilles, qu'il excitoit d'un profond sommeil, des réminiscences liées à de beaux jours; je trouvois, entre mon coeur & ma pensée, un voile qu'il m'auroit été doux, peut-être . . . triste, peut-être . . . de soulever; je me plaisois dans cette rêverie vague & voisine de la tristesse, qu'excitent les images du passé; j'étendois sur la nature l'illusion qu'elle avoit fait naître, en lui alliant, par un mouvement involontaire, les tems & les faits dont elle suscitoit la mémoire; je cessois d'être isolé dans ces sauvages lieux; une secrette & indéfinissable intelligence s'établissoit entre eux & moi; & seul, sur les bords du torrent de Gedro, seul, mais sous ce ciel qui voit s'écouler tous les âges, & qui enserre tous les climats, je me livrois avec attendrissement à cette sécurité si douce, à ce profond sentiment de co-existence qu'inspirent les champs de la patrie.

This is already, fully developed, the Proustian theory of memory: the most powerful and profound memories are those that cannot be consciously recovered, that can only be called up from the past involuntarily by sensations of taste or smell. The coincidence is not fortuitous: Proust knew this page of Ramond. (He even perfidiously attacked Sainte-Beuve for praising minor authors like Ramond de Carbonnières instead of major figures such as Stendhal and Balzac: in his essay on Ramond, in fact, Sainte-Beuve quotes from this page and comments on it.) Earlier eighteenth-century writers had made the connection between sensation and memory, notably Addison: "We may observe, that any single circumstance of what we have formerly seen often raises up a whole scene of Imagery, and awakens numberless Ideas that before slept in the Imagination; such a particular Smell or Colour is able to fill the Mind, on a sudden, with the Picture of the Fields or Garden where we first met with it" (*Spectator,* no. 417, June 28, 1712). But Addison does not take the final step and claim that the involuntary memory is more powerful than the one we can call up at will.

Ramond's prefiguration of twentieth-century thought would be merely a curiosity if it did not arise directly from the attempt to read a complex sense of time into the description of a landscape. A site has a sentimental as well as a geological history: the buried strata of the past are directly evoked by the sensations of the present. When Ramond writes of the "fragrance that the rays of the sun had developed and that its presence no longer dissipated," three scales of time coalesce: the weeks and months of growth, the diurnal movement from daylight to sunset, and the brief moments of evening when we are most strongly aware of the odors of the countryside, when Nature makes herself felt. (There was much eighteenth-century speculation on the role of association, purely mechanical and involuntary, in the process of thinking, notably by philosophers like David Hartley, so much admired for a while by Coleridge, and by the French *idéologues* (such as Maine de Biran), who were a major influence on Stendhal.) For Ramond, memory is built into landscape like its geological structure: the landscape reveals its past to the present observer, and his own past as well. The movement between nature and observer is convoluted: "I extended on to Nature the illusion that she had caused to be born, uniting with her—by an involuntary movement—the times and events of which she had stirred up the memory."

This is not merely the mind of the critical enlightenment that is speaking but also the essential self-alienation of the early Romantics, for whom classical art was a naive, direct response to the world, while modern art was critical and self-conscious (what Schiller called "sentimental"). Ramond yields gratefully to the urge to identify himself with the landscape which has acknowledged his presence, but he is, in passing, skeptical enough to analyze, and even to deconstruct, the mechanism that makes this possible.

At the heart of this passage there is a half lie: when Ramond claims that he did not know "what sweeter instants of [his] life the flowering lime tree witnessed," he knew perfectly well which happier days were being brought back: he had lived for a year in this valley of Gedro with the woman he loved. Nevertheless, it is important to him—and no doubt partially correct—that the memories recalled by the sensation of smell be imprecise. The immediate consciousness of the present moment expands to cover a whole range of the past: it does not pinpoint an event, but diffuses itself over the physical system of the individual until his entire body begins to stir with habits half remembered, long periods of time whose contours remain slightly blurred. I do not think it was possible to understand this before the end of the eighteenth century. A new way of looking at nature, which simultaneously superimposes different scales of time, an awareness of the great antiquity of the earth, and an original way of describing landscape combined to create a new kind of psychology.

These perceptions of the past within the present are not singular but commonplace, an everyday habit of viewing the world and nature. They are at once a style of description and a normal part of late eighteenth-century sensibility. The mixture of scientific observation and nostalgia that we find in Ramond is typical of his age. Reading the past into the direct experience of the present had, one might say, become second nature to the early Romantics—not just the past but many different kinds of past: millennial, annual, seasonal, diurnal, momentary.

Goethe's *Letters from Switzerland* of 1779 begin typically with a synthesis of immediate sensation and long-range time:

Through the back of a high, broad chain of mountains, the Birs, a massive river, sought a way for itself in primeval time. Some ages later necessity anxiously clambered through its gorges. The Romans widened the road, and now it is easily negotiated. The water rushing across boulders and the road go side by side, and in most places make up the entire breadth of the pass, closed on both sides by cliffs, which can be taken in by slightly raising one's eyes. Toward the rear the slopes of mountains gently rose and the peaks were hidden from us by mist.

Durch den Rücken einer hohen und breiten Gebirgkette hat die Birsch, ein mässiger Fluss, sich einen Weg von uralters gesucht. Das Bedürfnis mag nachher durch ihre Schluchten ängstlich nachgeklettert sein. Die Römer erweiterten schon den Weg, und nun ist er sehr bequem durchgeführt. Das über Felsstücke rauschende Wasser und der Weg gehen neben einander hin und machen an den meisten Orten die ganze Breite des Passes, der auf beiden Seiten von Felsen beschlossen ist, die ein gemächlich aufgehobenes Auge fassen kann. Hinterwärts heben Gebirge sanft ihre Rücken, deren Gipfel uns vom Nebel bedeckt waren.

Only the magisterial ease with which Goethe comprehends the creation of the landscape and its history along with the sense of moving through it is out of the ordinary for its age.

The landscape contains its past, has its memories buried within its forms, and Goethe tries to seize these memories in the darkness, like the traveller of Schubert's *Winterreise,* who closes his eyes to the lime tree and confuses the winter wind of the present with the remembered summer's breeze:

At the end of the gorge I descended and turned back alone for a space. Yet I continued to develop inwardly a profound feeling through which the pleasure is highly magnified for an attentive spirit. In the darkness one senses the origin and the life of these strange forms. Whenever and however it happened, these masses, by the weight and similarities of their parts, grandly and simply came together. Whatever revolutions afterwards moved, separated, and split them apart, these shattered masses were, however, only created by individual quakes, and even the thought of so monstrous a movement gives one an elevated feeling of eternal stability. Time, bound to eternal laws, has worked now more, now less, upon them.

On the inside they seem to be of a yellowish color; but weather and air alter the surface into gray-blue, so that only here and there is the original color visible in streaks and fresh breaks. The stone itself weathered slowly and its angles were rounded . . . The vegetation asserted its rights: on each projection, surface, and crevice fig trees take root, moss and herbs are sown about the cliffs. One feels deeply that there is nothing arbitrary here, a slowly moving eternal law works upon everything, and the only sign of the hand of man is the convenient road along which one moves through these strange surroundings.

Am Ende der Schlucht stieg ich ab und kehrt einen Teil allein zurück. Ich entwickelte mir noch ein tiefes Gefühl, durch welches das Vergnügen auf einen hohen Grad für den aufmerksamen Geist vermehrt wird. Man ahndet im Dunkeln die Entstehung und das Leben dieser seltsamen Gestalten. Es mag geschehen sein wie und wann es wolle, so haben sich diese Massen, nach der Schwere und Ähnlichkeit ihrer Teile, groß und einfach zusammengesetzt. Was für Revolutionen sie nachher bewegt, getrennt, gespalten haben, so sind auch diese noch nur einzelne Erschütterungen gewesen, und selbst der Gedanke einer so ungeheuren Bewegung gibt ein hohes Gefühl von ewiger Festigkeit. Die Zeit hat auch, gebunden an die ewigen Gesetze, bald mehr bald weniger auf sie gewirkt.

Sie scheinen innerlich von gelblicher Farbe zu sein; allein das Wetter und die Luft verändern die Oberfläche in graublau, daß nur hier und da in Streifen und in frischen Spalten die erste Farbe sichtbar ist. Langsam verwittert der Stein selbst und rundet sich an den Ecken ab . . . Die Vegetation behauptet ihr Recht; auf jedem Vorsprung, Fläche und Spalt fassen Fichten Wurzel, Moos und Kräuter säumen die Felsen. Man fühlt tief, hier ist nichts Willkürliches, hier wirkt ein Alles langsam bewegendes, ewiges Gesetz, und nur von Menschenhand ist der bequeme Weg, über den man durch diese seltsamen Gegenden durchschleicht.

Goethe is trying here to feel—or, better, to represent and convey to the reader—the rhythm of millennial change, and to incorporate it into the rhythm of the observer who walks through it—literally incorporate, and to inspire the bodily sensation of long-range movement polyphonically with the immediate sense of observation:

> Now walls hanging together rose straight up, now powerful layers stretched out towards river and highway, broad masses are laid over one another, and immediately beside them stand sheer cliffs. Great crevices split upwards, and plaques as strong as masonry have sprung themselves loose from the rest of the rock. Pieces of the cliff have plunged below, others hang over, and their position makes one fear that in the future they too will similarly fall in.
>
> *Bald steigen aneinanderhängende Wande senkrecht auf, bald streichen gewaltige Lagen schief nach dem Fluß und dem Weg ein, breite Massen sind aufeinander gelegt, und gleich daneben stehen scharfe Klippen abgesetzt. Große Klüfte spalten sich aufwärts, und Platten von Mauerstärke haben sich von dem übrigen Gesteine losgetrennt. Einzelne Felsstücke sind herunter gestürzt, andere hängen noch über und lassen nach ihrer Lage fürchten, daß sie dereinst gleichfalls herein kommen werden.*

The scene is all in movement, and all visual evidence of an earlier condition. It is not, however, the primitive state that Goethe attempts to recreate but the continuous movement from past to present, and it is not the poet but the landscape itself that remembers its past and affirms the unity of ancient and present time. In this new form of memory lies the difference between classical or historical landscape and the new modern sense of the sublime in a landscape with only minimal human presence and with no suggestion of human history. The classical vision of Poussin and Claude conjures up an earlier world now irrevocably past; even the great Dutch genre landscapes of the seventeenth century, with few exceptions, present a recent present frozen into a kind of pastoral of the Golden Age: in the Romantic landscape of Thomas Girtin, Turner, and Constable, however, the past is even now with us, in fragments, eroding, still decaying, and transforming itself into new life.

The forces that caused the decline of "historical" landscape and shaped the modern outlook are evident in Goethe's famous *Italian Journey,* written a few years after the trip to Switzerland of 1779 (the 1786–87 diary and letters of the trip to Rome, Naples, and Sicily were, however, not published until two decades later). On the fourth of April 1787 he found himself in a pleasant valley near Palermo:

> The most beautiful spring weather and a fruitfulness that streamed forth broadened the sense of an invigorating peace over the whole valley, which was spoiled by the pedantry of the tactless guide, who recounted in detail how Hannibal had waged a battle here and what monstrous actions of

war had taken place on this site. I reproached him disagreeably for his fatal raising of such departed spirits. It was bad enough that the soil from time to time had to be stamped upon by horses and men if not always by elephants. At least one should not rudely awaken the power of imagination from its peaceful dreams with such noises from the past. He was very surprised that I was irritated by classical reminiscenses in such a place, and I was indeed unable to explain clearly how such a mixture of past and present felt unwelcome to me.

Even more astonishing did I appear to this guide when I looked for little stones on all the low banks (of which the river left many dry), and took away with me the different kinds. I could not, however, explain to him that there is no faster way to arrive at an idea of a mountainous region than by investigating the kinds of stone that have been pushed into the streams, and that right here the task was to create by means of these scraps a representation of those eternally classical heights of the antiquity of the earth.

Die schönste Frühlingswitterung und eine hervorquellende Fruchtbarkeit verbreitete das Gefühl eines belebenden Friedens über das ganze Tal, welches mir der ungeschickte Führer durch seine Gelehrsamkeit verkümmerte, umständlich erzählend, wie Hannibal hier vormals eine Schlacht geliefert und was für ungeheure Kriegstaten an dieser Stelle geschehen. Unfreundlich verwies ich ihm das fatale Hervorrufen solcher abgeschiedenen Gespenster. Es sei schlimm genug, meinte ich, daß von Zeit zu Zeit die Saaten, wo nicht immer von Elefanten, doch von Pferden und Menschen zerstampft werden müßten. Man solle wenigstens die Einbildungskraft nicht mit solchem Nachgetümmel aus ihrem friedlichen Traume aufschrecken. Er verwunderte sich sehr, daß ich das klassische Andenken an so einer Stelle verschmähte, und ich konnte ihm freilich nicht deutlich machen, wie mir bei einer solchen Vermischung des Vergangenen und des Gegen wärtigen zumute sei.

Noch wunderlicher erschien ich diesem Begleiter, als ich auf allen seichten Stellen, deren der Fluß gar viele trocken läßt, nach Steinchen suchte und die verschiedenen Arten derselben mit mir forttrug. Ich konnte ihm abermals nicht erklären, daß man sich von einer gebirgigen Gegend nicht schneller einen Begriff machen kann, als wenn man die Gesteinarten untersucht, die in den Bächen herabgeschoben werden, und daß hier auch die Aufgabe sei, durch Trümmer sich eine Vorstellung von jenen ewig klassischen Höhen des Erd-Altertums zu verschaffen.

Goethe is at a loss to account for his distaste at this mixture of past and present, particularly as he himself was seeking out the traces of the past in the landscape itself. He had no lack of interest in classical history, and his appreciation of ancient ruins was as passionate as any other tourist's. It is, however, the continued existence of the past within the present that holds him, the living past that is still visible, that can still be a part of experience. He cannot bear the guide's anecdote of Hannibal, a kind of commemorative plaque that states that Hannibal once slept here, in a valley from which all trace of Hannibal has disappeared. In painting, the historical landscape of the academic tradition began to pale before the more powerful evocation of long-range time in the modern school. Like Goethe, John Constable and Caspar David Friedrich wished to eliminate historical references from their landscapes: classical temples, figures in togas and armor were intrusions, dissonances that marred the harmony of Nature.

Clearly, Goethe found the geological past nobler and more poetic than human history. For a number of years he played with the idea of writing what he called a "novel" about the history of the earth. In his sketches for it he produced some of his most extraordinary prose, above all the essay on granite, finally published more than a century after it had been composed. If in the end the project came to nothing, the reason may have been that for Goethe, long-range time had to be seized directly through the visible present: this gave a distinctive power to the new cosmological speculations. When Goethe made a report on the geology of the mountains of Saxony, he wrote to Count Ernst von Gotha on December 12, 1780:

> Your Highness will remark from the whole that we have not allowed ourselves a word about the origin of mountains. It is generally the foolishness of those who describe a couple of mountains to try immediately to drag in something about the creation of the world. I should like, however, to add one thing. In this case, as in a thousand similar, the concept arrived at by observation is infinitely superior to that attained by theoretical science. When I am above, or in front of, or in the midst of mountains, and I consider the form, the kind, the power of the layers and shapes, and vividly call up the contents and the contour in their natural shape and placement, then with the lively perception of *this is the way it is,* the spirit feels a dark hint of *this was the way it came about.*

> *Ew. Durchlaucht werden durch das Ganze finden, daß wir uns über die Entstehung unserer Gebirge kein Wort erlaubt haben. Es ist dies meist die Torheit derjenigen, die ein paar Berge beschrieben, daß sie zugleich etwas zur Erschaffung der Welt mit beitragen wollen. Noch eins muß ich freilich mit beifügen. Bei dieser Sache, wie bei tausend ähnlichen, ist der anschauende Begriff dem wissenschaftlichen unendlich vorzuziehen. Wenn ich auf, vor oder in einem Berge stehe, die Gestalt, die Art, die Mächtigkeit seiner Schichten und Gänge betrachte und mir Bestandteile und Form in ihrer natürlichen Gestalt und Lage gleichsam noch lebendig entgegenrufe,*

und man mit dem lebhaften Anschauen so ist's *einen dunklen Wink in der Seele fühlt* so ist's erstanden!

Goethe's defensive remarks reveal how fashionable cosmological speculation was, and they present a new ideal of scientific writing and of landscape description. Long-term process is represented by the accuracy, the ordering, and above all the vivacity of direct observation. Deep structure is inferred from the way it makes itself visible at the surface. This ideal spread rapidly to the visual arts as the antique grandeurs of historical painting faded for such artists as Constable and Friedrich. One painter, indeed, went even further. In a letter to Ludwig Tieck of December 1, 1802, Philipp Otto Runge set as a goal the almost impossible visual representation of the way theories of Nature develop:

> I wanted specifically to represent in images how I have arrived at the conceptions of flowers and of the whole of Nature; not what I think and what I am forced to feel, nor what is true and can be seen to cohere with that: but how I came—and still come—to see, think, and feel that; in other words the road I have taken—and then it would be strange if other men did not grasp it in the same way.

> *Ich wollte nämlich das, wie ich zu den Begriffen von den Blumen und der ganze Natur gelangt bin, wiedergeben in Bildern; nicht was ich mir denke und was ich empfinden muss, und was wahr und zusammenhangen darin zu sehen ist: sondern, wie ich dazu gekommen bin, und noch dazu komme, das zu sehen zu denken und zu empfinden, so den Weg, den ich gegangen bin, und da musste es doch curios seyn, dass andere Menschen das so gar nicht begreifen sollten.*

In short, it is less the truth of Nature than the way of arriving at the truth that interests the artist. The portrayal of the hidden processes of thought, however, is achieved by the images of Nature themselves and by the vivacity of the representation. In music, too, composers were often unsatisfied by the static representation of a sentiment by simple musical analogy, but sought to portray the processes of feeling and even, as we have seen with the end of Schumann's *Frauenliebe und Leben,* the actual functioning of memory.

The landscape of the Romantic poet and painter was saturated with memory, geological as well as sentimental: the essential condition of the new style was the visible presence of the past in the present. Opposition of past and present was not felt as a contradiction, paradox, or oxymoron—or only apparently so, since the relation was conceived above all as a dynamic continuity. Wordsworth's famous line in his account of crossing the Alps—"The woods decaying, never to be decayed"—is almost too simple an expression of this conviction. Perhaps the unbroken working of past time in the present Alpine landscape was even more powerfully conveyed by the striking image in the preceding verse: "The stationary blasts of waterfalls." Like Goethe, Wordsworth is trying to grasp the slow rhythm of long development of the earth within the immediate vision of Nature, a rhythm that Sénancour, at almost the same moment, caught with his wonderful phrase "this earth, which vegetates and mineralizes under our feet."

This is the landscape's memory of itself, an unconscious presence: ideally, for these poets, our sense of Nature should be equally unconscious, seized physically rather than called up at will. The memories of landscape to which Wordsworth returns are those for which the significance remained generally uncomprehended at the moment of perception:[13]

> The visible scene
> Would enter unawares into his mind
> With all its solemn imagery, its rocks,
> Its woods, and that uncertain heaven received
> Into the bosom of the steady lake.

The last line reverses the traditional symbols of sky and water for which the heavens should be fixed and eternal, the water fluid and unstable: heaven is uncertain here, the lake steady. Sky and lake absorb each other, exchange meanings. This image, which Coleridge found so typical of the poet that he claimed he would have cried out "Wordsworth!" if he had met these verses traveling alone in the Sahara desert, was also invented independently by Sénancour in a description of a sunset on a lake seen above the clouds, from the third fragment of *Oberman* (1804), "On Romantic Expression and the *Ranz des Vaches*":

The last rays of the sun turn yellow the numerous chestnut trees on the wild rocks; . . . they turn the mountains brown; they set the snow alight; they fire the air; and the water without waves, brilliant with light and confounded with the heavens, has become infinite like them, still more pure, more ethereal, more beautiful. Its calm astonishes, its limpidity was a delusion, the airy splendor it repeats seems to hollow out its depths; and under the mountains separated from the globe and as if suspended in air, you find at your feet the void of the heavens and the immensity of the world. This is a moment of prestige and oblivion.

Ses derniers feux jaunissent les nombreux chataigniers sur les rocs sauvages; [. . .] ils brunissent les monts; ils allument les neiges; ils embrasent les airs; et l'eau sans vagues, brillante de lumière et confondue avec les cieux, est devenue infinie comme eux, et plus pure encore, plus éthérée,

---

13. William Wordsworth, "There was a boy," in *Lyrical Ballads* (1800).

plus belle. Son calme etonne, sa limpidité trompe, et sous ces monts séparés du globe et comme suspendus dans les airs, vous trouvez a vos pieds le vide des cieux et l'immensité du monde. Il y a là un temps de prestige et d'oubli.

The sensation of floating over the clouds above a void is also described by Wordsworth elsewhere, and was portrayed by Caspar David Friedrich. It was a sensation cultivated at the time, and gave one the illusion of physical contact with infinity. These are accurate and evocative descriptions not of landscape seen but of landscape remembered, of landscape reexperienced as a memory. At the moment of actual experience, Wordsworth's boy is unaware of what lies before him, Sénancour's hero is oblivious in his contemplation.

For both, indeed, a remembered image can often be a substitute for one that is suppressed. In a famous passage, the wind and the rain return to Wordsworth the memory of the misty day he waited at a crossroads, beside a dead tree, a ruined wall, and a sheep, to see from which direction the carriage would come that would take him home from school. During the vacation his father died, but it is not an image of death to which Wordsworth later turns:[14]

> And, afterwards, the wind, and sleety rain,
> And all the business of the elements,
> The single sheep, and the one blasted tree,
> And the bleak music from that old stone wall,
> The noise of wood and water, and the mist
> That on the line of each of those two roads
> Advanced in such indisputable shapes,
> All these were spectacles and sounds to which
> I often would repair, and thence would drink
> As at a fountain.

No doubt, to a small boy, the anxiety and anticipated delight of his holidays would become a source of guilt when the holidays turned out to be the occasion of a father's death. Displacing the remembrance of death with the drear landscape and the memory of anticipation, now forever connected with the death almost as a cause, is both punishment and consolation. In fact, Wordsworth leaves the significance of his image undefined, and so should we: its function is expansive, to absorb new meanings not to narrow down or to specify. This is not imprecision: a memory for Wordsworth is not a verifiable quotation from the past but a return that takes new forms and new colors.

The interplay of memories is even more complex in the eleventh letter of

---

14. William Wordsworth, *The Prelude,* ed. Stephen Parrish (Ithaca, 1977), version of 1798–99, p. 52.

Sénancour's *Oberman,* which mingles memories of the Orient, the National Library in Paris, and the landscapes of Fontainebleau and Switzerland with deliberate incongruity. This book, which originally sold only a few copies, gradually acquired an almost legendary prestige, and became known as the Bible of French Romanticism; its influence extended from Balzac and George Sand to Matthew Arnold. It is here that landscape became the means of creating large structures in prose that foreshadow the song cycles to come a few years later. It is above all the scale of Sénancour's conception which is imposing. In these excerpts from letter XI Sénancour uses his complex of memories the way a composer uses themes, which recall one another and create new harmonies by their combination:

> Fairly often I pass two hours at the library, not exactly to learn something—that desire has considerably cooled—but because, not knowing exactly what to do with the hours that however drain away irreparably, I find them less painful when I employ them outside than when I have to spend them at home. Forced occupations suit me in my discouragement; too much liberty would leave me in indolence. I am more at peace among those who are silent as I am than alone in the middle of a tumultuous populace. I love these long halls, some lonely, others filled with attentive people, ancient and cold depository of human striving and all human vanities.
>
> When I read Bougainville, Chardin, Laloubère, I am possessed by the ancient memory of exhausted lands, of the fame of a distant wisdom, or of the youth of happy islands; but finally forgetting Persepolis, and Benares, and even Tinian, I reunite times and places in the present point where human conceptions can perceive them all. I see those avid spirits who ripen in silence and contention, while eternal oblivion, rolling over their wise and fascinated heads, brings their necessary death, and will dissipate in one moment of nature at once their being, their thought, and their century.
>
> The halls surround a long tranquil court, covered with grass [. . .] I like to dream while walking on these old paving stones that one has taken from quarries to prepare for men's feet a dry and sterile surface. But time and neglect have, in a way, put them back in the earth by covering them with a new layer, and by giving back to the ground its vegetation and the hues of its natural aspect. Sometimes I find these paving stones more eloquent than the books I have just admired.
>
> Yesterday, consulting the encyclopedia, I opened the volume to a place I was not looking for, and I do not remember what the article was; but it concerned a man who, tired with unrest and disappointment, threw himself into an absolute solitude [. . .] The idea of that independent life recalled to my imagination not the free solitudes of Imaüs nor the easy-

going isles of the Pacific, nor the more accessible Alps [. . .] But a distinct memory presented to me in a striking way, and with a kind of surprise and inspiration, the sterile rocks and the woods of Fontainebleau [. . .]

I was, I think, fourteen, fifteen, and seventeen years old when I saw Fontainebleau [. . .] Awkward, uncertain; apprehensive of everything, but knowing nothing; stranger to all that surrounded me, I had no other fixed character than that of being restless and unhappy [. . .] When I found an open place surrounded on all sides, where I saw only sand and juniper trees, I experienced a feeling of peace, of liberty, of savage joy, power of nature felt for the first time at an age easily happy. I was not gay, however: almost happy, I had only the agitation of well-being. I was bored when playing, and I always returned with sadness. Many times I was in the woods before the sun had appeared. I climbed the still shadowy summits: I was wet with the heather full of dew; and when the sun rose, I regretted the uncertain light which precedes the dawn. I loved the bogs, the dark valleys, the thick woods; I loved the hills covered with heather; I greatly loved the sandstones overturned and the crumbly rocks; I loved even more those vast and mobile tracts of sand, unmarked by the foot of man but streaked here and there by the uneasy trace of the doe or hare in flight. When I heard a squirrel, when I frightened a deer, I stopped. I was content, and for the moment I looked for nothing more. It was at this epoch that I noticed the birch, solitary tree which already made me sad and which I have never seen since without pleasure. I love the birch; I love that white, smooth, and cracked bark; that uncultivated stalk, those branches which bend to the earth; the mobility of the leaves, and all that abandon, simplicity of nature, attitude of the deserts.

Time lost, and which cannot be forgotten. Illusion only too vain of an expansive sensibility. [. . .] The brilliant magical illusion born with man's heart and which seems as if it should endure with him revived one day: I came to the point of believing that my desires would be satisfied. The sudden and too impetuous fire burned in the void and went out after having illuminated nothing. Thus, in the season of storms momentary flashes to fright the living being appear in the shadowy night.

It was in March: I was in Lu . . . There were violets at the foot of the bushes and lilacs, in the springtime in a little field, tranquil, sloping toward the southern sun. The house was above, much higher. A terraced garden blocked the view from the windows. Below the field, difficult rocks, straight as walls; and, beyond, other rocks covered with meadows, hedges, and fir trees. The ancient walls of the city passed across all that; there was an owl in their old towers. In the evening, the moon was shining; in the distance horn call answered horn call; and the voice I shall never hear again . . . ! All that deceived me. It was so far the only error of my life. Why then this memory of Fontainebleau and not that of Lu . . .?

Lettre XI
Paris, 27 juin, II.

Je passe assez souvent deux heures à la bibliothèque; non pas précisément pour m'instruire, ce désir-la se refroidit sensiblement; mais parce que ne sachant trop avec quoi remplir ces heures qui pourtant coulent irréparables, je les trouve moins pénibles quand je les emploie au dehors, que s'il faut les consumer chez moi. Des occupations un peu commandées me conviennent dans mon découragement: trop de liberté me laisserait dans l'indolence. J'ai plus de tranquillité entre des gens silencieux comme moi, que seul au milieu d'une population tumultueuse. J'aime ces longues salles, les unes solitaires, les autres remplies de gens attentifs, antique et froid dépôt des efforts et de toutes les vanités humaines.

Quand je lis Bougainville, Chardin, Laloubère, je me pénètre de l'ancienne mémoire des terres épuisées, de la renommée d'une sagesse lointaine, ou de la jeunesse des îles heureuses; mais oubliant enfin et Persépolis, et Bénarès, et Tinian même, je réunis les temps et les lieux dans le point présent où les conceptions humaines les perçoivent tous. Je vois ces esprits avides qui acquièrent dans le silence et la contention, tandis que l'éternel oubli, roulant sur leurs têtes savantes et séduites, amène leur mort nécessaire, et va dissiper en un moment de la nature, et leur être, et leur pensée, et leur siècle.

Les salles environnent une cour longue, tranquille, couverte d'herbe [. . .] J'aime à rêver en marchant sur ces vieux pavés que l'on a tirés des carrières, pour préparer aux pieds de l'homme une surface sèche et stérile. Mais le temps et l'abandon les remettent en quelque sorte sous la terre en les recouvrant d'une couche nouvelle, et en redonnant su sol sa végétation et des teintes de son aspect naturel. Quelquefois je trouve ces pavés plus éloquens que les livres que je viens d'admirer.

Hier, en consultant l'Encyclopédie, j'ouvris le volume à un endroit que je ne cherchais pas, et je ne me rappelle pas quel était cet article; mais il s'agissait d'un homme qui, fatigué d'agitations et de revers, se jeta dans une solitude absolue [. . .] L'idée de cette vie indépendante n'a rappelé à mon imagination ni les libres solitudes de l'Imaüs, ni les îles faciles de la Pacifique, ni les Alpes plus accessibles [. . .] Mais un souvenir distinct m'a présenté d'une manière frappante, et avec une sorte de surprise et d'inspiration, les rochers stériles et les bois de Fontainebleau [. . .]

J'avais, je crois, quatorze, quinze et dix-sept ans, lorsque je vis Fontainebleau [. . .] Embarrassé, incertain; pressentant tout peut-être, mais ne connaissant rien; étranger à ce qui m'environnait, je n'avais d'autre caractère décidé que d'être inquiet et malheureux [. . .] Quand je trouvais un endroit découvert et fermé de toutes parts, où je ne voyais que des sables et des genièvres, j'éprouvais un sentiment de paix, de liberté, de joie sauvage, pouvoir de la nature sentie pour la première fois dans l'âge facilement heureux. Je n'étais pas gai pourtant: presque heureux, je n'avais que l'agitation du bien-être. Je m'ennuyais en jouissant, et je rentrais toujours triste. Plusieurs fois j'étais dans les bois avant que le soleil parût. Je gravissais les sommets encore dans l'ombre, je me mouillais dans la bruyère pleine de rosée; et quand le soleil paraissait, je regrettais la clarté incertaine qui précède l'aurore. J'aimais les fondrières, les vallons obscurs, les bois épais; j'aimais les collines couvertes de bruyère; j'aimais beaucoup les grès renversés et les rocs ruineux; j'aimais bien plus ces sables mobiles, dont nul pas d'homme ne marquait l'aride surface sillonnée çà et là par la trace inquiète de la biche ou du lièvre en fuite. Quand j'entendais un écureuil, quand je faisais partir un daim, je m'arrêtais, j'étais mieux, et pour un moment je ne cherchais plus rien. C'est à cette époque que je remarquai le bouleau, arbre solitaire qui m'attristait déjà, et que depuis je ne rencontre jamais sans plaisir. J'aime le bouleau; j'aime cette écorce blanche, lisse et crevassée; cette tige agreste; ces branches qui s'inclinent vers la terre; la mobilité des feuilles, et tout cet abandon, simplicité de la nature, attitude des déserts.

Temps perdus, et qu'on ne saurait oublier! Illusion trop vaine d'une sensibilité expansive! [. . .] Le prestige spécieux, infini, qui naît avec le coeur de l'homme, et qui semblait devoir subsister autant que lui, se ranima un jour: j'allai jusqu'à croire que j'aurais des désirs safisfaits. Ce feu subit et trop impétueux brûla dans le vide, et s'éteignit sans avoir rien éclairé. Ainsi, dans la saison des orages, apparaissent, pour l'effroi de l'être vivant, des éclairs instantanés dans la nuit ténébreuse.

C'était en mars: j'étais a Lu . . . Il y avait des violettes au pied des buissons, et des lilas dans un petit pré bien printanier, bien tranquille, incliné au soleil du midi. La maison était au-dessus, beaucoup plus haut. Un jardin en terrasse ôtait la vue des fenêtres. Sous le pré, des rocs difficiles et droits comme des murs: au fond, un large torrent, et par-delà, d'autres rochers couverts de près, de haies et de sapins! Les murs antiques de la ville passaient à travers tout cela: il y avait un hibou dans leurs vieilles tours. Le soir, la lune éclairait; des cors se répondaient dans l'éloignement; et la voix que je n'entendrai plus . . . ! Tout cela m'a trompé. Ma vie n'a encore eu que cette seule erreur. Pourquoi donc ce souvenir de Fontainebleau, et non pas celui de Lu . . . ?

The transition to the final landscape of "Lu . . ." (certainly Lucerne) is violently abrupt, almost surrealist in its juxtaposition to what precedes. The abruptness prepares Sénancour's last puzzling question. The initial substitution of the adolescent memories of Fontainebleau for the travel images out of books is a brilliant illustration of Romantic ideology, and we are led into it by the stones of the courtyard's dead pavement in the National Library which appear to remember the living Nature from which they came. The birch becomes a symbol of the melancholy of Sénancour's adolescence and of his isolation. The splendor of the final paragraph lies in its change of style: after the rich flow of detail in the description of Fontainebleau with the long sentences encompassing several seasons and three years of experience, we find a portrait-landscape of a limited space during a few days in March—a landscape which comes to us in discontinuous fragments. The phrases are short and broken, the details isolated from each other: this is not a memory that arises spontaneously, physically, but one that is called up with an effort of will. The memories of Fontainebleau return unasked, but Sénancour is forcing himself to remember Lucerne. It is, paradoxically, even more moving, more poetic in its willfulness, in its inability to achieve organic movement. This letter is a profound example of a technique invented at the time and which effectively challenged composers to find a musical equivalent: to charge two images with all the power of memory and then to overlay one with the other, multiplying associations.

Music and memory

Beethoven is the first composer to represent the complex process of memory—not merely the sense of loss and regret that accompanies visions of the past, but the physical experience of calling up the past within the present. The first song of *An die ferne Geliebte* (To the Distant Beloved) of 1816 is about the pain of distance. Each one of the six songs of the cycle except the last is a landscape, and the opening landscape is one that separates:

> Upon the hill I sit
> Gazing into the blue land of mist
> Looking towards the far pastures
> Where I found thee, beloved.

> Far from thee am I removed
> Cutting off lie mountain and valley
> Between us and our peace
> Our happiness and our suffering.

> *Auf dem Hügel sitz ich spähend*
> *In das blaue Nebelland*
> *Nach den fernen Triften sehend*
> *Wo ich dich, Geliebte, fand.*

> *Weit bin ich von dir geschieden*
> *Trennend liegen Berg und Thal*
> *Zwischen uns und unsre Frieden*
> *Unserm Glück und uns'rer Qual.*

This is the traditional melancholy of separation, familiar to song and aria; and Beethoven sets the stanzas to a simple strophic melody sung five times. It is only with the second song that the process of remembering begins, and with it the familiar horn calls as well and the musical echoes:

Where the mountains so blue
From the misty gray
Look out towards here,
Where the sun glows
The clouds drive
Would I be.

This opening stanza of the second song only moves towards memory, as if the horn calls awakened it. It is with the second stanza that memory begins to flow, that the past becomes half present, musically as well as poetically:

There in the peaceful valley
Grief and suffering are silenced:
Where in the mass of rocks
The primrose dreams quietly there
The wind blows so lightly
Would I be.

The setting of this stanza is unique in Beethoven's cycle: the first five songs all have a short strophic melody simply repeated by the singer for each stanza. The accompaniments, indeed, are elaborately rewritten, but the only changes in the vocal parts are alterations of mode from major to minor, an occasional echoing repeat of the end of a phrase, and (at the conclusion of the third song) an additional few notes as a transition to the next song. Otherwise the strophic form reigns absolute until the last song, and the vocal melody is identical from stanza to stanza. The only exception is this second stanza of the second song: here the melody is not exactly altered but simply displaced from voice to piano.

The singer now repeats a single note, a kind of inner pedal point below the melody—in front of the melody, indeed, would be the more accurate way of describing the effect. The melody comes from a distance, and the singer is reduced to meditating on a single note, as if lost in the act of recollection. As far as I know, this is the first attempt to exploit the fact—psychological as well as acoustic—that singer and pianist are in different spaces. The feeling of distance in time is translated, as we have seen before, as distance in space, but here a doubly literal separation in space, as the beloved is distant from the lover, and melody is distant from the singer.

Beethoven imposes this feeling of distance by dynamics, sonority, and tonality. There are seven indications of *pianissimo* in this stanza, where the first stanza marks only two, and both of those are echo effects (the opening chord of the first stanza is also *pianissimo,* but the rest of the stanza must rise to *piano* if the echoes are to make sense). In the second stanza everything is hushed. Two of the indications of *pianissimo* are within bars 27 and 28, where the new sonority of a drone bass softly and delicately reinforces the repeated G of the voice, like the soft wind that blows. The voice remains on the tonic G, but the melody is no longer in the fundamental key: it is now transposed to the subdominant C major, and this too is the only example of a transposition in the entire cycle. The use of a change of key with a mysterious hushed sonority to represent a movement away from reality was to be imitated later, most notably by Schumann. Here it serves to portray the separation of present reality and past memory. The genius of Beethoven is revealed best of all by the restriction of the voice to a single note: it seems as if the lover, now completely passive, is submitting almost involuntarily to the incursion of memory.

One other change should be noted in this second stanza. The third line echoes the last half of the second one. In the first stanza, this echo was followed by another in the piano alone: since the third line is shorter than each of the first two, the result was a four-bar phrase with two echoes of one bar. All this play of sonority is removed in the second stanza, which runs everything together in a continuous *pianissimo,* the six-bar phrase is reduced to five (four and a single echo), and the new rhythm corresponds very subtly to the prosody. In this second stanza, too, the short third line runs into what follows. The new unity increases the wonderful effect of stillness: everything that happens seems far distant, motionless.

The last stanza of the first song of the cycle begins:

> Before the sound of song
> All space and all time retreat
>
> *Denn vor Liedesklang entweichet*
> *Jeder Raum and jede Zeit*

and the final song wonderfully illustrates this victory of song over space and time as the first song returns (the words have now become "Before these songs yield / what kept us so far apart" *(Dann vor diesen Liedern weichet / was geschieden uns so weit).* However, the first song returns only gradually: what actually comes back as the last song opens is a distorted memory of the past, a new melody so much like the initial song that when the opening of the cycle almost literally returns, it seems to arise directly out of the last song. It might reasonably be claimed that Beethoven is illustrating the words of the final poem, which opens:

Take them, then, these songs,
Which I sang to you, beloved.

The thematic kinship of the first and last songs is perceptible, but not obvious at first hearing, and it is a very different thematic relationship from those found elsewhere in Beethoven. In general, in his music two themes are related by coming from the same motivic nucleus, as if they had sprung from the same seed: this was the aspect of Beethoven's technique that was already most striking to his contemporaries, and E. T. A. Hoffmann remarked on it in his famous articles of 1811. Individual themes and, indeed, whole movements in Beethoven were perceived as being created from the development of a short motif. A single process seems to generate a multiplicity of related themes: sometimes, too, a new theme is only a variation of one previously heard. But the first and last songs of *An die ferne Geliebte* are not related that way: it is not the same short motif that generates them, nor is one strictly a variation of the other—at least not a variation in Beethoven's sense, in which essential parts of the motivic structure of the original are preserved. What the two songs have in common is not motivic development, or even any significant rhythmic detail, but general contour. They have similar shapes: the last song is not derived from the first but recalls it—indeed, at the end, literally calls it back.

The last song is, therefore, not a variant of the first but a new melody that suggests the first, brings it to mind. The opening of this final song is only a secret return; it makes its effect because the first song is hidden behind the new melody as a memory which in fact later reappears clearly. This hidden presence makes the relationship seem, at first hearing, to be an occult one, a secret revealed only little by little. With the direction *Molto adagio* and the words "Und du singst, und du singst, was ich gesungen" ("And you sing, and you sing what I sang"), the motif of the new melody approaches more closely to the first song:

This *molto adagio* is the emotional climax, the moment of most intense expression—the precise instant when past becomes indistinguisable from present. (It also prepares the return of the melody of the first song in its original form that follows shortly.) It is not simply the presence of the beloved but the songs of regret and longing which are remembered and become present, and these songs are themselves already the expression of memories. The past twice removed, the memory of memories, seems briefly tangible, and the sense of loss is all the more moving.

In its psychological complexity and its ambition, Beethoven's cycle is a rival to the great landscapes of his contemporaries: like the works of Constable, Friedrich, Wordsworth, Hölderlin, and Sénancour, it aspires to the sublime, and it does so with the landscapes of everyday life. The awesome and terrible precipices of the Alps have been replaced by the ordinary scenes of Nature. The magnificent picturesque grandeur of Nature did not, of course, entirely disappear: Turner continued to practice heroic landscape; Constable drew Stonehenge; Wordsworth crossed the Alps; Hölderlin celebrated the course of the Rhine. Nevertheless, the new style of landscape was more at ease with the familiar. Sénancour in fact made the transformation of the familiar the touch-stone of Romantic description, and established the essential distinction between the Romantic and the picturesque (or *romantique* and *romanesque*, two words whose meanings tended to blur before 1800, although they had begun to move apart). For Sénancour, writing in his preface to *Oberman*, the "Romantic" was an elitist concept, destined to be understood only by "a few scattered people in Europe" ("quelque personnes éparses dans l'Europe"). These happy few turned away from the spectacular landscapes that pleased the vulgar, and the scenes they loved defined a language that the crowd could not understand:

> When the October sun appears in the mist over the yellowing woods; when a small brook flows and falls in a field closed by trees, as the moon sets; when under the summer sky, on a cloudless day, a woman's voice sings, a little distant, at four o'clock in the midst of the walls and roofs of a large city.

> *Quand le soleil d'octobre parait dans les brouillards sur les bois jaunis; quand un filet d'eau coule et tombe dans un pré fermé d'arbres, au coucher de la lune; quand sous le ciel d'été, dans un jour sans nuages, une voix de femme chante à quatre heures, un peu au loin, au milieu des murs et des toits d'une grande ville.*[15]

Sénancour never disavowed his taste for magnificent mountain scenery, and for the sensation of finding at his feet "the void of heaven and the immensity of the world." But the scenes here are so modest and antipicturesque as to include a simple cityscape. Like Wordsworth's "spots of time," they modestly hide a very grand ambition. Sénancour's images are almost bare: the few details are chosen with precision to characterize, significantly, those instants of the present which betray a sense of the movement of time. If the immediate moment seems almost frozen, it is only to allow us a glimpse of a much larger scale of movement.

Constable made the preoccupation with the familiar even more imperative. In a letter to his friend, Archdeacon Fisher, he wrote on 29 August 1824:

> Last Tuesday the finest day that ever was we went to the Dyke—which is in fact a Roman remains of an embankment, overlooking—perhaps the most grand affecting natural landscape in the world—and consequently a scene most unfit for a picture. It is the business of a painter not to contend with nature & put this scene (a valley filled with imagery 50 miles long) on a canvas of a few inches, but to make something out of nothing, in attempting which he must almost of necessity become poetical.[16]

15. Etienne Pivert de Sénancour, *Oberman: Lettres* (Paris, 1965), xvi, 3.
16. *John Constable's Correspondence*, vol. 6, ed. R. B. Beckett (Ipswich, 1968), p. 172.

The sublime here comes not from the content of the picture, or from Nature, but from art: the traditional harmony between content and style—the sublime subject treated in a sublime manner—is destroyed, and along with it is destroyed the decorum of the system of genres. In its place we have the Romantic art as defined by Novalis: "Making the familiar strange, and the strange familiar."

The individual songs of *An die ferne Geliebte* are not only simple but relentlessly, willfully simple. The melodies are in many ways very like the tunes that Beethoven's contemporary J. F. Reichardt wrote for children. Only the last song reveals a musical and psychological complexity suggested by the half-hearted structural complexity of the text. The rich accompaniment plays a role throughout in developing these emphatically naive melodies, but it is above all the changes of tonality and the extraordinary final song which endows the cycle with a monumental grandeur. The cycle is, indeed, comparable as an achievement to Blake's *Songs of Innocence and Experience,* in which the simple doggerel style of didactic poems for children is similarly ennobled. We can see how essential for Beethoven's project was the familiar style of the individual melodies: it is the structure of the whole cycle that transfigures the details. Most of Beethoven's forms retain, even while they expand, Classical principles, but *An die ferne Geliebte* is his most openly Romantic work. Even the last phrase (which is the first phrase rewritten)

is both decisive and, by Classical standards, inconclusive. The end of the cycle with the return of the first phrase needs to suggest the incomplete: it is only the anguish of separation that returns. The last song is not a memory of the distant beloved but a memory of grief and of absence. Even if, as the words claim, the distance in time and space is vanquished by song, the effect of transcendence depends on our understanding that the absence persists.

Landscape and death: Schubert

The most signal triumphs of the Romantic portrayal of memory are not those which recall past happiness, but remembrances of those moments when future happiness still seemed possible, when hopes were not yet frustrated. There is no greater pain than to remember past happiness in a time of grief—but that is the Classical tradition of the tragedy of memory. Romantic memories are often those of absence, of that which never was. Out of all of Chateaubriand's virtuoso descriptions of his triumphs and his sorrows, his memory of the odor of heliotrope in a vegetable garden in the Ile St. Pierre stands out. After a dinner with the governor of the island, the young Chateaubriand, who was on his way to America, walked in the garden:[17]

> A subtle, sweet smell of heliotrope came from a little plot of flowering fava beans; it was brought to us not by a breeze from our native land, but by an uncivilized wind from Newfoundland, a wind with no relation to the exiled plant, without sympathy of reminiscence or of sensuous delight. In this odor that beauty had not breathed, that had not been purified in its breast or diffused over its footsteps, in this odor that had passed into another dawn, another culture, another world, there was all the various melancholy of regret, of absence, and of youth.

> *Une odeur fine et suave d'héliotrope s'exhalait d'un petit carré de fèves en fleurs; elle ne nous était point apportée par une brise de la patrie, mais par un vent sauvage de Terre-Neuve, sans relation avec la plante exilée, sans sympathie de réminiscence et de volupté. Dans ce parfum non respiré de la beauté, non épuré dans son sein, non répandu sur ses traces, dans ce parfum changé d'aurore, de culture et de monde, il y avait toutes les mélancolies des regrets, de l'absence et de la jeunesse.*

The odor of heliotrope transfigures the fava beans, makes poetry out of the familiar. The wind is from the wrong direction, from Newfoundland, not from France, and that is the source of its pathos. The memories it awakens come from somewhere else. They do not belong to the wind, and that makes them seem even more distant: their irrelevance to the present gives them a new power, out of place as well as out of time. These memories do not cause the past to live again; they make us feel its death.

A song cycle cannot tell a story directly—at best it can hint at one that remains untold. We do not know why lover and beloved remain separated in *An die ferne Geliebte,* just as we do not know why Oberman's love is fated to remain unhappy; in both those works, more specific detail would only distract. It may be thought that Schumann's *Frauenliebe und Leben* is an exception, but there is in fact no narrative: the songs only mark each important event in the typical life of an ideal woman—ideal from the male point of view: the woman's life starts when she meets the man who will marry her and ends with his death, leaving her only with memories. (The only important song cycle which genuinely tries to tell a story is the miscalculated *Magelone* cycle of Johannes

---

17. Chateaubriand, *Mémoires d'Outretombe,* Book 6, chap. 5.

Brahms: even here, most of the narrative takes place in prose between the songs.)

A skeleton of a narrative lies behind *Die schöne Müllerin* by Schubert: the poet, a miller's apprentice, follows a stream and in his wandering comes upon a mill; he loves the miller's daughter and believes his love returned; she, however, loves a huntsman and the poet drowns himself in the stream. No dramatic incident is related in the songs, which are lyric outbursts, poetic commentary. The poet Wilhelm Müller had found a way to create by purely lyric means what he himself in his prologue to the set called a monodrama.

Schubert intensified the lyricism. He eliminated the prologue and epilogue, both discursive in style, and three poems, two of which depart from the lyric tone by their narrative detail: in one, the miller's daughter flirts openly with other apprentices; in the second the poet sees her through the window with the huntsman in her arms. All the moments of dramatic action have disappeared. The only events left by Schubert are the trivial incidents of everyday life, invested with significance by the lyric context: the poet comes upon the mill in his wandering; he puts aside his lute and hangs it on the wall with a green ribbon; the girl remarks that the color of the ribbon is fading. With a sureness of touch that far surpasses Müller's, Schubert removed everything that would interfere with lyric expression (although elsewhere he produced many songs in narrative or ballad form). One should not underestimate Müller, however: even if rendering the commonplace details of daily existence in an ambitiously elevated lyric tone was already an important part of Romantic tradition by 1817, when the set of poems was written, the idea of a monodrama conveyed through a series of lyrics was his. It made it possible to endow the song cycle with dimensions even larger than Beethoven had envisaged.

Both of Schubert's cycles move towards death. The movement is progressive in *Die schöne Müllerin,* but the first intimation is crucial. It is found exactly halfway through the cycle, in the tenth of the twenty songs, called "Thränenregen" (Shower of Tears), and it immediately precedes the consummation of the poet's love in the eleventh song, "Mein" (Mine). "Thränenregen" is the only song with all the verbs in the past tense;[18] it is presented not as an immediate experience but as a memory. The poet and the miller's daughter were sitting at night looking at the reflections in the stream—their own reflections, the moon and the stars. The first three stanzas are set strophically, and the third opens with a premonition of suicide:

> And sunk within the stream
> All heaven appeared

---

18. I am indebted to Dr. Kristina Muxfeldt for this observation, as well as for material about the relation of Schubert's texts to the original texts of Müller's cycles.

And wished to draw me down with it
Into its depths.

Und in den Bach versunken
Der ganze Himmel schien
Und wollte mich mit hinunter
In seine Tiefe zich'n.

Schubert's music for these stanzas sets in relief the ambiguity of tone with his most exquisite display of three- and four-part polyphonic writing. It is the often-repeated E♯ in the first four bars that hints at the minor mode:

The expressive chromatic alterations are emphasized by the accents on weak beats, which delicately inflect the rhythm (they require an almost imperceptible rubato). The stream enters musically only in bar 12. The words of the second half of the third stanza hint more strongly at the temptation of death, the suicide by drowning of the final songs:

And over the clouds and the stars
The stream babbled cheerfully,
And called with singing and ringing
After me, Comrade, Comrade.

Und über den Wolken und Sternen
Da rieselte munter der Bah,
Und rief mit Singen und Klingen:
Geselle, Geselle, mir nach.

Müller's diction lacks refinement, but the image of the stream *above* the clouds and the stars is beautiful and striking; the stream explicitly calls the poet into its depths. Schubert's music for this part of the stanza exploits further the latent melancholy by expanding the suggestion of the minor mode; the E♯ now becomes the vehicle of a half cadence on the dominant of F sharp minor. The music only flirts with F sharp minor, however, and a full cadence is evaded: Schubert reserves the E♯ for a greater effect in the fourth stanza.

In the last stanza,[19] the melancholy is no longer half repressed; it breaks out—but only, in Müller's most subtle touch of genius, to be inhibited by the matter-of-fact words of the girl:

> Then my eyes overflowed
> Then everything blurred in the mirror,
> She spoke: "It's going to rain.
> Adieu I'm going home."

Schubert's music deals with every opposition and nuance of tone and meaning:

19. I have numbered the stanzas based on the musical setting. In fact, there are seven stanzas, which Schubert arranges into three groups of two and a final section. As in "Der Lindenbaum," the prosody is not the ultimate determinant of form.

The E♯, now written as F♮, turns the mode fully into minor, but more powerfully into the tonic minor, not the relative. The pathetic nature of the new mode appears with the B♭ in the piano at bar 28, but the E♯ / F♮ is still the principal vehicle of expression. In bars 29 and 30 the return to major with the prosaic words of the girl is accomplished by raising the F♮ to an F♯ The dissonant E♯/ F♮ appears throughout the song only in the piano, and the contrast between the simple diatonic vocal part and the chromatically expressive accompaniment is felt less as a source of tension than as an image of an innocent surface unaffected by the troubled depths that it covers. At the end, the postlude restates all the ambiguities, returns to the minor mode, and sums up the song. It looks forward, like the poem, to the tragic ending.

This song displays a sense of musical time different from that found in Classical form. A Classical work forecasts its own resolution: the dissonances of its large-scale form are similar and even parallel to small-scale dissonance; the final resolution to the tonic follows the "laws" of harmony and counterpoint.[20] The end of Schubert's "Thränenregen," however, does not point towards resolution. The return to the minor mode at the end of the postlude is, by the harmonic standards of the time, strictly a dissonant ending. The dissonant opposition of the major-minor ending predicts the tragedy to come. We know that Schubert liked an ambiguity of major and minor, and played with it frequently throughout his life. Did he find a precedent in the minuet of Beethoven's Trio in E flat Major, op. 70, no. 2?

20. Schenker's demonstration of this still seems to me irrefutable, and no criticism of his system or emendations can undermine the stability of his contribution to music theory in this respect.

This is an effect so Schubertian that one suspects some knowledge on the part of the younger composer. The source, however, does not matter. What is important to recognize is the variety of Schubert's use of the opposition, the different kinds of meaning he could draw from it. At the opening of the great Quartet in G Major, op. 166, it creates an initial and fundamental shock; it is the principal source of motor energy in the drama that follows:

In "Thränenregen," however, it is slowly and carefully prepared. The song as a whole gradually realizes the potentiality of an initial dissonance; the postlude presents the contradiction of major and minor as itself almost a resolution—or, better, as a recognition that resolution is not fully possible.

The listener will be particularly sensitive to the unreconciled opposition of tonic major and minor in "Thränenregen," as it is the first time in the cycle a song is immediately preceded by one in the same key: the stability of tonality makes the instability of mode all the more telling. It is also the first time in the cycle that the ambiguity of mode is not merely an interior detail but actually determines the large form. The change from major to minor is implied by the opening chord, and this augmented triad is played and accented six times in the first dozen bars.

A previous appearance in the cycle of Schubert's beloved shift from tonic major to minor is in the second part of the sixth song, "Der Neugierige"; it reveals the more drastic use in "Thränenregen" by comparison. The poet asks the stream if his heart is fooling him. Does the girl love him? The stream is silent:

The process here reverses the one in "Thränenregen": the shift is unprepared, but then resolved, as Schubert transforms the D♮ of the B minor chord into an agent of modulation to the flatted submediant, G major. The D♮ is used first for the silence of nature ("O stream of my love, why are you today so silent"), and then for the word "no" ("Nein!"). The cadence, however, leaves us with no sense of opposition, and then the return to B major completes the resolution. (The rest of the song, indeed, resolves the G♮ or F𝄪 within a B major context.) Even here, however, the major-minor opposition is introduced by Schubert to exploit a question, an uncertainty about the future.

The time of this song cycle is that of Romantic landscape: not the successive events of narrative but a succession of images, of lyrical reflections which reveal the traces of past and future within the present. What we directly perceive as happening is the change of meaning of the motifs from picture to picture.

Müller is economical with these basic symbols. Essentially there are only two: the stream that taught the poet to wander, that leads him to the miller's daughter, and that brings him to death; and the color green. It is with the color that Müller (and then Schubert) reveals himself at his most subtle: green is the color of hope, the color of the fading ribbon with which the poet hangs his lute upon the wall, the traditional color of the huntsman's costume, the color of cypress, of rosemary, the color of the grass that will grow upon the poet's grave. Fluctuations of meaning replace narrative: they stand duty for action.

The color green begins its dominant role in songs 12 to 14, and has the chief dramatic role in songs 16 and 17: "The Beloved Color" ("Die liebe Farbe"), and the "The Evil Color" ("Die böse Farbe"). Schubert sets "Die liebe Farbe" as an interior ostinato on one note, F♯:

This is the first song in which death is faced directly. As in "The Signpost" ("Der Wegweiser") of *Winter's Journey*, the monotonous repetition of a single note is a symbol of the finality of death:

> In green will I dress myself,
> In green weeping willows:
> My love is so fond of green.
> Will seek a cypress grove
> A hedge of green rosemary.
> My love is so fond of green.

The harmony is false when the singer is a woman instead of a man, as the vocal part must begin by providing a bass for the accompaniment. The relation of voice to piano is ambiguous: it is rare that we accept the voice as a real bass below the accompanying instrument—we hear the vocal part as in front of the piano, and the effect of providing a bass lends an eerie sonority to the initial bars. The voice, however, quickly rises above the piano bass, but never above the incessantly repeated F♯'s.

With the words "Mein Schatz hat's Grün so gern" in bars 10 and 11, there is an unprepared switch to the major mode, and voice and piano combine to create a series of horn sonorities:

This symbol of absence and separation is like a brief, distant memory, contradicted at once in bar 12 by the sudden return to minor. In this extraordinary song it is the composer even more than the poet who brings the weight of the past as well as the future to bear on present grief, but these horn sounds do indeed represent a memory of an earlier poem. Schubert has underlined the sense of the past by the simplest of means: a bare sonority and a change of mode. The melodic line even resembles the contour of the phrase in the thirteenth song, when the girl remarks that she is so fond of green:

Ich hab das Grün so   gern

The phrase in the later song is like a distant, simplified echo of the earlier.

Attempts have been made to find motivic and tonal unity in the cycle, but this is to misunderstand the source of its power. Many of the songs have similar opening motifs, the third, seventh, and eighth songs, for example, or the second and ninth:

The relationship between some of the motifs is striking, but oddly, Schubert makes no attempt to exploit any resemblance, as Beethoven had done and Schumann was to do; and if the effectiveness of *Die schöne Müllerin* was to depend to any great extent on motivic relationship, then Schubert's cycle would be less impressive than Beethoven's or Schumann's.

Similarly, it may be observed that the second and nineteenth of the twenty songs are both in the key of G, and this is comparable to Schumann's *Davidsbündlertänze,* op. 6, where the second and seventeenth of the eighteen pieces are both in the key of B minor. Nevertheless, as we shall see, Schumann goes to great pains in the *Davidsbündlertänze* to make the listener understand that these pieces are the true beginning and end of his cycle, and that the first and last pieces are outside the principal structure—or, following the aesthetic of the fragment, both outside and in. Schubert makes no such attempt, except for a similar but by no means identical representation of the flowing rhythm of the stream in the middle of the later song. Any perception of a return to G major would depend on the listener's having both perfect pitch and a memory that G major could be found sixteen songs back. It is not impossible to train oneself to listen to music that way, but the concentrated dramatic intensity of Schubert's cycle is not based on any such symmetrical organization, and, above all, it does not require any sense of a return. It is cumulative.

Die schöne Müllerin falls into a series of tonal groups, somewhat like the movements of a symphony, but these groups are only relatively autonomous. They are defined partly by how dramatic are the key changes from one song to another, and by the character of the music and the poem. For clarity, I summarize these groups:

Song 1. Introduction: B flat

Songs 2–4. Arrival and meeting: G, C, G

Songs 5–10. Progress and anxiety: a, B, A, C, A, A–a

Song 11. Triumph: D

Songs 12–15. Pause, jealousy: B flat, B flat, c, g–G

Songs 16–20. Towards death: b–B, B–b, e–E–e, g–G, E

The groups articulate the implied narrative that lies behind the cycle; they do not impose a rigid formal scheme but give a loose yet clearly defined shape which allows the story to unfold. Songs 2 to 4 describe the poet following the stream, the first view of the mill, and his thanks to the stream for leading him to the miller's daughter, and they constitute a tonal group of G major, C major, and a return to G major that sets them apart from the B flat of the opening song. The mediant change from B flat to G, in fact, forms a brilliant contrast with the simple key relationships that follow.

The dramatic new character that succeeds in song 5, "Am Feierabend" (Holiday Eve), initiates a group of six songs (numbers 5–10) that relate the attempt of the poet to make the girl notice him, his impatience, and the growth and progress of his love, ending with the ambiguous presentiments of "Thränenregen." The first of this group is clearly a new beginning.

The central key of the new group is a well-defined A in the sequence A minor, B major, A major, C major, A major, A major–minor. This A major is the dominant of the triumphant D major of song 11, "Mein," where the poet rejoices in having won his beloved. His joy even expresses itself in a series of yodel figures:

The next song, "Pause" (number 12), clearly means what its title says, and is marked by a change of key to B flat: the dramatic effect of the mediant change from D major and the extraordinary contrast of texture is more important than the fact that B flat was the key of the first song and that the two open with similar motifs. In his happiness the poet can no longer compose songs; he has hung up his lute. Schubert sets the words wonderfully to a counterrhythm that quietly but emphatically contradicts the pianist's simple square phrasing:

"I can sing no more, my heart is too full." The standard four-bar phrases have become three, and the vocal rhythm has its down-beat in the middle of the bar. This vocal cross-accent to a basic instrumental pattern gives a kind of prose rhythm to the musical prosody, a technique that was later exploited by Wagner. Even more Wagnerian is the passage toward the end of the song, with the familiar leap from major to minor:

Once again this shift of mode is used to represent the dimension of time, an uncertain irruption of both past and future into the present:

> Why have I let the ribbon hang so low?
> It often flies over the strings with a sighing sound.
> Is it the after-sound of my pains of love?
> Might it be the prelude of new songs?

This forecast of the harmonies of *Tristan* arises from the attempt to portray a complex sense of simultaneous happiness and frustration.

"Pause" closes the first part of the cycle, but it also starts a new group of four songs: the disquieting silence of the poet (12), the fading of the ribbon (13), the sudden appearance of the hunter (14), and the jealous rage of the poet (15). The keys of these four songs are closely related: B flat major, B flat major, C minor, G minor–major. Not only does the minor mode naturally become more frequent in the second half of the cycle, but the inner contrasts between major and minor become more startling, beginning with the first and last songs of this group.

The last five songs (16–20) go from despair to suicide and may be considered as a group. The B minor of "The Beloved Color," the opening song of this final set, follows without much of a jolt from the related G major ending of the previous song, but the monotonous regularity of its single repeated note announces a different turn: the movement towards death. The desire for death only hinted at before is now open and direct. Each of the songs brings death closer. In "The Evil Color" ("Die böse Farbe"), the alternation of major to minor, which is found in all these songs except the last, becomes ugly and brutal. It is an apt complement to "Die liebe Farbe," which was a song in minor with a poetic reminiscence in major. Now we have a song in major into which the minor mode forces itself intrusively:

The dynamics create the brutality: the unprepared change to minor in bar 3 is a sudden *forte,* the reappearance of the major mode in bar 5 an equally sudden *fortissimo.* The turn to F sharp minor of bar 11 is indeed extremely disconcerting by the standards of Schubert's time:

> I would go out into the world
> Into the wide world
> If it were not so green, so green, out there
> In wood and field.

In "Withered Flowers" ("Trockne Blumen"), the initial E minor of the poet's present despair changes to E major with a vision of the future and the flowers of May that will bloom on the poet's grave. The ecstatic sense of self-pity is brought abruptly back to reality in the postlude:

The unexpected minor of the final cadence is at once emphatic and indecisive. It destroys what was clearly the illusion of the major (the poet will never see the return of spring), but the final tonic chord arrives at first on a weak beat: the song dies away but does not properly conclude.

The opening in G minor of the next song, "Der Müller und der Bach," is the greatest harmonic shock of the cycle. No previous change of key from one song to another, no interior progression, has been as daring as this rare juxtaposition of E minor and G minor triads. To appreciate the affective meaning, we may look ahead to Liszt's use of this progression in the revised version of the principal melody of *La Vallée d'Obermann.* The original form, from *L'Album d'un voyageur,* began by moving simply from E minor to its relative major:

More than a decade later, in *Les Années de pèlerinage,* book 2, Liszt replaced the conventional shift from E minor to G major with the more dramatic modulation from E minor to G minor:

Here he continued the progression one step further, from G minor to B flat minor, and this reveals its enharmonic power, as it ends an augmented fourth away from the opening E, creating the most dissonant harmonic tension. In both Liszt and Schubert the emotion is the utmost despair: specifically, in "Die Schöne Müllerin," it confirms the decision for suicide.

The G minor tonality of the penultimate song seems to break with the tonal area defined by the three previous songs (B minor, B major, E minor–major), and its structure (G minor ending in major) parallels that of the fifteenth song, "Jealousy and Pride" ("Eifersucht und Stolz"); the turn to G major allows it, however, to remain partly within the E minor tonal area. The unity of the group is then reaffirmed by the E major of the final song, "The Stream's Lullaby" ("Des Baches Wiegenlied"). Nevertheless, the tonal relationships of the last five songs are the most complex of the cycle:

B minor (major)

B major (minor)

E minor–major–minor

G minor–major

E major

The modal purity of the last song is a consolation, the lullaby that the stream sings as a requiem.

I have gone into such extensive detail about tonal definition only to demonstrate that although no simple formal scheme governs the harmony of *Die schöne Müllerin,* it does not fall into twenty separate and successive key centers: it moves with great suppleness through sets of key regions, and the length of each of these sets is defined by the poetic text.

The comparison of these sets I made above to the movements of a symphony is deeply misleading in one respect. Songs 5 to 10, for example, are clearly centered on the key of A, but we do not understand this fully until we reach the last of these songs. The tonality of a movement from a classical symphony, however, is perceptible at once: its definition may be postponed for a few seconds at most. The perception of the large-scale tonal structure of the song cycle is like our experience of reading a novel or moving through a landscape: it is realized and defined progressively.

The song cycle is the most original musical form created in the first half of the nineteenth century. It most clearly embodies the Romantic conception of experience as a gradual unfolding and illumination of reality in place of the Classical insistence on an initial clarity. The form of Schubert's song cycle is not less precise than that of a Classical sonata, but its precision is only gradually comprehended as it unfolds. The significance of many of the elements can be realized only retrospectively in a way that is fundamentally different from the realization in time of an eighteenth-century musical form. The contrapuntal possibilities of the theme of a Bach fugue are displayed one by one, but they are already present in the initial bars, and an experienced musician would be able to predict the most important musical developments. The famous dissonant C♯ in bar 7 of Beethoven's *Eroica* Symphony may not find its implications fully realized until 397 bars later, but its harmonic significance and its importance in the harmonic framework are immediately felt. In *Die schöne Müllerin,* however, the harmonic structure of the last five songs is defined by the final one, the stream's requiem and lullaby, and consequently the harmonic function of the opening of this set can be perceived only after the fact. Just as the travelers of the last decades of the eighteenth century looked back and saw a landscape almost unrecognizable, astonishingly different from the one they believed themselves to have passed through, so the listener must listen back in his memory to the earlier songs, and only then can he perceive how the cycle is taking shape. The movement towards death that begins with a suggestion in the tenth song becomes fully intelligible in the last pages.

In the second of Schubert's cycles, *Winterreise,* all the events take place before the cycle begins, and we are not even sure what they were. There are only allusions to a girl who spoke of love, and a mother who had schemes of marriage. Twenty-four landscapes awaken memories and lead the poet to an acceptance of death. In this cycle not even death is an event. It is an image in the last song, the organ-grinder who mechanically and monotonously turns the handle of his instrument in the frozen winter landscape. Melody and accompaniment turn in steady, inexpressive circles, like the arm of the musician. All the phrases revolve: they mimic the gestures of the organ-grinder. The harmony is as frozen as the landscape, reduced almost to numbing alternation of tonic and dominant:

With this song the poet welcomes his death.

As the last song of a long cycle, this one is a magnificent, laconic, tragic ending. If it were performed on its own, its repetitive monotony would seem absurd, unmotivated. The songs of *Winterreise* are only apparently separate works: even those which are effective outside the cycle lose in character and significance when so performed. Within the context of the cycle, "The Lime

Tree" is the first intimation that death is a grave consolation after despair: as a separate song, it is merely sentimental and even pretty. The Schubert song cycle embodies a paradox: each song is a completely independent form, well rounded and finished, which nevertheless makes imperfect sense on its own.

The reduction of narrative almost to zero brings a greater lyric intensity to *Winterreise* than to *Die schöne Müllerin*. Indeed, in its first version, the first twelve songs alone, it had a more striking concentration, although lacking the tragic power of the second part. This first version was tonally closed, beginning and ending in D minor (and songs number 2 and 11 were both in the related key of A, making the closure more emphatic: DA–AD). It is difficult to speak of the larger tonal plan, however, as several songs of *Winterreise* were transposed down a whole step or a minor third, and we cannot know whether this was done to make the music easier to sing or for harmonic reasons; whether these were spontaneous decisions on Schubert's part or a response to demands from the publisher or singers—or even if the transpositions were made after Schubert conceived the second part, and this made the symmetrical closure of the first part less important.

The history of the composition of *Winterreise* is complex. In February 1827 Schubert saw the twelve poems published as *Winterreise* by Müller early in 1823 and set them to music. Müller, however, had added another twelve poems and integrated them in 1824 into the first set. When Schubert came upon the enlarged version of twenty-four poems in October 1827, he set to music all those he had not previously composed. He did not, however, follow Müller's new grouping but picked out the twelve new poems one by one in the order that he found them: he made only one change, inverting the order of the tenth and eleventh poems, "Die Nebensonnen" and "Muth." He conceived the new songs as a second part after the first twelve. Schubert's new arrangement, in fact, reduces the narrative sense of Müller's, who had placed "Die Post" (The Mail) as the sixth song after "The Lime Tree." "Die Post" opens Schubert's second book, but it would be more reasonable for the poet to hope for a letter (which never comes) from his beloved soon after he has left the city than some time later, after the intervention of several songs which have testified to his hopeless acceptance of isolation. Schubert, however, had other and more important considerations than narrative coherence. What these were may be suggested by his inversion of the order of "Die Nebensonnen" and "Muth" just before the final song. This order gives him a more intensely lyric finale. "Muth" (Courage) is a blasphemy, full of false cheer and bravado:

> If there be no God on earth
> We ourselves are gods.
>
> *Will kein Gott auf Erde sein*
> *Sind wir selber Götter.*

"Die Nebensonnen" (The Lesser Suns), on the other hand, is a cryptic lament that all light has set, gone out of the poet's life; as the penultimate song, it gives a more purely meditative introduction to the ultimate despair of "The Organ-Grinder."

Musical images of walking dominate the first half of the cycle: songs 1, 3, 7, 10, and 12 all have the easygoing rhythm of a walk through the countryside. The country walk, and its ideology of a direct contact with Nature through physical activity often pushed to the point of exhaustion, dominated German and, less powerfully, English culture from the mid-eighteenth century until the Second World War. Over this movement of walking Schubert imposes the musical images of landscape—in the seventh song, for example, the ice of the frozen stream, under which passion still flows. This is a symbol of the poet's heart:

The *pianissimo* of bar 45 recalls the apparent stillness of the frozen stream, for which it was explicitly used in the first stanza:

The later appearance refers back and prepares the sense of the violent swell under the surface that follows. The complex images of walking, stillness, and repressed passion are already almost completely intelligible in the music without the words:

My heart, in this stream
Do you recognize your image?
As if under its crust
It also swells so violently.

The last two of these walking songs, numbers 10 and 12, have a more tired, even exhausted pace. Other textures intrude, above all the hurried walk over snow and ice of songs 4 and 8. The movement of the latter begins with a certain brutality:

It burns under both my soles
As I already tread on ice and snow

but with the return of memories, there is a change to the major mode and the
presence of the familiar horn calls that symbolize the distant past (once again
the horn sonorities depend on a tenor voice that lies between the left and right
hands of the pianist):

> How differently did you once receive me
> You town of infidelity.

Images of death dominate the second part of the cycle. In the second song,
"The Raven" ("Die Krähe"), the opening accompaniment hovers above the
voice, and remains in this register almost throughout:

At the end, however, it descends into the tomb:

Raven, let me finally see
Fidelity unto the grave!

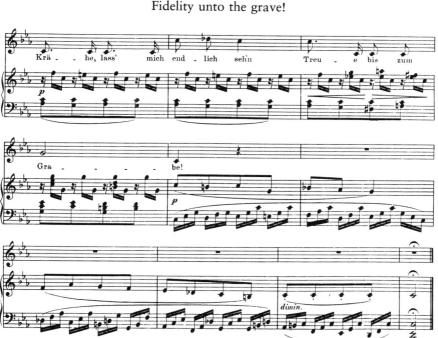

Winterreise is unsurpassed in the art of musical representation. Perhaps most remarkable is the picture of the single leaves that remain isolated on the trees in winter, and in the end fall to the ground. This is the beginning of "Last Hope" ("Letzte Hoffnung"), where the two-note motif is isolated, tentative, and fragile:

The vocal line is built over the motifs in the piano, and constructed out of them as well:

> Here and there on the trees
> Is many an isolated leaf to be seen.

The fall of the leaf is the death of hope:

> And I myself fall with it to the ground
> Weep, weep, on the grave of my hope.

> *Fall ich selber mit zu Boden,*
> *Wein', wein' auf meiner Hoffnung Grab.*

"The Signpost" ("Der Wegweiser") of song 20 is the formal announcement of death. The last stanza presents the final immobility, as in "Die liebe Farbe" from *Die schöne Müllerin,* by the obstinate repetition of one note:

This is a parallel to the monotonous repetition of the last song, and induces by its rigidity a sense of the terror of imminent death. The repeated notes are already present at the opening of the song, but only in the last stanza do they reach their full insistent power. This kind of musical imagery does not so much represent or even express emotion as provoke it. It does not work upon the listener's imagination but upon his nerves.

Throughout *Winterreise*, the dynamic processes of Nature are represented by musical landscape painting of extraordinary suggestion and even precision: the pivoting of the weathervane, the flowing water under the ice, the rustling of leaves, the winter wind, the will-o'-the-wisp, the slowly moving clouds, the quiet village street, a stormy morning—all these receive a remarkable musical contour. As in the great landscape tradition, present sensation and memory are superimposed and confounded. Above all, it is the sense of future time that Müller and Schubert have added to the physical sense of the present and the past.

The oncoming presence of death fills the last five songs: the signpost that points to the road from which there is no return; the cemetery that appears as an inn; the blasphemy and the false cheer in the face of despair; the mysterious subsidiary suns from which the light goes out on life as they set; and finally the organ-grinder as Death himself. The succession of these apparently unre-lated images all moving to the same point has a cumulative power. It is, in fact, an advantage here for Schubert that the cycle lacks the strict large-scale har-monic scheme or the subtle motivic relations we find in Beethoven and Schu-mann: they would have drawn attention away from the disparity of poetic image, each represented by an almost exaggerated contrast of musical texture. The disparity is essential to the emotional power; too tight a web, too formal

a scheme would have been irrelevant, out of place. Even the final image of
death does not close except with a question of the poet, now the composer:
"Wonderful old man, should I go with you? Will you play my songs?"

Schubert singles out this question with striking emphasis: it identifies death
with the music itself, and it forces the autobiographical interpretation to the
surface. This was, by his time, already a tradition: even the poet Wilhelm
Müller insists on it in the earlier cycle by making the poet a miller. By the end
of *Winterreise,* the subject is the composer's own imminent death, its approach
already visible.

The unfinished workings of the past

In Schumann's song cycles of 1839–40, set to poems by Heine, Eichendorff,
and Kerner, the immediate experience of landscape has almost disappeared.
For Heine, the elements of Nature—nightingales, roses, lilies—have become a
kind of emotional bric-a-brac, and they work simply as part of a psychological
system of signs: nightingales are only a symbol of the lover's sorrow; lilies
make present the whiteness of the beloved's skin. The banality of his poetic
paraphernalia does not disturb Heine—quite the contrary: he uses it expertly
to reflect a bitter irony onto a genuine passion, a passion that is forced to use
such commonplace modes of expression in order to reveal itself. In Eichendorff
and Kerner the general presence of Nature has still a great power, but the
details have become obscured: trees, moonlight, wind all have only an ideal
form—they do not exist except as they rise from the depths of the poet's mind.
Müller's lime tree by the city gate is far too specific for Schumann's poets:

details are now limited to the complex of emotions awakened. What these poets retain (even in the poems with no reference to Nature) from the tradition of landscape poetry from which they spring is the complex sense of time in which past, present, and future coexist and interpenetrate each other. Memory and premonition are as immediate and powerful as direct perception—which serves, indeed, for the most part simply to recall and to predict. The poet in *Dichterliebe* weeps when he dreams that his beloved is dead; weeps when he dreams that she has left him; and weeps most bitterly when he dreams she still loves him. Only the second dream reflects present reality; the first is of the future, and the third is a memory of what is irrevocably past. The first two dreams of future and present are set in strophic form: the only change made in the second stanza merely accommodates as usual the different number of syllables in the line. It is to the third dream of the past, however, that Schumann gives the greatest sense of a solid presence:

Mir träumt, du ver-liessest mich. Ich wach-te auf und ich

ritard.   pp
wein - te noch lan - ge bit - ter - lich.   Ich

                                                                       ritard.
hab' im Traum ge - wei - net, mir träum - te, du wärst mir noch

gut. Ich wach - te auf___ und noch im - mer___ strömt mei - ne Thrä - nen -

Only with the dream of an irrecoverable past are the notes of the piano sustained, and the shadowy form of the dream begins at last to take on substance. Future and present are almost unreal: only the past within the present has any force. Illusion and memory act with a power that makes them indistinguishable from reality.

The illusion explodes, however: the singer cannot finish the song. He ends on a tonic note, but it is the tonic turned into a dissonance. Then the void of the opening stanzas returns. This is perhaps the first piece of music in which empty silence plays a role as great as or even greater than that of the notes. For two stanzas voice and piano are isolated: they come together only with the resurgence of memory.

The Beethoven song cycle runs all the songs together into one uninterrupted sequence, with a return that rounds off the form. The two Schubert cycles are large sets of separate songs: it is not immediately apparent that very few of them can stand on their own. Nevertheless, for their full power and sometimes even their basic significance to be revealed, they must appear in the sequence determined by Schubert, even when, as in *Winterreise,* almost all narrative meaning has been removed from the set. The succession of images in *Winterreise* determines a musical and subjective time, but it refers only in the most perfunctory, offhand way to time in the world of events.

Schumann's technique is a synthesis of both practices. As I have remarked, in his cycles the songs are apparently separate as in Schubert, but several have endings either so dissonant or inconclusive that they must be resolved by the opening of the following song. Moreover, there are sometimes close and evident thematic relationships among the songs, and music from earlier songs appears at the end of the two cycles *Frauenliebe und Leben* and *Dichterliebe.*

These are the only two sets which Schumann himself called *Cyclus.* To all the other sets of related songs, he gave the title *Liederkreis,* "circle of songs" (or *Liederreihe,* "row of songs"). The "cycles" are those sets in which all the songs have the same protagonist, and in which the order is chronological, each successive song representing a later moment than the preceding one. (This essentially was the definition made explicit by Wilhelm Müller, the poet so richly set by Schubert.) In short, where a *Liederkreis* is a set of related songs, often with a literary and musical structure that holds them together, a cycle is a monodrama, in which there is a single speaker and at least the skeletal suggestion of a narrative. *Dichterliebe,* for example, moves from the awakening of desire, through love, deception, rage, and despair, to a bittersweet ending of cynicism and regret.

On the last page of *Dichterliebe* the piano returns to one of the earlier songs in the cycle, but the nature of this return sets it apart from that in Beethoven's cycle or in Schumann's own *Frauenliebe und Leben:* it is not a return to the opening page. *Dichterliebe* originally had twenty songs: Schumann cancelled four of them before publication (the first and more complete version seems to me both more original and more moving). What returns at the end of the last song (now the sixteenth) is the final section of the twelfth song.

We must not think of the postlude as a return of the twelfth song itself, and the words of that song are irrelevant to the end of the cycle. The melody that returns as a coda was already a postlude to the twelfth song, a new theme not motivically related to the main body of the piece:

Schumann does not allow the singer to finish here, but suspends the vocal line on a half cadence. The piano does not so much continue the song as offer a melody of its own, which is like a meditation or commentary on what had preceded.

At the end of the cycle the vocal line is once again suspended, and the piano returns to its earlier meditation, this time elaborately extending it into an extraordinarily expressive cadence:

In this postlude Schumann withholds the full resolution on the tonic in root position which seems imminent throughout, until three bars before the end. The return, like the one in Beethoven's *An die ferne Geliebte,* is neither a *da capo* nor a formal close but a memory, and the lack of formal justification is even more striking in Schumann: what returns is a postlude heard only a few songs back, three quarters of the way through the cycle. The return is consequently unmotivated by any convention of form or even by the demands of the text. It seems to be spontaneous, an involuntary memory, governed by a law of its own.

In no other work does Schumann appear to violate conventional expectations of form so flagrantly. Yet there is a logic to it that is convincing enough even at first hearing. The last notes of the singer demand instrumental resolution even more urgently than his final phrase in the earlier song; the elaborate improvisatory cadence which now rounds off the reappearance of the postlude is more satisfying than its initially laconic and more mysterious playing.

Schumann was not the first composer to introduce a new and independent melody in the last bars of a piece, but he exploited this for a greater sense of shock than any before him. Earlier in the cycle *Dichterliebe* the eighth song had an instrumental ending even more startling:

This is, indeed, unprecendented; it is also, here, directly motivated by the text. "She herself has broken my heart" are the words of the last line of the poem which give rise to the raging storm that follows. In the final song, however, we must take the postlude as a commentary not on the last song but on the cycle as a whole—above all because it is an earlier instrumental phrase that returns for a longer development.

Schumann unifies the set of songs by this return. To serve his purpose it had to be a return unjustified by any traditional formal convention, and at the same time to satisfy the individual formal considerations invented for this particular work by the composer, to seem both unprecedented and right. Part of the individual justification lies in the character of the last song. It stands outside the lyric mode as one of two satirical songs (the other being number 11, "Ein Jüngling liebt ein Mädchen," "A Young Man Loved a Girl"). There are indeed also two scherzos (numbers 3, "Die Rose, die Lilie," "The Rose, The Lily"; and 15, "Aus alten Märchen," "From Old Tales"), and two dramatic songs (numbers 9, "Das ist ein Flöten und Geigen," or "That Is a Fluting and

Fiddling"; and 13, "Ich hab im Traum geweinet," "I wept in a Dream"). But in all the others a lyric mode prevails, and in most of them the lyricism is exclusive—and markedly, even defiantly, simple. The postlude reestablishes at length, like an ultimate song without words, the basic lyric tone of the cycle, and it reestablishes this tone as a memory of the past. The lyric character is like a tonic chord to which one returns, and the final D flat major chord of the postlude to the cycle brings back the final harmony of the first song but without the dissonant seventh.

Many of the songs of *Dichterliebe* begin with similar motifs:

but this not an effect that Schumann sets into relief. It is perhaps interesting solely as an example of his tendency to write melodies circumscribed by a small interval, like a third or a fourth. He takes great care, however, that each song shall follow the preceding one in a closely related key, generally tonic to dominant, or minor to relative major (or, more rarely, from tonic to mediant and this only in the middle of the cycle). The same harmonic consistency may be found in all five of the important sets: the three *Liederkreis* of Eichendorff, Kerner, and Heine, as well as *Dichterliebe* and *Frauenliebe und Leben*.

The song cycle is the embodiment of a Romantic ideal: to find—or to create—a natural unity out of a collection of different objects without compromising the independence or the disparity of each member. By a "natural" unity I mean one which is not imposed in advance by convention or tradition: the large form must appear to grow directly from the smaller forms, and this preserves their individuality. It smacks a little of having one's cake and eating it too, but it is better thought of as a parallel to the scientific ideal of finding an order for experience which is not factitious; there was already a concern at that time of the folly of imposing a physical or mathematical order on a biological universe.

In *Dichterliebe*, Schumann refuses all the easy ways out. There is no central tonal unity as in Beethoven's song cycle, nor even the grouping of the songs into different tonal regions which we found in Schubert: rather there is a continuous sense of movement and even growth from one tonal center to the next, each successive step preparing the following one. A unique tonal center is replaced by a controlled movement of tonal change. There is also no omnipresent motif or set of motifs on which all the songs are based. The melody of many of the songs, however, appears to derive from the previous song, without rising (or descending, if one likes) to the level of actual quotation. The only true quotation is the final postlude, and here one point must be insisted upon: in the twelfth song the instrumental melody is presented when the song is over; at the end, the postlude arrives when the cycle is finished, when there is nothing more to be sung. The only "return" in the cycle is therefore both inside and outside the work. I remarked earlier that the first song of *Dichterliebe* is in reality a closed form that appears open: the cycle as a whole is an open-ended form that has an apparent instrumental closure. Vocally *Dichterliebe* begins in the middle and does not end. "Why is this coffin so large and so heavy?" asks the poet in the last verse of the cycle; "I have sunk within it my love and my sorrow." But neither the love nor the sorrow ever comes to an end.

The *Liederkreis* of both Heine and Eichendorff are tonally closed. Circles as well as cycles for Schumann demanded some kind of return, and in these two sets the return is tonal. The first two songs of the Eichendorff set are in F sharp minor and A major, the last two in A major and F sharp major. The intention of symmetry is evident. Further, successive songs are based on similar motifs. Songs 5 and 6, "Mondnacht" (Moonlit Night) and "Schöne Fremde" (Beautiful Foreign Land), open with clearly related phrases. Song 7, "Auf einer Burg" (On a Fortress), begins with a simple motif displayed contrapuntally in all voices:

The first stanza ends with a half cadence on the dominant interrupted by the motif in the bass which completely disrupts the harmony by putting a tonic A against the singer's G♯, one of the more spectacular examples of Schumann's delight in making harmony and melody work out of phase. The final cadence is still, in Baroque style, on the dominant (the tonality of the song is wonderfully ambiguous: it starts as if in E minor, but by the end, the key is A minor and the E major chord is clearly a dominant). This cadence is an ending both complete in Baroque terms and incomplete for early nineteenth-century harmony, and the E major cadence leads directly into the A minor of the next song, "In der Fremde" (In a Foreign Land), which uses exactly the same motif as the preceding, although the poems are not related at all by subject:

"In der Fremde," in fact, reciprocates by acknowledging its dependence on the previous song: although it begins in A minor, it returns immediately to the E minor of "Auf einer Burg." It is not until the end of the song that we know which was the main tonality.

A similar and equally extraordinary combination of independence and continuity is found in the Heine *Liederkreis*. The last bars of the seventh song die away, leaving only a note which provides a dominant to the chorale that follows:

This chorale, in turn, ends with a question on the dominant, and prepares the way for the last song:

More striking than these endings on a dominant are the full tonic cadences which Schumann manages ingeniously to render inconclusive. The ending of the fourth song, for example, would be completely closed if voice and piano were in phase—but they are not. They are out of phase throughout the song:

and they distance themselves even further at the end, as the singer continues for three beats after the piano has finished the song:

"So that I may soon fall asleep" ("Damit ich balde schlafen kann"). Schumann's setting wittily suggests the probability of insomnia.

The last bars of the fifth song of the Kerner *Liederreihe,* the most underestimated of Schumann's sets, is equally remarkable. This moving song, "Sehnsucht nach der Waldgegend" (Nostalgia for the Woodlands), is one of Schumann's finest. Nature has here been reduced to a childhood memory, and Schumann's ending as a fragment suggests the unbridgeable distance:

"Only the song, as the bird only half sings, that separates one from leaf and tree." The first five bars of this ending repeat the opening of the song, but the last three bars are new. The voice finishes in the relative major but on a D, which is the dominant of the original G minor key, and the piano turns regretfully back to the tonic but in a way that leaves the vocal melody still suspended. The piano does not end but disappears. The last bars are harmonically closed and rhythmically open, the last notes a memory that cannot finish, an echo of the opening in the right hand that is echoed in turn in the bass.

Most of these songs, particularly the Eichendorff "circle," are songs of alienation, absence, and regret. The unfinished workings of the past within the present weighs on almost all of them. Schumann's elaborate display of out-of-phase effects, dislocating harmony and melody and using syncopated accents deliberately to trouble and confuse the lucidity of classical voice leading, contrives to express some of this alienation with great power. Sometimes the form of expressive alienation is almost purely stylistic, as in the use of Baroque style. The expressionistic picture of the wedding dance in *Dichterliebe* depends on musical parody:

This is, surprisingly enough, in the form of a Baroque chorale-prelude of a type like Bach's famous "Wachet auf!" in which *cantus firmus* and prelude seem to ignore each other and move in different spaces. The point of the verses here is the poet as outsider, and the music keeps up the dance rhythm relentlessly throughout the song. But hidden inside the accompanying part is the *cantus firmus*. We can observe the parallel octaves:

In the sixth song of *Dichterliebe,* Baroque style explicitly represents an image from the past:

The subject of the poem is a picture in Cologne Cathedral. The dotted rhythm came to Schumann as a legacy from the Bach revival, and derives from French overture style. For an early nineteenth-century musician, Bach was anachronistically like a Gothic cathedral, and the song equates a Gothic church with antique (Baroque) sacred organ music. (Schumann's beloved author E. T. A. Hoffmann likened Bach's music to Gothic architecture.) The music transforms Heine's impudent sentimentality (the famous Madonna in Cologne Cathedral looks like his girl) into a grave style. (The suggestion has absurdly been made that the dotted rhythm represents the waves of the Rhine. If the waters of the Rhine ever remotely resembled that rhythm, it would be time to take cover on high ground.) The parody of Baroque harmony and rhythm is an ironic commentary of the past on the present, but the continuation of the song into a long postlude allows the musical representation of Cologne Cathedral to continue to resonate after Heine's witty blasphemy has died away.

Song cycles without words

The landscape cycle was to return to Schumann's work late in his career—but without words, in the *Waldscenen* (Forest Scenes) for piano. This time, however, the elements of landscape are not the purely symbolic commonplaces of Heine's poems or even the mythical presences in Eichendorff—with the exception of "Vogel als Prophet" (Bird as Prophet), which stands out in the cycle as a return to the eccentric inspiration of Schumann's early work. The other pieces are from a more comfortable age, and the landscape is the amiable Biedermeier countryside of a middle-class flight from urban care: "The Friendly Landscape," "The Wayside Inn." Even the melancholy of this cycle—in "Lonely Flowers" and "The Haunted Spot"—are the harmless urban fictions of country life. *Waldscenen* is one of Schumann's most exquisite achievements: it gives the lie to anyone who thinks that Schumann's genius disappeared after the great year and a half of *Lieder* writing—but it also betrays how true it is that much of the earlier energy had abandoned his genius. This energy is not merely the kind that reveals itself in the character of an individual piece, but the power that gives a succession of pieces its vitality, the energy that manifests itself over a whole cycle and drives from one piece to the next. Schumann's earlier *Kinderscenen* (Scenes of Childhood) had this energy, so it is not the tame subject matter of the *Waldscenen* which would entirely account for its absence there. The *Waldscenen* are autumnal in character, the work of a truly aging composer, although Schumann was not yet forty when he wrote them.

The landscape pieces of the *Waldscenen* do not have the extraordinary synthesis of past and present that the cycle had learned from the poetry of landscape: they are all set in neither past nor present but in some kind of mythical time zone, in which one can feel a passionate nostalgia for a nonexistent present. That this song cycle is without words, however, should alert us to the fact that the structure of a Schumann song cycle was worked out long before he began to write any of the songs he later published. His transformation of the genre begins with the great decade of piano music he composed from the age of nineteen to twenty-nine.

What was to become Schumann's new conception of the song cycle is already evident in such works of the 1830s as the *Papillons,* op. 2; *Kinderscenen,* op. 15; *Fantasiestücke,* op. 12; *Carnaval,* op. 9; *Davidsbündlertänze,* op. 6; and *Humoresk,* op. 20. All of the different ways he later used to unite the songs of a cycle into a single coherent work are found in these early piano sets, and in several of them he even succeeded in inventing a musical technique for representing the idiosyncratic sense of time that was the legacy of Romantic landscape.

More openly than any other work of Schumann, *Carnaval* is tied together by its motifs. These are three in number, but they resemble each other closely, two of them to the point of near-identity. They are spelled out towards the center of the work by the "Sphinxes," which look like cryptic bits of medieval chant and were not intended to be played:

SPHINXES.

"S.C.H.A." is the first one; *S* is for *Es,* the German for E♭, and *H* is the German for the note B in English; the four notes are the musically playable letters in

Schumann's name. These four notes, permuted, give the third Sphinx, "A.S.C.H.," and spell the name of the town in which Ernestine von Fricken (Schumann's fiancée for a brief time) was born. The second Sphinx, "As.C.H." (A♭, C, B in English) also spells out the town, and has two notes in common with the other two Sphinxes. These motifs provide a basis for the masked personages of *Carnaval*. Although the opening and closing numbers are derived from some variations on a Schubert waltz that Schumann had been working on, all the central pieces are based on the Sphinxes—with two exceptions, "Chopin" and "Paganini," and these are the only two characters who appear undisguised and under their real names. (A modest allusion to Sphinx 3 appears in the last two bars of "Chopin," but this does not seem to me to affect the principle of its independence.) The others are either characters from the commedia dell'arte or else idealized fictional names masking Schumann and his friends.

The Sphinxes do not simply provide a way of constructing similar tunes; rather, they organize the whole work in a remarkable way. Sphinxes 1 and 3 have an A♮, Sphinx 2 an A♭. The tonality of *Carnaval* is centered around A flat major. Schumann uses Sphinxes 1 and 3 in the order of the notes given by Sphinx 3 for the first half of the work (numbers 2 through 9); in the rest (10 through 21) he uses only Sphinx 2. The A♮ in 1 and 3 acts almost always as a dissonance resolved by B♭, and pushes the work toward the dominant key of E flat or to closely related keys in the dominant region, B flat major and G minor: the A♭ in Sphinx 2, however, completely takes over and draws the second half of the work back towards the tonic and the subdominant (D flat) and the relative minor (F minor). This gives *Carnaval* the traditional tonal structure that we find in any moderately complex work of tonal music from the fugues of the *Well-Tempered Keyboard* in the early eighteenth century of to the sonatas of the classical period: an initial move from the tonic to the dominant followed by a return to the tonic with the use of a subdominant emphasis.

We may think that Schumann was lucky to find such accommodating Sphinxes in his own name and that of Ernestine von Fricken's town, or we may decide that Schumann chose his cryptograms with a large structure in view. We may doubt that the Sphinxes have a deep significance with regard to any of the individual pieces when we reflect that "Chiarina" has always been accepted as a portrait of the very young Clara Wieck, and yet it is based on Sphinx 2, "As.C.H.," which spells out Ernestine's birthplace—Clara, after all, had perfectly playable letters in her own name. It may even be—as Schumann contended about his method of composition of the *Kinderscenen*—that the pieces of *Carnaval* were first written as variations on the three mottos and then given names afterward as the composer reflected on their aptness. An exception must be made, of course, to the self-portraits of "Florestan" and "Eusebius," expressly and eccentrically designed as representations of the divided personality of the composer.

We have in *Carnaval,* and on an even larger scale, the use of recurring motifs that we found in the Eichendorff song cycle. The end of *Carnaval* is also a precursor of the later vocal works: the beginning does not so much return as it is integrated into a finale conceived on a large scale. Passages of the opening Préambule keep recurring in the final march (in 3/4 time!), and at last bring about a full-scale return, considerably magnified, of the end of the first piece. *Carnaval* contains many of Schumann's most personal and eccentric inspirations, but its eccentricity is tempered in the large-scale harmony by a conservative classicism often at odds with the small details. That, however, is a contradiction typical of the age in which it was composed.

Written in 1838 after *Carnaval,* op. 9, but published earlier with the lower opus number 6, *Davidsbündlertänze* is outwardly less cryptic but inwardly much more so: it is the subtlest, most mysterious, and most complex of all Schumann's large works. Essentially it is simply a set of eighteen dances, most of them of a popular nature. They are based on the first two bars of a mazurka by Clara Wieck:

but this motto is harmonically much more commonplace than the Sphinxes of *Carnaval,* and it is treated by Schumann in a way that removes what little individual character it had—it becomes merely an excuse for writing melodies that emphasize initially the third degree of the scale, and then the fifth. The second piece of the set, a slow *Ländler,* shows clearly how abstractly the motto is handled and how this allows Schumann to develop strongly defined characterizations of his own for each successive piece:

The second dance plays the crucial role in the large structure, as it, and not the opening mazurka, returns at the end—and not even exactly at the end either, but interrupts the sixteenth of the eighteen pieces. There is a tradition for the theme of a set of variations to return at the close, and the

Davidsbündlertänze is, in a limited sense, a set of variations; but the distorted, not to say perverse, manner in which Schumann realizes the convention is less a way of acknowledging the tradition than of violating it.

This perversity is reflected in the details of the pieces: hardly one of them does not distort the traditional rhythm of the different dances. The opening mazurka, gradually transformed by Schumann into something more like a waltz, never places a sustained melody note on a downbeat but always on the weak beats two and three:

The second dance, a *Ländler,* pits a clear duple time in the melody against the traditional 3/4, and in the third, the four-bar groupings necessary to the waltz are disconcertingly out of phase between the two hands throughout the middle section—sometimes the left hand is one bar ahead of the right, sometimes two:

With the fourth dance, the two hands are now consistently half a beat apart:

Schumann translates these popular dance forms into his most personal language. The most violent dislocation is found in the tarantella, number 6. Normally the six beats of a tarantella have two accents, on beats one and four: in Schumann, here, the right hand emphasizes beats three and six, the left hand beats two and five, a double subversion of the traditional accent:

(This is difficult to render clearly, particularly with Schumann's direction *"Sehr rasch und in sich hinein,"*[21] "Very fast, and within itself," i.e., repressed). These cross-accents continue throughout and develop a wonderful tension. In the trio section the accents become exceedingly complex, the syncopations irregular and dramatic:

21. *Und in sich hinein* is a direction found only in the first edition.

(Considering Schumann's growing conservatism, one can see why the word "dances" was removed from the title in the second edition.)

In the seventh dance the bar line is made so ambiguous by the phrase structure of the middle section that the third beat begins to sound like a downbeat:

This is one of the most powerful examples of the way Schumann works on the psychology of the listener. We only gradually feel that the bar line is shifting, and a momentary conviction does not arrive before bar 32: our sense of rhythm is neither fooled nor bewildered but troubled, and little by little this creates an emotional disturbance.

The eighth dance is made up of irregular seven-bar phrases (see p. 274), and the tenth dance opposes duple rhythm in the right hand to triple in the left:

In number thirteen, the two hands are out of phase by half a bar, and the result is a wonderfully Schumannesque opposition of phrasing:

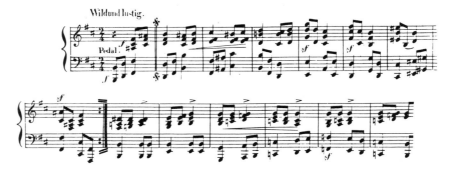

Most outrageously, the trio of number 16 presents the melody *pianissimo* and the accompaniment *forte:*

All of this is determinedly willful, and it is put into the service of a radical new view of large-scale harmony. The ambiguities of rhythm reflect a deeper ambiguity of structure. The *Davidsbündlertänze* are divided into two books with nine dances in each. Both books end in C major, yet the basic tonality of the whole work is clearly B minor. The way this fundamental harmonic contradiction functions not only reveals the originality of Schumann's technique but is also a key to the work's emotional power.

The essence of Schumann's conception is the replacement of the Classical location of a key at the outset by a gradual realization: the definition of a center of harmonic stability becomes part of the progressive experience of the work. The opening piece is unstable, shifting at once from G major to E minor, continuing to oscillate, and finally reaching B minor:

This brief reference to B minor is made important by the wonderful invention of the opening phrase, where a single B emerges from a chord and is sustained to become the first note of the succeeding melody. The music continues to return to this B, which alters the harmonic center of gravity of the piece from

G to E and back again. The restlessness and anxiety of this opening come from
the harmonic indecision as much as from the rhythmic ambiguity.

The lyrical second piece, in strong contrast, is absolutely stable, changing
only from B minor to B major. The feeling of a point of rest begins to define
itself; and it is confirmed by the instability of the third piece, which starts again
in G major only to go at once to B minor (see above) and then to D and even
to B flat; the fourth piece returns to B minor, and it not only never leaves B
minor even briefly but consists largely of tonic and dominant chords (see
pp. 225–226). For this piece Schumann directs *da capo ad libitum.* In fact,
all the dances in B minor—and only those—are played twice in the
Davidsbündlertänze. In the opening numbers it becomes clear little by little
that the central key is B minor, and the second half of the work confirms this.

The second book, like the first, begins outside the key of B, but the second
and fourth pieces are, as in the first book, in the key of B minor (although the
first of these has its cadence in the relative major)—and both are marked *da
capo ad libitum.* The *ad libitum* direction has, I think, been misunderstood, as
a glance at the eleventh piece will show:

The pianist is not "at liberty" to disregard the *da capo*, as this piece must end with the replaying of the first phrase, marked *Schluss* (or *fine*). *Ad libitum* can only mean that the pianist may go round again a second time if he wishes. We know that Schumann was fond of playing his best tunes (and this is one) over and over again for hours. The thirteenth piece is also in B minor, and is the most brilliant, even violent, of all—in spite of its length, it is played twice and followed by a continuously accelerating coda in B major.

The final confirmation of B minor as the central harmony of the entire work is the occasion for one of Schumann's greatest inspirations, and is among the most moving pages in early nineteenth-century music. The finale begins with the sixteenth piece, in an unstable G major that like the first piece keeps veering to E minor:

This is more jovial and good-humored than the opening piece, but when—once again as in the opening—B minor appears, the good humor disappears, and something more ominous takes its place, as the repeated F♯'s of the accompaniment are hammered out against a *pianissimo* melody (see p. 229). The reversal of significance between melody and accompaniment gives force to the F♯'s, which become a pedal point from which the last piece—or what should be the last piece—arises without pause:

This is marked "As if from a distance" ("Wie aus der Ferne"), and sounds doubly so because each phrase has an echo, and the pedal necessary to enforce the sustained notes casts a mysterious blur over the soft and deliberate sonorities. The creation of a sense of distance is an extraordinary innovation, but what follows is the greatest stroke. To the distance in space is added a distance in time, as the slow *Ländler* of the second piece begins again, directly from the echoing sounds of the repeated F♯'s:

A distance in time of more than twenty-five minutes separates the second from the seventeenth piece, and within the context of a work like the *Davidsbündlertänze* this is a genuine return of the past—not a formal return, or a *da capo* or a recapitulation, but a memory. It was Schumann's genius to have seen that the simple, unexpected memory of the slow, sad *Ländler* is heartbreaking. So far the only piece in B minor not yet played twice, the *Ländler* is now heard straight through, unchanged, with all of its repeats, leading this time to an impassioned development, a powerful and brilliantly accelerated climax, and a sad, plagal B minor final cadence.

Final? "Superfluously, Eusebius added the following," Schumann wrote over the eighteenth piece, "and his eyes filled with tears of happiness." The German is "Ganz zum Überfluss," that is, superfluous and flowing over, and the eighteenth piece takes the final B in the bass of the "final" piece and transfers it to the soprano of a C major chord:

The end is open. Like the first piece, this slow waltz in C major is outside the main B minor structure—a Neapolitan relationship of traditional pathos. It is a measure of the greatness of the conception of the work as a whole that this charming postultimate dance reveals its pathos only when played after the rest of the work—on its own it has grace and charm but little depth. Its dramatic force depends upon its being heard only after the work is over: in the final bars, middle C repeated twelve times signals the hour of midnight.

The final dance is therefore both within and without the formal structure. A rival tonality that remains unresolved, the concluding C major is, in fact, almost, but not quite, adequately prepared by the C major at the end of the first book, the only other piece to have a dramatic superscript ("Here Florestan stopped and his lips quivered in pain"); it is prepared, too, by the dominant G major which initiates both the work as a whole and the finale proper. The C major, however, never has enough power to challenge the principal B minor, but it sets up a symmetrical ending to both books which is half independent of, and half integrated into, the main structure. It is this subsidiary pattern which gives such conviction to the final dance as postlude.

The return of the second dance as if from a distance in space as a metaphor for a long absence in time alters our traditional conceptions of musical form. It is bound up with the way Schumann signed each piece in the first edition with the initials F and E, to indicate which part of his divided personality, "Florestan" or "Eusebius" (or sometimes both together), was responsible for the composition. It suggests a significance that is intended to appear private—a part of life and not of art. The return of the *Ländler* is not motivated by an abstract pattern, nor is it justified by tradition, but seems to be evoked naturally by the sense of distance. It is, for this reason, considerably more affecting on its second appearance: its return is like that of a memory that is not called up by design or by an act of will but by the course of nature.

The *Ländler* gave the cycle its first sound of the central tonality of B minor, but we only realize as the work progresses that this is the main key, and our realization is not confirmed until the reappearance of the *Ländler* in the seventeenth piece. Tonality here is not a prerequisite of musical logic but a progressive experience. The continuity of the return of the *Ländler* with what proceeds is very intensely and elaborately worked out: the *Ländler* is only a part of the seventeenth piece—and this, too, does not begin after a short pause but as if it were an integral part of the sixteenth piece. Even this join violates a formal requirement, as if to make the natural continuity more powerful: the seventeenth dance interrupts the so-called Trio of the sixteenth, as if to prevent the proper function of a trio, which normally implies the replaying of the initial section. Schumann does everything possible to make the return of the *Ländler* sound like the involuntary resurfacing of a buried memory, the rediscovered existence of the past within the present.

The sense of time of the *Davidsbündlertänze* determines the idiosyncratic formal structure, and it rests on the palpable traces of the past in immediate consciousness. Even the way Clara's motto is used works to that end: it is not a theme that one recognizes at each transformation but a continuous presence of which we are only partially conscious. That is why Schumann had to use a motto that had so little character of its own, or, rather, why he purges Clara's motto of its individuality. The more clearly defined character of the *Ländler* (although derived like every other dance from the motto) makes its return felt, and even this return is introduced dramatically by the tone color "As if from a distance." The setting prepares the sense of distance in time that the *Ländler* itself releases.

A work of pure instrumental music with no visible program recreates the sense of time and memory of Romantic landscape. The discovery of a hidden program, if one existed, would only distract the listener from an appreciation of the way Schumann's long-range treatment of harmony and thematic return are a substitute for narrative, and of how they turn a series of miniatures into a single work. The magnitude of Schumann's achievement is measured by the extent to which the *Davidsbündlertänze* can make its dramatic effect with no hint of a narrative, no reference beyond the music: even the initials of "Florestan" and "Eusebius" and the stage directions presented as superscripts to the finales of books 1 and 2 are more directions to the interpreter than hints of a secret. (The stage directions are not, in fact, cryptic but must be taken as a statement of fact. "Quite superfluously, Eusebius," i.e., the composer, "added the following," is the simple truth.) This work no more needs a program than the great Romantic representations of landscape needed historical reference, an intrigue, or a plot.

In Schumann's song cycles without words the wheel has come full circle. It was Schiller's counsel earlier that landscape take on musical form. Landscape had been reconceived in terms of its geological history, its development in time. To ennoble both landscape poetry and painting, the late eighteenth century turned to the example of music, preeminent as the art of time, and this gave landscape literally a new dimension and allowed the revolutionary conceptions of Nature to be carried out in the arts of painting, prose, and poetry. From the poems, the song cycles of Beethoven and Schubert inherited the new sense of time and found the most striking musical expression for it. With the piano cycles of Schumann, the modern understanding of time that had been revealed in painting and literature was realized in instrumental music by a purely musical structure. We do not hear the *Davidsbündlertänze* as the working out, however dramatic and surprising, of an initial musical idea, but as a structure experienced progressively as one moves through it: the apparent disparity of the individual dances reveals the sense of a larger unity only little by little as the series continues. The reappearance of the melancholy second dance is not only a return but more specifically a looking-back, as the Romantic travelers delighted to look back to perceive the different appearance of what they had seen before, a meaning altered and transfigured by distance and a new perspective. In Beethoven's instrumental works the return of an initial theme had often been transformed and radically altered by rescoring and rewriting: but in the *Davidsbündlertänze* the *Ländler* is apparently unaltered, transformed simply by distance in time and space, by the preceding sonorities, by everything that has taken place since the opening. An age that began with the attempt to realize landscape as music was finally able, in the most radical and eccentric productions of Schumann, to experience music as landscape.

CHAPTER FOUR

Formal Interlude

Mediants

The relation of tonic to dominant is the foundation of Western triadic tonality. The attempt of the early nineteenth century to substitute third or mediant relationships for the classical dominant amounted to a frontal attack on the principles of tonality, and it eventually contributed to the ruin of triadic tonality. This ruin was accomplished from within the system, however, as mediant relationships were essential to tonality as conceived in the eighteenth century.

What the new power of the mediant relationships attacked was the coherence of the tonal hierarchy, which in the eighteenth century gave opposing functions to the chords of the dominant and the subdominant. Movement to the dominant raised the tension of the music; an allusion to the subdominant decreased it. That is why, in a Bach fugue or a Mozart sonata, the music first goes to the dominant, and generally emphasizes subdominant harmony only in the latter half of the form. This distinction, wonderfully useful for dramatic expression throughout the eighteenth century, practically disappeared for the generation of composers born around 1810. A new chromaticism, largely arrived at through the use of mediant relations, blurs the clarity of the tonal system: one is no longer so certain which harmonies are most distant from the central tonic, a doubt which never arises with the music of Bach, Haydn, or Beethoven.

A sudden shift to the mediant or submediant was a dramatic effect in the late eighteenth century; it was generally reserved for the center of a piece, as when Mozart moves suddenly from the dominant to its mediant in the sextet from *Don Giovanni* at the moment when Donna Anna and Don Ottavio enter and prevent Leporello from escaping. Within Mozart's style this new harmony is electrifying, and is magnified by a *pianissimo* drum roll and a soft trumpet sonority.

Perhaps only Mozart at that time could have achieved the following progression in an exposition of a sonata form, as any other composer would have reserved it for a development:

This, from the E Major Trio, K.542, following the passage to be quoted on p. 260, goes from the dominant to its flatted submediant, then to this flatted submediant minor, and back elegantly to the dominant (B major–G major–G minor–B major). Haydn can be equally dramatic in his E Major Trio, H.28, but he waits for the development to pull it off. He goes first from the dominant to its submediant minor, and then with unexpected dynamic emphasis to the major:

In the second half of the exposition of this E major movement, Haydn does go, like Mozart, from B major to the flat submediant G major, and with equally surprising effect:

but he cannot parallel Mozart's exotic modulation to G minor, and instead returns to B major through the more conventional relative minor, G sharp minor.

None of these examples, although wonderfully dramatic, affect the basic tonal language: they are essentially coloristic, and make no attempt to set up the kind of polar opposition to the tonic reserved for the dominant, or, in the minor mode, for the mediant major. (It is, in fact, largely the minor mode, with its dependence on mediants, which is the source of the later developments in harmony during the nineteenth century.)

Beethoven, however, did often attempt to substitute third relationships for dominants, and to set up a direct polarized tension from a mediant to the tonic. One should, I suppose, make basic distinctions among these third relationships: major and minor mediant, flatted mediant, submediant, and flatted submediant (for C major, these are E, E flat, A, and A flat, respectively). But Beethoven employs all of these in similar fashion. The *Waldstein* Sonata goes to the mediant, the *Hammerklavier* Sonata to the submediant, the String Quartet in B flat Major, op. 130, to the flatted submediant. (Beethoven does not ordinarily use the flatted mediant except for a major-minor relationship.)

In these expositions Beethoven prepares the mediants exactly as he would prepare a dominant. The focus is on the dominant of the mediant, just as, in the more standard form, the focus is on the dominant of the dominant (V of V). The *Waldstein* Sonata, in C major, goes to III, E major, after a pedal point on V of III, B major. The music remains on this B major harmony for a full twelve bars:

and the repeated A♯ functions classically to impose the dominant of the dominant of the mediant (V of V of III).

Similarly the *Hammerklavier*, in B flat major, sets up the submediant G major, VI, by a long pedal on V of VI, a D major chord, and remains on this pedal for twenty-four bars. All the standard procedures for establishing a dominant are now diverted to the mediants:

In the *Archduke* Trio of Beethoven, the exposition also goes from B flat major to the submediant G major, and the preparation of the submediant by its dominant is lengthy, leisurely, and emphatic:

Clearly, the preparation of a mediant was a source of genuine musical pleasure. The mediants for Beethoven were not primarily coloristic episodes, as they were for Mozart, but a harmony of greater tension than the more ordinary dominant. Beethoven replaced the polar opposition of the dominant with a mediant, and established it with equivalent weight. This is one of the essential characteristics of eighteenth-century harmony that is weakened in the new style: a classical form of opposition is retained, but it has become slightly blurred. The new keys are not formally established: the music slides from tonic to mediant. The articulations, with Chopin and Schumann, are often so covert as to disappear.

Other aspects of classical tonality also disappeared in the music of the 1830s as the sense of a polarized tonal opposition lost its importance. When Beethoven used a mediant instead of a dominant in an exposition, he not only prepared it in the way he prepared a dominant, as we have seen; he also resolved it similarly. In a classical recapitulation, a passing use of the subdominant (without, however, a formal cadence) was almost inevitable and was remarked on by eighteenth-century theorists like Koch. On the rare occasions when Beethoven does not use the subdominant or a subdominant-related key in a recapitulation, he makes a striking use of it in the coda (see, for example, the Sonata for Piano, op. 31, no. 3, in E flat major). He requires the same balance for the mediant, and a sharp or dominant harmony in an exposition is offset in the recapitulation by a flat or subdominant harmony, the mediant by the submediant.

In the *Waldstein* Sonata, in C major, the E major mediant of the exposition is balanced by the submediant A major/minor in the recapitulation. In the Sonata for Piano in G Major, op. 31, no. 1, the second group in the mediant B major returns in the submediant E major. In the E flat Major Quartet, op. 127, the mediant G major is balanced later by submediant C major. In the Quartet in A Minor, op. 132, all the material first played in F major is repeated in C major. In the *Hammerklavier,* op. 106, the opposition of B flat major and G major in the exposition is resolved in the recapitulation by the flat coloring of G flat major, related to the subdominant. (There are other forces at work in all these cases: the G flat of the *Hammerklavier* is part of the tonal plan which emphasizes B major—or C flat major—as the goal of the development; the subdominant in opus 31, no. 3, has to be postponed from the recapitulation to the coda as the opening theme is already too strongly characterized by the subdominant harmony.)

Only once, in the Quartet in B flat Major, op. 130, does Beethoven simply slide chromatically into a mediant harmony (here the flat submediant G flat major), following the more modern fashion (even here, the slide is to the dominant of the submediant):

and a laconic move to the mediant D major balances the submediant and opens the development:

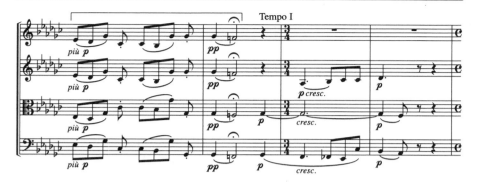

As we can see, even at the end of his career he keeps a strong grip on the distinctive classical functions of every harmony and allows no chromatic blurring.

The generation that followed Beethoven could dispense with such procedures, and set up what amounted to a powerful change of tonality in the simple way that Mozart used mediants episodically for coloristic effect. In the duet from the first act of *William Tell,*

Rossini uses only mediant shifts:

E flat	I
G flat	III flatted
D	VII
F	II
A flat	IV

and the tonic E flat returns with the cabaletta. Here is the first of the changes:

No dominant preparation of the new tonality of G flat major is employed; it is the dominant of I, not of the flat mediant, that appears, and the shift to the new key is made with ostentatious simplicity. The next two shifts use the dominant of the new key with only the most perfunctory emphasis, first to D major:

then to F major:

The last modulation parallels the first:

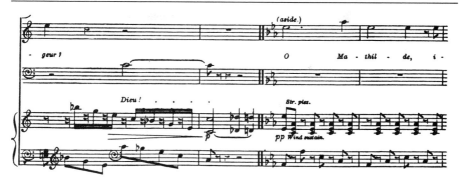

The series of rapid, surprising shifts are in stark contrast to classical practice. The articulated balances and resolutions in Beethoven became almost a dead letter for the generation of composers born around 1810. They reconceived modulation not as the establishment of an opposition but as a chromatic coloration of the original tonic—and this original tonic was often loosely enough defined to contain both its own minor mode and the relative minor as well.

Chopin's Scherzo in B flat Minor is essentially in the relative major D flat, which allows the mediant relationship of A major for the central section (not only the end of the scherzo but also the end of the opening section is in D flat major). Within this A major central section there are episodes in the closely related keys of E major and C sharp minor (the latter is, after all, the tonic minor). The nature of the mediant relationship D flat / A natural is brilliantly exploited in detail in the coda:

The return of A major here is a shock but not a real modulation; it merely adds chromatic excitement to the simple diatonic V/I cadences that precede. From then on, A♮ / B♭♭ dominates the rest of the coda:

The final cadence, which employs the A♮ with an F major chord in a D flat major cadence, was impossible in the eighteenth century; by 1840 its harmonic excitement had not yet become quite ordinary, but it was easily acceptable.

Chopin's Mazurka in B Major, op. 56, no. 1, an extraordinarily imaginative work, goes straight to the flatted submediant G major even before the tonic has been truly established, and resolves the G major into the dominant of B major:

It is, in fact, not clear before bar 13 that B major is the tonic. Its harmony is stated in the second bar but only as a part of an ongoing series of sequences. This is one of the most interesting experiments in postponing the full definition of the tonic, here put in the service of a more fluid sense of harmony and a feeling of improvisation. The third relationships are exploited in the rest of the piece. A trio section starts immediately in E flat major, the mediant of B, and alternates this harmony with its own subdominant, A flat major, the submediant of B:

After a repetition of the opening section, the trio returns, now in G major, the flat submediant of B. It alternates, not with its subdominant as before, but with its dominant, D major, which is the flat mediant of B:

In this way, all possible mediant relationships of the tonic B major are called into play in this mazurka: mediant, flat mediant, submediant, and flat submediant—or E flat, D, A flat, and G. I do not think that one should interpret this as an attempt like Beethoven's to balance mediant with submediant for resolution, but as a complex synthesis of mediant harmony and chromaticism. The resolution of D major back to B is accomplished in pure chromatic fashion, using the opening bar as a motif that is transposed a scale of half steps:

The tendency to move to the mediant without creating any sense of opposition can be seen in the attempt by various composers, Chopin above all, to make these moves imperceptible, as in this example from the Nocturne in D flat Major, where he introduces A major into a sustained chord of D flat major by changing as few notes as possible. It carries out Chopin's ideal of evading any emphatic articulation of the phrase:

The four mediants are unique in realizing this effect, as only dominant, subdominant, and the four mediants have a note of their major triads in common with the tonic triad. Changing to a dominant creates a sense of opposition, and a move to the subdominant is generally weak: in addition, both of these moves are purely diatonic. The mediants alone can give both a new color and an effortless change of harmony.

The use of mediants for the large structures may often be paralleled on a small scale. The beautiful principal melody of Liszt's *Sonetto del Petrarca*, no. 104, develops a series of mediant shifts:

The bass line of the second phrase moves by thirds from D to B♭, then to G and a dominant seventh on B♮, and that gives this phrase greater movement and power than the first. The E major cadence is followed at once by the chord of the mediant G sharp major.

Chopin's Mazurka in C sharp Minor, op. 50, no. 3, climbs up a series of mediants in the coda (quoted on p. 438), and so does the Nocturne in G Major in bars 7 to 12 (quoted on p. 273). These rise by minor triads. A slightly slower series may be found in the Polonaise-Fantaisie, in which the harmony goes from A flat major to C major and finally to E major:

Here the A♭ in the bass is a tonic, the C a dominant, and the E a tonic which turns into a dominant seventh after several bars, and quickly blends with another dominant seventh on B♭. The key structure (if that is what to call it) is therefore A flat major, F minor, and then E major moving into E flat major. In essence, these moves by thirds are linear and chromatic in nature even more than they are tonal, and they show that in Chopin's style, counterpoint or voice leading rules over harmony.

In all these examples from the first half of the nineteenth century, musical style is moving from the dissonant passing notes of classical tonality towards the dissonant "passing phrases" (to use Bernard Shaw's excellent term about Strauss's music) of the early twentieth century. Renouncing the force of tonal opposition may eventually have weakened the tonal language, but it did not weaken the music, which in fact had gained a new source of power.

Since the complementary function of dominant and subdominant was almost forgotten by 1830, its essential role in eighteenth-century sonata forms went largely unrecognized by nineteenth-century theorists. The strictly defined hierarchy of diatonic relationships was traded for a new conception of the chromatic continuum, in which a dazzling variety of harmonies could blend with one another in a kaleidoscopic exchange of energy. This opened up not only new harmonic possibilities but also a novel and much more fluid conception of rhythm and tempo.

Four-bar phrases

The four-bar phrase has had a bad press in our time. Grouping all the bars in fours is often considered mechanical and even thoughtless, and historians of music will hold up three- and five-bar phrases for our admiration as if they were gems of inspiration. The periodic phrase—whether in bar groups of three or (most often) four—is essentially a system of controlling large-scale rhythm by imposing a steady, slower beat over the beats of the individual bar.

The system of four-bar phrasing was already in frequent use in the early part of the eighteenth century—dance patterns demanded this kind of regularity; by the last quarter of the eighteenth century it dominated almost all composition. The slower beat imposed over the music should not mislead us: the music of the late eighteenth century actually seems to move faster than that of the Baroque. The rate of change of the harmony was slower; this is reflected in the four-bar groupings, and it controls the sense of large-scale movement. The technique works very like the motor of a car: in a higher gear, the motor turns over more slowly, but the car moves faster. The slow harmonic rhythm and the periodic phrase are the main aspects of the move to a higher gear, and they allow the more largely conceived dramatic structures to unfold effectively and avoid the concentration on the small-scale rhythmic motion within the bar.

In the late eighteenth century the module of four bars can be altered in various ways. The phrase can be introduced by one or two bars of accompaniment, and the last bar can be extended by echoes. Haydn's String Quartet in C Major, op. 33, no. 3, opens with an example of both of these devices:

Two four-bar phrases are extended to six here by one bar of introduction and by replaying the last bar an octave lower. What makes the repeated note accompaniment of the opening bar so effectives is that it is not mere accompaniment: the melody, too, begins with a repeated G (o | ♩♩) as if the first bar were first augmented and then accelerated. In any case, this is essentially a four-bar phrase extended.

Later in this movement another method of extension is employed—expanding the center of the phrase—a more sophisticated technique quite advanced for its time:

This phrase is, of course, derived from the opening theme played twice as fast. The second bar is repeated a half step lower in an obvious echo, and turns a four-bar group into five bars. (When the phrase is repeated, Haydn further surprises us by extending the movement for two more bars.)

Mozart was to employ the technique of inner expansion with great subtlety. In the Trio for Piano and Strings in E Major, K.542, the initial theme of the B major second group expands what might have been a four-bar phrase to six bars:

I have deliberately chosen this example because it is what might be called a hard case, a convincing six-bar phrase. Nevertheless, one gets a clear sense in listening to it of a phrase being stretched out, with a resulting increase of tension. In the majority of Mozart's themes there is an increase in harmonic motion after the second or fourth bars. Consider the opening theme of this trio, for example:

For the B major theme above, the commonplace pattern would have been:

or in outline:

In the six-bar phrase this structure augments the rhythm:

This gives a commonplace pattern a greater breadth and more intense character, and accounts for the effect of a line sustained beyond the listener's expectations.

For Beethoven, the four-bar rhythm takes on an even greater effect of motor energy than for the composers of the previous generation, propelling the music forward; his deviations from it seem almost always like an act of will: they require an effort. Nonetheless, we should abandon the general prejudice that the deviations are more important than the formidable stretches of conformity. It ought to seem odd that deviating from the four-bar system should be considered more creative than using it imaginatively—as if we were to reproach a composer for not throwing a few five- or three-beat measures into his standard 4/4 or common time.

On the whole, it is clear that by the 1820s the four-bar period has extended its dominion over musical composition. The large-scale structure may no longer be said simply to organize the rhythm shaped by the periods: it is now the four-bar periods themselves which have become the basic elements of musical material, as attention is deflected away from the bar and to the whole phrase as a unit. Deviations from the four-bar grouping tend, therefore, to develop very different aspects from those I have sketchily summarized for the late eighteenth century. Chopin's G Major Prelude has a fine example of the new technique:

After the two bars of introduction, only bar 11 is an exception to the four-bar pattern, and interrupts the regularity set up by bars 3–6 and 7–10. Bar 11 is not, however, an extension in the classical sense, either echo or further development. It simply prolongs the harmony of bar 10, acting as a fermata over the upbeat back to the strong bar that opens the next phrase. Bar 11 is a kind of rubato, an expressive suspense.[1]

A similar example may be found in the Scherzo in B flat Minor by Chopin. The middle section opens with a new twenty-bar *sostenuto* theme, repeated immediately with one extra bar:

1. Carl Schachter has interestingly analyzed bar 11 as an augmentation of the important motif of the melody E–D in bar 3, in *Music Forum V* (New York, 1980), pp. 202–210.

The extra bar does not, in reality, affect the periodic structure: it is only a rubato. The orchestra waits briefly while the singer adds a little expressive decoration. The operatic origin of this passage is obvious, particularly in its later appearance, where the decoration becomes more elaborate:

What these examples show is that the suppleness of the four-bar phrase under Haydn and Mozart gives way to a certain rigidity: the four-bar period is no longer so malleable, so easily extensible, but it can still be inflected by a rhythmic freedom which does not alter the basic shape.

The danger of periodic phrasing (in four bars, or, more rarely, in three) is, of course, monotony, above all the sense of the invariable downbeat on bar 1. It is when the system is employed with understanding, or when the deviations are not merely local eccentricities but contribute to the larger plan, that the music tends to be most successful. When the phrase lengths are uniform, the sense of monotony may be countered by varying the accent of the bar, and avoiding the relentless alternation of strong and weak bars. The interplay between phrase length and accent allows the composer to organize his structure with freedom.

We can see this in the simplest but most spectacular form in the famous *ritmo di tre battute* from the Scherzo of Beethoven's Ninth Symphony:

At the beginning of the passage, the emphasis, defined by the motto, lies on the first of the three-bar groups (bars 177–206). Then the emphasis shifts, and the motif is found on the second of the three-bar sets (bars 207–224), and then shifts again back to the first bar (225). Putting the accent on the second of three bars is a destabilizing force, and Beethoven creates a miniature ternary structure of stability–instability–stability. The return to four-bar grouping (bar 234) is achieved by placing the motto on each of the four bars in succession, and the quadruple rhythm is defined by shifts of harmony. It is typical of Beethoven that each shift of rhythm is determined almost solely by the way the principal motif is placed. I have chosen this exceptional three-bar rhythm as its suppleness characterizes Beethoven's practice with the more common four-bar form.

A passage from the finale of Schubert's Sonata in C Minor, D.958, written shortly before his death in 1828, shows a very different interplay between accent and phrase length, but one of equal mastery:

This lyrical interlude in this tarantella movement consists of two phrases, of fifteen and seventeen bars respectively—or 4 + 11 and 8 + 8 + 1. There is no suggestion of irregularity in performance, however, as the accent remains steady: the strong bar here is always the odd-numbered one. The contrast is one of a trochaic structure followed by an iambic one. In other words, in the first part of the theme, an accented bar is followed by an unaccented one: bars 247–250 have a feminine ending with the accent on the first and third bars, and bars 251–257 continue the pattern. The second part of the theme (bars 258–273) is the reverse: an accented bar is preceded by an unaccented one. Bar 273 leads back to the opening pattern. It is not merely that the whole passage adds up to thirty-two bars which gives the impression of regularity, but that the irregularities balance symmetrically and keep the pulse steady. We must remember that (exactly as in 4/4 time) bars 1 and 3 are generally strong (or downbeat), bars 2 and 4 weak (or upbeat). (Bars 258 to 273 start with a fourth bar accent.) Schubert retains the regularity of the module but varies the accent of the phrases.

It should be evident that in the 1820s, at least in the work of a master like Schubert, the deviation from the four-bar module can have as systematic a purpose as the standard form. The basic distinction should not be between composers who slavishly followed the standard form and those who abandoned it creatively, but between those who employed it (or not) unthinkingly and those who exploited the superimposition of a larger and slower beat on the music to realize a new temporal perspective on the entire form.

The secret of avoiding monotony with the four-bar module was to vary the accent and the weight of the bars to avoid giving a similar emphatic accent on the first bar of every group, as if one were accenting a downbeat. After Beethoven and before Brahms, perhaps the greatest master of the technique was Chopin, as one can see from the opening of the Nocturne in D flat Major, op. 27, no. 2, of 1836:

After a bar of introductory accompaniment (which hints at the contour of the melody), we find a five-bar phrase followed by a three-bar answer—or better, four and a half bars followed by three and a half. Basically, the fourth bar of the melody (bar 5) has been lengthened. Instead of

we find a surprisingly long A♮ with a wonderfully expressive effect, and this forces an accelerated movement in the following bar with a sense of greater passion. The Etude in E Major, op. 10, no. 3, also opens with a similar group of five and three bars, but different forces are at work:

Bar 6, which should be a second or weak bar, has the weight of a downbeat, and crowding the whole second phrase into three bars creates an agitated contrast with the simpler opening.

We can see that the module of four is generally constant with Chopin but that it is partly independent of the length of the phrase, which Chopin can vary with great suppleness. The opening of the Scherzo no. 2 in B flat Minor, op. 31, shows a very sophisticated use of syncopation within the four-bar pattern:

The downbeats or first bars of the group are placed at 5, 9, 13, 17, 21, and 25. Bars 5 and 13 have powerful *fortissimo* accents but act almost as upbeats to the next bars, and the ties from 6 to 7 and 14 to 15 are essentially syncopations. Bar 17 is much weaker than 13; bar 21 has no accent at all, merely sustaining a tied note; and bar 25 commences as a void. Nevertheless, there is no sense of irregularity, and the larger four-bar rhythm is relentless. This makes possible the effect in bars 22 and 45, where a violent off-beat accent in a "weak" measure results in a double off-beat effect. It is evident that this syncopation requires a strict tempo; any expressive freedom can take place only within the four-bar group, but the first bar must always arrive with metronomic regularity, and bars 16 to 24 permit no freedom at all to be completely intelligible.

In the fourth Scherzo in E Major, op. 54, what seems to be an irregular nine-bar phrase after a brilliant climax (bars 384–393) is in fact an absolutely strict carrying out of an eight-bar pattern:

Here the first bars or downbeats of the phrases are at 353, 361, 369, 377, 385, and 393. Bars 385 and 387 are therefore strong bars, and at 384 Chopin has begun the phrase a bar before the downbeat of the phrase. Bars 384 and 386 are syncopated; they anticipate the metrical accents and act as upbeats. This dramatic effect works only if the pause in bar 383 is not lengthened as it so often is in concert, since most pianists find it convenient to heave a long sigh of relief after the virtuosity of bars 369 to 382. The temptation should be resisted, as the phrase 384 to 393 is considerably more expressive if it sounds like a syncopation to the central beat. When this introductory phrase reappears, it is preceded once again by an arpeggio that begins within the middle of a four-bar group, arching over the systematic rhythm:

How concerned Chopin was for the large-scale beat to be perceived can be seen by his notation of the end of the scherzo:

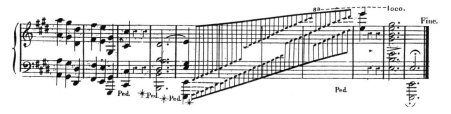

The scale, which must be played more or less as fast as one can, is still measured out by Chopin in four bars, each beginning with a note of the tonic triad.

Chopin's mastery comes from his ability to retain the four-bar grouping while varying the metrical significance of the bars. The opening of the Nocturne in G Minor, op. 37, no. 1, reveals his ability to manipulate a commonplace technique:

The first phrase seems to be over at bar 4, but is then extended and carried forcefully into what follows. Bar 5 appears to be the completion of this process, but then suddenly with the second beat becomes a return of the first four bars, now more dramatic and more expressive. The new force comes partly from Chopin's ability to fuse the two playings of the theme into one, to make bar 5 both a resolving completion and a new beginning.

Chopin's exquisite manipulation of the inner accents of a four-bar group can be demonstrated with extraordinary clarity in the central section of the B flat Minor Scherzo in a passage shortly after the one quoted earlier:

Here the same motif is used both for emphasis:

and for release:

The emphasis is placed initially on the first bar of the four-bar groups, or the downbeat, the release on the third. This pattern is played three times. The fourth time, the third bar is also given the emphatic form, and in the next four-bar group the accents are reversed, with the release on the first bar, the emphasis on the third. (We could consider this whole passage as three four-bar groups followed by two six-bar groups, but this does not alter the essential rhythm of four bars.) If performed correctly, this passage has the effect of an expressive syncopation, a shift from a fully stable version to an unstable one comparable to the form observed in the *ritmo di tre battute* we found in Beethoven's Ninth Symphony. Few composers were capable of this craftsmanship.

If we keep in mind this ability both to retain and to override the four-bar rhythm, we can understand the more complex of Chopin's experiments, like the second nocturne of opus 37, in G major. This is one of Chopin's rare uses of a three-bar period:

In these three-bar periods of bars 1–12, the left and right hands are out of phase, the left being consistently a half bar ahead of the right. The left hand begins a new period with bar 4 while the right hand ends its phrase (and this process continues through bar 12, the left hand always ahead of the right). Bar 4 is therefore a new first bar and a fourth bar at the same time, and what is implied is an overlapping system of four-bar groups so reduced to three. At the second half of bar 13, the pattern changes to an open four-bar phrase, which ends on bar 17, but a new four-bar pattern overlaps here starting on the second sixteenth note. An analysis may be fussy, but the result of Chopin's play of rhythmic structure is a fluid motion that enhances the barcarole character of this nocturne.

This kind of mastery was denied to Schumann, but in his concern to make the four-bar structure interesting, he was forced into solutions that are as original as Chopin's, and perhaps more dramatic. The eighth piece of the *Davidsbündlertänze* is in seven-bar phrases:

There is clearly a bar missing in these phrases, with a wonderfully eccentric effect. This is because bar 4 (and bar 11) is at the same time both an answer to the preceding bar, in parallel with bar 2 (and with bar 9), and a beginning of a new four-bar phrase that accelerates the harmonic rhythm to the end of the seventh bar. Schumann underlines the eccentricity with his final bar, which is a one-beat bar in a two-beat metric. Not only do we feel that a bar is missing, but—when the repeat begins, as it should—a beat has also disappeared.

This structure—three seven-bar phrases plus one four-bar phrase extended by a written-out *ritardando* into five bars with a beat lopped off is unusual for Schumann; what is typical is the extravagance. Even more typical, and in some ways equally extravagant, is Schumann's frequent attempts to inflect the rhythm by obscuring the downbeats with an insistent emphasis on weak beats or else with a continuous employment of *rubato*. The seventh piece of the *Davidsbündlertänze* provides one of the finest examples:

The indication *ritenuto* arrives even before tempo or basic rhythm has had a chance to establish itself, and is repeated every two bars. The absence of an indication *a tempo* is also typical of Schumann. It does not mean that the original tempo should not return, but it is evidently impossible to make clear to the listener just where the tempo has been reestablished. What comes out most convincingly is a flexible movement in which the rhythm is continuously bent according to the caprice of the performer, on whom the coherence depends as well.

In songs, the four-bar phrase can be ambiguously treated: the piano can add bars to the singer's four-bar phrase, and the extra bars most often sound as if they were in a different rhythmic space, subordinate to the principal one. In *Der Einsame* (The Solitary Man) by Schubert, the vocal part is perfectly regular in sets of four half bars. The interruptions of the piano make it more complex, but the regularity is not genuinely upset:

Nevertheless, the interruption of the accompaniment can be integrated with the vocal melody to form a unified phrase together as in Schubert's *An die Musik* (To Music):

The first vocal phrase is four bars in length. The second phrase overlaps with the first and starts in the piano; three bars of voice continue the line to form a new four-bar version, more expressive and more complex, of the first phrase.

With greater intensity, the interruption of the piano part can appear to begin a new four-bar group, and then the return of the voice starts a new four-bar phrase of its own, half independent and half integrated with the initial piano line, as in "Der Wegweiser" (The Signpost) from *Winterreise*:

There is no way to decide, from bars 10 to 14, whether we have a four-bar or a five-bar phrase: both have equal claims. (For another example of this impressive technique from *Im Frühling,* see p. 62). Bars 15 to 19 are a four-bar phrase lengthened to five by a repetition of the third bar.

The four-bar phrase enlarged the time scale of music. In the newly systematic use developed in the early nineteenth century, it turned short pieces into genuine miniatures, as if Chopin's Prelude in G Major were only seven bars long and not thirty-one (that is, seven times four plus two bars of introduction and one bar of suspension). It gave a larger sense of motion to long works and altered the significance of the smaller details. Eventually this larger sense was to make possible the gigantic forms of the Wagnerian music dramas.

Chopin: Counterpoint and the Narrative Forms

Poetic inspiration and craft

In almost every edition (and consequently most performances) of Chopin's Sonata in B flat Minor, op. 35, there is a serious error that makes awkward nonsense of an important moment in the first movement. The repeat of the exposition begins in the wrong place. A double bar meant to indicate the beginning of a new and faster tempo in measure 5 is generally decorated on both staves with the two dots that indicate the opening of a section to be played twice. Here is the mistake in the first German edition printed in Leipzig:

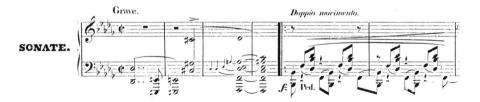

A glance at the photograph of the manuscript in Warsaw will assure us that these dots are an engraver's embellishment. (The manuscript is not autograph, but it has additions and corrections in Chopin's hand. A facsimile of the first page is printed in the notorious "Paderewski" edition.) The mistake was made in one of the early editions. Chopin's works were almost always published simultaneously in three cities—Paris, Leipzig, and London; the German edition is faulty in this place. The London and Paris editions of the opening of the sonata are, nevertheless, correct. This is the London edition, in conformity with the manuscript:

All twentieth-century editions that I have seen, however, are wrong. One other nineteenth-century edition, reprinted in the twentieth, gets it right: the critical edition published by Breitkopf & Härtel late in the century and edited by Liszt, Reinecke, Brahms, et al. The sonatas were revised by Brahms, and he was too intelligent to perpetuate the error.[1]

We should not, however, need to glance at the documentary evidence. The faulty indication is musically impossible: it interrupts a triumphant cadence in D flat major with an accompanimental figure in B flat minor, a harmonic effect which is not even piquant enough to be interesting, and merely sounds perfunctory. The repeat is clearly intended to begin with the first note of the movement: the opening four bars are not a slow introduction but an integral part of the exposition. The performances I have heard that do not perpetuate the foolish misprint have omitted the repetition altogether. This makes the movement too short, but better that than musical nonsense. I am sure, however, that there are pianists who have discovered the right version from either the manuscript or the old Breitkopf publication edited by Brahms.

The opening is a shock, beginning with a suggestion of the wrong key, D flat, which turns quickly to B flat minor. When the first bar comes back, it is now the right key, as the exposition has closed in D flat. The opening four bars have a double function—a dramatic beginning, and a transition from the end of the exposition back to the tonic:

1. The edition of Ignaz Friedman of 1912 is also correct at this place, but it was evidently based on Brahms's edition, as it repeats the addition of two extra bars of recapitulation in the finale (a variant plausible enough to have been made by Chopin himself, but which was probably made by the printer of the Leipzig edition in miscounting the number of bars to copy). This means that Brahms was using the Leipzig printing as a basis; in spite of this, he was able to correct the gross error of the opening page.

The left hand, unharmonized, resolves the cadence a measure before the right. This is a device used with equally astonishing effect by Chopin a few years before the sonata in the Scherzo in B Minor, op. 20, written in 1832. It occurs in bar 569 at the beginning of the coda:

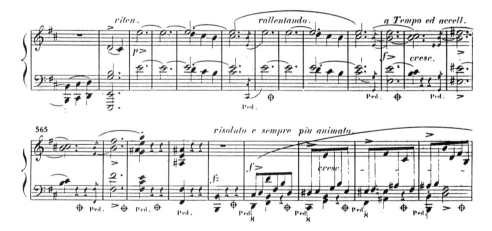

The effect here is perhaps even more startling because it is not prepared rhythmically as in the sonata. The opening of the sonata is exactly twice as slow as the rest of the exposition. (Chopin's direction for the new tempo is *doppio movimento*, and the usual concert performance of the first phrase as three or four times as slow is a thoughtless attempt to make the beginning more pretentious.) Two bars of the quick tempo equal one of the slow (marked *grave*), and at the end of the exposition Chopin returns to the original slow tempo with long notes two bars in length so that the transition is wonderfully smooth.

A phrase that is both an initial dramatic motto and a modulation from the secondary tonality of the exposition back to the tonic is a remarkable conception. Even more significant is the carefully worked out realization in terms of rhythm, harmony, and texture. When we reflect that the misprint in almost all editions has gone not only uncorrected but seemingly unnoticed for more than a century, I think we may reasonably decide to give very little weight to the standard critical opinion that Chopin's treatment of sonata form is uninteresting.[2]

The Sonata in C Major, op. 24, by Carl Maria von Weber, one of the few composers of his time whom Chopin admired, provided a precedent, if not a model. The first movement starts, like Chopin's, with a four-bar "motto" that begins outside the tonic harmony and then resolves into the tonic. On its return, when the exposition is repeated, the motto now appears as a clear extension of the final bars of the exposition. Chopin's version is tighter and more dramatic, as the beginning of his motto is the resolution of the unfinished cadence at the end of the exposition. (Weber's movement has a further affinity with Chopin's work, as the tonic harmony returns in the recapitulation not with the opening bars or even with the main theme at bar 5, but with the new material of bar 20.) This is Weber's opening:

and the end of his exposition with the initiation of the development (this also has a good deal in common with Chopin's conception):

2. Margaret Bent has pointed out to me that Edward T. Cone originally defended the erroneous reading (in *Musical Form and Musical Performance* [New York, 1968]) but then wrote in an article called "Editorial Responsibility and Schoenberg's Troublesome 'Misprints,'" *Perspectives in New Music,* vol. 11, no. 1 (1972), p. 65, that the repeat signs "result in nonsense."

Schumann's review of Chopin's Sonata in B flat Minor, op. 35, is only too well known, but it remains a model until our day of both the appreciation and misunderstanding of Chopin's style. Schumann was clearly sensitive to the work's power and conscious of its importance; he complained, however, that Chopin had yoked four of his strangest and most heterogeneous children together to make a sonata. The musical world of 1840 was even smaller than that of today, and Schumann was undoubtedly aware that the third movement, the *Marche Funèbre,* had been written two years before the rest of the sonata. Nevertheless, the unity of tone and of harmonic color that holds Chopin's four movements together is not only impressive, but far surpasses the more arbitrary technique of achieving unity by quoting literally from earlier movements in the later ones, a technique that was popular with many of Chopin's contemporaries including Mendelssohn and Schumann himself.

The chief stumbling block for Schumann was the last two movements of Chopin's sonata. The funeral march, he wrote, had something repulsive about it. The finale is a single line of triplets doubled at the octave, *presto, pianissimo, sotto voce,* and *legato,* with no added harmony until the last measure (a B flat minor chord *fortissimo* and with pedal) and no other indication of dynamics or pedal except for a crescendo in bars 13 and 14. It created a stir at its publication. Schumann made a generous attempt to appreciate what he felt was "more like an irony than a kind of music." He wrote that "from this musical line without melody and without joy, there breathes a strange, horrible spirit which annihilates with its heavy fist anything that resists it, and we listen with fascination and without protesting until the end—but without, nevertheless, being able to praise: for this is not music."

It is perhaps unwise to take too seriously the pronouncements of one composer about another. Mendelssohn, too, hated this finale of Chopin's, but then he detested many of the mazurkas as well. When a copy of Schumann's *Kreisleriana* was sent to Chopin, to whom it had been dedicated, he commented favorably only on the design of the title page (which was, indeed, impressive). Chopin's general contempt for most of his colleagues, including Liszt and Berlioz, is well documented. Composers are chiefly interested in music they can turn to their own profit or steal from, and then they are unwilling to discuss the matter in any detail. Schumann's resistance to the novelty of Chopin's finale is understandable, although this movement displays a mastery of long-established eighteenth-century formal procedures which Schumann rarely equalled. It was not the kind of music that he himself aspired to write, and he may be easily pardoned for not recognizing the traditional elements and the conservative craftsmanship that sustained Chopin's most radical experiments. Nevertheless, Schumann's reaction sets the pattern for most later criticism of Chopin: an acknowledgment of imaginative power along with an assertion of technical limitations.

For Schumann, the limitation of Chopin's technique was a clear incapacity for attaining the unity necessary in a large work, an inability to realize his imaginative vision in acceptable musical terms. More recent critics have defined Chopin's deficiencies somewhat differently but with even less intelligence. It is more or less a commonplace of Chopin criticism[3] to write that he was incapable of dealing with large forms, although it might be more reasonably maintained that he was the only musician of his generation who felt invariably at ease with them—each of the Ballades and Scherzi is, after all, as long as, or longer than, an average movement of Beethoven, and the two mature piano sonatas of Chopin are more satisfactory in public performance than any other comparable works of the 1830s and 1840s. Another commonplace, equally foolish, of Chopin criticism is that his works are almost all examples of ternary form. The terms "binary" and "ternary" are already awkward when used about eighteenth-century music; when "ternary" is applied to one of Chopin's Ballades or even to the Polonaise-Fantaisie, it is mischievously uninformative, and even actively misleading. Our technical vocabulary is ludicrous when it comes to dealing with Chopin's inventions.

Chopin's poetic genius was based on a professional technique that was without equal in his generation. His craftsmanship exceeded even Mendelssohn's. After he reached the age of twenty, there are almost no miscalculations in his works, including the most ambitious, as there are frequently enough in the music of his greatest contemporaries, Schumann and Berlioz. Even when he wished to give the effect of improvisation, his forms are tightly organized, never loose to the point of disintegration, as we find so often with

3. Nicholas Temperley's article on Chopin in the *New Grove's* is an honorable exception to this, and the recent studies by Jim Samson, Jeffrey Kallberg, and others have shown greater understanding.

Liszt. The only craft he never bothered to perfect was orchestration. On the other hand, unlike Schumann, Liszt, and Berlioz, he mastered Italian operatic forms: there are many examples in his work of perfectly formed melodies in the Italian style, and even, in the F Minor Concerto, a complete *scena*. It is, in fact, the constructive use of Italian operatic technique that may puzzle critics, most of whose tools of analysis are derived from German instrumental music.

Above all, Chopin was the greatest master of counterpoint since Mozart. This will appear paradoxical only if we equate counterpoint with strict fugue, and Chopin wrote no formal fugues except as an academic exercise. His chief training, in both composition and keyboard playing, however, came from a study of Bach, and it was a study that engaged him all his life and which he always recommended to his pupils. His pupils attest to his idolization of Bach. The *Well-Tempered Keyboard* was the the only music he took with him on his famous trip to Majorca with George Sand, and he generally warmed up for concerts by playing some of the preludes and fugues. It is the facility of Chopin's voice leading or part writing which is dazzling. Beethoven's mastery of this art was achieved with much more evident difficulty; in fact, the very awkwardness is responsible for some the power. Chopin's ease of part writing was unmatched by any of his contemporaries.

As a student, Chopin knew the solo works of Mozart, but probably none of the concertos: his ideas of concerto form came from Johann Nepomuk Hummel, Frédéric Kalkbrenner, and John Field. Italian opera must have been his greatest delight: it was certainly the most popular form of music of his time. He very quickly transmuted the salon style of composers like Field into something much closer to Italian opera. The influence of Hummel waned early in his music, although he never ceased to admire him, and in the 1840s Hummel's Sonata for Piano in F sharp Minor is still the easily recognizable model for Chopin's Third Sonata in B Minor. Chopin's music is largely derived from his early experience of opera, the rhythms and harmonies of native Polish dances, and Bach. The art that held all this together came above all from the last, in particular the *Well-Tempered Keyboard*. If he ever knew the religious music of Bach, it was at a moment too late to be of any use to him. In order to disabuse ourselves of the impossible image of Chopin as an imaginative genius seriously limited by a deficient technique, it is with the craft that we must start, not the genius, even if, in the end, it is the genius that we hope to illuminate.

Counterpoint and the single line

One of the extreme points of Chopin's craft is the monophonic finale of the Sonata in B flat Minor that so disturbed Schumann and other musicians. What was disquieting about such a piece (and it retains some of its shock effect even today) is that certain of the elements of the art of music are reduced almost to zero; this enables us, however, to see more clearly how the other elements work, and how they can be called upon to replace the functions of those which have disappeared. (We might add in passing that to have been told that one had exceeded the bounds of music while holding listeners fascinated to the end may not have been an unwelcome criticism to a young and ambitious composer.) There are the other "monophonic" pages in Chopin, including the Prelude in E flat Minor, and a wonderful central section of the Polonaise in F sharp Minor, op. 44. This latter page is in some respects more radical than the finale of the sonata, and I shall use it as a starting point: not only are melody and polyphony here reduced to a minimum, but there is an obstinate insistence on a single note unparalleled elsewhere in Chopin. The long passage occurs after the first part of the polonaise has ended on an F sharp minor cadence, and it serves as a transition to the middle section:

This is the greatest military passage in Chopin's Polonaises, although it is not the most famous (those in the Polonaises in A Major, op. 40, no. 1, and in A flat Major, op. 53, are better known). Chopin transformed the polonaise from a stately processional dance into an image of heroism, and even, in opus 53, into what might appear the representation of a cavalry charge—all this without recourse to what is generally called program music, the nonmusical elements in his Polonaises being no more and no less important than they are in a Haydn string quartet. Here, in opus 44, the effect is as purely percussive as any composer of the time had dared to write. The four thirty-second notes in each bar reproduce a snare-drum roll, and the eighth notes that follow at the end of the bar are written as hard timpani strokes (and Chopin directs that they be played without pedal throughout). The only dynamic mark is the initial *forte* and the accents on every first beat: it is clear that the dynamics should be *sempre forte* until the *poco a poco diminuendo* that begins in bar 117. In bars 103–110 the replaying of the second theme of the opening section should be *forte* and *sostenuto,* as it was marked on its first appearance, although the *sostenuto* implies a tone color of *cantabile.* Any attempt by the pianist to provide large contrasts of dynamics would be misguided: the *forte* need not be insensitive or uninflected, but it must be as relentless as the rhythm, or the *diminuendo* beginning at bar 117 would be spoiled. It is good to be reminded of how brutal Chopin's music could be; there are pages in the Etudes and the Scherzi that go even farther, but none that hammer away at one sound so fiercely.

It is precisely the obstinate repetition that makes the return of an earlier theme so effective: after twenty accented repetitions of an A, the G♯ which begins the theme in bar 103 comes not only as a relief but as an inevitable consequence. The continuous repetition of a note is the simplest way of turning it into a dissonance—that is, into a sound that must be resolved—and the most common classical form of resolution is a downward moving second, like an appoggiatura, in this case from A to G♯. The psychological effect of repetition had been understood before Chopin (by Handel, Haydn, and Beethoven in particular), but no one had exploited it on the scale we find here. The drop of a second to G♯, written as if all the registers had been taken down simultaneously, gives the impression that the twenty bars of A major were dissonant to the G♯, a kind of large-scale Neapolitan relationship. That this is an illusion is shown by the triumphant return to A major eight bars later, with the highest registers now taken up an octave. The return to A major is made both simple and convincing by the most banal sequential pattern derived from going around the circle of fifths (the bass line is the simple succession G♯–C♯–F♯–B–E–A):

This theme at bar 103 is designed, here and at its two previous appearances, to start with a shock: a drop of a second, initially unharmonized and then quickly explained as a 6/4 chord. Its second phrase begins (bar 107) not in 6/4

position but in the more stable root position, as the sequential bass movement
now takes priority and serves to lead directly back to the harmony which ended
the previous section. Its modulating character only reaffirms the stability of
the A major that precedes and follows.

There is nothing unusual in the technique of implying perfect four-part
harmony by means of a single line of music, as we see in the outer sections of
this quoted passage. It is part of the stock-in-trade of all composers since the
early eighteenth century: we find it not only in the solo flute sonatas of J. S.
Bach and in the caprices of Paganini, but also in any fugue theme. (Dozens of
arias in the operas and oratorios of Handel and other composers are monophonic, without continuo or figured bass; the effect was very popular early in
the eighteenth century.) In fact, one might say that the test of a great contra-
puntist is the ability to compose a single unaccompanied line that makes
harmonic sense. The successive notes of a tonal melody are dissonant or
consonant with respect to each other and to the tonic triad which is almost
invariably defined by the opening: in a well-formed melody the dissonances
are gracefully resolved into consonances as it proceeds. The opening of Bach's
Fugue in A Minor for Organ, BWV 543, provides a clear example:

The first bar defines the A minor triad; the dissonant note is the B, and it is
immediately resolved at the opening of bar 2 into the C; the initial A and the
low E in bar 1 are not only part of the soprano melody but provide a bass
line as well which gives the root positions of the harmony. From bar 3 the
four-part harmony is explicit. Bach himself notates a parallel voice later in two
parts:

The last six notes in the left hand may be expanded into four voices, and every
listener's understanding of this passage entails an instinctive acceptance of these
six notes as a simultaneous unit, just as we accept the successive plucked notes
of a chord played on a guitar or harp as a unit even after many of the notes
have ceased to resonate. Arpeggiated harmony is perhaps the most ancient
harmonic form, and arpeggiating the harmony by means of the melody is not

much more sophisticated. There is nothing very original about Chopin's exploitation of the technique as such in the F sharp Minor Polonaise.

More original is the electrifying moment at bar 95 when bass and soprano separate from one line into two. After twelve bars of a repeated A, the appearance of F♮ in the bass comes with great effect. We realize here that the pedal point on A is not primarily in the bass but in the treble, which continues to sustain it without change. The dissonance that this creates in bar 96 seems at first hearing willful and even arbitrary but—for this reason—extraordinarily powerful. Maintaining the A in the soprano against a B flat major chord is ruthless here: it makes no concessions to the listener's comfort, but this only increases the delight, even exhilaration, that comes from the rhythmic energy of this page.

Most radical of all, however, is Chopin's use of octave doubling and register. Each of the three motifs of the "monophonic" line is associated with a different registral timbre. In bar 112, for example,

the opening beat is sharply separated from the rest not only by accent but by octave quadrupling; it unites the highest and lowest registers. The motif in thirty-second notes uses the middle registers, and the three heavy staccato eighth notes that close the bar leap into the bass. Not only do the successive notes imply different voices united in one line, as in Bach, but each voice is given a distinct and individual instrumental sonority. This is emphasized when the upper registers are taken up an octave in bar 111. In spite of the displacements of register, the line remains unified by the somewhat neutral resonance of the piano, and by Chopin's indications of pedal. Nevertheless, we may say that Chopin has translated a standard classical technique into a novel conception of sound in which the registers are clearly distinguished.

Clear distinctions inevitably present a tempting opportunity for a play of ambiguity. We can see how Chopin exploits the ambiguity if we score the different motifs separately; this illuminates the separation of registers. Normally the dissonant harmony implied by one of the motifs is resolved within the next appearance of the same motif in the same register in the following bar: for example, the C♭ in bar 98 is resolved in the corresponding part of the same motif in the next bar with a C♮. But in bars 122 to 124 there is an exchange of register:

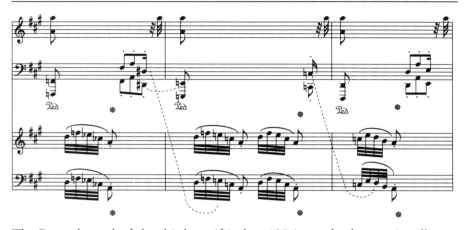

The D♯ at the end of the third motif in bar 122 is resolved exceptionally not by the C♮ at the end of bar 123 but by the E in the bass and tenor parts, and the low C♯'s at the end of bar 123 move into the B in 124 at the end of the group of thirty-second notes in the middle register. If Chopin had not characterized the different motifs of his line with such precision, this would pass without notice: here it gives the sense of one voice resolving another. In terms of standard polyphonic technique, Chopin's procedure is impeccably orthodox: it is his scoring that is original, the sound that is new.

The replacement of harmony by melody, therefore, is conservative, although the sonority is unprecedented. The replacement of some of the functions of melody by rhythm is considerably more startling. It is accomplished largely by the four-bar cadential structure of the harmony, and by this uncomplicated motif

which plays an important role in the structure. Bars 83 through 86 are an introductory phrase, which appears to be only an accompaniment: we do not at first realize that this accompaniment is almost all that we are going to get. The detail that is added in order to give the impression of melody is the tiny upbeat, a thirty-second note drum tap before bars 89, 91, 93, 95, 97, 99, 100, and 101—every two bars except at the end, when the rhythm goes twice as fast. Bar 87 initiates the pattern: although it has no upbeat, it gives the impression of a new beginning an octave higher after the four bars of introduction. The result is the following rhythm (notated with one bar for every four of the original):

Taken together with the changes of harmony, which contrive cadences to articulate the phrases at the right places, this gives the absolute minimum necessary for a correctly formed Romantic melody, a tune in proper symmetrical four-bar groups.

We must admire an economy of means which results in such extravagance. It works above all through the hypnotic effect of the unyielding repetition of note and rhythm. It is evidently intended as a bravura display of composition which requires an equally bravura execution from the pianist. Its brutality is justified by its place in the structure of the Polonaise: it is an interlude that stands between the tragic nobility and passion of the outer section and the lyrical trio that follows, the *Tempo di Mazurka* marked *sotto voce*. The Polonaise and trio are a simple ternary form, but the military interlude alters this in a way that is easy enough to appreciate but difficult to characterize with a vocabulary invented largely for eighteenth-century forms.

The military interlude itself is a ternary form, but only on paper: its middle section, a simple binary structure (two phrases, bars 103–110, modulating downward by whole steps), is placed between two playings of a theme that previously appeared nowhere in the Polonaise. This central section, however, does not act simply like the contrasting middle section of an *ABA* form: it enters as a resolution of the insistently repeated note A, and it leads by sequence directly back to this note. It links the interlude by quotation, to the opening section of the Polonaise. The military interlude as a whole is tied harmonically by its key of A Major to the mazurka trio, but it destroys much of the effect of contrast between polonaise and trio; it leads, after twenty-nine bars of unremitting *forte*, into the mazurka by a long diminuendo of ten bars, and seems to exhaust itself as it prepares the mazurka rhythm. It breaks up the ternary dance form with an extraneous element: it does not belong to the trio, the mazurka, as it contains a reminiscence from the opening dance as an essential element of its form; it is also outside the initial polonaise section, as it begins in a new key and with a strikingly different character after the initial polonaise has clearly ended.

The additive construction that dislocates an established form, the dramatic interruption with a brief but literal quotation of a phrase from an earlier section—the technique comes directly out of Chopin's experience of Italian opera. It may be compared to the way composers like Rossini, Donizetti, and Bellini broke up conventional forms, interrupting the traditional slow-fast sequence of the aria, for example, with a chorus or even an entire scene. This kind of interruption was itself a tradition in opera by Chopin's day, but he applied it to pure instrumental music with a dramatic force that was unprecedented. Violating a traditional form as it does, it has the significance and effect of program music, but we need no program to understand it musically. The interruption is so well integrated that, from a slightly longer perspective than the academic one, it creates a new and completely acceptable form. Unlike the classical forms, however, it is not easily reproducible: it can only be done once.

The completely monophonic finale of the Sonata in B flat Minor is so much
less radical than this Polonaise that it may be difficult at first to put one's finger
on just why Schumann and his contemporaries were shocked by it to the point
of considering it unmusical, although it is easy to understand why they were
fascinated. Formally it is a one-part invention, a *perpetuum mobile* in relatively
simple binary form. The first four bars are clearly an introduction on the
dominant of B flat minor:

and their harmonic outline recalls the opening four bars of the first movement:

The main theme that follows in bars 5 to 8 is chromatic, but bars 5 and 6
define the tonic and dominant:

The chromaticism becomes more insistent, but the harmony gradually defines
the dominant of the relative major with increasing clarity, and a new theme
enters in that key at bar 23 and is repeated an octave higher beginning at bar
27:

The dominant of B flat minor is then carefully prepared, in the most respectable Classical fashion, by its own dominant:

and the recapitulation begins with a literal replaying of bars 1–8 starting at bar 39. There are seventy-five bars of music in the whole movement, and bar 39 is close to the exact center.

The recapitulation of bars 11–30 is much more freely worked with elements of the transition and the "second theme" developed toward a cadence. For example, bars 63 and 64 clearly recall bars 23 and 27, as these are the only two examples of unbroken scale motion in the movement. Bars 17 and 18 are recalled in the inversion by bars 57 and 58, and bars 61 and 62. A coda on an implied dominant pedal begins at bar 65.

The parallelism of the two parts even extends to the phrase structure, which is all in four-bar groups except for one ambiguous two-bar phrase in both parts—ambiguous because in both cases it is unclear whether it is attached more closely to what precedes or to what follows. In the first half, bars 21 and 22 have this transitional role (bar 21 begins like bar 20, and bar 22 leads motivically to 23); in the second, the same function is taken over by bars 67 and 68, which complete 65 and 66 but are slurred with 69 and 70. This slur overrides a new phrase, which begins with the change of harmony at the opening of 69. The low F of bar 65 is to be interpreted as harmonically valid until bar 69 and even beyond—it is only resolved with the final *fortissimo*. The full force of the V–I cadence is undermined by what follows: the first tonic resolution is on a weak beat with only a bare fifth at the end of bar 68, and immediately falls into the unstable 6/4 position. Chopin's phrase mark (from bars 67 through 70) overrides (as so often) the rhythmic grouping, as 67 and 68 belong harmonically with 65 and 66, and a new harmonic group starts with 69; the composer was concerned to avoid too clear an articulation. The final cadence is clearly an anticipated tonic: the fundamental bass note is reached tentatively and inconclusively four times over on a weak beat in bars 72 to 74. Harmonically, however, the piece is ended by bar 73, and that makes the pedalled *fortissimo* of the last bar all the more brutal.

This kind of binary "sonata" form without development was very common from 1750 to 1800, and after that it continued to appear frequently in opera overtures, including most of those by Rossini and Berlioz. It might be best called cavatina form because it is the normal basis for the outer sections of a *da capo* aria (an aria without middle section and no *da capo* was called a *cavatina* in the eighteenth century). Few of the other elements of Chopin's finale were uncommon in the 1830s, including Chopin's rich chromaticism, which can easily be paralleled in works of other contemporaries like Louis Spohr. What was disconcerting then, and is still somewhat disconcerting today, is the uncompromising, almost austere way that Chopin realized the musical idea, and the speed with which the dissonances implied by the single line move past.

The rhythm is unrelenting, with nothing set in relief; the sonority is *sotto voce* and legato throughout, with almost no dynamic emphasis; a complicated chromaticism is worked out in implied three- and four-part harmony entirely by means of one doubled monophonic line; and the tempo is *presto*—the movement goes by like lightning. All this makes the music difficult for the listener to grasp in spite of the traditional clarity of structure.

The finale is popularly supposed to represent the wind sweeping over the graves of the cemetery after the departure of the funeral procession. This was a view that at least one contemporary interpreter, Liszt, rejected with indignation; he remarked on hearing Anton Rubinstein's performance of this sonata (which, as described by Moriz Rosenthal, resembled Rachmaninoff's recording—obviously a Russian tradition) that it was the unfortunate result of imposing a literary reading on pure music. The effect of wind over the graves is generally achieved with a heavy wash of pedal: Rosenthal, however, who had studied with Chopin's pupil Mikuli and with Liszt, claimed that this movement should be played entirely without pedal, except in the final bar. Chopin's indications of pedal are very often heavy, but he directs pedal here only in the last measure (it is interesting, too, that there are no signs for the pedal in the *Marche Funèbre* until measure 11, which implies an opening that is somewhat dry and withdrawn). It should be added, nevertheless, that wind is traditionally represented in music by the kind of rapid chromatic motion found in the finale, but in any case Chopin always repudiated programmatic interpretations of his works, and there is no reason to think he would have made an exception for this movement.

The great art of the Romantic generation was to imply the existence of a program without realizing the details in any specifically extramusical sense. The emotional power of this finale is evident enough: the sense of terror and anguish after the funeral march is too apt to require any material detail for support. The power comes from the density of the writing, the refusal of Chopin to make any compromise for the comfort of the listener, to afford any relief from the continuous *pianissimo,* the extreme velocity, the swift changes of harmony that must be caught by the ear through the movement of a single line. The intensity, the extraordinary demands made on the listener's concentration, are hypnotic.

Implying three- or four-part polyphony with one line inevitably produces certain ambiguities in voice leading. Part of the effectiveness of this finale rests on Chopin's genius in exploiting these contrapuntal ambiguities. He does this

with slight variations of pattern in the figuration: these variations go by so
quickly that the listener seizes their import a split second after they have
disappeared. The delay in full understanding is inherent in the form. The single
line sustains nothing but only suggests: confirmation of the harmonic sense is
always slightly late. Chopin carried the technique of suggestion further than
any other composer, but even the uneducated listener grasps the meaning. For
example, in bars 13 to 16:

The harmonic sense of all the details in the first bar is immediately obvious,

and the remaining notes, E♮ and G♭/F♯, are subsidiary, either appoggiaturas to
the F or, with the final F♯ in the bar, a passing note to the G♮ in the next bar.
Bar 14 appears identical to the previous one, only transposed up a whole tone,
but the harmonic sense is very different because of what succeeds. The F♯ and
A♭ are subsidiary to the G♮, or seem so at first—but the final A♭ in the bar is
not a passing note; it is the initiation of the harmony of the next bar, and it
attracts the harmonic weight to itself. The harmonic sense becomes:

On the final beat of bar 14 the G♮ is devalued by the new sense conferred on
the A♭ by the following bar, and in consequence the F♯ in an accented position
on the fourth beat gains in importance, since it too is no longer felt as an
appoggiatura to the G—but this is sensed only in retrospect. The new significance of the F♯ is confirmed, however, by the two following bars, at the end
of which it has become the main element in the bass line:

There is no difficulty in grasping Chopin's procedure intuitively (every pianist
gives a little extra weight to the final A♭ of bar 14, partly because the figuration

requires it, and the expressive potential of the F♯ is sometimes realized with the proper delicacy); but to describe it, one must understand that its basis is a simple harmonic progression, rather like the realization of a figured bass in Bach (or like a Schenkerian graph of the middle ground), which is expressively ornamental and projected over the whole range of the keyboard.

The flickering sense, momentarily indeterminate, of harmonic change which gives this movement its sinister, repressed excitement comes from the technique of suggestion, realized retrospectively (although the delay is always slight): it is reinforced by the sotto voce sonority, the speed, and the absence of accent. The harmonic meaning is in the end almost always completely determined, rarely left ambiguous. In bars 61 to 63,

we may be initially unsure whether 61 is meant to be interpreted—played and heard—as:

An ear accustomed to tonal music will search out the simplest triadic explanation. Bar 62 tells us, however, that the G♭ is the sustained note in the harmony throughout both bars, and that we are to hear:

or, with more detail:

It may seem astonishing to be able to suggest so much harmony with slight variations in simple scale passages, although, as I have said, Chopin is extending a long tradition. Repetition clearly plays an important role in determining the basic harmony, along with the high and low limits of the figuration. The relation of a note to the beat is another factor, and Chopin obtains interesting effects in this passage by placing the high and low voices on the strongest and weakest beats, respectively: the upper line on the beginning of the first and third beats, the lower on the end of the second and fourth (no pianist can resist setting the bass line here in relief, either by a light accent or a slight rubato, or by sustaining the note into part of the next triplet). In the end, the traditional system of academic counterpoint—rules of dissonance and its correct resolution to consonance—determines how we hear the harmony. Even when we do not know the rules, our ears have been trained by three centuries of melodies created to be harmonized according to the rules, and their existence is always implied by the flow and the articulation of the melodies.

There are places where a momentary ambiguity is exploited with great richness, most strikingly in bars 5 to 8 (page 294). The basic harmony is:

but in bar 7 the figuration clearly emphasizes two subsidiary chords:

which act upon the main harmonic movement like chromatic grace notes. All the dissonant notes are resolved correctly, but the intricacy of the chromatic movement is so great that the dissonant notes in different voices tend to form new harmonies with each other that momentarily delight the ear as they superimpose themselves on the fundamental progression.

As we have observed, the most banal way of indicating polyphony with a monophonic line is with an arpeggio or an arpeggiated figure: the Alberti bass is only the best-known form (probably because it was christened while many others remained anonymous). Chopin took over from Bach the craft of doing the same thing with scale passages; with the chromatic development of his harmony he achieved an even greater richness. In some respects he went further than his master in giving polyphonic life to the arpeggio. Take bars 9 to 12 of the finale:

Bars 11 and 12 seem almost identical to 9 and 10, but the harmonic rhythm is faster and the harmony more dissonant. The arpeggios are arranged to imply bass and soprano lines which are parallel but out of phase. It is this delayed parallelism which creates the dissonance, as we wait for the resolution. The first two bars, therefore, produce:

which outlines differently the descent of a minor third in both voices, and the difference makes us aware of two lines and creates the clashes at the end of bar 9 and beginning of 10. Here the upper line is resolved against the lower, and consonance is reestablished throughout. Not so in bars 11 and 12, which give a different reading of the two voices:

The descent is now enlarged to a fourth, the harmonic rhythm accelerates, and the clash is a movement of minor ninths only the last of which is resolved: it is a simple chromatic scale given a strange dissonant cast by shifts from one register to another. Chopin exemplifies in this passage one of the great lessons of Bach's counterpoint: not only can many voices be produced out of one, but one can be produced out of many. What we had just previously been forced to accept in bars 9 and 10 as two voices (soprano and bass) now turns back into a single line in bar 11. The swift, shadowy touches of dissonance give this passage an uneasy harshness which, even softened by a performance that is truly *sotto voce,* can still astonish today.

I have started with these "monophonic" pieces because they reveal with great clarity two of the most impressive aspects of Chopin's art: the projection of a single line over different registers with an unprecedented play of sonority and tone color, and the creation of individual lines in the inner parts and the bass of such great expressive power that every part of the texture of his music seems alive. These two aspects are, in fact, the opposing faces of the same coin: the reinvention of Classical counterpoint, its reconception in terms of Romantic color.

Narrative form: the ballade

We find a similar transformation of Classical counterpoint in music of more "normal" aspect, the opening bars of the Ballade in A flat Major, op. 47, for example:

This is a single eight-bar melody divided into simple two-bar groups: it starts in the upper voice and then moves to the tenor register an octave below in bar 3, and acts as a bass to the harmony; it then moves down again an octave in bar 5, and returns to the soprano in bar 7. The subtlety of the procedure is most evident at the last shift from bar 6 to 7: the E♭ in the upper voice has already been sounded as an accompaniment to the melody in the bass at the end of bar 6, and it becomes a melody note only in retrospect as the upper voice takes over the exposition. This is a technique that Chopin learned, I think, from those fugues of J. S. Bach where one sometimes finds the initial note of the fugue subject tied to the previous note of the episode. These passages would have struck an early nineteenth-century performer as problematical in a way incomprehensible to a contemporary of Bach: performance was by Chopin's time geared to making a work effective and completely intelligible to a listener. Chopin, indeed, makes Bach's procedure here unusually effective: the upper voice rises naturally out of the sonority of the previous chord. The importance of the E♭ is, in fact, prepared: the whole of these eight bars is a pedal point on E♭, starting with the inner voice in the first bar and shifting an octave below and then above in the second. There are only the briefest of passing moments in this phrase where an E♭ is not either struck or still sounding. The shift of the pedal point from one register to another is as characteristic of Chopin's thought as the shift of the melody or principal voice.

The displacement of registers is even greater at the next appearance of the melody a page later, reaching over more than six octaves, or almost the full length of the keyboard:

The bars that lead to this return dwell for a long time on the C major chord that will dominate the next section, and they are a brilliant example of a special kind of illusory counterpoint typical of the Romantic period: the heterophonic accompaniment, in which both principal and secondary voices outline the same motif, but out of phase with each other. Here, the left-hand phrase

reappears in different form in the right hand:

The effect is not one of canon or imitation but of the simultaneous playing of a clearly defined simple phrase and its freely decorated, fluid form, the decoration displaced upward over three octaves and then gracefully descending into the lowest bass. The opening theme then leaps with its first note from bass to treble, as it comes out of the chromatic ascent in bar 36, returns to the bass in bar 41 with part of its initial motif as a counterpoint in the soprano (bars 43–44), and then rises as high (bar 47) and falls as low (bar 48) as Chopin's piano would allow.

These changes of register are not simply a fanciful play of sonority but are essential to the conception of the melody, which cannot be played effectively throughout in the same register. Each one of its four two-bar phrases is based on the same motif, a simple sixth Eb/C, played in varied forms. Heard always in the same register, this motif would be intolerable, and the melody is formed by its displacement. It appears first as a rising scale:

then as a descent:

once more in its initial form as a rising scale, and finally in varied form in bars 7 and 8:

The subsequent themes in this Ballade are derived from this opening sixth.

In bar 2, a second motif appears, equally simple:

I have quoted this falling second where it is used as a counterpoint in bars 43 and 44. It appears relentlessly in the left hand in every bar from 9 to 25:

It is also implied by the right hand in bars 10–11, 14–15, 19, and elsewhere. This motif is generally heard as coming after the sixth,

not so much in this way:

as:

The falling second has, naturally, less of an independent existence in this work than the various ways of outlining the sixth, which play a more fundamental role.

The opening of this passage (bars 9–10) shows a melodic line constructed by what appears to be two independent voices, as what we hear is (reduced to one line and one register):

That we are intended to hear these two voices as a unity is made clear when the motif is varied a few bars later:

It is true that many of Chopin's melodies fit into the space defined by these two motifs.

Two examples from the Nocturnes can be given:

and this contour may be considered typical of Chopin's style. Nevertheless, the consistency of the thematic relationships in this Ballade is very remarkable— the two motifs are repeated almost obsessively throughout—and it is to be expected that such consistency should have been achieved with a type of melody most congenial to him.

The second section of the Ballade changes to F major; it has three themes, all derived from the initial motif. First the motif of the sixth is inverted in two different ways, B^1 and B^2:

A third theme, C^1, projects the sixth over several octaves[4] after a magical change of harmony, a return to the original tonality of A flat major:

and this theme is immediately transformed by a variation, C^2:

4. In *The Chopin Companion* (London, 1966), pp. 236–239, Alan Walker gives a detailed analysis of the motifs in the opening pages but omits any reference to their transformation in what follows, except for bars 115–123. He considers the motif of the sixth only in its original form from E♭ to C, and does not admits its transpositions. This insistence on a fixed pitch for the motif possibly arises from a Schenkerian approach, and it should be admitted that the original form naturally plays a slightly more influential role in the larger structure than the transposed variants. The importance of the transposition to the original form, however, becomes crucial in the later development from bars 183 on, as we shall see, and it is upon the equivalence of the original and transposed forms that the preparation of the final climax depends.

Chopin directed the initial E♭ of the grace note arpeggio at the opening of bar 116 to be played on the beat together with the left hand. This makes the change from E♮ to E♭ an exquisite effect, and it emphasizes the motif, as the arabesque sweeps up from E♭ to C and then returns gracefully downward: the left hand expressively echoes the motif in bar 117. This passage, more than anything else in the Ballade, discloses to us Chopin's transformation of contemporary salon style into a purely instrumental version of bel canto coloratura, and he surpassed both his sources of inspiration.

This extraordinary moment of return to the tonic A flat major with a theme that is apparently new and yet related to everything that has gone before will repay our lingering over it for a moment—just as almost every pianist will pull back the tempo slightly here (he is almost forced to do so by Chopin's arpeggiated opening) in order to let the new sonority expand. The return to A flat seems unprepared and yet perfectly convincing: there is less a sense of surprise than of fulfillment. Part of this sense derives from Chopin's art of dwelling insistently and hypnotically so long on one harmony that the change comes as a relief and seems inevitable—a characteristic we have observed less delicately employed in the F sharp Minor Polonaise. Although bars 54 to 114 of the Ballade remain throughout in the key of F, and begin and end in the major, there are no F major cadences anywhere. There are three F *minor* cadences in the center of this section, all placed with a certain rhythmic ambiguity, but it is the half cadence on the C major dominant of F that insistently returns—ten times in all, generally over a pedal point on C, and with the C major chord obsessively repeated. (This obsessive concentration on a C major chord has already provided the climax to the opening pages from bars 29 to 36, leading directly back to A flat, as in bar 115.) When the repeated C is reinterpreted in bar 116 over an A flat chord, we seem to be returning from an unresolved, unstable section to the more firm ground of the opening pages:

The enchanting sense of fulfillment of this moment of return at bar 115 depends, too, on Chopin's mastery of polyphonic movement. The E♮ of the C major chord descends to become the E♭ of the opening motif of the sixth; but that is not the end of the story. It then rises in the inner voice for the E♮ to return as an F♭. This inner voice is easy to trace, as it continues on its way:

Other polyphonic relations sustain the impression of absolute continuity, a closely knit web of kaleidoscopically changing harmony. We are not always aware of all of these different voices at once, but if one of them becomes the bearer of harmonic significance, we hear instantly where it has come from and where it is going.

Another factor that makes the return to A flat major at bar 115 so stable is the contrast with the ambiguity of phrase rhythm in the previous long section from bar 54 to 116, where right and left hands are consistently out of phase—so much so, in fact, that it is sometimes not clear for a moment precisely where the phrases begin. This blurred contour produces a delicate set of fleeting harmonic nuances lit by the half light of *mezza voce:*

The bass begins on the first beat in bar 54, but the right hand is briefly delayed, and at the opening of the next bar it has still not resolved its dominant chord while the left hand is already sounding the tonic. There is a play between strong and weak measures, accented and unaccented downbeats, which is very subtle, lending itself to different nuances in performance, but which is firmly controlled by the underlying structure.

This play is signalled by an arithmetic anomaly: the theme which begins on an even-numbered bar at 54 returns at an odd-numbered bar at 105. This means that one bar is missing from one of the four-bar groups which are otherwise in force throughout the work. The first time I noticed this, I was puzzled because the phrase rhythm does not, in fact, appear to be irregular. We are not conscious of an alteration of the four-bar period, which seems to flow without a break. It is worth going into the way in which Chopin can impose upon an anomaly a convincing impression of regularity. The details may seem complex, but the principles are extremely simple, and they are fundamental to Chopin's mastery.

As we have seen, the left hand starts its four-bar group on the first of the six beats of bars 54 and 58, while the right starts its period two beats later, and finishes its four-bar groups on the downbeats of 58 and 62, where the bass (or left hand) is already starting a new group. The conclusion of the right-hand group coincides with the commencement of the left-hand group. The pivot is found in bars 62 to 73. Bar 65 begins a new four-bar group in the bass, while the right hand now dramatically begins not two beats later but almost a full bar later with the upbeat to bar 66. In other words, the right hand continues the initial four-bar grouping, but the left hand has moved ahead: the displacement is all the more convincing because the left hand was already slightly ahead at the outset; the right hand begins its melody after the bar line in bar 54 and bar 58, but then anticipates the downbeat from bars 66 on, and this makes the development so smooth. The shift in the bass is prepared in bars 57 and 61, which foreshadow the strong downbeat effect of bars 73 and 81.

The right hand joins the new articulation of the bass at bar 73. Soprano and bass are suddenly in phase for a moment, and the transition is made beautifully smooth by the syncopated melodic shape of bars 70 and 71, where the principal melodic line begins in the middle of bar 70, and is displaced from the right into the left hand in bars 71 and 72. The effect is already prepared by bars 67 and 69, where the movement of the bass shifts the weight of the downbeat to the second half of the bar, and once again the right conforms to the left only later in bar 70. The passage could be notated:

The displacement is first contrapuntal and then monophonic, as one voice disappears into the other after they meet in an octave G: this is complex only on paper, but sounds wonderfully straightforward in performance. The weight given here to different bars inside each four-bar period is supple and varied.[5] What continually shifts is the emphasis within the period. We may compare bars 81 and 85–86 to see clearly the shift of emphasis from odd- to even-numbered bar.

The interplay between harmony and melody is very sophisticated. Bars 65 and 81 have a strong downbeat only in the bass, a new beginning in the left hand, while in the right there is a graceful rounding-off of the end of the melody. The new strong beginnings of the melodic phrase are at the upbeats to bars 66 and 82, where, however, the bass accents are weaker; a further new melodic attack is the middle of 86, which displaces the emphasis more radically. This ebb and flow of accent and its sensitive displacement from one part of the period to another, and the out-of-phase interweaving of harmonic rhythm and melodic structure, give this passage a wonderfully fluid atmosphere, a sense of floating which fits so perfectly with the rhythm of the barcarole.

The large-scale movement may be summed up: the bass anticipates a new four-bar period at 65, overlapping by one bar with the old one; the treble continues the old period until 73, when it conforms to the bass. These phrases are then repeated more intensely starting at bar 81. In short, a strong underlying continuity is varied on the surface with a subtle overlapping system of phrasing. Among his contemporaries Chopin is the supreme master of phrase rhythm, and he brings a smooth surface to an underlying passionate agitation.

The extraordinary tranquillity of the return to A flat major in bar 116, its sense of breadth, comes from the sudden disappearance of all this elaborate dovetailing. Treble and bass are now in phase; the four-bar period is untroubled. Chopin was unique among the composers of his generation in his mastery of large-scale rhythm, his ability to vary rhythmic textures and to make them correspond to long-range harmonic movement. Here he moves almost imperceptibly and with no effort from tension to stability. There is, however, no resolution of the tension, only a momentary turning away from it. The texture becomes, in fact, more complex, more brilliant, and more unsettled. Full resolution is postponed until the last page.

The tension of this inner section, bars 50 to 115, comes from something more than the rhythmic instability or from the move away from the tonic A flat. The music shifts from A flat major to F major at bar 54, but, as I have

5. Bars 58 to 62 may be considered a five-bar phrase in the right hand, followed by three bars (63–65). Bars 66 to 70 form an irregular four-and-a-half bar shape, although Chopin's slur (end of bar 69 to middle of 71) overrides this and insists on the periodic rhythm. When the passage returns at bar 86, the pedal (middle of 85 to middle of 86) plays the role of a slur, but it is even more evident here that a new phrase begins in the middle of bar 86. Bars 86 to 88, indeed, expand and intensify the motif of the falling sixth of bars 82 and 83.

said, there is nowhere from bar 54 to 115 (or, indeed, anywhere else in the work) a cadence on F major: there is nothing but half cadences on the dominant of F until the arrival at F minor, which remains in force from bar 65 to 102, when F major returns, but still only with a resolution to the dominant. Since Chopin tends to treat A flat major and F minor as the same key, we might say that until bar 145, more than half the length of the Ballade, there is no modulation at all, merely a series of shifts of mode.

Every shift is accomplished by a two-bar repetition of an octave C, heard either as the dominant of F or the mediant of A flat. This recurrent pattern acts like a refrain between successive stanzas of a verse narrative. Here are the different points:

a)

b) 62

c) 102

d) 111

Each of these moments is less a modulation than a reharmonization of the C, which remains fixed as the end point of all the different versions of the basic motif. The sense of forward movement starts up again only when this presentation had been finished. This is the point of greatest difference between Chopin's forms and those of his Classical predecessors, for whom the exposition of material required not merely contrast but a clear heightening of tension. Chopin delays this large-scale increase of tension until all the thematic material has been heard, just as he delays resolution until the last possible moment.

A new departure occurs at the end of themes C^1 and C^2 in the tonic, and it sounds as if the second section were simply to be repeated at the subdominant D flat major with the theme I have called B^1:

The first thirty-three bars of the second section are indeed repeated at the subdominant in this way,[6] although with the arrival of B^2 and the minor mode, a more agitated obbligato is added in the bass:

6. Gerald Abraham, who gives a cursory and appreciative summary of the work, seems to think that bars 146 to 178 are in A flat rather than D flat and not to have noticed that this "development" is a strict and undeviating variation of bars 54 to 86; see *Chopin's Musical Style* (London, 1939), p. 108. Abraham's "gigantic sequence through B major, C, D, and E flat" that follows bar 178 is a series of dominant pedals, and the keys are, of course, respectively E, F, G, and A flat. It is astonishing how even the finest writers lose their wits at moments when confronted with Chopin.

This new texture already gives something of the character of a development to the reexposition at the subdominant, and at bar 178 a development section starts in earnest, with all the earmarks of the Classical development: sequential modulation, fragmentation and recombination of themes, increase of dramatic tension. It ends, too, like so many of Mozart's and Beethoven's developments, with a pedal point on the dominant that leads back to the triumphant playing of the main theme.

The relation of the two principal themes which begin the first and second sections of the Ballade is clarified by this development: the kinship of A and B^1 is neither fortuitous nor an effect of the composer's unconscious. Chopin wants us to know that B^1 is the inversion of A:

Here the opening theme *A* appears to grow almost organically out of *B*^{1}, and the triumphant return of *A* in the original key at the end is made to seem inevitable. The relationship of *A* and *B* is the material of the rising sequence which leads to the return of the tonic. The development draws the two opening sections together, and the final return completes the synthesis.

This return is so idiosyncratic as to defeat our vocabulary of analysis. We have no term handy to describe it: it is neither a Classical recapitulation nor a return of *A* in a ternary or *ABA* form. The opening section of the Ballade is fifty-two bars long: at the end of the work, only eight bars of it return, this time played *fortissimo,* followed by ten bars of development and stretto which lead triumphantly to the theme of the middle section I have called *C,* played at a faster tempo and concluding with a brilliant cadence. Throughout the return of *A* the tension of the previous dominant pedal is partially sustained, and a full sense of resolution comes, in fact, only with the arrival at *C* in bar 231. The abridgment of *C* is as drastic as that of *A;* only four bars are needed.

To make the synthesis complete, the truncated version of *C* is succeeded by a final reminiscence of section *A* in conclusion; the ultimate version of the opening motif

in bars 237 and 239 derives from the passage in the first section, bars 29–32, and bars 235–236 from 35 (see pp. 303–304). The brevity of this final section, the radical shortening of both themes, and the synthesis of the opening and middle section of the Ballade make these last pages not so much an orthodox return as the climax of the long development that preceded it (even if we consider the return of *C,* with the new tempo of *più mosso,* as a coda). In many respects, the conception of form that this reveals is original with Chopin, and he was to vary this formula later in some of the greatest works, notably the Polonaise-Fantaisie and the Barcarolle.

The form of the A flat Ballade may be summed up roughly, and it will show us how the reprise of B^1 and B^2 is dovetailed with the stretto:

Bars 1–52	1. Opening section	Theme A	A flat major
52–65	2. a) Second section	Theme B^1	F major
65–104		Theme B^2	F minor
105–115		Theme B^1	F major
116–145	b) Variation or return?	Theme C	A flat major
146–156	3. Third section	Theme B^1	D flat major
156–178	Variation	Theme B^2	C sharp major
178–212	Development, stretto, and retransition	Themes B^1 and A	Rising bass and domi-nant pedal
213–221	4. Conclusion	Theme A	A flat major
222–230	Short development and stretto		Dominant pedal
231–240	Piu mosso	Theme C (brief reference to opening and final cadence)	A flat major

Although this form cannot be described either as ternary or as sonata, it clearly borrows from both. Its originality lies above all in placing a development section so close to the end, as well as in the revolutionary telescoping of the final tonic area, and the masterly combination of themes from opening and middle sections. Maximum tension is placed very near the end, and final resolution is powerfully compressed. It is significant, too, that the dominant of A flat plays no large-scale structural role except for the dominant pedal point that starts just before the return and continues through it (in bars 205–230), and that the dominant of F minor is substituted for it at crucial moments with wonderfully dramatic effect. This implies that some important aspects of Classical harmony have been cast aside, along with Classical proportions.

The anomalous role of bars 116 to 145 (theme C) shows how irrelevant the Classical categories of form have become for Chopin. Thematically these bars cannot be adequately described as either a new theme or a varied form of the opening theme. This ambiguity may, indeed, be derived from Classical technique, but it is puzzling because of the harmony: in a Classical work the return to the tonic generally implies the reappearance of previous material in its original form, and these bars, at once novel and familiar, are disconcerting. The harmonic ambiguity of the tonic here is profoundly un-Classical: the return to A flat major at bar 116 is both unprepared and too early for the proportions of the work—too early because unprepared; on the other hand, the spectacular final return at bar 213, this one massively prepared, is too late in Classical terms for a form that has only 242 bars. It makes one realize that the first return to A flat at bar 116 was not a return at all because there had been no true departure. As I have remarked, the second section (from bars 52 to 115) does not really leave the tonic, since Chopin (like many of his contemporaries) tended to treat a major key and its relative minor (A flat major and F minor in this instance) as the same tonality. Chopin's long-range vision becomes manifest when we reflect that he sustains interest for 145 bars without any real change of key, and follows this with the genuine modulations and the complex chromatic movements that precede the return of A flat and the extraordinarily intense combination of all sections of the work in the final pages. The music gathers momentum slowly, like a story that takes its time getting under way. Until the great swell of excitement and intensity in the last third of the Ballade, there are only fluctuations of intensity, waves of lyric passion that break up and come together again.

The fusion of narrative and lyric in the Ballades is perhaps Chopin's greatest achievement: he realized in music one of the major ambitions of the Romantic poets and novelists. It is largely for this reason that Classical criteria of form apply so awkwardly to the Ballades, although we cannot entirely dismiss them as the composer was still working with them, or, more interestingly, against them. The Ballades are in narrative form but without a program: if there ever was a program that inspired them (they have been said to be based on poems by Adam Mickiewicz, but this is very doubtful), it is no longer relevant for their understanding. There is no narrative sense of opposition and developing struggle: the narrative form is filled by a lyric content. The movement of the Ballades is that of a story (an old story in verse with a refrain), but there are no events, only elegiac expression. This was Chopin's individual solution to the pseudo-problem of Romantic program music that Schumann, Liszt, and Berlioz fretted over.

*   *   *

The third Ballade avoids both the clear-cut dramatic opposition of sonata style and the conventional balance of ternary form. The ambiguities are essential to its sense of narrative flow. It is structured not by harmonic events or by thematic contrast but by fluctuations of sentiment, by variations of intensity. These are conveyed by variations of texture, sonority, and periodic phrasing; furthermore, these variations are not highly articulated as in sonata style but apparently continuous. In the Classical sonata a new section starts from the unresolved tension of the previous one: the so-called second group generally resolves a half-cadence on V of V; the development is a response to the opposition of tonic and dominant established by the exposition. In Chopin's Ballades, however, the end of one section is relaxed but incomplete: what follows does not contrast with it but grows out of it. We find ourselves at bar

146 in a reprise of B^1, the subdominant, without any break in continuity, and a complex development and retransition follow without our being able to say just at what point they begin. (The only decisive break is at the end of the first section at bar 52, and Chopin in one version directs the pianist to carry over the pedal for several bars into the second section.) There may be no story to the A flat Ballade, but there is the growth of urgency and intensity that properly accompanies the telling of a tale as we move from the simple phrase groups of the opening to the interlocking out-of-phase periods of the second section. It is, however, less the extraordinary continuity of the movement that is so impressive than the lyricism, the effect of continuous song. Even the few passages of brilliant figuration sustain and prolong an uninterrupted melody. The lyrical sense depends on the continuity both of the periodic phrase structure and of the polyphonic web. A genuinely conservative technique made possible the revolutionary innovation of the synthesis of narrative and lyrical expression.

It is clear that we must take the title Ballade seriously: an antique verse narrative in stanzas with a refrain. In his creation of the genre as an instrumental form, Chopin interpreted it much more freely than Brahms was later to do, in whose ballades the archaic effect of stanza and refrain is more literally indicated. Chopin's form is the Romantic ballade, modern in conception although influenced by the medieval originals: Brahms's is more thoroughly neo-Gothic. Chopin's genius was, above all, to have conceived of imitating with an instrument not a particular narrative but the technique of ballad narration: the formal periods and the refrain and the sense of story that overrides these formal divisions with increasing tension—as if he were carrying out Hegel's characterization of music as formal structure with indeterminate content. The ballade is a sung narration, and throughout all of his Ballades, Chopin retains a feeling for a continuous, uninterrupted flow of repetitive melody that he almost never employs in other large works like the Scherzos and the Polonaises—with the exception of the Barcarolle and the Polonaise-Fantaisie, which might almost be called fifth and sixth Ballades. (Both the Polonaise-Fantaisie and Barcarolle, in fact, never lose their essential genre character, but they take over from the third Ballade the wonderful conception of the final pages as a concentrated synthesis of the first and second parts: an excessively abbreviated return of the first theme followed by a triumphal apotheosis of an important melody from the second section, now appearing in the tonic.)

It is in the first two Ballades that the sense of an old story and the technique of refrain appear most clearly. After the opening page the main theme of the Ballade no. 1 in G Minor never reappears completely, and the first four bars alone come back as a refrain; the theme itself already has something of a refrain structure in the simple repetition of its opening figure. Above all there is the sense of a formal opening of a narrative:

The formality is inflected by the subtle relationship between the two motifs that make up the melody: an arpeggiated figure and a sigh. They start almost as separate contrasting entities and draw gradually closer together. The first motif completes with a tonic cadence the imperfect half cadence that precedes:

The second motif

makes an answer like a new beginning, and is itself resolved by the last notes of the first motif:

For the first five bars the two remain relatively independent; in bars 14 to 16 they draw together:

Until bar 15 the second motif has always been phrased separately: here it is explicitly joined to the first. In bar 14 the first motif begins for the first and only time on the beat, so that no pause divides it from what precedes. The two motifs act at first as if they had been assigned to different voices, which are then fused into a single line: the change of phrasing of bar 15 imposes a new color and demands a new touch. The expression is more intense, but it is once again resolved by the opening figure:

The changes in phrasing set the descending scale into relief:

The motifs are separated by leaps at the opening, and then shaped into an absolute continuity. This increasing continuity of phrasing is a very up-to-date version of a basic classical pattern in which the second part of a phrase, made up of shorter motivic groups than the first, is put together with greater continuity and intensity. A good example of the standard procedure is Chopin's second theme (quoted in Chapter 1, p. 23), comparable in this respect to the practice of the preceding age: in the first theme the increase of intensity and continuity are similar, but the technique is incomparably more subtle and elegant.

A cadential theme to conclude this opening section of the G Minor Ballade gives us a beautiful example of Chopin's heterophonic polyphony, in which two apparently separate voices outline in different rhythms the same motif (derived from the second motif of the main theme), an operatic sob:

That is:

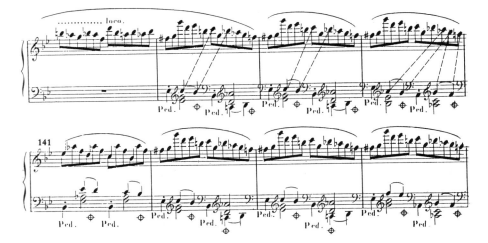

This reappears later in much more complex form:

I have marked the out-of-phase parallel octaves, emphasized by Chopin himself in bar 141 by the extra stems in the right hand, and should add that the right hand arpeggiates the harmony of the left but finishes its arpeggiation only when the left has gone on to a new chord.

The form of the G Minor Ballade is as innovative as that of the A flat, if somewhat less refined.[7] A short outline should make clear its originality:

Introduction (Largo)

Theme I^A (Moderato) *(piano)*   } G minor

Cadential Theme I^B (*piano* and then *forte agitato*)

Transition and development (*sempre più mosso*
   forte, then *calando*)

---

7. Gerald Abraham (see ibid., p. 54) thinks that "even the most enthusiastic admirers of Chopin would hardly claim that [the G Minor Ballade] is a masterpiece of form." Why not? He seems to object to a development that "consists rather of variation and improvisation than 'true development.'" I have no idea what "true development" can mean here, but am sure that it would not be an improvement on Chopin.

Theme II^A (*meno mosso,* Tempo I) *(pianissimo)*	
Cadential Theme II^B *(sempre pianissimo)*	E flat major
Theme I^A abridged, as refrain *(pianissimo, crescendo)*	A minor
Theme II^A *(fortissimo)*	A major
Transition *(sempre più animato)*	
Theme I^B varied *(scherzando)*	E flat major
Transition and development	
Theme II^A *(fortissimo)*	
Theme II^B *(fortissimo)*	E flat major
Theme I^A as refrain *(pianissimo, crescendo)*	
Cadence *(il più forte possibile)*	G minor
Presto con fuoco, new thematic material	

Even such a schematic presentation makes evident some unexpected aspects, above all the crucial role of dynamics in Chopin's conception of form. There are two groups of themes, both initially presented softly; the sections that follow combine the two groups in a novel way. The climaxes, both *fortissimo,* are provided by the second group, first in A major—with a surprising relation of a tritone to the surrounding E flat—and then again in E flat major. The themes of group 1 only reappear abridged and varied: Theme I^A acts as a ritornello, or, as I have said, a refrain; it returns twice not only shortened but also both times over a dominant pedal. It is typical of Chopin's third conception of form that this refrain should act as a transition. At its last appearance, it leads to an enormous climax *(il più forte possibile)* but only with new melodic material just before the coda, itself made up of new motifs.

The coda in fast tempo, created entirely of material that makes no reference to the main body of the work, is at once innovative and traditional. It is inspired by the operatic stretto, the concluding fast section of an ensemble: it stays entirely in the tonic and provides a brilliant conclusion with new themes to the slower music that precedes it. Chopin's coda is wonderfully orchestral in conception, with something like an accompanied recitative towards the end in an alternating *ritenuto-accelerando* rhythm. Chopin found this coda form with new thematic material exceptionally useful, and he employed it again in the second and fourth Ballades, the first and third Scherzi, and the Barcarolle.

Also operatic in origin is the structure of both groups of themes. It is easy to find prototypes for Theme I with its cadential theme and perhaps even easier for Themes II^A and II^B in contemporary Italian operas, including those of

Bellini, whose music Chopin is known to have admired. Both groups correspond to verse patterns often found in opera libretti, and the expansion of the end of I^A with its beautiful cadenza into I^B is directly modelled on operatic practice. This influence goes some way towards explaining Chopin's ability, unique among instrumental composers, to sustain melodies at great length. In this he was the equal of Bellini, and the borrowings from the Italian stage make the G Minor Ballade the most operatic of the four, the most overtly melodramatic.

*   *   *

The exquisite opening melody of the second Ballade owes nothing to the opera aria. It arrives as if from a distant past, and, in its repetitive simplicity and its imitation of folk style, most obviously recalls the medieval ballad:

It is hard to know what to admire most about this page, the impassive surface or the extraordinary activity that takes place beneath. It begins in the middle, as if it had been going on for some time, and it is less a folk song than an idealized memory of a folk song. Few dynamic indications disturb the delicate sonority, and it would be a mistake to add any to those supplied by Chopin. The phrasing was originally somewhat more articulated, and was altered by

Chopin in proof to an almost unbroken continuity. Sustaining this unbroken continuity is a triumph of composition.

The triumph is a formidable one: underneath the apparent simplicity—the naive melody, the artless rhythm, the suggestion of modal harmony—the next section of the Ballade is being prepared. The A minor of the *Presto con fuoco* that follows comes suddenly without modulation from the F major of the *Andantino*, but no modulation is needed; the A minor has already been implied within the *Andantino*. It is not simply that A minor is the only other tonality besides F major and its dominant C major that is suggested in the forty-six bars of *Andantino*: the way A minor appears and the emphasis that is given to it in the otherwise unbroken and almost undifferentiated movement of the *Andantino* alerts us to the role that it is about to take on. In the *Presto con fuoco* the A minor is very unstable and lasts only for six bars, but it is, so to speak, the only landmark in an otherwise flat landscape.

The form of the opening melody is traditional. After one and a half bars of introduction (which Chopin clearly intends to blend imperceptibly with what follows), the tune has eight four-bar phrases and a twelve-bar coda: only the coda has something unconventional about it. I give a schematic analysis of the melody which shows both the simple traditional form and the role of A minor (iii):

Motif	A	B	C	C	B	A	B	B	B¹
Harmony	I	I	iii	V	V	I	iii	iii	I
Bar	2–5	*6–9	*18–19	*20–21	*22–25	26–29	*30–32	33–37	*38–45
	*10–13	*14–17							

(Starred references indicate that the period starts with the second half of the previous bar. Bar 33 is linked to the phrases before and after, 25 to the beginning of the phrase that follows.) The structure and harmony of this opening melody could not appear to be less sophisticated: first part played twice; second part; first part again; and closing phrase—or tonic, tonic, dominant, tonic. The sophistication lies in the smallest details: the artful and accomplished voice leading, the coda, the placing of the few indications of dynamics, and, above all, the way the phrases open either on the bar line or on an upbeat. Chopin's decision on publishing to remove most of the articulations of phrasing in the manuscript deliberately glosses over the slight variations of surface in order to make them as smooth as possible.

The melody proper begins on the first beat at bar 2, but the continuation is ambiguous: the original articulation indicated by Chopin as beginning on the last eighth note (B♭) of bar 5 is a beautifully expressive effect but convinces no one that the phrase begins there—the motif of which it is a part starts on the preceding A, but this note is itself the resolution of the previous harmony. However it is played (unless the performer makes a doctrinaire attempt to force our understanding), we hear:

In other words: the A in bar 5 is both an end to the first part of the phrase and a beginning of the second. By contrast, the end of the second phrase and of the first section in bar 9 is clear-cut. The repeat of the first eight bars of melody begins with a long upbeat of a dotted quarter on an F major chord.

The long upbeat returns in bar 17 after the first section has been repeated, and with it comes the first important change of harmony, the first indication of dynamics, and the first A minor chord. This suggests an importance for A minor that has until then only been given to the tonic F major. The cadence at the dominant of F major in bar 21 is marked by a renewal of the *pianissimo (sotto voce)* of the opening with an added diminuendo for the return to the first section in bars 25–26.

The grand effect is reserved for bar 33, the end of the reprise of the first section and the end of the conventional form. The final chord, however, is not a resolution downward to the tonic F major but a leap upward into A minor, set into relief by a crescendo. Most significant is that the unexpected appearance of A minor is the first disturbance of the four-bar periodic structure. The surprise cadence has almost the effect of cutting off the previous phrase and starting the new one too soon; the four-bar period is preserved by a group of three and five. In fact, the upbeat of bars 9 and 17 (and also 25, where the B♭ is both a continuation of the previous phrase and a new beginning) has been lengthened. Instead of

we have:

as if the harmony of A minor were so impatient to start that it could not wait. The metaphor is not as absurd as it may seem: Chopin establishes A minor by giving independent vitality to the new harmony as if it had a life of its own.

It remains only to sustain that impression of vitality through the conventional F major cadence that follows the phrase in A minor of bars 34 to 37. The method seems simple and even obvious, although I doubt that it would have occurred to anyone except Chopin: a series of accents on the A in bars 38, 40, 41, and 42—if there are no accents written in 43, 44, and 45, that is because none is needed. In bars 41 to 45 the A is played over and over—a dozen times, in fact, all of them with emphasis. The *fortissimo* A minor that follows may be startling, but it has been amply justified. The opening of the second Ballade is a model of how to allow one tonality to grow out of another without the formal modulation and opposition of a sonata exposition.

At the return of the opening section, the F major is abandoned poetically almost at once (no one can claim to understand Chopin's style who does not appreciate how the phrase slur is carried through and beyond the fermata and the pause):

The calm diatonic movement is succeeded by an elaborate and stormy development in the same rhythm (going quickly through harmonies as remote as D flat major, G flat major, E major, and C major). The *Presto con fuoco* reappears (now starting not in A minor but in D minor—in 6/4 harmonization, however, with A in the bass, and then returning to A minor), but this time after only sixteen bars it incorporates the opening *Andantino* in one of the most dramatic passages Chopin ever wrote:

Here, for the first time, we may say that A minor is fully established, and has become the principal tonality. It is remarkable that in a work of 205 bars, we must wait until bar 150 for this to be cleared up, and it is significant that Chopin makes the moment of harmonic decision coincide with his synthesis of the material from the two contrasting tempi. This passage reveals, however, that the *Andantino* and the *Presto* are, oddly enough, almost exactly identical tempi.

The synthesis is succeeded by a long *agitato* coda in A minor, which (once again like the final stretto of an operatic ensemble) does not leave the tonic and is made up of new thematic material until sixteen bars from the end, where the main theme of the *Presto con fuoco* reappears wonderfully transformed, and is followed by the initial material of tempo I:

The resonance of the *Presto* coda is sustained by the pedal through the initial bars of the return of the opening page, this time now solidly in A minor. The ending is of an extreme simplicity, and Chopin, indeed, wrote an even simpler version:

Each one of the Ballades that we have so far examined has a unique form, different from all the others, but it is possible to define certain principles of construction. Two thematic groups in contrasting tonalities or modes are presented separately, like successive stages of a narrative and with little of the close-knit opposition of sonata style. In what follows, the two groups do not remain independent but contaminate each other (either by development or combination). The level of tension and excitement is raised, by variation, development, and generally by something like an operatic stretto (acceleration, repetition of short motifs, and a rising sequence). The original material, above all that of the second group, reappears with greatly heightened brilliance, glorified and often drastically abridged. The climactic return is placed as close to the end as possible, like the denouement of a tale, but may be rounded off by a virtuoso coda based on new material.

To comprehend the originality of Chopin's large forms, we must realize that neither development nor return has the same function as in Classical sonata style. Chopin's return, or recapitulation, does not resolve previous tensions or reconcile harmonic and melodic oppositions; the original material returns with greater intensity and concentration—an intensity so great, in fact, that the material is often condensed to a small fraction of its original proportions. The purpose of Chopin's form is to bring back some of the main themes with a magnified aura of brilliance, complexity, tension, violence, and pathos (a more subtle version—and not always so subtle—of the way Liszt brings back his themes five times as loud and with ten times as many notes). Development for Chopin, consequently, does not prepare for resolution but for further excitement: it plays a role similar to stretto, and is often associated with stretto.

We have seen how short the ultimate return of the opening section is in the second and third Ballades, and the unusual transformations undergone by the material in the first Ballade. The return of the main theme in the Polonaise-Fantaisie resembles that of the A flat Ballade, even more concentrated and more spectacular. The first appearance is lyrical:

It is also leisurely: the first statement finishes with a half cadence after twenty
bars and is followed at once by a second statement, more developed and
impassioned, of twenty-two bars that closes now with a full tonic cadence,
ample and satisfying.

The return drastically reduces all of this to eight bars, which lead without
delay to a surprising reappearance of B major, the key of the central section
of the work, but now with entirely new material. The tonic A flat major returns
almost at once after a fierce two-bar stretto, and serves to realize not the first
theme but a transcendent version of the second section:

When originally in B major, this theme was *sempre piano* over a tonic pedal, and is now *sempre fortissimo* over a dominant pedal. Even with the return to A flat major, full harmonic resolution is withheld for fourteen bars. The most radical innovation of Chopin is his refusal to allow the return of the opening theme at the tonic to lower the dramatic tension even for a moment—this may account for his omission of the first theme from the recapitulations of his mature sonatas. In the Polonaise-Fantaisie, as in the third Ballade, final resolution is postponed for as long as the contemporary harmonic language would allow. A similar process can be seen at work in the final sections of the other long works, in particular the third and fourth Scherzos and the Barcarolle.

To what extent does Ballade no. 4 in F Minor conform to this model? The final coda with new material is there, as well as the two sets of themes. The second set initially appears in B flat major, and I can think of no other work in the minor mode which uses the *subdominant major* as the principal secondary key. After quiet, meditative expositions, both thematic groups return at the end with greater brilliance, and the second group, now in the submediant D flat major, leads to a stretto and a massive climax. The two thematic groups are presented separately, except that an extension of the second group at its first appearance leads seamlessly into a development of the first theme.

The end of this brief development is the occasion of the work's most striking moment, the reappearance of the introduction and the return, out of phase, to the tonic and the opening theme. The variation technique in this Ballade is more elaborate than in any other, and both the introduction and main theme come back with a display of counterpoint and a coloristic transformation which is one of the most moving pages in all nineteenth-century music. The character of the introduction and opening theme makes the later inspiration possible:

The opening, Chopin's masterpiece of elegiac style, demands a radical alteration in our emotional experience of tonality, which depends in its Classical form on a fundamental distinction between the firmness of a full cadence on the tonic and the more tentative half cadence on the dominant. The introduction has a series of half cadences on the dominant C major. It is clear at every point that this is a dominant (it opens, in fact, by implying a clear dominant seventh), but with all its dreamlike atmosphere the music nevertheless suggests the stability of a more powerful full cadence. Without quite reaching the status of a full cadence, the half closes on the C major chord are too strong; they are insistently approached at the end by the dominant seventh of C major, a V^7 on G. The repeated rounding-off of the plagal F major / C major ambiguously makes the C major too stable and yet anticipates the tonic F.

The main theme, one of Chopin's most original inventions, extends the harmonic ambiguity—an ambiguity of surface, as the tonic F minor is never really called into question. There is, however, no cadence on the tonic but only, *mezza voce,* a floating movement to the harmonies of the relative major, A flat, and then to the subdominant minor, B flat (bar 16). It is, in fact, the subdominant which then receives all the emphasis without rising even for a moment to the status of a new tonic: a weak half cadence on its dominant F major (bar 18) is followed by a full cadence on B flat minor—which then delicately, and at the last possible moment, slips back to the central F minor. The tonality is sketched by half lights on the surface, while the underlying structure remains absolutely transparent.

The dynamics also evade any determinate emphasis. The repeated notes that open the introduction reappear with operatic pathos in the theme at bars 11, 15, 17, and 21. The harmonic climax is always on the last of these four repeated notes, and is so marked by a crescendo, but paradoxically, before the end of the crescendo is reached, a diminuendo is indicated in the melody for the last two notes. It is clear from manuscript and edition that Chopin intended the diminuendo to commence in the middle of the crescendo and to coexist with it briefly although almost all editors, puzzled by the anomaly, remove it. (The execution demands a rubato which gently rounds off the melody as the harmony reaches its apex.)

Even the rhythm adds an apparent ambiguity to an underlying regularity. The phrases of the melody (starting from the middle of bar 8) are respectively eight half bars long, then again eight half bars, and finally twelve half bars. This is a perfectly Classical pattern, but an extra half bar of accompaniment is added in bar 12 between the first and second phrases (exactly as Schubert often did in his songs); and bars 17 to 20 reverse the two halves of the melody, now making the opening two bars the answer (or consequent) to bars 3 and 4. The process is completed in turn by the second half of the melody reestablishing itself in its right function. Everything—harmony, melody, and phrase rhythm—is contrived to give strength to the classically weaker elements, and this softening of the structural contours contributes to the extraordinary sense of melancholy that the character of the theme sets out from its first notes.

The return of the introduction later rises out of the development, but it comes without our being aware of it, and in the wrong key:

A recapitulation that begins in the wrong key is a familiar device to amateurs of Haydn and Beethoven, but never has the deception been carried so far or executed with such secret art, combined paradoxically with an overt and almost obtrusive display of contrapuntal skill. One finds oneself (bar 129) in the introduction again without realizing it—but in the wrong key, and then one finds oneself (bar 139) in the right key, once again without being immediately aware of it. All this craft is placed in the service of a meditative sadness, a resigned melancholy half perceived as if in a dream. The effect of a dream depends on the extraordinary skill of the transition, on the way Chopin brings us from one point to the other without allowing us to notice how each has been prepared. Part of the skill is the voice leading learned from a study of Bach: voices turn out to have thematic significance only as we realize that they have been there all the time, waiting with that potential for vital movement which is the essence of traditional counterpoint.

The repeated notes of the first bar of the introduction reappear in the development (bar 125) before the introduction returns: when we perceive that the introduction has come back, we are already well into its second bar. These repeated notes characterize the main theme as well, and they seem in the development to be a reworking of the main theme. It is the development, in fact, that makes us understand the relation of introduction and main theme. The introduction continues the new, rich sonority of the development, and with new harmonies that exploit this, emphasized by the fact that everything is transposed down a minor third from the beginning. After an exquisite cadenza that develops the last bars of the introduction, the first theme returns in imitative counterpoint. The effect of this learned display is to heighten the pathos of the main theme. The modulation back to the original pitch is achieved in four bars, but Chopin does not allow us to understand this for another eight bars, in which we appear to be still moving towards the opening. Chopin never surpassed this page, and he rarely equalled it. The wonderfully floating harmonies of the introduction, with its evasion of a full tonic cadence, make the poetic return possible. There is no other moment in the music of his time which so combines a deeply moving simplicity with such complex art. It stands once again as a demonstration of the way Chopin's most radical genius came directly out of his most conservative skill.

Changes of mode

In Ballade no. 4, the key of B flat major for the second theme makes a strange, indeed unprecedented, companion for the F minor tonic, but it does not sound strange. To grasp why it seems so convincing is essential to an understanding of Chopin's innovations in large-scale harmony. The main theme, as I remarked, may be in F minor, but it moves firmly to a cadence on the subdominant minor, B flat minor: at the end of the first playing of the theme, the harmony slips unassumingly back to F minor, but the second time the B flat minor cadence is allowed to stand. The third playing ends with a passionate climax on the dominant of B flat, and the new theme is introduced. The dominant pedal seems to be preparing a new tonality, but in fact we have been almost as much in B flat minor all the time as in F minor.

What we hear, in short, is less a change of key than a change of mode, from minor to major. We have already observed the same phenomenon in Ballade no. 3 in A flat Major, where Chopin treated the tonic and its relative minor (F minor) as essentially the same key and slipped back and forth from one mode to another, starting in this case in the major, and using F major and F minor as harmonic colors of the tonic A flat. In the F minor Ballade no. 4, the second theme appears later in the new key of D flat major, the relative major of B flat minor, only after the extraordinary recapitulation of the opening theme that I have quoted at length.

This is a basic principle for the way Chopin conceives many of his large forms: he does not oppose tonalities by the Classical technique of modulation but uses related tonalities for coloristic purposes as if they were different modes of the same tonality—or the same tonal region would be a better term. Even in Ballade no. 2, the relation of the opening F major to the final A minor operates in the same way, as if the A minor were only a modal variant in an area that includes F major and D minor. The second and third scherzos both apply his principle with wonderful effect: in the Scherzo no. 2, both B flat minor and D flat major are used as the same tonality with a contrast of mode; the harmonic structure of Scherzo no. 3 progresses from C sharp minor to D flat major (or C sharp major renotated), and then recapitulates in C sharp minor and E major, the relative major. In all of these works, more traditional harmonic modulation is always reserved for the creation of tension later in the piece.

One of Chopin's last works, the Polonaise-Fantaisie, employs the same innovative conception with the greatest mastery: the main sections are in A flat major for the first theme and B major for the second. The fact that B major is used here essentially as a modal variant of the main key (B natural, after all, is the minor third in an A flat chord) is shown by the way that a third melody immediately extends the second: it begins in G sharp minor (or A flat minor renotated). Perhaps the subtlest demonstration of the technique here, its capacity for achieving an effect of great poetry, is reserved for the return of the opening: the introduction begins once again but is interrupted, *pianissimo*, by the third theme now in F minor, the relative minor of the opening A flat key. All the tonalities—A flat major, B major, G sharp minor, and F minor—belong together as major and minor modal variations of each other.

This accounts in part for the complete success of Chopin's large forms in spite of his defiance of the main Classical methods of structure. He had found a way of contrasting not tonalities but modes, and he did this by extending the way major and minor modes were conceived far beyond the more limited uses made before him. Fundamentally, he turned the mediant shifts into changes of mode instead of changes of key. That gave him the possibility of sustaining interest over a large structure without the clear-cut oppositions and tensions of Classical modulation, and he could postpone the true increase of tension until the last part of the work with dramatic effect. (The only emphasis on the dominant is often reserved for the final stretto; and in the third Scherzo, the third Ballade, and the Polonaise-Fantaisie, he could forcefully telescope the dominant preparation with the return to the opening theme.) Chopin has been criticized for his disregard of Classical proportions and structures, and it was paradoxically this disregard which accounts for his greatest triumphs. (In the Classical sonata in a minor key, the relative major is almost always the secondary key, but the initial direction is from minor to major, while in his large-scale works Chopin can slip back and forth from major to minor.) It is only recently that critics have begun to realize that Classical tonal theory needs to be considerably overhauled if it is to deal with Chopin's innovations.

Above all, it was this harmonic originality that enabled him to create narrative-like forms that were continuously lyrical in feeling: substituting shifts of major and minor modes for the more hard-edged dominant/tonic oppositions and redefining the mediants as changes of modes allowed him to appear to stay within the same tonal area (this, too, redefined with greater breadth) and yet to achieve a rich and complex sense of movement that was consistently expressive and delicately nuanced. He rarely needed those neutral moments of cadential definition at the end of a modulation that were clearly indispensable to Mozart and Beethoven, and from which Mendelssohn and Schumann could not free themselves. His large works, even the most violent, never lose a sense of intensely refined poetry.

Italian opera and J. S. Bach

There is a paradox at the heart of Chopin's style, in its unlikely combination of a rich chromatic web of polyphony, based on a profound experience of J. S. Bach, with a sense of melody and a way of sustaining the melodic line derived directly from Italian opera. The paradox is only apparent, and it is never felt as such when one hears the music. The two influences are perfectly synthesized, and they give each other a new kind of power.

Chopin used Italian opera as he used Bach, discreetly, and, for the most part, without ostentation, absorbing it into his own style. There are a few open references, however. The Etude in C sharp Minor, op. 25, no. 7, the so-called Cello Etude, is derived from the *scena* in the third act of Bellini's *Norma*, with a melody originally destined for solo cello but then altered to the full cello section:

Chopin has turned this into a duet between solo cello and soprano, but the relationship with Bellini is clear enough. Nevertheless, the character of the Etude is more instrumental, and it exquisitely develops figuration typical of the cello (the only instrument besides the piano that ever interested Chopin):

More specifically operatic is the coda to the Nocturne in B Major, op. 32, no. 1, with its dramatic recitative (quoted on p. 82), and above all the final section of the Nocturne in G Minor, op. 15, no. 3, where an offstage chorus is heard softly chanting a hymn after a tolling bell has sounded:

This is no doubt program music, but once again no program is necessary for understanding: the discovery of a program, if there ever had been one, would only be a nuisance.

An article by Jeffrey Kallberg, "The Rhetoric of Genre: Chopin's Nocturne in G Minor," raises the level of discussion of this work above the naive and even primitive question of program music to considerations of genre. He points out that this nocturne begins clearly with mazurka rhythm, and that its indication of *rubato* is more typical of the mazurka for Chopin than for any other type of piece. He writes: "At one level, the fusion of the nocturne, the mazurka, and the *religioso* into one heterodox work can be understood as an experiment in the combination of seemingly uncombinable types, one designed to broaden the expressive range of the genre of the nocturne."[8] Kallberg adds convincingly that the association of the nationalistic dance with the religious atmosphere is a reflection of the religious consciousness associated with Polish nationalism among Chopin's contemporaries.

It may also be said that the operatic character of the chorale may have been influenced by the urgings of Chopin's friends that he write a Polish national opera.[9] Further, the indication of *rubato* in the opening bar of a work can be found elsewhere in Chopin only in the Mazurka in G Minor, op. 24, no. 1, which resembles the nocturne not only in its tonality but also in the character of its opening phrases.

Typical of the orchestral writing in contemporary Italian opera is the fast section of the first movement of the Sonata in B flat Minor. It can be found in agitated moments of operas from Rossini to Verdi, and it is not keyboard but string figuration:

8. Jeffrey Kallberg, "The Rhetoric of Genre: Chopin's Nocturne in G Minor," *Nineteenth-Century Music*, vol. 11, no. 3 (Spring 1988), pp. 238–261, at 255.

9. Ibid., p. 257.

Chopin turns the counterstatement of this theme some bars later into a more specifically pianistic effect by the relentless offbeat accents, which would not be as effective on string instruments:

This demands the slight percussive capacity of the piano, but increases the tension in a way that is still basically operatic in feeling.

One work, indeed, the slow movement of the Sonata for Piano in B minor, op. 58, is openly a homage to the Italian stage—and, I think, specifically to Bellini. Here, for the only time in Chopin, the accompaniment is a literal pastiche of Italian opera orchestration—a pastiche full of affection and admiration. The movement opens with a four-bar transition from the E flat major of the scherzo to the B major which is the fundamental tonality of the work. These opening bars represent the short modulating improvisation between pieces of different tonality that remained in vogue even well into the twentieth century with pianists of an older generation, and Chopin's must be one of the rare examples to have been written down and incorporated into the text:

The main theme is as fine a specimen of Bellini's cantabile technique as any that came from the original model, and displays a mastery of that effect of never-ending melody for which Bellini was so famous. The unbroken movement at the end of each four-bar period contains the secret, as we can see at bars 8 to 9 and 12 to 13. (The phrase line may be broken at the end of bar 12, but the next bar follows as part of the previous sequence: there is no pause even for breath.)

This is almost pure opera, but there is one moment where Chopin's idiosyncratic polyphonic technique leads him to an effect foreign to the Italian tradition. In bars 16 and 17 the descending bass with a crescendo reaches the tonic B—but a half bar too soon, as part of a G sharp minor six chord. Chopin seizes upon this with an extremely rapid diminuendo to *pianissimo*. The bass remains stationary on the B for more than two bars, and the music seems to melt into the return of the tonic chord and of the opening bars of the theme. Making this moment of color more striking is the movement of the voices: at the opening of bar 17, the melodic line in the upper voice of the previous bar becomes a lower voice that expressively alternates an F♯ and a G♯ in a primitively simple counterpoint, while a new soprano line begins the melody—the aria turns into a duet. The change without warning from aria into duet is, of course, an operatic trick, but the harmonic movement combined with the alteration of tone color is pure instrumental style—specifically piano style, as only an instrument capable of rapid dynamic change on which all the voices resemble each other in tone color so that one blends into the rest can conceivably execute this passage. The sudden *pianissimo* corresponds to the new function of the B in the bass as the tonic comes back and emphasizes the return of the theme: but the sense of unbroken motion requires that the resonance of the G sharp minor chord blur very slightly with the new harmony—and if the rapidity of the diminuendo is not enough to guarantee this, which it should be, the G♯ is prolonged throughout the next two bars by the counterpoint in the inner part which leads to the A♮ and the change of harmony (bar 19). This counterpoint is therefore at once an outgrowth of the original melody, an emphasis to the harmonic and melodic structure, and a necessary part of a contrast of color.

The synthesis of long-breathed melody and polyphonic movement is never this subtle in Italian opera—or in German, for that matter, where the feeling for melody is not as long-range, nor is melody so determinate an element of structure. This synthesis accounts for the effectiveness of much of what I have called Chopin's heterophonic counterpoint, two voices playing the same melody together in different rhythms. The next section of this movement, marked *Sostenuto,* furnishes us with a fine example:

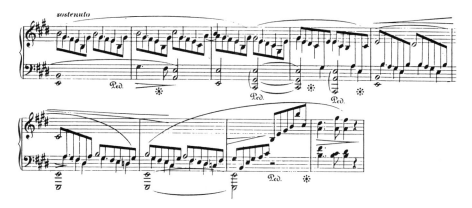

Here the right hand outlines in half a bar what it takes the left hand two full bars to encompass. The right-hand arpeggiated figure is typically a three-voice structure. The melody augmented in one voice against a more fluid form in the accompaniment is a technique that Chopin used elsewhere, most remarkably in the Prelude in G Major, op. 28, no. 3:

but the interplay, deliciously witty as it is, appears more academic here than in the sonata. At the end of the slow movement of the sonata, the textures of the main theme and of the middle section are fused in a coda which at its climax offers one of the most beautiful moments of heterophony:

The parallel octaves make themselves heard as they are delayed by the expressive ornament:

Once again, the expressive tone color arrives as a direct and natural outgrowth of voice leading.

The importance of the heterophonic texture for Chopin—the single melodic line simultaneously displayed in different rhythms in two voices or more—is that it preserves the supremacy of the Italian-style melody while allowing a richly interesting polyphonic development. It also allows the accompaniment to become melody at any moment, and maintains the implicit existence of melody in the subsidiary layers. The Nocturne in D flat Major, op. 27, no. 2, shows this art at its finest:

The Italianate melody (which once again changes from aria to duet in specifically operatic fashion in bar 10) is already hidden in the opening bar of accompaniment:

Relationships like this make most performances of Chopin either fussy or insensitive—often both: if the pianist tries hard to bring out this relationship, the result is pedantic; if he plays without being aware of the implicit melody in the accompaniment, the left hand becomes trivial or mechanical. Perhaps the effect is best achieved by the kind of tact which is unconscious, ingrained—semiconscious at best. No doubt, some kind of awareness is necessary, as

Chopin's notation makes clear later, when the return of the theme is prepared, and the counterpoint hidden in the subsidiary comes to the surface of the page at bar 23:

Here at bars 29–30, well into the return, the implicit becomes explicit for the ear, with the interior rising motion D♭–D♮–E♭. Accompaniment has become melody: our attention is attracted to the tenor voice at the moment when the soprano ceases to move. Melodic interest appears in the subsidiary voices when there are holes in the melody. This is not independent counterpoint, although it maintains the independence of voices.

Chopin is in this only the greatest master of a technique widespread in his time: the *effect* of counterpoint without any "real" counterpoint. For the Romantic composer, the experience of counterpoint comes first: the working-out on paper takes second place. In the development section of the early Mendelssohn Capriccio in F sharp Minor, op. 1, for piano, there is even a fugue with almost no counterpoint:

The development is the traditional place in classical form to experience fugue, and Mendelssohn economically provides a homophonic "fugue"—that is, the effect of fugue in one voice with chordal accompaniment. The fugue is realized in the right hand alone, the running bass contributing nothing to the fugal illusion. The successive entries are all there (and continue for several pages more), and for the ear there is only the structure of a fugue—a hollow structure. "Hollow" is a pejorative word, and that is the wrong attitude to take to such skill and such inspiration. Only pedantry would insist on real counterpoint when none is necessary. This kind of skill, however, discovers a conception of the art of music profoundly alien to the generations that came before Mendelssohn and Chopin.

The homophonic "fugue" is one extreme of the period. Another is the melody achieved through a complex interplay of two or more voices, but without any sense of contrapuntal opposition. The trio from the scherzo of the Sonata in B Minor, op. 58, is an exceptionally skilful example:

Here the melody proper is divided over four voices. Where the soprano moves, the other voices with melodic interest remain briefly static: they either repeat the previous note or hold it tied over from the preceding beat. The result is paradoxical; we retain a sense of the separate individual voices, but at the same time, we cannot avoid hearing:

and later:

The importance of this technique may be understood if we reflect that in this passage the individual voices in the original notation are not very interesting by themselves, while the rescoring for one voice I have given is awkward and even ungainly—but the combination of the different voices produces a melody which is both beautiful and fascinating. It is obvious that the composer here wants to have the best of both worlds, polyphonic and monophonic; and this page is only intelligible as both a single unified melody and a complex many-voiced web. Chopin has transferred Italian operatic melody to a keyboard texture and combined it with his study of Bach. It was from Bach that Chopin learned to make many voices out of one, but he went even further than his model in the art of making one melodic line out of many voices, the art of projecting a single line to distant regions of the musical space.

Even the rudiments of this aspect of his art were learned from Bach, I suppose, but we may conjecture that it was not so much from a study as from an experience of his music—experience of playing as well as hearing. We have seen in the Mendelssohn Capriccio how a Romantic composer could reproduce the audible experience of fugue without actually constructing one. The generation of composers born around 1810 were all brought up to the music of J. S. Bach: they did not so much learn music from the *Well-Tempered Keyboard* as they learned to play the piano. For Schumann, Mendelssohn, Liszt, and Chopin—and for many generations of musicians since that time—part of the earliest musical experience was that of playing Bach on a modern keyboard, and their conception of the nature of music—of polyphony and counterpoint above all—was fundamentally determined by the sound of Bach on a modern instrument. If present-day purists ever have their way and the music of Bach is restricted entirely to early eighteenth-century instruments, the history of nineteenth-century music will become in large part unintelligible. So far it remains at least unconsciously simple to grasp because so many musicians are still educated today on the music of Bach.

Played on the piano, the fugues of Bach may be interpreted with a kind of execution denied to organists or harpsichordists (unless they engage in tricks of phrasing for which there is no evidence in Baroque performance practice): successive parts of the polyphonic texture may be brought to the fore, selectively emphasized. There are very few pianists who resist the temptation (and why should they?) to set different voices into relief, to clarify the structure of a Bach fugue for the public by marking the entries of the principal theme with a slight emphasis. All too frequently, however, this leads to the most foolish and simpleminded of performances, in which the theme is played *mezzo forte* at each appearance and everything else appears as a backdrop—as if the most expressive aspect of a fugue were the theme and not the multiple ways in which the theme is combined and blended with the other voices.

On paper a fugue is a set of independent voices, but that is not quite the way it is experienced. Played on whatever keyboard instrument, the fugue most of the time seems to the ear now one voice and now another coming to the fore, not all of them with the main theme. As the activity changes from one part of the texture to another, we are conscious of one voice emerging and another reentering the general harmony—sometimes so briefly that we are aware of the movement of only two or three notes. This is particularly true of the fugues of Bach, above all those of the *Well-Tempered Keyboard*. In the fugues of Beethoven and Mozart, we are too often forced to perceive a more continuous and independent activity in many of the voices simultaneously, while in Bach they blend into the general harmony more readily, with less opposition and contrast. The basic sonority may often change very little in Bach, but we are all the more aware of delicate alterations of harmony and color as our attention is drawn successively to different details in one voice after another. This characteristic of Bach's style is inescapable on any keyboard instrument, but it is brought forward with striking clarity by the piano, and it was deeply important for the Romantic composer, Chopin in particular.

What Chopin reproduces of Bach, therefore, is not the theoretical structure on paper but the aural experience. This reproduction is so extraordinary within the terms of Chopin's more modern style that we can reconstruct the theoretical independence of the voices and renotate them in full score with a consistency that could never be achieved with the piano music of Schumann or Liszt—or rarely with the piano music of Mozart and Beethoven for that matter. If we do this, however, we rarely find that the different voices have, simultaneously, an equivalent motivic interest as in Bach: in Chopin, as I have said, even in the most complex polyphonic passage each voice tends to wait for the others, and insert itself in the spaces left when the other voices pause or sustain their notes. This is counterpoint calculated purely for the experience of listening.

There are, of course, in Chopin's music as in the work of all other composers of his time, many passages which are the simultaneous statement of two clear motifs, as in the dramatic explosion of the *Presto con fuoco* section of the second Ballade:

Even here, however, the relation between right- and left-hand motifs is intimate. In the first bar quoted, the right-hand motif is simply an inversion and diminution of the left-hand, and in the second bar both hands outline a rising diminished seventh chord in a combination of cross-rhythm and syncopation.

There is also the slightly less familiar classical technique of starting a motif which becomes an accompaniment, as in the opening of the Impromptu in F sharp Major:

For an analogue, compare the slow movement of Mozart's Serenade in B flat Major for wind instruments and double bass. In the impromptu, the melody begins by inverting the line of the opening bars and ends (bars 10–11)

by echoing them. The emphasis on the motif of D♯–C♯ in the left hand gives
the expressive impetus to the end of the right-hand melody. Even more interesting is the accompaniment which suddenly turns out to be an independent
voice with an interest of its own. In the Nocturne in F Major, op. 15, no. 1,
the upper voice in the left hand starts out as a simple doubling of the melody,
but in the third and fourth bars it goes off on its own, first by echoing the
melody of the second bar:

The most original invention of Chopin's polyphony, however, is the melody
displaced over two voices, which I discussed earlier. One of the most famous
examples of this, with the two voices more than an octave apart, comes from
the Scherzo in B Minor, op. 20, in the section *Molto più lento*:

The principal voice is mostly the alto, but in bars 310 and 311—and 319 and
320—the melodic interest moves to the soprano (note the neutral role played

just preceding the shift by bars 309 and 317–318). It is typical of Chopin that later at the return even the left-hand figure should take on momentarily a quasi-melodic interest in bar 374, as our attention is drawn delicately and fleetingly to the tenor by the accents within the pianissimo:

What Chopin achieved, therefore, was not the constant independence of the voices in classical counterpoint, but a latent independence of each voice, consistent and continuous, which could break into full independence at any moment. This latent independence, however, corresponds to the experience of listening to counterpoint, if not to the theory. In Chopin, the voices reach full independence only when the listener need be aware of them: elsewhere they remain buried in an apparently homophonic texture. When only latent, they may be hidden but they can always be uncovered—which has given so many pianists the delicious possibility to bring out apparently irrelevant and insignificant inner voices in Chopin, a practice almost traditional earlier in our century. In bars 361 to 368 of the page of the scherzo quoted here, the preparation of the return of the melody shows how Chopin himself on occasion even directs the performer to emphasize an inner voice when it seems to have still only a harmonic function, and becomes fully melodic five bars later. The voice is standing in the wings, so to speak, waiting to makes its entrance on the stage—for once, Chopin wants us to catch a glimpse of it behind the scenes.

This idiosyncratic but powerful approach to contrapuntal detail can help us understand Chopin's mastery of large forms. He is one of the rare composers who knew how to sustain not only a melody and a bass but the inner parts as well. Perhaps this interest in the inner parts accounts for Chopin's idolization of Mozart's music, where the inner part writing is richer than in any of Mozart's contemporaries. There is a persistent sense of inner movement in his works which takes priority over breaks in phrasing, and it bridges over from one section to the next. We are often only half aware of this inner movement because it does not always have melodic or motivic significance, but it is everywhere present, ready to break through the surface of the musical texture.

The music of Chopin—although more intimately expressive than the keyboard works of Bach—is not conceived for the solitary performer. Chopin's counterpoint is public. He selected from Bach only those aspects of contrapuntal art that have a direct effect, conscious or half conscious, on listening. He borrowed what he could hear. The *Well-Tempered Keyboard,* while effective enough in the modern concert hall, was not composed for an audience but for the pleasure and instruction of the performer: any public performance is certain to leave the audience in the dark about the many aspects of the work perceptible only to the performer, who sees them in the score, and above all feels them through the muscles of his hand and arm. The music of Chopin, no matter how personal and how intimate, is calculated for an audience, even if only a small one. It is true, with Chopin, the listener often feels, not that he is being spoken to, but that he is eavesdropping. Chopin, indeed, generally played in small halls and preferred weaker, more lyrical instruments than the Erards used by Liszt, but we must not make the mistake of thinking that a composer's limitations as a performer are a reliable guide to the way his music should be played. The *fff* found twice at the end of the first Scherzo, and the direction *il più forte possibile* of Ballade no. 1, are only two of the many indications that Chopin's music often requires a vehemence and a power in performance that equals and even surpasses the demands made by Liszt. Not only do the last pages of the Polonaise-Fantaisie go by implication beyond any instrument available to Chopin, but even the modern nine-foot steel-frame concert grand is inadequate:

This needs both keyboard sonority and orchestral power: every performance will seem puny compared to the idea conveyed by the notation of these bars. It is generally believed that Chopin's music is pianistic, but often enough this is true only in conception. He is ruthless, capable of asking the pianist to try for the unrealizable in delicacy as well as violence. The unrealizable in Chopin, however, is always perfectly imagined as sound. His structures are rarely beautiful or interesting in themselves on paper, as are those of Bach or Mozart (to name his favorite composers): they are conceived for their effect, even if the intended public was a small and very private one in some cases. That is why his long works have been underestimated: forms like the third Ballade or the Polonaise-Fantaisie appear lopsided on the page. They are justified by performance, although Chopin is among the most difficult of all composers to interpret. His music, never calculated, like much of Bach, for solitary meditation, works directly on the nerves of the listener, sometimes by the most delicate and fleeting suggestion, sometimes with an obsessive, hammered violence:

CHAPTER SIX

Chopin: Virtuosity Transformed

Keyboard exercises

Only once in Chopin's music is there a direct reference to Bach, and that is, appropriately, at the beginning of his only educational work, the two sets of Etudes, op. 10 and 25, and the three Nouvelles Etudes for Moscheles. In the first Etude, op. 10, in C major, we find a modernized version of the Prelude no. 1 of the *Well-Tempered Keyboard*:

Chopin's version is projected over the whole range of the contemporary keyboard. Like Bach's introductory piece, Chopin's is nothing but a string of
arpeggios with an almost absolute rhythmic uniformity, and a sense of melodic
line that is considerably reduced and seems to spring only from the succession
of chords. It is, of course, traditional to start a set of pieces with arpeggios, a
standard way of beginning an improvisation: toccatas, fantasies, and suites
often open that way, and Liszt begins both of his great suites of Etudes, the
Transcendental and the *Paganini,* with arpeggios. Nevertheless, Chopin's Etude
is so close to Bach's Prelude in its unity of construction, in its insistence on a
single form of arpeggiation throughout, and in its harmonic shape, that we
must conclude that an allusion to Bach was intended.

In the first half of the eighteenth century, the masterpieces of keyboard music
appear for the most part as works of instruction: Leçons, Klavierübung, or
Essercizi. Almost all of Bach's published music is printed under the title of
keyboard exercises: the Partitas, Italian Concerto, Four Duets, the Chorale
Preludes arranged in the order of the mass, and the *Goldberg* Variations. These
are instructive works for composers as well as players (the difference was not
marked at the time), and to the published music must be added the Inventions
for two and three voices, the *Art of Fugue,* and the *Well-Tempered Keyboard*—
all of these specifically for the keyboard player, and almost all requiring great
virtuosity. A similar virtuosity is demanded by the only sonatas of Domenico
Scarlatti published by the composer himself: they were titled Essercizi. In the
later eighteenth century this extravagant virtuosity almost disappears: it finds
a minor outlet in the concerto (although even the most brilliant of Mozart's
are technically less dazzling and less arduous than the *Goldberg* Variations or
Scarlatti). Keyboard music had become more sociable, less professional: the
amateur's interest was now the primary consideration, particularly if one
wished to make a profit from the sale of sheet music. Mozart's publisher
cancelled his order for six piano quartets after the first two proved to be too
difficult for the average pianist. Carl Philipp Emanuel Bach carried on the old
tradition, but the technical requirements of his works were considerably tempered by the effects of sensibility essential to the sentimental style then in
vogue. Keyboard virtuosity reappears in the last quarter of the century with
Muzio Clementi, famous for playing parallel thirds in one hand: he was later
to write the educational *Gradus ad Parnassum.*

Between the instructional works of the late Baroque and the Romantic etude lies the development and spread of the public concert. The volumes of the Klavierübung of Bach are meant for private study, even for meditation. The great Romantic finger exercises are public. The more private educational works of the Romantic composer produced little of any considerable musical interest, even for those of us with a nostalgic feeling for the days when we played "The Happy Farmer" and other pieces from Schumann's *Album for the Young*. By the late eighteenth century, there is a sad and permanent decline in the quality of music written for young performers or beginners: one has only to compare Bach's *Album for Anna Magdalena Bach* and the Two-Part Inventions with anything that came later. No composer of importance between Bach and Schumann turned his hand to writing for children, and Schumann's essays came after his years of greatest inspiration for piano writing had gone. (Mozart is the odd exception, but then he was, in fact, almost incapable of writing really easy pieces: he no doubt believed that his Sonata in D Major, K.576, was easy, perhaps because all the hard passages in the first movement were in simple two-part counterpoint, one voice in each hand, but he was wrong.) By 1800 music for piano was public, and anything interesting in the genuinely private sector was confined largely to compositions for four hands.

Chopin is the true inventor of the concert etude, at least in the sense of being the first to give it complete artistic form—a form in which musical substance and technical difficulty coincide. His first etudes were written in the late 1820s, and the complete set of opus 10 was published in 1833 and dedicated to Liszt. Etudes of musical interest were written before him: in 1804 by John Baptist Cramer, an anglicized German and friend of Beethoven; by Muzio Clementi, an anglicized Italian, whose *Steps to Parnassus* (1817–1826) was so important in the training of young pianists; and by Carl Czerny, Liszt's teacher. Etudes specifically intended for concert performance rather than for didactic purposes were published by Ignaz Moscheles, a famous Czech pianist, in 1825, just before Chopin began to compose his opus 10. In all of these, as in Liszt's first set of 1825, either the musical value is minimal, or else it is partially or wholly independent of the technical problems. (In some of the later parts of Clementi's *Steps to Parnassus*, the musical value is high but execution is relatively easy.)

The etude is a Romantic idea. It appeared in the early nineteenth century as a new genre: a short piece in which the musical interest is derived almost entirely from a single technical problem. A mechanical difficulty directly produces the music, its charm, and its pathos. Beauty and technique are united, but the creative stimulus is the hand, with its arrangement of muscles and tendons, its idiosyncratic shape.

The opening of Chopin's first Etude lies well for the hand, but when the tension rises we have:

a passage so difficult for pianists with only moderate sized hands that many
change the fingering from the 124 5124 prescribed by the composer to the
considerably simpler 125 2125—unfortunately, one can always hear the change
in the phrasing of the arpeggio that this entails. (In this respect Chopin is one
of the least pianistic composers: a change of harmony that makes the original
figuration exceedingly awkward does not lead him to change the figuration,
and he always refuses to adapt his musical thought to the convenience of the
hand.) The original fingering enforces a painful stretch between the second and
fourth fingers, and there is no question that practicing it sensibly and without
excessive force develops the muscles of the hand. It is in this respect that the
Romantic etude is a genuine finger exercise. The keyboard exercises of Scarlatti
and Bach are often as difficult as Chopin's and require as much practice, but
studying them is not very different from learning to play any difficult work.
Practicing an etude of Chopin or Liszt is an athletic exercise: it stretches the
hand, develops the muscles, increases suppleness, enlarges physical capacity.

In no form of Romantic music is the intimacy of musical idea and realization
demonstrated so powerfully as in the etude. Chopin may not allow the hand
to dictate the development and the flow of musical thought, which had their
own logic for him, but the original inspiration behind every etude is still the
physical configuration of hand and arm: this is what determines the opening
bars, and these in turn determine the character of the piece. No one understood
better than Chopin the advantage of basing an etude on a single technical
difficulty: piano technique and musical thought are so clearly identified in the
etude that this is the only way to ensure the unity of style. With its homogeneous texture, in which the figuration of the opening bars is generally devel-

oped without ceasing until the end, the etude is the most striking product of
the nineteenth-century Baroque revival.

Chopin's two most idiosyncratic fingerings are oddly similar: the first is the
realization of a delicate chromatic line entirely with the fourth and fifth fingers
(or with the third, fourth, and fifth in more complicated passages); the second
is the playing of a series of melodic notes entirely with the thumb. An example
of the first is found as early as Piano Concerto in F Minor, finished by the time
he was eighteen,

and the second may be found in the slow movement of the same work. At the
end of the last arabesque the direction to use the thumb three times in a row
slows the notes down and makes them expressive:

The second Etude of opus 10 in A Minor is an exercise in playing the chromatic
scale with only the three weakest fingers:

and the second of the three Nouvelles Etudes in D flat Major enforces a flexible
use of the thumb for several notes in a row five bars before the end:

In fact, the original printer misread the indications of the thumb in bar 69 as a sharp *staccato,* and this mistake is still carried over into most modern editions. The first Nouvelle Etude, in F minor, offers a more characteristic use of this fingering:

Here the thumb is used, as in the slow movement of the Piano Concerto, to bring out the most expressive notes.

In using the thumb, Chopin is only extending an old tradition in which the most important notes are set in relief by slightly detaching them. Two example show the classic practice, the first from the slow variation of Mozart's Sonata in A Major, K.331:

The detached notes carry the expressive weight: playing them this way enforces a kind of *rubato,* a very slight holding back of the tempo for a fraction of a second. This is equally clear in the slow movement of the *Waldstein* Sonata by Beethoven:

The detached sound is paradoxically a way of dwelling on the note, and there is no reason why in all of these passages we should not play the successive notes with one finger, as Chopin was later to do. Perhaps it was already an accepted technique before he was to require it in print.

The effect is midway between a staccato and an accent: this is why at the end of the eighteenth century there is a confusion between the signs for the two, a confusion which is in fact irremediable. Beethoven admonished his publishers to distinguish carefully between a dot over a note and a vertical stroke—the vertical stroke being a sign for an accent somewhat less than the mathematician's sign "greater than" (>). It is, however, impossible to make the distinction in Beethoven's own manuscripts, as the dot turned easily into the stroke in his handwriting: the decision must always be a musical one. It is obvious that the dots in the following passage from the opening movement of the Sonata in A flat Major, op. 110, cannot refer to a staccato but must indicate the slightest of accents within the indications *piano* and *leggermente,* enough to mark the beat with subtlety:

The confusion between *staccato* and a slight accent is historically understandable, given the limited dynamic range and fast decay of sound on the early pianos: detaching a note was an admirable and indispensable way of setting it slightly in relief without exaggeration, and it still works well on modern instruments. Chopin uses the fifth finger to do this with extraordinary delicacy in the Nocturne in E flat, op. 9, no. 2:

The directions *poco rubato* and *dolcissimo* give us the sense of this fingering. Using the thumb on successive notes is equally expressive, although naturally more emphatic, as the central section of the F Minor Ballade reveals:

We need not restrict ourselves to passages where Chopin has specifically indicated the fingering. There are many places where playing the melody with the thumb is the only possible solution. The Prelude in F sharp Minor, op. 28, no. 8, is an example throughout:

This sort of writing has always been considered one of the triumphs of Chopin's style. It was certainly not innovative to ask the pianist to play the melody louder than everything else, as the notation here implies. What was original was to bury the melody within a polyphonic texture of such richness, with chromatic passing tones and complex cross-rhythms, and to arrange for it to stand out with such clarity from the shadowy mass enveloping it. This polyphonic chiaroscuro was perhaps Chopin's highest achievement in the play of sonorities.

His use of fifth finger and thumb put Chopin in direct opposition to the reigning contemporary piano pedagogy, the ideal of which was to make all fingers equally powerful and nimble. Chopin insisted that each finger was fundamentally different in character, and that the performer should try to exploit that difference. His use of the fourth and fifth fingers for delicate chromatic effects became almost a trademark (and, in fact, the Etude "in thirds," op. 25, no. 6, depends on this technique): it was parodied by Schumann in the piece in *Carnaval* titled "Chopin":

The bar with the fingering is the most successfully Chopinesque detail of the imitation. This sense of the different character of each finger reveals something of the nature of Chopin's musical thought: it was subtle gradations of color, inflections of phrasing, that interested him, and it was what he expected from performers.

Some of the Etudes in the first set, opus 10, were written by the time Chopin was twenty. It is with these pieces that Chopin's style was fully revealed in all its power and subtlety. Later works are sometimes more ambitious and, in a few cases, more audacious, but there were no radical changes of style, nothing to compare to the later revolutions we find in the careers of Haydn and Beethoven, or even in the shorter lives of Mozart and Schubert. Chopin's mastery was proven with the twelve Etudes of opus 10.

The second dozen, opus 25, are even more impressive, in part because the poetry is more intense, the chromaticism more pronounced, but also because Chopin arranged the set to work as a whole: every successive etude seems to spring directly out of the preceding. The tonality of each is closely related to that of the succeeding one, with the exception of the last two, where this pattern breaks down. The way the end of an etude appears to prepare the opening of the next is sometimes striking. The repeated C's at the end of opus 25, no. 2, leads directly in to number 3:

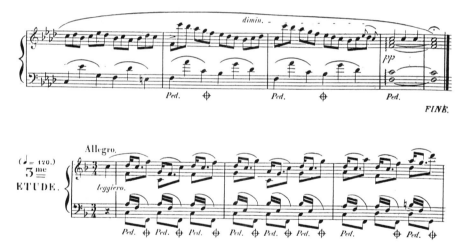

and the last bars of number 3, in F major, prepare the A minor of number 4:

Pianists are often understandably tempted to make no pause between these etudes when they play the opus as a whole.

The succession of numbers 5, 6, and 7 is extraordinary. The trill on the G♯ anticipates the next etude, and the *sotto voce* trill of the opening of 6 comes like an echo of the *fff* sonority of the preceding passage, which should be held until it dies away:

At the end of Etude no. 6 it is even possible to let the pedal last until after the first note of the introductory recitative of number 7 has been sounded:

It is evident that Chopin was attempting to make one unified work out of a series of different pieces: that this attempt was not planned in advance but imposed afterwards on previously written etudes is suggested by the breakdown of the order at the end, as the last three etudes are the only ones not in closely related keys. There is no general consistency to the scheme of keys (A flat major, F minor, F major, A minor, E major, G sharp minor, C sharp minor, D flat major, G flat major, B minor, A minor, C minor) but only local coherence: we start with a contrast of major and minor; a succession of dominant to tonic follows (D flat to G flat to B); and the bravura violence of the last three etudes makes a tremendous finale. Although there is no evidence that the set was played as a whole or even intended for such a complete performance, it is clear that the composer thought in terms of selecting a group of succeeding numbers. Played as a whole, however, opus 25 can make a grand effect. Chopin had already shown a similar concern at ordering the etudes of opus 10 (the manuscript of the third Etude indicates that the fourth was to be attacked without pause), but it was somewhat less consistent: the set makes a more disparate impression, and the succession falls into distinct groups. (Not even the final major chord of opus 10, no. 6 will make its E flat minor sound compatible with the C major that follows.) By contrast, the dramatic structure and the progression of virtuoso brilliance of opus 25 are a remarkable achievement of both unity and variety.

This achievement is comprehensible only if we realize that Chopin's approach to the etude had very little in common with that of his most important predecessors—Cramer, Czerny, Kalkbrenner, and Moscheles. Essentially, he does not simply do what they did, only better: make interesting and brilliant music out of a motif or figuration technically difficult to execute (this is true only of a few Etudes, such as the heroic and dramatic C sharp Minor Etude, op. 10, no. 4). For the most part (and this includes some of the earliest) Chopin's etudes are studies in color, and the technical difficulties concern the quality of touch more often than accuracy or speed. This concern with tone color gives importance to Chopin's insistence on the different functions of different fingers.

Opus 25 begins with a spectacular essay in color:

Only the notes written large are intended to rise out of the mist created by the arpeggios. The small notes must only just speak, at the limit of the audible. Later subsidiary voices are to appear, detaching themselves from the inner parts:

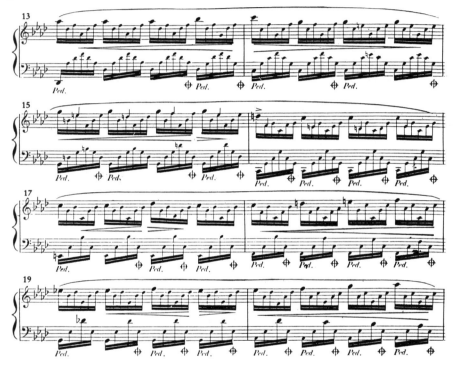

As we might expect, the inner voice in small notes marked by separate stems in bar 15 is already present in bar 14, but it is only latent, not yet intended to come completely into the light. Even more revealing of Chopin's technique is bar 16: the large notes in the soprano line do not continue the large notes of the previous one; they take over from the inner voice marked by separate stems, and the new voice marked by separate stems in this bar has been prepared by the four F's hidden within the arpeggios of bar 16. In what follows, tenor and soprano have almost equal prominence. Chopin's counterpoint is a counterpoint of color, and this etude is an exercise in gradations of touch, from the almost imperceptible to a full cantabile.

The next piece of opus 25 is equally subtle.

This is an etude not of figuration but of delicate cross-accents: it must be played softly, yet with the beats of the right hand gently marked. The mistake of performing the right hand in six beats instead of four is made all too often:

The music falls easily into this false rhythm if the four C's are not very slightly accented: the difficulty of the etude lies in keeping these accents to the absolute minimum which will still both clarify the rhythm and allow an even flow. Chopin's pedal, introduced only in bars 5 and 7, has an extraordinarily poetic effect, the release making the resolutions onto the tonic of bars 6 and 8 graceful and light.

The etudes that follow are also studies in contrasting touch. Number 4 in A minor opposes a relentless, leaping staccato in the left hand to three different kinds of texture in the right, consistently offbeat. First, staccato:

then a typical Chopinesque effect, legato and staccato combined in one hand (in which the lyricism of the cantabile legato line is given great pathos by the contrast of the scherzando accompaniment):

finally, staccato, full legato and semilegato juxtaposed dramatically:

Etude no. 5 similarly takes a simple motif—an interval and a single note—and treats it in a succession of colors, all requiring a different kind of touch. First in dotted separate groups of two:

then even groups of two:

groups of two with the upper voice sustained (the acciaccatura in the lower voice must be played on the beat):

with an even legato:

and then with a light legato *(leggiero)* as accompaniment to an obbligato melody played *sostenuto:*

This etude requires a progression from a distinctly contoured detached sound to a texture *più lento* in which the basic motif blends into a continuous background and becomes indistinguishable as a separate entity.

The Etude in E Minor is partly inspired by Hummel's Etude in E Minor, op. 125, no. 7, published between Chopin's opus 10 and his opus 25. This is a rare example of Chopin's borrowing from another composer in a mature work:

Bars 9 and 10 are almost literally quoted by Chopin. There is, however, little in Hummel's Etude of the subtle gradations of touch, tone color, and phrasing that distinguish Chopin's conception.

In these etudes, Chopin invents sounds with an imagination comparable in power to Liszt's but essentially different. Liszt's invention is basically imitative: he makes piano sonorities that resemble sleigh bells, horses' hooves, fountains, rustling leaves, or that imitate instruments of the orchestra—flute, violin, trombone, trumpet, percussion. This imitative effect is rare in Chopin, although we have seen an exceptional example of his representation of percussion instruments in the F sharp Minor Polonaise. In the Etudes, Chopin invents pure piano sound—abstract piano sound, in fact. It would be naive to identify the original conceptions of Chopin with the sonority of a particular instrument: he may have preferred the Pleyel, but he also performed on Erards and on Broadwoods, almost as different from the Pleyel as from the modern Steinway. In any case, Chopin's intentions—even if they were, improbably, specific and private—are irrelevant to the power and effectiveness of his ideas. It is not material sounds that he invented but a structure of subtle gradations, layers of sonority, a counterpoint of color.

This coloristic approach is already evident in the earliest etudes, written before he was twenty. Opus 10, no. 10, in A flat major, is a remarkable example, and makes the most elaborate demands on the performer in varying a single pattern by changes of accent and touch:

The opening bars already contain a clash of accent between the hands, using the motif of a sixth and a single note that Chopin employed in several of the later etudes. The four accents per bar change to a new pattern of six, but without altering the figuration, and shift the accents from offbeat to on, making a new cross-rhythm between the hands, as the left stays *legatissimo* in four beats per bar against six in the right:

The touch then changes from *legatissimo* to *staccato*:

Chopin's primary concern is for the widest possible variety of touch that can be given to a single pattern. The continuous changes of accent highlight different parts of the figuration, and emphasize the polyphonic nature of the pattern.

One etude, opus 10, no. 6, in E flat minor, written when Chopin had just turned twenty, should be mentioned, as it reveals Chopin's later interests already fully developed, and is often misinterpreted:

Chopin's metronome mark ($\quarternote. = 69$) is more than twice as fast as the usual performance—as fast as the Etude "in thirds," as a matter of fact. The tempo is indeed Andante, but it is intended not as a slow six to the bar but as a slow two. The music is a genuine etude, not a nocturne, as it is often conceived, although it is derived from John Field's Nocturne in A flat Major:

At Chopin's tempo, the richly chromatic inner voice is surprisingly difficult—
above all to play evenly, quietly, and with the delicate fluctuations that make
it expressive without overpowering the melody:

Here we have Chopin's already mature conception of layers of sound, which
interact chromatically and move from voice to voice.

It is difficult to appreciate today how radical was the synthesis embodied in
Chopin's etudes. The major technical problems in these pieces are most often
ones of touch and balance: they increase the strength and the suppleness of the
hand, but they also develop the performer's ear. Chopin's coloristic invention
is at its highest in the Etudes, and nowhere is it more evident that this coloristic
imagination is fundamentally contrapuntal in nature—or, rather, that the counterpoint is fundamentally coloristic, the interweaving of different kinds of
texture:

The difficulty of such a passage from opus 25, no. 6, lies in balancing, *sotto voce,* two different kinds of legato. This kind of tone color is pure keyboard writing: contrast of timbre is produced by touch alone and not by contrast of instrument. For this reason, Chopin's tone color is as abstract as pitch or rhythm: it is based on the relationship between different kinds of texture realized with the neutral sound of the piano—neutral in that it is relatively uniform from top to bottom, or, better, that changes of tone color from bass to treble are produced without a perceptible break. The ideal piano—for which every composer writes, not for the imperfect instrument at his home—provides a continuum of sound, and the Romantic composer generally requires a use of the pedal which ensures that some of that continuum will actually be realized on our imperfect instruments, and that the real differences in timbre between high and low notes will be glossed over. These questions of balance and contrast make the etudes supremely difficult—that and the problem of endurance. Like the preludes of the *Well-Tempered Keyboard* from which they largely derive, which served as models, most of the etudes develop the initial motif without pause until the end. No doubt the heavier action of the twentieth-century concert grand has made these pieces even harder to play than they were during Chopin's lifetime, but they were a challenge from the beginning—too great a challenge in some cases, it is said, for Chopin himself, who, exceptionally, preferred Liszt's execution of these works to his own.

The challenge comes from Chopin's ruthlessness: he makes, as I have said, no concession. The etudes (and the preludes as well) generally begin easily enough—at least the opening bars tend to fit the hand extremely well. But sometimes, with the increase of tension and dissonance, the figuration quickly becomes almost unbearably awkward to play. The Prelude in G Major gives us a typical example. The opening bar is as comfortable as one could want:

A few bars later, however, the black keys turn the figure into a steeplechase, yet the hurdles of the black keys must be negotiated with elegance and ease, and without interrupting the flow:

Played with the absolute evenness and lightness demanded by the context, these two bars are among the most difficult ever written.

Even more significant a contrast is offered by the Etude in A Minor, op. 25, no. 11. It sets off, in spite of all its complexity, with passage work that lies comfortably and does not stretch the hand:

but the climax twists both hands unmercifully:

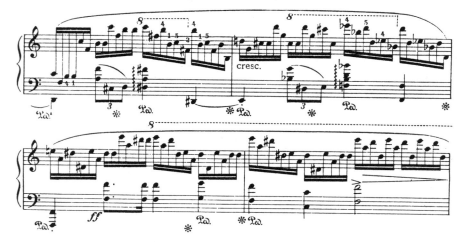

The very positions into which the hands are forced here are like gestures of exasperated despair. It would seem as if the physical awkwardness is itself an expression of emotional tension. The public does not, I think, generally realize the amount of pain actually attendant upon virtuoso pianism; the intense muscular exertion is comparable to a sport like tennis, and brings with it a battery of physical ills, like tendinitis, that have incapacitated pianists for short periods or even permanently ruined their careers. There have, of course, been pianists, such as Josef Hofmann, whose control of a relaxed technique was so great that they perhaps never felt real discomfort, but they are rare, and most performers find it hard to relax so completely. Such relaxation is the supreme form of technique and is not always attainable. Many of the finest pianists today are clearly driving themselves to bear pain. We must not, as I have remarked, blame the heavy action of modern pianos: Chopin himself had to warn students to cease playing when they felt genuine pain. The infliction of pain on keyboard performers begins, in fact, in the early nineteenth century, with the accompaniment to Schubert's *Erlkönig,* which seems to have caused the composer himself some problems to perform. Several Scarlatti sonatas are as difficult to play with accuracy as any work by Liszt, but none of them has ever caused physical anguish to a performer. The most famous danger to health comes from the brilliant displays of staccato octaves, like the finale to the Hungarian Rhapsody no. 6 of Liszt, but such passages are very short in Chopin, with the exception of the left-hand octaves in the Polonaise in A flat Major, op. 53. However, the legato octaves of the Etude in B Minor, op. 25, no. 10, are even more punishing than anything in Liszt. Chopin's sadism is usually more subtle than that of his contemporaries, and in most of his work actual pain is associated with emotional violence.

In the etudes of Chopin, the moment of greatest emotional tension is generally the one that stretches the hand most painfully, so that the muscular sensation becomes—even without the sound—a mimesis of passion. Perhaps this is what lies behind Rachmaninoff's reported reaction to Alfred Cortot's recording of the etudes, almost the cruellest observation ever made by one pianist about another: "Whenever it gets difficult, he adds a little sentiment." There is no question that the gradual increase of difficulty in a Chopin etude generally corresponds to the degree of emotional tension—although this does not mean that slowing down is invariably the most satisfactory way of interpreting such passages. It does imply an intimate relationship between virtuosity and emotional force in the mature works of Chopin. The hand of the performer literally feels the sentiment. This is another reason why Chopin often wanted the most delicate passage played with the fifth finger alone, the most powerful cantabile with the thumb. There is in his music an identity of physical realization and emotional content that is paralleled by the identity of tone-color and contrapuntal structure.

Virtuosity and decoration (salon music?)

There is an urbane, worldly aspect to Chopin's style that partly accounts for his immense popularity; it has also given him a bad name among amateurs who take their music earnestly. Chopin's urbanity has two strongly contrasting facets: a virtuoso glitter, above all the use of fast, brilliant passage work in the upper reaches of the piano; and a fashionable sentimentality, employed directly and openly, without humor—there is, in fact, irony and wit but not a trace of humor in Chopin's music, neither the diabolical humor of Liszt nor the ambiguous poetic humor so striking in Schumann.

Superficial brilliance and sentimentality are generally assumed to be the typical characteristics of salon music: I am not sure just why this is supposed to distinguish it from the rest of music. Glittering passage work in the upper octaves of the keyboard is found above all in the concertos played in large concert halls (and this is as true of Chopin as it was of Hummel, Field, and Weber); and sentimentality is as much operatic as instrumental. "Salon music" is usually a pejorative term, and there is no doubt that a great deal of bad music was played in salons—but not, I think, more than was played in public concerts, in the home, or in the opera house. It is not clear whether there is, in fact, any such thing as salon music, or at least whether any satisfactory definition of such a genre can be found. It is, nevertheless, a useful term only as long as we do not try to attach too limited a meaning or determine too nicely who listens to it.

Music may be performed to a large audience that has paid for admission, to an audience strolling casually by in the street or in the park, to a small private audience, for a small group of friends, for musicians only, for oneself. There is chamber music, popularly supposed to be written above all for the pleasure of the performers, although during the lifetimes of Haydn and Beethoven the string quartet was a considerably more public form than the piano sonata (critics have even remarked that the openings of many of the late Haydn quartets were designed to silence an inattentive audience). *Hausmusik*—music for the home—was designed for the pleasure of the amateur, like the easy piano sonatas and the compositions and arrangements for piano four hands so popular until the advent of recording.

The conditions under which music is performed influence the way it is written, but this influence is rarely simple, and it is impossible to confine music to its social function. Just as some of the most idiomatic keyboard music mimics other instruments, as Scarlatti imitates the trumpet and the guitar, and Liszt the flute and the cymbalum, so the most characteristic chamber music imitates the public genre, as the finale of Mozart's Sonata in B flat Major, K.333, reproduces the entire structure and sound of a concerto finale, and Beethoven's String Quartets, op. 59, magnificently employ the texture of orchestral writing. These works would not, of course, make their effect if there were not a normal or standard chamber style against which they react. Nevertheless, many works partly, and some works wholly, transcend the conditions for which they were designed. Schubert's *Winterreise* makes the amiable gathering of friends in which *Lieder* were generally performed seem an inauspicious and inadequate framework (although modern performance in public recital has its own musical awkwardness and discomfort), just as Bach's *Mass in B Minor* is not easy to conceive satisfactorily in any of the conditions of performance open to the composer.

An attempt by Nicholas Temperley in the *New Grove* to classify Chopin's production in three groups—works for concert performance, works for teaching and salon performance, and works both personal and esoteric, which escape both from pedagogy and the salon—is interesting but not completely convincing. The etudes, for example, are in the end not really pedagogical in intent; most of them demand a level of technique that Chopin can never have found among his students, and they are no more teaching pieces than Blake's *Songs of Innocence* are poems for small children. They quickly became concert display pieces. The Nocturnes, on the other hand, supposedly "salon music" of the most evident kind, were used for teaching by Chopin himself perhaps more often than any other works. It is not the purpose for which the work was written that determines its style but the genre within which the composer works, and which he may alter and even create as he writes: what demands attention is less the immediate intent of the composer than the tradition in and on which he is acting. Both etude and nocturne existed as genres before Chopin took them up (although Chopin was to write the first musically viable etudes), and it is true that the nocturne started in the salon, the etude in the practice room, but Chopin's versions leave behind both salon and practice room. The style of the genre may have been determined by its original function, but the style of the individual examples is not only more personal but even transcends any personal intent. Over the years Chopin's etudes and nocturnes have become essential elements in a tradition of performance that he can never have foreseen—on instruments, in immense concert halls, and through recordings that he could not even have imagined. The historicist attempt to bring these works back to their original social functions runs the risk of a double misunderstanding: it severely and unnecessarily reduces the significance of the achievement, since posterity was to discover certain important aspects of the music only dimly visible to contemporaries; and it even tends more often than not to misrepresent these original conditions. Structurally the etudes were practice pieces; athietic training was inherent in their form but that was not their artistic purpose. The nocturnes were as much private meditations as light, social entertainment—in fact, both etude and nocturne draw some of their power from the way they overwhelm the modest expectations aroused by an apparently unpretentious genre.

In any case, the so-called salon style, the brilliant passage work of Chopin's early works, principally the Rondos and the works with orchestra, largely disappears in the music he composed after the age of twenty—disappears or is transformed: either the brilliance is an essential part of the motivic structure, or it becomes the vehicle of passion. The Rondos provide us with moments like the following, essentially derived from concerto style:

These bars from the Rondo, op. 16, are very close to much of Hummel—this passage, for example, from the Piano Trio in E, op. 83, of 1819:

Similar examples can be found in the piano music of Weber and the concertos of Field.

For the writing of mechanical passage work intended to dazzle, Chopin's superiority to his predecessors lay chiefly in the delicacy of his ear, his ability to make the piano vibrate with delicious sonorities. The trick consisted above all in the spacing of chords and the use of the pedal. At times Field came close to Chopin in his feeling for sound, but the sonority is less refined, the virtuosity less complex and less inventive:

This lovely passage from Field's Concerto no. 2 in A flat Major shows his sense of spacing and pedal, which had such a great influence on Chopin. A page later Field combines brilliance and delicacy:

This is beautifully laid out, but the left-hand writing is even less imaginative than the accompaniments found in the Italian opera of the time, all too justly famous for their banality (although dramatically effective and, in Bellini, sensitively orchestrated). The agreeable sonority that Field creates often relies on unyielding strings of parallel tenths, sixths, and thirds, as in the finale of the same concerto:

Parallel thirds, sixths, and, above all, tenths make up the easiest and most superficial formula for creating a pretty sound. Like Schubert, Chopin did not disdain it, but generally built it into a less naive structure—or else isolated the parallel lines for their effect as pure sound, as in the slow movement of the E Minor Concerto:

Two further examples of parallel motion from Chopin's Concerto in F Minor show this simple delight in sound even more strikingly, the first from the slow movement:

The second is from the finale:

These are not very different from Mozart's use of the glockenspiel in *The Magic Flute,* except that Chopin is even more uninhibited and musically less interest-

ing. The pleasure obviously needed no justification for him—no complex
relation of motif or process of modulation: the occasion for both examples is
a simple transition back into the opening theme.

Chopin's exquisite ear saved him from the ugly repetition of thick chords in
the bass that frequently disfigure the work of Mendelssohn, Weber, and Hummel—and even of Field. The first movement of Field's Concerto no. 3 in E flat
Major shows this kind of unimaginative accompaniment:

Even in Chopin's early works, where this kind of texture is still found, it is
always tempered by adding a bass note below the repeated chords. The spacing
lets some air into the texture, and allows the harmony to vibrate against the
fundamental tone in the bass, as in the opening movement of Chopin's Concerto no. 1 in E Minor:

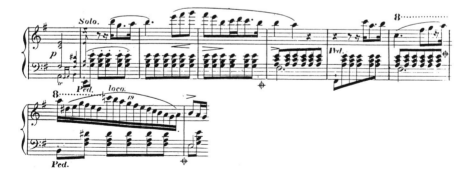

This is a technique learned probably from Field, who often employed it, and
whose ear was generally fine, his sense of spacing sensitive. Both Weber and
Mendelssohn, however, in an attempt to make a loud noise, use textures that
were unacceptable to Chopin, much as he was influenced by Weber. Two

examples can be offered: the end of the first movement of Weber's Sonata no. 1 in C Major:

and the opening of the finale of Mendelssohn's Sonata in E Major:

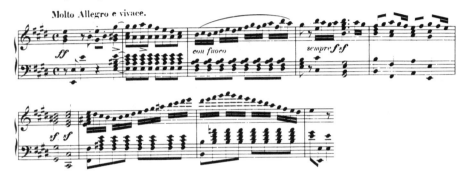

These accompaniments sounded considerably less hideous on an early nineteenth-century instrument, but they do not respect and exploit the overtones of the piano as Chopin's music always does. Even at the most brutal climaxes in his works, the inner parts, although thick, vibrate against a lower bass note. Chopin's extraordinary feeling for the open spacing of chords on the keyboard and the creation of enchanting sonorities was rivalled perhaps only by Schubert, largely in the music for four hands (and we know from Chopin's students of his admiration for some of the four-hand compositions of Schubert).

For most of his exploitation of mechanical virtuosity, Chopin was able to call upon an extraordinarily varied invention in the accompaniments as well as in the principal voices. This is true of the compositions finished by the time he was twenty, like the two concertos: this, from the finale of the F minor Concerto:

and this, from the opening movement of the Concerto in E Minor:

The second example shows the use of virtuosity for drama, but in both the accompanying figures have an energy of their own that complements the ornamental invention in the right hand.

In the latest works this richness of invention of virtuoso figuration is even more remarkable. In the scherzo of the Sonata in B Minor, op. 58, the counterpoint is partly built into the figuration:

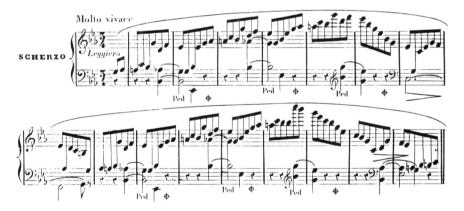

The accompaniment is almost minimal (although not completely devoid of motivic interest) because of the complexity of the figuration, which realizes much of the harmony through an implied polyphonic structure of three voices. The art is clearly related to the monophonic technique of the finale of the Sonata in B flat Minor, but here it sweeps through all the registers of the piano.

Three very similar late examples of figuration intended to dazzle show the consistency of principle that guided Chopin's variety. The first comes from the second group of the rondo finale of the B Minor Sonata:

The second opens the coda of the Impromptu in F sharp Major:

The last example is the final page of the Barcarolle:

From the middle of the first example, at bar 78, the bass line acquires an independent melodic interest, which is present from the beginning of the others. The scale passages hover between true melody and embroidery. They are not the essentially ornamental arabesques of Baroque style, although the technique is partly modeled on them (and we must remember that a Baroque revival was in full swing when Chopin was writing). These passages are basically derived from finger exercises, and they transform simple practice formulas into wonderful effects of tone color. Much of Chopin's ornament may be operatic—most decoration is operatic in origin—but not here. These are finger exercises not only conceived as decoration but further translated into melody, pure keyboard melody in which there is no mimesis of the voice, no cantabile. The cantabile is reserved for the lower and inner parts, which are played off against the figuration in a counterpoint of color as well as of line. In the first two examples the principal melodic voice is in the right-hand figuration, and the bass line comes into prominence above all when it parallels the right in a kind of heterophony (note the implied parallel octaves at the end of third bar quoted from the Impromptu). The page of the Barcarolle is more ambiguous, and the voices are almost equally balanced in interest: the rocking motion of the barcarole rhythm in the left hand is a foil to the fluid scales of the right, which, however, takes over more completely with the last beats of its ascent. The final cascade outlines the following cadence:

and its full sonority justifies the bare octaves at the end.

All these virtuoso effects could, with some justice, be characterized as salon style. They develop directly out of techniques found in the opera fantasies and potpourri display pieces that Chopin himself wrote before he was twenty: the Fantaisie on Polish Airs, the Introduction and Variations on a Theme from an opera by Louis-Joseph-Ferdinand Hérold. The label of salon style, however, does not help us to see Chopin's originality: the passages have a complexity of tone color realized infrequently by Chopin's predecessors or contemporaries, with the significant exception of Berlioz and Liszt, and Chopin's are achieved with a purity of voice leading beyond the reach of any contemporary. It is a rare combination of tone color and polyphonic structure that raises his virtuoso figuration above the level of similar passages in Field, Moscheles, and Hummel—not to speak of the once-famous virtuoso hackwork of Thalberg and Kalkbrenner. And when we reach the virtuoso conceptions of the scherzos, the dramatic force leaves any sense of the salon behind:

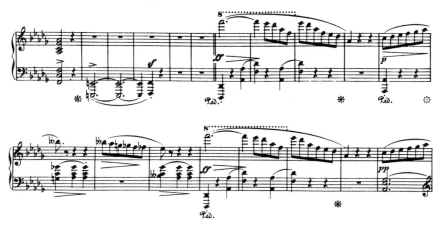

Here we have technical figuration as motif: the virtuoso glitter is necessary to the sense of violence and the brutal contrasts of dynamics.

Technical display in Chopin, after the early works, is transmuted into tone color or dramatic gesture—we may say, to accept the prejudices of Chopin's own generation, that it has been ennobled. This is the source of much of the poetry in Chopin's music: it comes from the transformation of the vulgar into something aristocratic. Its power depends in part on our unconscious sense of how commonplace the material originally was before it reappears with an aura of iridescent sonority. The metamorphosis of the finger exercise into a play of sound is demonstrated best not by the etudes but by a late piece, the Berceuse of 1844. The work is pure tone color. Structure—conceived as harmony and melody—is close to minimal, but then structure in this piece has largely become texture. The harmony is painfully simple: a rigid alternation, once per bar, of a tonic chord and a dominant seventh; a sustained pedal D flat is implied in the bass throughout (even if it must disappear at moments to avoid blurring); a coda adds a lengthy cadence with subdominant chords, the only harmonic change in the piece. The rhythm is the relentless rocking motion of the lullaby.

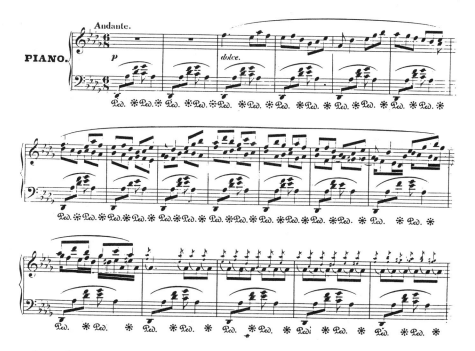

Over this monotonous underpinning the right hand delicately plays a series of minuscule etudes, two- and four-bar structures in each of which a simple but tricky figuration rises or falls sequentially over the keyboard almost independently of the basic harmony:

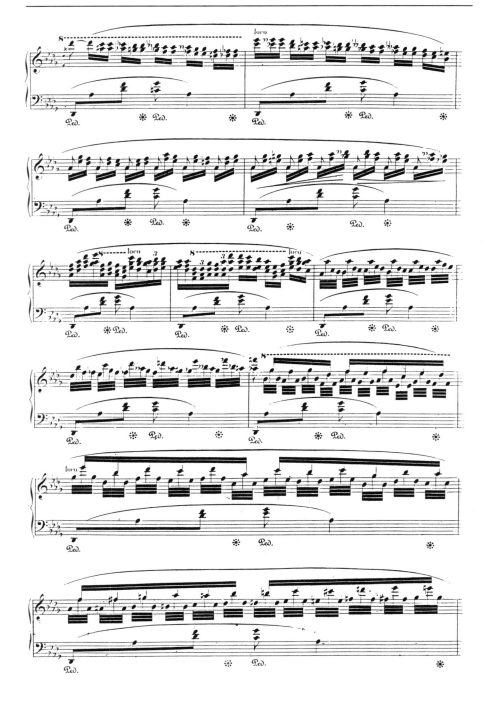

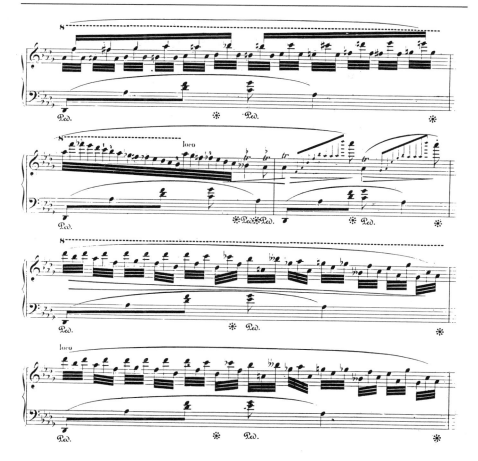

The apparent indifference of the right hand to the left, of the figuration to the
underlying harmony, creates a web of delicate dissonances, a grill of sonority
like the mixtures on a Baroque organ that never disturbs the insistently repeating harmonic structure but seems to have a life of its own. These tiny two-bar
finger exercises vary from the most banal scales to the most original patterns.
The choice of a lullaby for a display of extraordinary technical skill in execution is significant. All overt excitement has been removed from virtuosity,
leaving only the breathless tension which is the homage paid to supreme grace.
The marvel of this piece is that the virtuosity is largely inexpressive, as if
illustrating the thoughtless, unself-conscious mechanical control that was
Kleist's definition of grace in the most famous of all Romantic essays on
aesthetics, "On the Marionette Theater."

Morbid intensity

Chopin escaped the dangers of superficial virtuosity either by ennobling it, as we have seen, or by employing it with consummate disdain. And yet he evaded the sentimentality of salon style more ambiguously—by magnifying and exaggerating it, by forcing it to the point of morbidity. It was a common reproach of Chopin's contemporaries that his music was sick—and this was not unjustified, but it ought not to have been a reproach. Indeed, the morbidity of Chopin's style is one of its claims to superiority, a kind of superiority that seems to escape all considerations of craft; it depends on an element of extravagance which is one of the virtues of Romantic style. This extravagance is a moral rather than an artistic quality, a quality that Mendelssohn lacked and that was largely irrelevant to Schubert, but that Chopin shared with Schumann, Liszt, and Berlioz, whose music he despised—perhaps at least partly because of the way that each of them eccentrically realized his own personal form of extravagance.

"Improvement makes strait roads," Blake wrote, "but the crooked roads without Improvement, are roads of Genius." Chopin's morbidity was his crooked road, and it saved him from good taste and from the bland neoclassicism that crippled the work of so many of his contemporaries. This morbidity has been traced by his biographers directly to his life: his unhappy existence as a Pole in exile, his stormy affair with George Sand, his physical frailty, his sickly constitution, his early death. Liszt claimed that Chopin himself had privately described the basis of his own character with the almost untranslatable Polish word *zal*: Liszt attempted to paraphrase the richness of meaning of this monosyllable elaborately as "inconsiderable regret after an irrevocable loss . . . a ferment of resentment, premeditation of vengeance, . . . sterile bitterness," and found all of this naturally in Chopin's music, and remarked on moments in the Etudes and Scherzos of "a concentrated exasperation, a despair sometimes ironic, sometimes disdainfully proud."

However we define this morbidity, it became clearly accentuated in the later works. When Liszt wrote his book on Chopin in 1850, a year after the latter's death (or the Princess Sayne-Wittgenstein wrote it for him), these late works were generally condemned as sickly, an opinion in which Liszt half concurred, remarking on a "sickly irascibility, arrived at the point of feverish trembling," but adding that in these final works, "from a technical point of view, one cannot deny that far from being diminished, the quality of the harmonic material has only become more interesting in itself, more curious to study." This alliance of rich harmonic interest and morbidity is found a few years later in Wagner's *Tristan und Isolde,* clearly part of the heritage of Chopin, transmitted through Liszt.

The description given by Liszt of Chopin's last large work, the Polonaise-Fantaisie, is naturally as overwritten as most of the musical descriptions of the period:

Despair rises to the brain like a large draught of Cyprus wine which gives a more instinctive rapidity to every gesture, a sharper point to every word, a more burning spark to every emotion, making the spirit reach a diapason of sensitivity close to delirium . . . Pictures largely unfavorable to art like all these of extreme moments, of agonies, of death rattles and the contractions in which the muscles lose all elasticity and the nerves, ceasing to be organs of will power, reduce man to the passive prey of pain. Deplorable aspects, which the artist should admit to his domain only with an extreme circumspection.

As a description of the Polonaise-Fantaisie, this is, to modern ears, absurd, but revealing both in the way it emphasizes the extreme aspect of Chopin's art, the tendency to go beyond what seems permissible, and in the way it brings out the heightened intensity of the music—"a more instinctive rapidity to every gesture, a sharper point to every word." It is this extraordinary intensity, this sharper point, that enabled Chopin, like Wagner, to escape from nineteenth-century sentimentality, as neither Schumann nor Liszt was completely able to do; emotionally he was more extravagant than they were.

Wagner's intensity, although partially learned from Chopin, and in fact inconceivable without Chopin's original inspiration, was totally public, even shameless in its lack of reticence; Chopin's remained private. In this respect, the salon, far from imposing its preference for artificial sweetness on Chopin, was paradoxically his means of escape from false sentiment: a painful intensity of sweetness often redeems the sentimentality by its pungency, gives it new force. His music remained after 1832 entirely in a salon format—or, at least, in a format possible for the salon. As a performer, he never conquered a large public: he depended on a small, select group of listeners, most of them from a fashionable Parisian world, and a few appreciative amateurs and connoisseurs. It was not a public that could really be judged superior (except in respect of birth) to the more democratic public of the grand concert, but its relative intimacy certainly made possible the kind of experimentation necessary to the development of Chopin's art. He was freed from public pressures, and, although the salon had its own insidious forms of coercion, they were of a kind that Chopin found easy to bear and even, largely, to ignore.

He made false sentiment real by intensifying it. What is generally meant by false sentiment is expression which has no profound hold on our lives—clichés with no psychological resonance, commonplaces which sound grand or handsome and can be uttered with no disturbing consciousness of their meaning. In this sense, "false" sentiment is as real as any other: it is expressed every day by all of us, and we believe what we are saying for the moment of speaking. To magnify these commonplaces, to give them rhetorical emphasis, is often to make them even more false, as sometimes happens in the music of Liszt and in much of the opera of the period. Chopin took his sentimental clichés where he found them, largely from Italian opera, charged them with a significance sometimes so complex that it made his public ill at ease, and then gave these clichés back, transformed, to composers of opera—German and French opera, that is, as Chopin's influence on the Italian stage was negligible.

Chopin's first published Nocturne, op. 9, no. 1, in B flat minor, displays the extravagance by which he forced sentimentality into a more immediate and less conventional expression of emotion:

The ornamentation in bars 2 and 3 is banal, derived largely from Italian opera: what is surprising is to find so much of it so soon, and, above all, its concentration. It turns the melancholy plaint of the opening bar into a surge of despair, complete with operatic sobs. (The pedalling of the first bar is clearly intended to continue, and the dots over the notes in bar 3 are not indications of staccato but of expressive emphasis, a direction to the pianist to linger delicately.) No doubt singers of the time began to improvise ornament as early as this in an aria, and it was not in the best of taste, I suppose, but Chopin had the genius to make some forms of bad taste a positive virtue. I do not know of another case where a composer requires decoration of such forceful expression so close to the opening of a modest piece. It has the effect of making the decoration seem less gratuitous, more an intensification of the phrase demanded by the structure of the melody.

Dividing the melody into two voices in bar 5 sustains this intensity by making it appear falsely as if the essential melodic structure were only in the upper voice: part of the tension derives from the difficulty of sustaining the A♭ in the upper voice until it rejoins the melody at the end of the bar. Difficult to sustain on a modern piano, and nearly impossible on a piano of the 1830s—in fact, absolutely impossible to hear when the left hand plays along, but the impossibility makes the passage all the more effective, as the sense must be conveyed by phrasing, and the ear then strives to hear a tone that has in reality died away by the end of the measure. The listener need not be aware of the notation: the pianist can make the division of voices clear by rhythm and phrasing. For the effect to work, however, the A♭ need last just long enough to establish that the D♭ is in another voice; the imagination of the pianist and the listener will take care of the rest. The leap downward and the indication *sforzando piano* set the A♭ sufficiently into relief. The ornamentation of many of Chopin's contemporaries, including Hummel and Field, could be equally lavish, but more rarely with the initial playing of the melody, and never with the same contrapuntal and radically chromatic intensity and abandon.

If these opening bars seem to be throwing away the most expressive variations at the very start, Chopin can go still further on the last page:

The indication *legatissimo* is purely expressive: almost all those notes in this passage are in the upper reaches of the keyboard, where Chopin's piano had no dampers anyway, and *legato* has no strictly acoustical meaning here. We must interpret *legatissimo* to mean a moderately slow and expressive rendering of the twenty-nine notes of the melody in this bar.

In the same opus, the Nocturne in B Major, no. 3, contains decoration that violates the normal conventions of ornament:

The chromaticism of the opening is conventional enough, although Chopin's notation of the inner part of the left hand (or the tenor) as a separate voice enforces a new and strange sonority, and creates interesting dissonances with the right hand's ornamental variant in bar 3. The strange variation in bar 9, however, is another matter: we could, no doubt, claim that the decoration resolves nicely according to the laws of harmony—in the first half of the bar, the F♮ resolves to the E, and both the E and C×resolve to the D♯—but that is not the way one hears it. Chopin has ordered the figure so that the resolution is ambiguous, or in fact it seems not to resolve at all but to resonate like an arpeggiated cluster. In Chopin's music, as in Baroque style, expression is largely conveyed through the ornamental notes, above all the appoggiaturas which carry the essential dissonances against the basic notes of the melody; the expressive force is concentrated in these dissonances. Here, however, these written-out appoggiaturas transcend their decorative function with a momentary sense of unresolved sonorities which take on a new and more powerful expressive force. Indeed, within the playful context they are overexpressive. To what an extent such decoration is a play of sonority for Chopin can be seen at the first return of this theme:

In bar 31 the high notes (C♮ and B) lie so far outside the main melodic register that they enter as isolated sonorities even though they are octave doublings of part of the main ornament. They are not only part of the ornamental figure but a counterpoint to it, a parallel to the inner voice in the left hand.

Chopin's power to transform banal appoggiatura, turns, and other graces into startlingly original figures is evident from the early works. One can see that the extravagance of his accomplishment would seem unhealthy to his right-thinking contemporaries. The later works are even more lavish, and the Nocturne in E flat Major, op. 55, no. 2, shows an extreme use of sentimental operatic formulas (as in bars 35–38):

The sequence is realized with hypercharged expressive ornament in a duet with both voices in the right hand, but even the left hand arpeggiation is given a vital expressive cast—doubly expressive, with the written-out appoggiaturas on the second and fourth beats of bars 35 and 36, and with the extraordinary range of the arpeggios which strain upward, crossing into the register of the melodic voices. The rich, overloaded texture was bound to seem morbid. The skeleton is found in the opening bars, which becomes in bars 9–12 something closer to the return of bars 35–38:

The extravagant version in bars 35 to 38, however, is not simply an overloading of ornament but a structural transformation, which makes the third and fourth bars of the phrase more intense. The progressive treatment shows:

The last two bars have now become an augmentation, a more slowly drawn-out version of the figure in each of the first two bars. The expressivity increases at the end of the phrase as the extravagance of the ornament disappears and the line becomes simpler.

It would be a mistake, therefore, to think that the intensity that burns off the sentimentality of Chopin's material is dependent solely upon lavishness, on a profusion of ornamental and contrapuntal detail. It comes even more often from a fierce concentration, one which could invest a single note with a wealth of meaning. As in Bellini, this note is generally the third degree of the scale; and the opening page of the Nocturne in F sharp Major, op. 15, no. 2, written before 1833, shows everything moving to a cadence in bar 24 on the A♯:

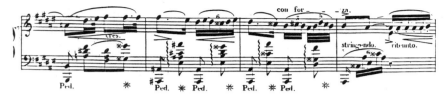

At the end the bass descends to the A♯, with a fourfold repetition on A♯ in the treble, but this resolution is prepared from the opening of the melody. The A♯ is continually set in relief by the phrasing (the end of bar 11 gives a refined example), but the secret of Chopin's technique is that almost every appearance of the A♯ has a different harmonic purpose, investing the note with a different tone color. Bars 7 and 8 are particularly subtle: all three A♯'s in the melody in bar 7 are equally important, but each has a different harmonic and melodic role, while in bar 8 the main harmonic movement is the chromatic descent in the tenor of A♯, A♮, G♯ (this voice leading is already prepared at the end of bar 7). The last beat of bar 8 emphasizes the reappearance of A♯ in the melody with a crescendo, a sweep upward, an octave doubling, and a firm tonic chord in root position—a sudden moment of rich sonority that adds great tension to the second playing of the opening theme. This concentration prepares the cadence in bar 24, where the voices converge on A♯; the underlying structure of this convergence is:

Chopin's exploitation of the power of insistence is similar here to the way he produced a modulation from F major to A minor at the opening of Ballade no. 2 or to the ostinato passage of the Polonaise in F sharp Minor (both discussed earlier). In the Nocturne, it purges the material of everything that might seem merely pretty and brings an edge of passion to the arabesque lines. The return of the opening section at the end confirms this concentration, and the point of greatest intensity is reached with the highest A♯ on the keyboard available to Chopin:

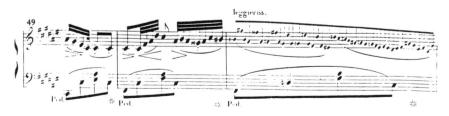

Bar 54, where the highest A♯ is played, was marked *con forza:* in an emendation of genius in a pupil's copy, Chopin added a sudden pianissimo on the third beat just before the A♯, giving it even greater prominence with an effect of extraordinary beauty. A detail of equal mastery is found in the movement from bar 57 to 58: the tenor part is left with an unresolved B at the end of 57, which is picked up and resolved into an A♯ a beat late in 58 with the accompaniment figure that sustains the A♯ until the end. The last bar is remarkable as all sonority disappears except for the tonic in the bass and the A♯ in the treble. This is an effect of great poetry—and a sufficiently radical ending to have inspired a banal variant pencilled into the copy of one of Chopin's students, which adds a full chord and brings the melody down to the tonic. I do not know anyone who really thinks that this regrettable variant is by Chopin, but it is interesting that the original ending should have disturbed a contemporary, even if it was, after all, the composer himself in a moment of self-doubt.

It is not repetition alone that gives such intensity to this composition but
the wonderful variety of harmonies and textures evoked by the repetition. A
basis for comparison would be the opening of the slow movement of the
Symphony in D Minor of César Franck:

Darius Milhaud used to give this to his students as a horrid example of a
composer's inability to get off a note. In the Franck, almost every appearance
of the F is harmonized by a perfect triad in root position, and most are tonic
triads. The resourcefulness of Chopin's repetition is a remarkable contrast: it
works imperceptibly, and it is only with the cadences in bar 24 and in the last
bar of the piece that one feels the mechanics of the elaborate preparation.

On occasion, Bellini and Verdi—more rarely, Donizetti—gave new life to the
banal and conventional motifs of Italian opera merely by letting them speak
directly, simply, and without shame, so that the conventionality seems to
disappear with an air of conviction. Chopin's way of purifying his motifs of
false sweetness was more sophisticated—and may, in fact, appear less coura-
geous. He brought all his command of classical polyphony and harmonic
invention to bear on material apparently simple. This gave his art an over-
charged complexity that made it often quite literally offensive to his contemporaries. It should be added that Bellini's ability to arrange his motifs to sustain
a melody for great lengths has a refinement if not a richness comparable to

Chopin's technique, as does Verdi's understanding of long-range dramatic organization. Nevertheless, the intensity of detail and the mastery of complex polyphonic form in Chopin's music have no parallel in his own time, and they make his work, in spite of its immense popularity, the most private and esoteric achievement of the period.

Chopin: From the Miniature Genre to the Sublime Style

Folk music?

Folk music is always considered a good thing. There is a catch, however: it has to be "real" folk music, anonymous, evoking not an individual but a communal personality, expressive of the soil. The Hungarian Rhapsodies of Liszt have been all too often condemned because they use Gypsy, not peasant, tunes. True folk music is produced only by farmers and shepherds; only this can guarantee its mythical status, its down-to-earth contrast with sophisticated urban music. Folk music, in fact, is not art but nature. The composer who turns to folk material is like the landscape artist who paints out of doors: they both reject the artificial for the natural; they start not with what is invented but with what is given by reality.

Folk tunes have been used in art music at least since the fifteenth century. However, the special status of folk music as fundamentally different from art music, as an innocent art that had not yet eaten of the Tree of Good and Evil and suffered the corruption of learned and sophisticated culture, dates from the latter part of the eighteenth century, when the industrial development of cities made a vacation in the country seem like a virtuous duty, an obligation to oneself and not just a simple pleasure. Pastoral poetry by the end of the eighteenth century was no longer a literary exercise that evoked a rustic Golden Age, but an evocation of a very recent past as mythical in its moral integrity and uncorrupted simplicity as the classical Golden Age. Collections of folk poetry, ancient legends, and fairy tales were made at this time in most European lands. They were a patriotic manifestation of Romantic nationalism, a protest against the authoritarian forms of academic classicism. The French and the Irish hoped to recover their legendary Celtic past. The Germans and the English attempted to revive their medieval and premedieval Nordic civilizations as a way of asserting an individual cultural identity against the dominance of modern French culture and the worn-out academic models of Greek and Roman art and literature. Folk art was not only picturesque but morally and politically liberating.

Along with the new consciousness of folk art and the attempt to recover national and local folk traditions came, naturally, the sophisticated imitation of folk art—the writing of songs in what was conceived to be a naive folk manner, the production of modern ballads in neomedieval style, the rustic elements in Haydn's symphonies, the popular folklike tunes given to Papageno in *Die Zauberflöte*—and the faking of folk art as well. James Macpherson's *Ossian* is only the most scandalous example of such forgery: of course, a high value placed on authenticity is an immediate stimulus to a forger. From the collection of authentic folk material to imitation and then to forgery is not a series of separate stages but an unbroken line, and it is hard to classify many of the examples, from Bishop Percy's tactless rewriting of old ballads to bring them into line with modern taste, to the literal transcriptions of the oral tradition of fairy tales made by the brothers Grimm and published, first with philological notes and then, in later editions, with artistic improvements—this after they had objected to Clemens Brentano's overly poetic treatment of fairy tales. The *Knaben Wunderhorn* of Brentano and Achim von Arnim contains new poems by the editors alongside the popular verses they had collected from past centuries. The concept of authenticity was ideologically important but it had very little practical application (except in the hands of a few irascible and eccentric bibliographers like Joseph Ritson).

It was perhaps above all in opera that folk elements were exploited with the greatest frequency, as they were so useful in creating picturesque effects of local color, of making heroic outbursts of patriotism most persuasive. Operas with Swiss backgrounds like Rossini's *Guillaume Tell* were filled with yodel phrases, and Berlioz cynically transported his Faust in one scene to Hungary in order to introduce a version of the Rákóczi March. Folk music provides an artificially picturesque atmosphere, and often resembles the rustic dialogue in eighteenth-century French and English comedy, which had little relation to the way peasants actually spoke. It does not matter that the folk elements are generally pure convention with no direct connection to any known folk style, like the Turkish music in Mozart's work—all that is necessary is that it seem exotic with lots of percussion (the choruses in *Die Entführung aus dem Serail* sound vaguely Hungarian more than anything else). It is mainly out of the French operatic tradition that the taste for exotic color grows, and both Chopin and Liszt worked in Paris, Chopin indeed for most of his creative life. The French have perhaps been the greatest masters of other national styles: they showed the Spaniards how to write Spanish music and the Russians how to write Russian. (In the hands of Edouard Lalo, in fact, the Russian and Spanish pieces sound surprisingly alike.) The Romantic form of the Hungarian Rhapsody, on the other hand, was invented by Schubert, and it was from him that Liszt inherited both the structure and the manner. No composer restricted himself to his own national style: Chopin, with a bolero and a tarantella, ventured into the Spanish and Neapolitan picturesque, and Liszt did some of his most considerable work in the Spanish, Venetian, Neapolitan, and Swiss veins.

Chopin's mazurkas stand apart from the rest of the considerable production inspired by folk music which reaches into all forms of Romantic music; they cannot conveniently be classified with any of the other manifestations. They are not arrangements of popular folk tunes, like Beethoven's arrangements of Scottish songs, Liszt's Hungarian Rhapsodies, or Brahms's Hungarian Dances; Chopin's mazurkas contain few, if any, Polish tunes—although one of them, indeed, contains an imitation of Scottish bagpipes. They are not evocations of landscape and local color like Liszt's Swiss and Italian pieces. Chopin's treatment of folk or national style is, in fact, very advanced, prophetic of Debussy's evocation of Spanish music. He uses only fragments of melody, Polish formulas, typical national rhythms, and he combines them in his own way with great originality. From early on, Chopin's mazurkas are much more elaborate than the few modest pieces employing mazurka rhythms by Chopin's Polish predecessors, and they soon became the occasion for some of the most complex and pretentious of Chopin's forms.

Furthermore, they are not brilliant salon dances like the waltzes. I do not mean that Chopin's waltzes were intended for practical dance use, and I presume that they were, in fact, rarely danced in a Parisian salon, but the waltz was a recognizable form for Chopin's audience, who knew the proper steps and understood the conventions of the rhythm. Not so the mazurka, which was considerably more ambiguous. As a matter of fact, the mazurka is not a dance but a number of very different kinds of dances. Descriptions tend to be deplorably vague: "The dance has the character of an improvisation, and is remarkable for the liberty and variety in its figures," we read in the *New Grove,* which adds that it is characterized by "a certain pride of bearing and sometimes a wildness" and that it "can express all kinds of feeling and even shades of mood." This left Chopin with all the freedom he could have wished.

Few of his mazurkas can be assigned unequivocally to one specific type: he combined the different kinds of rhythm with considerable liberty. Accounts of mazurka rhythms are comically confused. The three main types of mazurka are, we read in Gerald Abraham,[1] "all characterized by the accent on the third beat," and he appends a note: "According to some authority, the mazur takes the accent on the second beat." Not only the *mazur,* but also the *kujawiak* and the *oberek* (other varieties of mazurka) often take the accent on the second beat. The *New Harvard Dictionary of Music* (1986) is more hesitant; the different kinds of mazurka "are linked by common rhythmic traits, such as strong accents unsystematically placed on the second or third beat." Unsystematically? Not at all: there are different systems, or rhythmic figures, which are quite coherent. The most common is

1. Gerald Abraham, *Chopin's Musical Style* (London, 1939).

where the accent shifts from the third beat to the second at the fourth bar to provide a decisive close. The *New Harvard Dictionary* characterizes the *kujawiak* as "similar to the mazurka, but slower" (Abraham, too, calls it "slow and melancholy"), and gives three examples from Chopin, one (op. 6, no. 4) marked *Presto, ma non troppo* and with a metronome indication of ♩. = 76—this makes a quarter note equal to 228, which is the fastest indication ever given by Chopin to one of his mazurkas, most of which vary between 126 and 160 to the quarter. It is clear that Chopin took what he pleased from his native folk music and adapted it without inhibition. The mazurka provided him with a repertoire of motifs, rhythms, and sonorities outside the main Italian, French, and German traditions of European music: he used it to create a series of works within this tradition which are absolutely personal—marginal works which challenge the center.

They are the most eccentric and original of Chopin's works. We shall never know exactly what and how much Chopin took directly from the popular folk tradition and how much he invented, but it does not matter: his originality is revealed as much in what he selected as in what he imagined. The folk dances gave him the possibility of exploring new harmonies, of exploiting the emotional effect of obsessive repetition, and of developing a new form of rubato.

Rubato

Most of the written-out indications of rubato in Chopin are to be found in the mazurkas (although he ceased to use this direction after opus 24).[2] It is probable that Chopin used the older form of rubato so important to Mozart (as he writes in his letters) and classed as an ornament by late eighteenth-century writers. In this form, the melody note in the right hand is delayed until after the note in the bass. Mozart occasionally wrote this out in slow movements (see Chapter 1) and it is certain that he played this way in many passages where he did not write it out. We associate this manner of rubato with the early twentieth century, when it was used lavishly by Ignacy Paderewski and Harold Bauer, more sparingly by Josef Hofmann and Moriz Rosenthal, but it dates back at least to 1750 if not before, and was already called rubato, or *temps dérobé*. An allied form of this rubato is the arpeggiation of the chords thereby delaying the melody note; according to Chopin's pupil, Carl Mikuli, Chopin was firmly opposed to this practice. Brahms, however, arpeggiated most chords when he played, according to contemporary witnesses, but I do not suggest this as a guide to performing his works. It was in Chopin's playing of the mazurkas that his liberty of rhythm seems to have been most remarkable (although conductors, including Berlioz, complained when they had to accompany him in one of his concertos). It is improbable that this liberty was

2. Jeffrey Kallberg informs me that a manuscript of the waltz, op. 34, no. 1, contains the indication *rubato*.

capricious. Not only did Chopin insist to his students on the importance of working with a metronome, but there is the precious testimony of Sir Charles Hallé, who said that Chopin's rhythmic freedom in the mazurkas seemed so natural that he was not even struck by it for years. In 1845 or 1846, however, Hallé remarked to Chopin that he played most of his mazurkas as if they were notated in 4/4 and not 3/4. Chopin at first denied this energetically, but finally agreed when Hallé made him play a mazurka and counted aloud to him as he did so. Chopin then said, laughing, that the rhythm was the national character of the dance. A similar altercation between Chopin and Meyerbeer in front of one of Chopin's students ended less amicably, as Chopin on that occasion resented being told that he played his mazurkas in two instead of three.[3]

An observation of Hallé needs to be emphasized here: when one heard Chopin play, he remarked, one had the impression of a 3/4 rhythm and not a binary one even if objective measurement made it binary. It is clear that the lengthening of one of the three beats is a form of accent related to a specific rhythm, and Hallé never claimed that Chopin played all the mazurkas in this fashion. Which beat was so privileged and for which rhythmic form is another question, and Hallé's belief that Chopin insistently lengthened the first beat of the bar must be mistaken—this is only possible in some instances, and would make nonsense of the rhythm elsewhere. We have other witnesses, however, although they are too late to testify directly to Chopin's manner. Moriz Rosenthal, who studied not only with Liszt but also with Mikuli, always played one particular mazurka rhythm as if it were notated in 4/4, altering

| ♫ ♩ ♩ | to | ♫ ♩ ♩ |

The middle section of the Mazurka in A Minor, op. 17, no. 4, provides an example:

3. Jean-Jacques Eigeldinger, *Chopin vu par ses élèves* (Neuchâtel, 1979), pp. 110–112.

The deformation brings vitality to an otherwise bland rhythm, makes it more rustic, and emphasizes the drone, but we must be careful not to apply it across the board to every other rhythmic figure in the mazurkas. In an interview, Rosenthal once indignantly rejected the possibility of deforming the mazurka rhythm into duple time, but the evidence of his own recordings shows that he did.[4] Like Chopin, he was unaware of the *rubato,* and he felt it as triple time—as we all do.

This specific liberty of execution should not be confused with the written directions of *rubato* found, for example, at the last playing of the main theme in opus 7, no. 3:

Rubato here means a slightly slower, freer, and more expressive rendering, and the detached notes four bars after the indication of *rubato* make a similar point. Opus 24, no. 1, in G minor begins with this indication:

---

4. I am indebted to Richard Johnson for this information about Rosenthal's interview.

and we must assume that the pianist is to start with the freely expressive
inflections generally reserved for the second playing of the theme—and this
mazurka, indeed, begins as if already in the middle of a phrase.

Modal harmony?

We must not exaggerate Chopin's use of modal harmony in the mazurkas: in
every instance he rationalizes a modal form into something purely tonal. The
principal modal characteristic of Polish music seems to be Lydian—that is, a
scale on the white keys of the piano starting on F, consequently with a
sharpened fourth degree (or B♮). The modal sound does not impress by its
Polish individuality: a scale with a sharpened fourth seems to be common to
most Western folk cultures, not just Polish, and long before Chopin it was the
most ordinary way to make something sound rustic and folksy. Haydn employs
it to great effect in the slow movement of the *"Drum Roll"* Symphony, and
Rossini makes a similar use of it in the third section of the overture to
Guillaume Tell.

In the Mazurka in E Major, op. 6, no. 3, Chopin makes classical use of the
sharpened fourth in order to indicate country matters:

The pastoral effect includes the equally rustic drone bass, which has, in fact, been sounding since the beginning:

Notice the shift of accent in the first four bars—two bars with an accent on the third beat, and then two bars with what might be called a syncopated hemiola—that is, one 6/4 bar and three bars of 2/4 with the accent on the weak beat of each. This pattern is repeated in the Mazurka in C Major, op. 24, no. 2, bars 53–56:

(We can safely assume that this rhythm is derived directly from the Polish folk tradition.) In these mazurkas of opus 6, written when he was twenty, Chopin employs the traditional elements of the musical picturesque. He was shortly to make much more personal use of them.

The apparently "modal" harmony of opus 17, no. 4, in A minor, written two years later, is very much more individual. The Lydian harmony gives an exotic color:

At the end of bar 20—in fact, already at bar 12—it is clear that this is not Lydian but a solid minor.[5] The sixth chord on A

not only gives a strange plaintive character to the tonic, but also enables Chopin to accomplish the wonderful chromatic descent in bars 6 to 11 from F to D; further, the resolutions onto sixth chords in bars 9 and 10 help to transform any suggestion of modal harmony into an evocative chromatic resonance. The end shows Chopin experimenting with sonority, and produces an extraordinary series of tritones:

5. Similarly, the end of opus 24, no. 2, seems to me not "strict modality" (as Nicholas Temperley calls it in the *New Grove*) but strict tonal C major; what makes it sound wonderfully rustic is the splendid series of parallel fifths. The only real modality in the Mazurkas—perhaps the only real modality in Chopin—is found in bars 21 to 36 of this Mazurka, which have a genuine Lydian sound, not just an F major with a rustically sharpened fourth. Even here, indeed, the repeated dominant seventh chord of C major tends to undermine the modal effect.

The last bars, which return to the opening phrase, shake the firm plagal cadence in A minor but not the sense of tonality. They turn the piece into an ideal Romantic fragment: complete and provocative, well-rounded and yet open.

Mazurka as Romantic form

It is in the mazurkas that we find most of Chopin's essays in the fragment. There are mazurkas like opus 33, no. 1, that begin as if in the middle, with a final cadence,

and others with endings at once inconclusive yet wonderfully satisfying. Some of these fragments—opus 7, no. 5, in C major, opus 24, no. 4, in B flat minor—were published as the last mazurkas in their opus, as if to emphasize the open ending when the opus was played as a whole.

The end of opus 41, no. 3, is perhaps most remarkable; it simply stops in the middle of a phrase, as if Chopin had just discovered with surprise that nothing more was necessary:

This is both poetic and ironic, achieved with great delicacy and the minimum of emphasis.

The contrast we have found between naïveté and urbanity, simple folk motifs and sophisticated handling, may be put more paradoxically. The mazurkas are the most learned section of Chopin's work. Open displays of skill at classical counterpoint are rare in Chopin, but he amuses himself several times in the mazurkas after 1840 with examples of canonic imitation. Writing a strict fugue seems never to have caught Chopin's fancy sufficiently to have inspired a good one, but the Mazurka in C sharp Minor, op. 50, no. 3, adapts fugal technique freely to astonishing effect. It begins like a fugue, although tonic entries and dominant entries do not follow each other successively but are separated:

The texture is more elaborately fugal at the return of the opening theme:

Pages like these are interesting as they reveal how the counterpoint becomes more extrovert during the latter years of Chopin's lifetime. They do not convey the range of his contrapuntal thought, or its intensity, which lies hidden in apparently straightforward homophonic passages. We can see this already in Chopin's first published Mazurka, op. 6, no. 1, in F sharp minor (we may disregard two printed without opus number when Chopin was only sixteen):

Throughout we are conscious of the alto in counterpoint with the melody, partly because, in the first two bars, the melody divides into two voices:

and in bars 3 and 4 the alto continues to echo the opening descent at the same pitch, and then turns it into a chromatic descent:

All this is discreet enough, giving only an individual richness and coherence to the voice leading, but above all, it prepares the beautiful effect in bars 13 to 15, where the F♮ changes to an F♯ and gives a surprising new meaning to the twice-repeated melodic figure. The subtlest nuances of harmony in Chopin are so powerful because, like this one, they have been prepared contrapuntally many bars in advance.

The form of the initial section (bars 1 to 40) of this first mazurka is completely traditional, but it has nothing to do with Polish folk tradition: it is the conventional three-phrase binary form of the eighteenth-century minuet (in which the first part consists of the first phrase played twice, and the second part, also repeated, groups phrases two and three together, with the third phrase either identical with the first or similar to it). Minuets often end their first phrase on the dominant, but equally often we find a tonic cadence—for example, in the minuet-scherzos of Haydn's Quartets, op. 30, nos. 2, 3, 4, 5, and 6. Chopin frequently uses this form (it may be summed up as AABABA) as well as a variant in which the second part is not repeated (or AABA). This is almost always followed by a central section or trio and a return of the initial mazurka, most often abridged to its final phrase alone.

I give these details not for their intrinsic interest—they have none—but, first, to show that Chopin employs the most conventional forms of art music, and, second, to emphasize the rigid sectional structure of the mazurkas, characteristics quite normal and proper for dance music. Both these characteristics are associated with the mazurka throughout Chopin's life, but he begins very early on to play with both the conventional form and the sectional phrase structure in increasingly subtle and varied ways. It is, in fact, in studying the mazurka that one finds the greatest sense of gradual progress and stylistic change in his work.

Already with the second set of mazurkas Chopin begins to enlarge on the central or trio section. Opus 7, no. 3, in F minor, of 1831, has a central section of forty-eight bars, twice as long as the introduction and initial section. This center is made up of three clearly distinct eight-bar tunes, each played twice. The transition back to the introduction is particularly impressive. The Mazurka begins with the sonority of the bare fifth associated with a drone:

The drone is not simply rustic: its mysterious and even sinister sonority is an exercise in the Romantic grotesque. The last part of the middle section and the return to the beginning are remarkable:

Chopin exploits sonority here, doubling the A♭ in bar 74 so that the fifth with the D♭ in the bass is set in relief, and gives a mysterious coloring to this bar with the illusion of D flat minor—the F♭ being merely an anticipation of the E♮ in the C major triad.

This transition is grand, but it has nothing like the cohesion that Chopin was to reveal in the next set, opus 17. It is with these Mazurkas that he developed the effect of changing key almost imperceptibly by tying one note from the last chord of one section into the first of the next. Number 3 in A flat Major begins with a repeated F♭ in the alto:

The F♭ (E♮) prepares the trio section in E major. The movement from A flat to E major and then back again is accomplished by sustaining one note and changing the harmony. The modulation to E is as follows:

The accented C♭ turns into a B, and the soprano note remains stationary.[6] The return to A flat is even more delightfully poetic; it depends on the presence of an E♮ / F♭ as the last note of the middle section:

One section dissolves into the next, and passages like these offer a pianist who enjoys them a chance to exploit the harmony through tone color.

In the final dances of this opus, and, above all, of the next, opus 24, Chopin begins to transform the mazurka from a miniature salon piece into something more ambitious. In both these sets we find for the first time the long coda which radically alters the proportions and the significance of the mazurka. Opus 17, no. 4, in A Minor has already been quoted above (pp. 417–418), and opus 24, no. 4, in B flat Minor is on a still larger scale. The latter begins with four bars of introduction followed by a melody separated by the notation into two voices,[7] after which the second voice becomes an obbligato counterpoint:

6. For this kind of modulation to work, it is evident that the shift must be to a mediant, as that allows one of the notes of the main triad to remain stationary.

7. Misled by the notation, I suppose, Gerald Abraham considers bars 5 to 12 as still only introduction (*Chopin's Musical Style*, p. 48). He seems to sense how wrong this reading is as he continues: "The main part of the mazurka grows out of the introduction so spontaneously that one hardly realizes that the opening, after the first bars, is still only introduction, especially as the main theme is foreshadowed in bars 5 and 6"—and 7 to 12, he might have added. "One hardly realizes that the opening . . . is still only introduction" because it isn't, and I mention this odd error from an excellent book only to remark that the opening melody of this mazurka is one of those interesting phrases that must be played twice in order to seem complete, like the first themes of the Mazurkas, op. 6, no. 4 and op. 7, no. 4 (both played twice at every appearance)—and like the "Valse noble" of Schumann's *Carnaval,* for which most editions, including the first, mistakenly leave out the repeat sign for the opening phrase.

The division into two voices illuminates the thematic structure, the kind of hidden polyphony to which Chopin was more sensitive than any of his contemporaries. The expressive theme and the way it rises to a *fortissimo* climax reveal a deeply serious intensity.

The new seriousness is intensified in what follows. A motif in the next section (derived from the introduction) produces an extraordinary series of parallel sevenths that lead back to the main theme:

These dissonances are willfully harsh yet expressive; the Romantic grotesque, central to Schumann and Berlioz, is found nowhere else in Chopin with such clarity as in the mazurkas; even the Preludes are less radical. It was the "folk" character, real or invented, that liberated the grotesque in Chopin, that enabled him to break so sharply with ideals of decorum and respectability.

For the Romantic, the grotesque is a violation of the classical standards of beauty, an irruption of the ugly—the intrusion of life, in short, into art. The most famous justification for the grotesque was Victor Hugo's preface to his drama *Cromwell,* a preface which served for many years as a manifesto of the French Romantic movement; the grotesque was partly a reminiscence of medieval art, but it also encouraged a powerful movement toward realism. With this in mind, we can understand one of Chopin's most brilliant innovations, first revealed in the coda to this Mazurka:

Here we have a new kind of melody for the keyboard which recalls half-sung, half-spoken fragments of folk music. Presented as if dying away in the distance, or receding from consciousness with the coming of sleep, the obsessively repeated motifs cover a final cadence which they appear to ignore, continuing after the piece is over.

The boldness is extended in the next four Mazurkas, op. 30, and was remarked on with admiration by Schumann, above all the alternation of major and minor in no. 3 in D flat Major. The shock is the last bar, which resolves the ambiguity laconically in favor of the major mode:

The alternation is emphasized by the brutal juxtaposition of *fortissimo* and *pianissimo*, another element of the grotesque found only in the Mazurkas.

With this piece, however, Chopin develops an extraordinary fludity as well. The central section is once again expanded to forty-eight bars, three separate mazurka tunes, each immediately repeated:

At the end of the first playing of each mazurka tune, there is a clear break in the texture: at bars 32–33 the melody starts again only after a rest and a change in harmony; bars 48–49 change from *sotto voce* to a sudden *forte;* the third mazurka theme is first played softly, comes to a firm close in bar 64, and starts again *forte.* On the other hand, going from one mazurka tune to another, we find the most artful continuity: at bars 40 and 41, mazurka number one melts into number two; at 56–57, mazurka number two is suspended into the opening of number three, which (in bass 71 to 79) develops its final motif in a transition that returns to the opening. The sectional structure is emphasized within the dance, and the continuity is felt as one moves from one dance to the next.

This linear succession is typical of eight-bar phrases, dance forms from the late eighteenth century to Chopin's day, above all the suite of waltzes, *Ländler,* German dances (all these terms were more or less synonymous and all strings of one tune after another): Schubert's sets are the examples best known today, and they were known to Chopin as well. The wonderful continuity from one dance to the next, however, is an invention of Chopin, and he develops it, not at first with the waltz, but with the mazurka. If the string of short dance tunes is an old-fashioned structure in the 1830s, the continuity displayed is strikingly new: the mazurkas are both more reactionary and more innovative than the waltzes written by Chopin at the same time. Of all the short works of Chopin, it is the mazurkas that capture the full range of his genius.

It is, however, from the waltz that he derived the elaborate codas that begin to appear in the mazurkas only with opus 17: they are already found in his first published waltzes. They were, indeed, a convention in the waltz, and Chopin's codas in the waltzes are very much more traditional than his endings for the large-scale mazurkas. The structure of the mazurka proper remains the simple *ABA* of the old dance form, even with the frequent expansion of the central *B* section into a string of dances, but the coda is the place where

Chopin's imagination takes off freely. Nowhere else (certainly not in the Preludes, as has been claimed) is the sense of free improvisation so persuasive as in these codas. The end of the coda is often reserved for his most personal, most eccentric inventions, a new melody in which only a few notes are obsessively repeated, or where a sonority of bare fifths is exploited. Even if these effects are derived from folk music, Chopin's use is deeply personal.

Schumann was impressed by the originality of Chopin's opus 30, published in 1838, above all by the provocative series of parallel fifths at the end of the last and grandest of the set:

"The professors will throw up their hands in horror at this," Schumann wrote. We can see that, for both composer and critic, the mazurka provided a chance to taste forbidden pleasures.

In opus 33, the device of reiteration is carried still further. Number 2 in D major contains the following passage:

in which the repetition of one rhythm is used hypnotically. This is neither music as abstract structure or music as expression: it is music as an agent that acts directly on the nervous system, induces a kind of intoxication. The last piece in the set, number 4 in B minor, strips down the device of repetition to one voice:

The variety as well as the eccentricity of Chopin's final bars is demonstrated throughout these short dances.

Opus 41 was published two years later. In this opus, all the numbers equal and even surpass in originality any of the earlier mazurkas, and we find the first of Chopin's dramatic displays of imitative polyphony at the return of the opening theme, a technique which he was to employ later in other mazurkas and most spectacularly in the fourth Ballade. The opening of the fourth dance of the set

is rewritten on its return, and given a remarkable introduction in the submediant A major:

As counterpoint this is uncomplicated, but the poetic effect is profound. The music slips mysteriously back into the opening bars with a simple sequence of descending thirds (A major to F sharp minor and then D major); it is the D major chord at the end that prepares the harmonic inflection of the first theme away from the original "Phrygian" toward a more pathetic if less exotic Neapolitan.

Earlier in this set the use of hypnotic repetition reaches an extreme: repetition of a single note. The whole of number 1 must be quoted to show the effect this has on a simple ternary form:

This is a structure of *AA BB C BB A*. The harmony is the simplest possible: *A* (tonic, E minor); *B* (dominant, B major); *C* (appears to modulate on the surface, but actually remains in B major throughout). The first appearance of *A* is quiet through both playings, but it returns *fortissimo* in bar 57 only to end quietly again. Each section is an eight-bar phrase. *A* and *B* are played twice, *C* once, *B* again twice, and *A* once with a four-bar coda. The dynamic change is accomplished in the *B* section by the repetition of one melody note, D♯, which is repeated thirty-two times from bar 17 to 32. In this section the melody is one expressive four-bar phrase played four times: the bass throughout is a relentless tonic pedal on a B, except for two bars at the end of the second and fourth phrases where the harmony briefly changes. The dynamism of such an insistently static conception (similar to the "monophonic" passage from the F sharp Minor Polonaise, quoted earlier) is that change seems inevitable, comes as a relief: the moment of change gains in power and urgency. Prolonged repetition can turn even a tonic chord into a dissonance: what follows always seems like a resolution. It is this simple device which radically transforms the significance of ternary form: the central section is not a contrast but a release.

The lyrical melody at bar 33 (section C) derives its passionate force from the way it relieves the tension of the previous sixteen bars. It starts with the same D♯ that had been pounded into our consciousness and leads into a line of great sweetness; in place of the unchanging harmony, we have a simple sequence that starts to go round the circle of fifths:

Following the exasperated insistence of section *B*, this essentially lyric passage has a dramatic power that it would never possess in isolation. The lyricism comes wonderfully as an overflow of the tension, seems to spring inevitably without a break from the obsessively repeated D♯.

This technique, in which a cantabile line gains much of its passion from the tension generated by a long drawn-out ostinato preceding it, can be found in Chopin, some years before, as early as the Mazurka in C sharp Minor, op. 30, no. 4, of 1837, but it achieves its most striking realization here in opus 41 and somewhat later in opus 50, no. 3, in C sharp Minor. The opening section of this Mazurka has already been quoted. The middle section is worth quoting as an example of Chopin's phrasing, which appears to demand an almost unbroken continuity:

Once again the lyricism of the *sostenuto* springs with great intensity out of a passage of hypnotic repetition.

With this work of 1842 the basic form of the mazurka, as Chopin had ambitiously reconceived it, is in place. Opus 50, no. 3, displays the elements in exemplary fashion: the combination of folk rhythm and motive with sophisticated counterpoint; the use of ostinato both to give a pastoral or even a primitive flavor to the music and to build a climax; the picturesque "modal" harmonies resolved into a complex chromatic texture; the bold use of rare sonorities, parallel sevenths, bare fifths, and unaccompanied lines; the ingenious dovetailing which achieves an unprecedented continuity between sections of the dance; the addition of a long coda which improvises a development and meditation on the motifs of the more formal dance proper; and the return in the last few bars to the repetition of an extremely simple motif and the barest harmonies, as if to end with an allusion to the rustic origin of the mazurka—all this is achieved in opus 50, no. 3, in exemplary fashion. The last part of the coda shows Chopin's harmony at its most masterly:

Wagner was to be heavily in debt to passages such as this. The clarity of the writing is even more admirable than the complexity: when the bass line produces its most interesting harmonies, it receives an accent (as in the fifth bar of this illustration, where the accent emphasizes the lack of parallelism with the similar phrase two bars before, and the greater dissonance of the voice leading).

The late mazurkas

The structure of opus 50 as a whole establishes the type for the sets that follow: an impressive opening mazurka, a simple second one, and a grandly contrapuntal finale. Chopin was to publish three more sets of mazurkas during the last decade of his life and to compose at least two single pieces which he had no chance to send to an editor. There are few formal innovations in these works, but the genre, as Chopin had shaped it, is exploited more profoundly. Opus 56, no. 1, in B major is discussed at length in Chapter 4. After a more modest second Mazurka, which combines Polish rhythms with the sound of Scottish bagpipes (the opus was dedicated to a Miss Maberly), the third dance of opus 56 in C minor expands the form to the limits to which Chopin was to take it. The longest of all the mazurkas,[8] and in many ways the most ambitious, is rarely played and is perhaps not easily approachable by either listener or performer, but in harmony, texture, and phrase structure it is one of the most daring and original.

It begins astonishingly with an imitation of the entries of a fugue, in a contrapuntal texture—in spite of the counterpoint, however, it is only an imitation, as the successive entries which preserve the alternation of tonic and dominant do not go from one voice to another but are all in the same voice, descending from the middle of the keyboard to the bass:

---

8. Opus 33, no. 4, in B minor has more bars in almost all editions, but in four separate sources Chopin indicated a cut of twenty-four bars which clearly improves this work.

The experience of the *Well-Tempered Keyboard* is fully transformed here by Chopin into something completely individual. Still more remarkable is the treatment of the four-bar phrase: nothing shows better than this opening page the way a bar is conceived by Chopin as a single large beat. We start with an upbeat of a quarter note, which is expanded in bar 4 to an upbeat of four eighth notes, and to five eighth notes in bar 12. (In fact, bar 13, which must be considered a downbeat, continues to expand the previous bar to displace the effect of the downbeat to the following bar.) Finally, the upbeat is expanded to last the whole of bar 24. To sum up:

One could consider bars 12 through 16 a five-bar phrase, following the three bars 9 through 11, and then 17 to 20 reestablish the norm. These ambiguities are a tribute to the suppleness of Chopin's phrasing. It is given such importance here by the harmony: the apparent modulation to D minor (bar 14) turns out to be only an approach to the half cadence on V with the G major chord of bar 23—a picturesque "modal" approach with a flattened seventh, F♮ in place of F♯. It is fitting that the D minor chord should arrive on a weak measure, not on a "downbeat," and it makes the astonishing prolongation of this harmony over another eight bars all the more effective.

The D minor chord, however, prepares the next section in B flat major, the remote key of the flatted leading tone. The modulation is one of Chopin's displays of compositional virtuosity, both direct and devious at the same time:

The music goes at once to A flat and B flat major in eight bars, and then swerves to B major, only to return to B flat ten bars later. The process is emphatic enough for Chopin to frame this ten-bar parenthesis with changes of key signature, but the turn to B major in bars 56 to 57 is a ravishingly understated effect—not a modulation but an illusion. The B♭ at the end of 56 is sustained into an A♯, as the harmony changes color with a sudden *dolce*.

This transitional section (bars 49 to 72) has a weight equal to that of the opening dance; both are twenty-four bars long (although the opening is played twice). A sixteen-bar dance follows with two almost identical parts (an eight-bar phrase played twice, once with a half cadence and then with a full cadence). If the phrasing and harmony are less complex here, the polyphonic texture is considerably richer:

This is one of those tunes in which the melodic interest is displaced from one voice to another: bass and soprano in bars 73 and 75 to the alto in bars 74 and 76. This dance in B flat major has an elaborate thirty-two bar trio, one of Chopin's supreme inventions:

No page exhibits more strikingly the combination of rigor and freedom, of rustic dance and sophisticated art, which is the glory of Chopin's mazurkas. Moreover, nowhere is the relation between irregular phrase and four- or eight-bar module more crucial.

The irregularity is only on the surface: the melody is shaped by the underlying dance rhythm. The phrase lengths, starting from bar 89 (the last two beats of 88 are felt as a transition) are:

	Phrase group	4-bar structure
7 (4 + 3)	bars 89–95	89–92
		93–96
5 (2 + 3)	bars 96–100	97–100
5 (2 + 3)	bars 101–105	101–104
4	bars 106–109	105–108
4	bars 110–113	109–112
2	bars 114–115	113–116
5	bars 116–120	117–120

This all adds up to 32, quite proper for a dance tune, but the four-bar pulse is not sustained simply by the fact that the whole is divisible by four. Bars 89 to 92 are a melodic parallel to 97 to 100, the latter being a transposition up a whole tone of the former (and the parallel continues into the following phrases): yet the former are bars 1 to 4 of a seven-bar phrase, the latter bars 2 to 5 of a five-bar phrase. At the same time, however, they have the same position within an eight-bar construction—both of them are bars 1 to 4 of the divisions determined by the large pulse. The phrasing may be irregular, but the melodic pattern is completely regular with respect to the four-bar pulse, and the regularity helps us to sense the pulse against the phrase. This technique combines symmetry within the four-bar and eight-bar beat with asymmetry of phrase, regularity with free development. The "downbeats" of the four-bar module are on bars 89, 93, 97, 101, 105, 109, 113, and 117: we can see that the phrases beginning at bars 106, 110, and 114 all start on the second bar of the four-bar pattern, and we can appreciate how bar 117 reestablishes the sense of beginning on the first bar by starting a new melodic figure, although tying over the bass note with the pedal keeps the large rhythm fluid.

It is worth doing these exercises in simple arithmetic to appreciate the way phrase rhythm and four-bar rhythm are consistently out of phase and yet ultimately coordinated. In turn, this explains how Chopin achieves both the sense of improvised expression and the dynamic impetus of the regular dance step, how he combines the free play of imagination with a directed energy. The whole brilliant section is the longest of the Mazurka before the coda, and it is one of those central sections in which the expressive force appears almost to explode, to speak to us unrestrainedly and directly. Meanwhile, Chopin's slurs override both the phrase and four-bar structure to provide a counterpoint of articulation that enforces a larger unity.

After a full return of the B flat major theme, and then of the opening C minor section, the elaborate coda interrupts:

Counting from bar 173 to the end, we find forty-eight bars, starting with a sixteen-bar transition, made up of an impressive contrapuntal interplay and a chromatic structure that must, like several earlier ones, have been of great help to Wagner.[9] What follows (bar 189) is a long variation on a kind of plagal cadence; one hears the important presence throughout of an F minor chord while the dominant is constantly inflected by a D♭ (and the D flat chord

9. The relation of this page to Wagner's harmony is excellently discussed by Abraham, *Chopin's Musical Style*, p. 100.

reinforces, and sometimes substitutes for, the F minor). The dance structure is absolutely maintained: one eight-bar phrase (bars 189–196) repeated more intensely (197–204); a four-bar pedal point on the tonic, also repeated with greater intensity (205–208, 209–212); a two-bar cadence repeated (213–216); and a wonderful four-bar exploitation of a single note, E♮, with a dissonant plagal coloring (two one-bar units, each played twice, 217 to end). The successive shortening of the phrase unit creates an accelerated movement to the end.

This wonderful mazurka will never be a popular work: it is perhaps too complex, and certainly uningratiating. Even with the direct passion of the middle section it may seem somewhat austere. After this, the dances of the last two published sets appear less ambitious, but that is perhaps because they are informed above all by an aristocratic sense of ease and an extraordinary refinement. Opus 59, no. 2, in A flat Major displays an exquisite contrapuntal detail in its middle section:

Bars 46 and 50 contain in the alto a pre-echo of the next bar's soprano, a very urbane example of rustic repetition.

The grandest of the set is, as usual, the final one, in F sharp Minor. The main theme is

and the imitative return is as accomplished as that in the F Minor Ballade,

while the coda is one of the most intense, and rivals that in opus 50, no. 3, in C sharp Minor (quoted on pp. 438–439):

The transfer of the melody to the left hand takes place in bar 122 as an apparent interruption of the four-bar pattern, which remains nevertheless undisturbed, as we can see from the parallelism of bars 123 to 127 with bars 115 to 119. Perhaps most admirable of all is the invention of a new theme in the last bars, insistently repetitive, and both elegant and expressive. There are several examples in the Mazurkas of a new theme in markedly "folk" style at the end of the dance, above all in the more elaborate pieces, and this is perhaps the finest, certainly the most laconic:

These final bars have a beautiful melodic economy within a very small span of notes: we can see how the Polish heritage of the mazurka liberated Chopin from the Italianate melody of most of his other works.

Opus 63 is the last set published by Chopin. In number 1 in B Major, once again obsessive repetition blossoms into full-blown lyricism, this time without warning and with more subtlety than ever before:

The lyrical passage announced emphatically by the *tenuto* of bar 24 is only a transition, and slips with deceptive casualness into the strange key of the flatted leading tone, and the simple lilting rhythm of bars 33 on.

The third Mazurka of the set starts modestly with one of Chopin's most immediately affecting melodies, at once poignant and full of charm:

At the end the melody is reworked in a canon:

The technique of canon is ostentatiously applied here to a melody of great sweetness and pathos; the dissonant clashes of ninths and sevenths produced by the canon makes the melody even more expressive. The directions to arpeggiate in bars 67, 69 and 71 make it clear that Chopin wanted both voices realized with the right hand (although most editors try to circumvent this by suggesting a fingering that brings in the left hand and makes the piece easier to play). Rendering the pleasure of an intellectual difficulty by the delight of a physical effort reveals how much Chopin's counterpoint is absolutely pianistic. It is perhaps fitting that the last mazurka Chopin made public contains his most unashamed demonstration of academic craft.

It would be a pity, however, to leave the mazurkas with this less-than-subtle display. A detail from opus 50, no. 1, in G Major represents Chopin's contrapuntal art even better. Chopin considered this Mazurka difficult to interpret, according to one of his pupils, and set particular store on this passage:

The principal melody is in the left hand throughout until bar 53, emphasized by an unbroken phrase line: the right hand interjects some contrapuntal fragments. Yet the presence of the right hand's countermelody is always felt even when it pauses: the most telling detail is the indication *tenuto* in bar 48 on the A that will be sustained, and it also sustains our sense of the upper line through the five bars until, with the G♯ in bar 53, it becomes the principal voice. It is this kind of continued contrapuntal presence, latent even when inactive, that gives Chopin's style its sweep and its richness.

The mazurkas represent Chopin's supreme achievement in small form, just as the ballades do in the larger (and we must remember that the Barcarolle and the Polonaise-Fantaisie must be classed structurally with the ballades). I do not mean that the mazurkas are better music or more successful works than the preludes, etudes, or nocturnes. Nevertheless, the mazurkas show a significant stylistic development unmatched by the other forms. The reduced small-scale constraints of the dance, far from tying Chopin's hands, inspired several works which, in their grandeur, stand midway between the miniature form and the larger structure such as the ballade. The folk origins of the genre released an uninhibited display of contrapuntal virtuosity and of sophisticated invention. The popular character of the mazurka brought forth Chopin's most aristocratic and most personal creations. Perhaps nowhere else do we feel so powerfully his combination of fastidious craftsmanship and passionate intensity.

Freedom and tradition

The later mazurkas may help us understand Chopin's mastery of large forms. He was, in fact, the only composer of his generation who never, after the age of twenty-one, displayed the slightest awkwardness with longer works—and this is something that could not have been claimed, for all their important successes, by Schumann, Berlioz, Liszt, and Mendelssohn. The concertos, written by Chopin in early youth, have loomed too large in critical discussion and obscured the infallibility of his mature craft. His mastery, however, is idiosyncratic; many of the long forms resemble no one else's. The eccentricity of the larger Mazurkas give us some of the principles of his method.

Chopin's enlargement of the small mazurka form is not Classical in method—that is, he does not magnify each section and keep the relative proportions of the original. On the contrary, he generally preserves intact within a larger context the original small form, the banal structure of dance and trio, each made up of two, three, or four phrases of eight bars. Expansions within these patterns are minimal, and very traditional. There is often a succession of several dance melodies in the trios, but this, too, is conventional. The chief innovation is the lengthy coda, a kind of free contrapuntal meditation on the previous material. This transforms the short, conventional form into a more imposing work, and it is Chopin's most personal invention. The return of the opening section is sometimes given a complex contrapuntal preparation,[10] and this return is often drastically abridged. In the Mazurka in A flat Major, op. 50, no. 2, for example, the opening section of sixty bars is cut to twenty on its return. The abridgment generally turns the reprise of an opening section which was already itself an uncomplicated ternary form into a simple repetition of its opening phrase.

These expansions—and abridgments—leave the symmetry of the original melodic forms largely unaltered. It seems to me that this practice derives not only from Chopin's comprehension of traditional dance patterns but also from his love of Italian opera. The integrity of the melody or of the dance phrase is preserved: the expansion is a new section, which spins out the material into new forms, sometimes by an imitation of Classical development technique, at other times by forming new melodies with the motifs or by finding new motifs related in character. In a sense, Chopin does not properly expand the small forms; he adds to them, extends them. These additions—transitional passages or codas—are most often free in style and openly contrapuntal in texture, sometimes elaborately so. What keeps the large structure from falling apart is Chopin's art of blurring the frontiers between different sections, and his unfailing sense of polyphonic continuity, above all the rich continuity of the inner voices which is the hallmark of his style.

The free sections added to an underlying skeleton are responsible for much of the breadth and the magnificence of the Barcarolle, one of the most impressive of Chopin's longer movements. The underlying skeleton is one that Chopin had made most personal: two contrasting sections, juxtaposed, but not linked as in a sonata, the second with two distinct themes; then an abbreviated but triumphant reprise of the first section and a more complete one of the second theme of the second. This basic form is articulated rhythmically: the tempo of each theme is slightly faster than the preceding, although the quicker tempo that begins the second section gives an impression of great breadth by the slow rate of harmonic change, as if the barcarole had moved from a Venetian canal to the open sea. Here is the transition from the first to the second theme:

10. The central section, in a few rare cases, is also prepared by an elaborate transition, as in op. 56, no. 3 and op. 41, no. 1.

The abridged reprise of the first theme is grandly rescored, and the reprise of the third theme is perhaps Chopin's most powerful climax, an eloquent transformation.

The sustained grandeur of the reprise is prepared and then confirmed by the free sections. The return of the opening theme is introduced by a long passage that begins by developing the barcarole rhythm and then dissolves into an extraordinary cantilena marked *sfogato* ("unbound," or giving free play to feeling):

This is one of Chopin's most imaginative creations, with a sense of improvised poetry. An elaborate preparation of the return is found in the grandest mazurkas, as is a coda that is richly polyphonic. The coda of the Barcarolle, however, is Chopin's most orchestral conception, and uses largely new thematic material. It achieves one of the most fundamental goals of Romantic style, placing the climax near the end and sustaining the tension until the close:[11]

11. The final bars are quoted above, in Chapter 6.

This postponement of much of the dramatic working out until the final pages is characteristic of the ballades and most remarkably of Scherzo no. 3 in C sharp minor. Once again a traditional *ABA* structure is followed by a more elaborate and free section, although the ternary form is profoundly and radically altered by a device that Chopin used several times: the return of the first theme is succeeded by a grand reprise of the second. Even the harmonic structure of this scherzo shows a high-handed treatment of form:

A: C sharp minor

B: D flat major

A: C sharp minor

B: E major

Free continuation of *B:* E minor followed by a pedal point on V of C sharp major

Coda: C sharp minor

Most of the harmonic activity is left for the last pages, exactly as we have found in the most ambitious mazurkas. There is, indeed, no harmonic contrast at all for the first three quarters of the piece, only a simple change of mode (from C sharp minor to D flat major).

Perhaps nothing characterizes a style better than the way its composers try to sustain the interest in the return of a previously heard section. Most eighteenth-century musical forms can be defined precisely by the way the reprise is handled. The earliest practice was to make it more expressive by adding ornamentation. In the latter half of the eighteenth century the technique of sonata recapitulation became elaborate; return of the opening section of a movement was reconceived harmonically, moving towards resolution instead of towards large-scale structural dissonance, while the melodies retain their original shapes and even sometimes their original order. But after 1820, ornamentation was a weak solution for a composer with any ambition for creating a dynamic form, and sonata recapitulation was unwieldy to a generation that preferred to withhold the sense of resolution until the final bars.

This was perhaps the major formal difficulty for composers writing after

1825, and its intractability accounts for most of the failures in the work of, for example, Schubert and Schumann, both of whom often settled for literal repetition at great length (sometimes but not always transposed from the original keys), and who generally lacked the will to reconceive the material radically but had little taste for drastic abridgment. These literal repetitions have their reasons for existing, and one can find ways to justify them and to perform them effectively, but under modern concert conditions—which were already to some extent in force in the 1830s—they still create difficulties for audiences as well as performing musicians.

None of Chopin's contemporaries could rival him for the variety and effectiveness of his treatment of the return. We have seen the extraordinary telescoping of the opening material at the end of the second and third Ballades and the Polonaise-Fantaisie. This can be paralleled in several of the late Nocturnes, and clarifies Chopin's aesthetic. The last one he published, opus 62, no. 2, in E major, has an ample exposition of thirty-two bars:

The return abridges this considerably, and essentially skips, after repeating bars 1 and 2, to bar 27—and, in a more important transformation, intensifies the modulation in this bar, which had moved in the opening section to the flat submediant C major, by going, *pianissimo,* to a harmony more radically opposed to the tonic E major, the flatted leading tone D major:

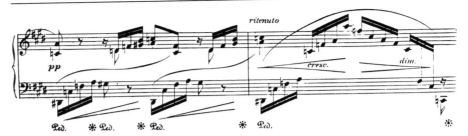

Introducing the most distant harmonies towards the end of a piece represents Chopin's most significant break with classical tradition.

In the G Major Nocturne, op. 37, no. 2 (discussed earlier, in Chapter 4), each return of the opening theme is less stable than the previous one. The first bars alternate tonic and dominant seventh chords in root position over a tonic pedal:

The first return places these harmonies over a dominant pedal:

The third and final return starts at the mediant B major, and reintroduces the tonic G major without emphasis, almost in passing, and continues the series of modulations up by minor thirds until, starting at bar 129, the bass goes down the complete circle of fifths: first G–C–F–B♭, and then more rapidly E♭–A♭–D♭–F♯–B–E–A–D:

Each return intensifies the kaleidoscopic variety of harmony in the opening section.

Bringing back the opening theme with more brilliant dynamics is a technique employed by many other composers, Liszt above all—the greatest influence here may have been Beethoven—and a corollary was the return with a richer and more complex texture. In spite of remarkable examples from other composers (the E Major Polonaise of Liszt, for example, and *La Vallée d'Obermann*), Chopin set a standard that was hard to equal. The C Minor Nocturne has an operatic opening of great pathos:

It is reported that the composer spent a full hour teaching a student how to play the first phrase alone. Its return comes with an elaborate orchestral accompaniment:

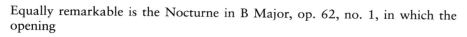

Equally remarkable is the Nocturne in B Major, op. 62, no. 1, in which the opening

returns with continuous trills:

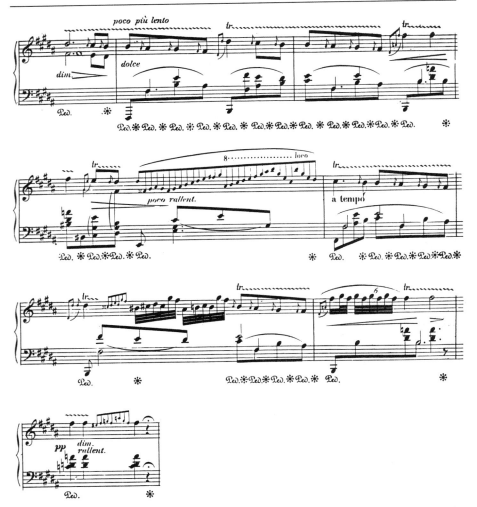

The trills here are not expressive decoration but textural, a sort of reorchestration. That is why Chopin directs that each trill begin with the main note instead of the more expressive trill that begins with the upper note. The return preserves the delicacy of the opening, but it is an analogue to the fortissimo returns of the third Ballade and the Polonaise-Fantaisie.

It is these final returns that often make it impossible to call Chopin's forms either binary or ternary. The Prelude in B flat Major seems at first to be a ternary form, with its cadence in the tonic at bar 16, and a sudden shift to G flat major for a new theme:

Nevertheless, the return to the opening material after another sixteen bars (at bar 33) is so dramatically recomposed to appear as the continuation and the climax to the central material that it is less a return than a final stretto that leads to the coda. In its way this is a kind of telescoping, but I know of no precedent for it.

The most idiosyncratic variety of these returns is the one in which the first theme is reworked contrapuntally: we have seen this in several of the mazurkas as well as in the fourth Ballade. We might say, however, that Chopin's most personal form is that in which the return is absolutely unaltered—perfunctory, so to speak—but prepares a surprising new development of its material, as in many of the later mazurkas.

Those are all attempts to combine the symmetry of a return with a dynamic increase of interest and tension. None can be easily exploited with sonata form. In Chopin's three mature sonatas—those for piano in B flat minor and B minor, and the undervalued masterpiece that is the late cello sonata—Chopin found solutions that compromised neither his sense of style nor the energy of the form. He returned to an older eighteenth-century tradition of eliminating most of the first group from the recapitulation, and placed the definitive moment of resolution with the return of the second group. In compensation, he made the development section largely an elaborately contrapuntal working out of the first theme. The development was the traditional place for chromatic harmony, but Chopin outdoes any previous composer here in richness, complexity, and a bewildering variety of surface change.

What holds this variety together is Chopin's unsurpassed feeling for a long line. This is shown by the development of the Sonata in B flat Minor, the most tightly organized of the three sonatas:

The Wagnerian character of these pages is easily remarked, and it is due not only to the harmony but to the treatment of rhythm and motif. In 1838 Chopin has anticipated the creation of a web of leitmotifs that Wagner was to find only with the *Ring* (*Lohengrin* in 1848 associates leitmotifs with characters and ideas, but does not yet combine them into a complex network). The development of the sonata uses two motifs, both from the first group of the exposition,

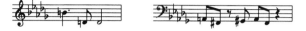

and there is hardly a bar from 105 to 160 that does not use one or both of them. (A correct reprise of the exposition with the opening motif clearly helps the listener to comprehend the development.) The motifs begin by alternating, and finally are woven together in a relentless sequence.

The unity of the different textures is enforced by a chromatic line that rises from bar 105 to 137 and then falls back to a pedal point on the dominant. The structural skeleton is skillfully transferred from voice to voice. The following diagram is intended not as an Ur-Linie, but as an attempt to indicate the voice leading:

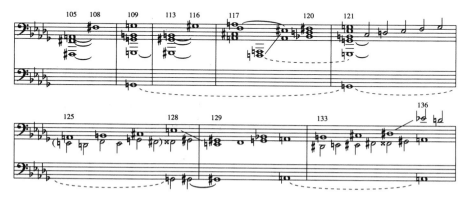

This large-scale rise and fall clarifies the rhythm. The phrase structure seems irregular at first sight—three bars, three bars, five bars, three bars, two bars. Not only, however, does this add up to sixteen, but the basic harmonic line enforces the sense of a four-bar structure with a downbeat at bars 105, 109, 113, 117, and 121. The underlying harmonic movement not only organizes the complexity of texture, it also overrides the melodic symmetry. Bars 121–124 are apparently parallel to 129–132, but the first phrase has a rising tenor over a pedal G, and the second a dynamic bass line that rises from E to A with a much greater energy.

Bars 121 to 124 round off the *Tristan*-like harmonies of the opening with a melody that anticipates the music of Amfortas in Wagner's *Parsifal;* this melody is freely derived from the second group of Chopin's exposition. The change in phrasing is remarkable: the irregular movement of the opening gives way at bar 121 to articulated four-bar phrases, and then to a lengthy and stormy climax of two-bar sequences (137–152), in which both motifs are combined throughout. This is the apex of the form: the chromatic line has reached the tonic B flat, harmonized as a G minor sixth chord, and it is the beginning of the descent. This climax on a B♭ bass note but not on a B flat harmony demonstrates the preeminence of contrapuntal line over harmony in Chopin's art.

The two-bar phrases pound relentlessly like a series of waves of continuously renewed force. Wagner was to begin to use an identical technique in the *Ring*. It is important, however, to see that Chopin's deployment of his motifs is subservient to the harmonic and contrapuntal structures (as it was also to be later with Wagner). The first motif disappears from the bass line in bars 149–150 at the only place where the bass is forced to move within the two-bar group in order to establish the arrival at the dominant F. After this arrival, Chopin broadens the rhythm, dovetailing the phrases from 153 to 161, so that each phrase finishes within the beginning of the new one. From bar 151 to 169, G♭ is suspended and then resolves into F repeatedly: this is the grandest dominant preparation in all of Chopin before the transition to the coda of the Scherzo in C sharp Minor.

What makes this development so powerful is the sense of line that organizes the changing rhythm, the supple phrasing, and the radically inventive chromaticism. The line controls the climax, and on it depend the incessantly repetitive appearances of the motifs. The foundation for the technique is Chopin's ability to shift line and motif from one voice to another over the entire range of the keyboard (note the way the D♯ in the tenor of 135 is transferred up an octave to the E♭, in the alto which then guides the harmonic movement).

This development section may make one of Chopin's most disconcerting statements less paradoxical. Delacroix, in his diary, reported that Chopin protested against the school of musicians who claimed that the charm of music lay in its sound, its sonority. This remark was evidently aimed at composers like Berlioz, but it upset Delacroix, who took it almost as an attack on himself; he copied it out twice. (It is true that Chopin admired Delacroix personally but disliked his painting.) In the contemporary battle in the visual arts over the importance of line as opposed to color, Delacroix was seen as the leader of the colorists. He tried weakly to answer Chopin in his diary by commenting that Chopin wrote only for piano and was not interested in orchestral color. Nevertheless, Chopin's mastery of tone color is incontestable: his works reveal a range of sonorities unsurpassed before Debussy.

The opposition between structure and sonority in music is almost as misleading as that between line and color in the visual arts. Baudelaire insisted, correctly, that Delacroix was one of the three greatest draftsmen of the century, and emphasized his mastery of line. In the same way, a study of Chopin demonstrates the intimate relation between line and color in music. In a Bellini opera, the sentiment that brings tears to the eyes of listeners depends on the composer's mastery of the long sustained line. The poetic force of Chopin depends similarly on his control of all the lines of a complex polyphony. On this was based the subtly shifting phrase accent and the astonishing experiments in harmony. The wonderful sonorities of Chopin's writing—the exquisite spacing, the vibrant inner voices—spring from an abstract structure of lines. The pianist is conscious, as he is in Bach, both of the way an individual line is sustained and of the passing of the melody from one voice to another. It is not only in small details that Chopin displayed this art but in the general outlines of the larger forms. The lyricism and the dramatic shock in his music are equally indebted to this craft. This is the true paradox of Chopin: he is most original in his use of the most fundamental and traditional technique. That is what made him at the same time the most conservative and the most radical composer of his generation.

CHAPTER EIGHT

Liszt: On Creation as Performance

Disreputable greatness

Berlioz and Liszt are assured of immortality. By now, their right to a place in the pantheon of nineteenth-century composers goes largely unchallenged. Yet this place is equivocal. The worst criticisms made during their lifetimes are still repeated by musicians today: Liszt is cheap and flashy, Berlioz incompetent. The charges are astonishingly heavy and detailed: Liszt's melodies are banal, his harmonies tawdry, his large forms repetitious and uninteresting; Berlioz was incapable of writing correct counterpoint, his harmony is full of grammatical solecisms that a second-year conservatory student would know how to avoid, and his sense of form was defective. One might well think that it is especially heroic to have achieved greatness against such odds.

Liszt and Berlioz were natural allies from the start. In 1830 the nineteen-year-old Liszt heard the premiere in Paris of the *Symphonie fantastique,* and he became one of the champions of Berlioz, his elder by eight years. It was the publication of Liszt's arrangement for piano of the symphony (an arrangement he played in public) that became the occasion for Schumann's famous review, the most appreciative and favorable criticism that Berlioz was ever to receive. Superficially, Liszt and Berlioz had much in common: they both exploited a satanic public image, and enjoyed a Gothic taste for the macabre with all its paraphernalia—witches' Sabbath, march to the scaffold, dance of death. They were both virtuoso conductors, and did perhaps more than anyone else of their time to create the modern image of the orchestral director as an international star. The music they wrote, however, was worlds apart, and the controversy each excited was of a very different nature.

The Romantic myth that great artists go unrecognized during their lifetimes has been pretty well dismantled by historians today. In its place, however, they have erected an anti-myth equally foolish: the belief that the artists whose works have survived the ravages of time were better understood by their contemporaries than by later generations. The truth lies generally the other way. Time tends to strip away old misunderstandings. (It also, of course, adds new misunderstandings, but these are rarely as pernicious or as tenacious as the original ones, and they evaporate easily with the rapid changes in critical fashion.) No one any longer thinks that Mozart's modulations are too complex or that his scores contain too many notes, that Beethoven was an undisciplined, barbaric genius, or that Wagner's music is unintelligible noise, yet these were the considered and well-established judgments of the composers' contemporaries, even the most enlightened ones. Other prejudices take even longer to disappear, but now there are only a few miserably isolated diehards who claim that Chopin could not handle large forms, that Beethoven was a poor melodist, or that Schoenberg's music is inexpressive. Remoteness has blunted, softened, and veiled whatever once seemed difficult and unacceptable from these composers, and it has rightly made them appear almost infallible—rightly, because the standards by which we can judge them are derived above all from a study of their works.

The controversy over Liszt and Berlioz, however, has not subsided, even though their greatness is acknowledged. The durability of the old criticism is exceptional, and suggests that the importance of these two composers is felt instinctively but only imperfectly grasped, and that we have not yet learned a critical approach to their work, a way of elucidating what they were up to.

Liszt has never needed revival; his music has always been an important part of the concert repertoire. Nevertheless, he has appeared to need rehabilitation. From the beginning he had his admirers as well as his critics, but the admiration has often been uneasy, qualified, even shamefaced—it has paradoxically been withheld from, or given only grudgingly to, the most successful works, those that have held their place in the pianist's repertoire for more than a century. In recent years his supporters have rested their case largely on that part of Liszt's very considerable production which has been, and still is, only rarely performed. These neglected works come from three groups. First the *Lieder*, still insufficiently appreciated: as a composer of songs, Liszt stands somewhat outside the German tradition of Schubert and Schumann, and closer to French style. The other two groups are mainly drawn from the music he composed after the age of forty: the liturgical works and the late piano pieces. The masses and the oratorio *Saint Elisabeth* lack the vulgarity of the early piano music, but that does not make them very interesting, in spite of a few fine moments. A better case can be made for the piano music of the last years, much of it published only in this century.

Most of the piano works by Liszt that have remained in the repertory today were written, at least in their initial form, before 1850, and the musical material is either invented by someone else or, with some very significant exceptions, it is shoddy and tired, likely to grate on the nerves of any musician of delicate sensibility. After 1850 Liszt's sense of material became more refined and, in later years, even austere. These last years were devoted above all to short piano pieces and to religious music (Liszt became an abbé when the Vatican revoked its sanction of the divorce of Princess Sayn-Wittgenstein, and he had to renounce all hopes of marrying her). Many of these late piano works are experimental, foreshadowing the music of Debussy and the atonal composers of the early twentieth century. They cannot have had much influence on these developments, however, since they were essentially private and little known, and the importance of Liszt to history cannot be explained by an appeal to his late style. In any case, even the best of the late works are less impressive than the music of Debussy and Schoenberg to which they appear to point. It is essentially the inspirations of the young Liszt of the 1830s and 1840s that remain alive today, and we still draw upon them for musical sustenance. They gave Liszt his stature. The early works are vulgar and great; the late works are admirable and minor. Liszt may be compared to an old ancestor who built up the family fortune by disreputable and shameful transactions in his youth and spent his last years in works of charity; recent criticism reads like an official family biography that glosses over the early life and dwells lovingly on the years of respectability.

Die Lorelei: the distraction of influence

Even if the late works made little impact and have only a small role to play in history, Liszt's influence on other composers was nevertheless very great indeed. In an odd way, however, his influence tends rather to diminish than to magnify his stature. This can be shown by one of his finest works, the setting of Heine's *Die Lorelei*. Here the influence of Liszt on one of his greatest contemporaries is flagrant. The beginning of the second version is as follows:

These opening bars, which so clearly evoke the prelude to Wagner's *Tristan und Isolde,* are not to be found in the first version, written in 1841 and published in 1843. The second version, however, was published in 1856, and on the nineteenth of December of that year Wagner began to sketch *Tristan.* The priority of Liszt is therefore certain, and Wagner even acknowledged his indebtedness on one occasion, according to an anecdote.

The relationship, unfortunately, is not entirely to Liszt's credit, as Wagner's reworking is both more interesting and more powerful:

The opening chord of Wagner's version of the motif excited bitter controversy when it was first heard, as musicians and theorists were not sure how to classify the chord in a tonal system: there is still some uninteresting discussion about what the name of the chord should be. If we take the position—as Chopin did, and probably Wagner, too—that voice leading, or counterpart, had clear priority over harmony, we may see the chord and Wagner's progression as a gradual alteration of Liszt's oversimple diminished sevenths:

The novelty of Wagner's version comes above all from the parallel minor sevenths in alto and bass (D♯ to D♮, F to E). Wagner's debt acts in the end to point up one of Liszt's greatest weaknesses, an insistent exploitation of the diminished seventh chord. (He shared this vice with contemporary composers of opera, who found the diminished seventh incomparably useful for effects of horror, rage, astonishment, and terror.)

Liszt returned to the "Lorelei" or "Tristan" motif many years later in 1877 in the third volume of *Années de Pèlerinage* with the second of the two pieces entitled "Aux Cyprès de la Villa d'Este" or "By the Cypresses of the Villa d'Este" (the first of the two pieces is one of Liszt's most impressive late works, and the second, although weaker, is not without merit). Once again the piece opens with the "Lorelei" motif, but we can see that Wagner has been there in the meantime:

The repeated diminished chord has given way now to a more interesting progression—although a diminished seventh harmony returns by implication in bars 7 to 10. Later Liszt harmonizes the motto with an inversion of Wagner's chord, only to follow it once more with his beloved diminished seventh:

Earlier in the work he had adapted the motto to a more imaginative treatment with a half cadence on a dominant that, indeed, recalls Wagner's half cadence on a dominant seventh:

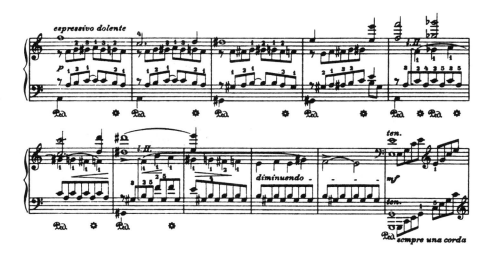

It should be evident that Liszt's stature is not magnified by observing that he did some of Wagner's work for him. Nor, on the other hand, is it diminished by his borrowings from Schubert, Beethoven, Rossini, and Chopin.

In short, the influence on Wagner is only a distraction if we wish to appreciate the greatness of Liszt's *Die Lorelei*. The principal melody is one of the composer's finest. The first version was considerably inferior to the revision of 1856. In 1841 the principal melody began:

This later became a broader triple time, more flowing and more powerful, with two asymmetrical ten-bar phrases:

The simple tonic cadence at the end of the first phrase has an unexpected pathos. In addition, it later serves, after the melody is immediately repeated, to make the cadence on the mediant of C sharp major all the more voluptuous, and the sudden swerve to B flat minor / major more moving as well as more dramatic.

These are all mediant relationships, and Liszt's most successful harmonic surprises are largely restricted to such mediant shifts. (He is, in fact, much less daring than, say, Schubert in his large-scale harmonic planning.) He handled these mediant relationships with great mastery, never more so than in the last page of *Die Lorelei*, where the introduction returns in the original key of E minor but the principal melody reappears no longer in E but in G major. This is one example among many of a composer of the 1830s treating a minor key and its relative major as more or less the same key, but Liszt is here more subtle than most of his contemporaries and, indeed, more sophisticated than he generally showed himself; in an exquisite prolongation of the final phrase of the melody in the concluding G major section, the key of E, now major, reappears suddenly and quietly, only to dissolve back into G major:

This brief recall of the initial tonality is a coloristic device here, one which suspends the musical motion for a few seconds before allowing a resolution. *Die Lorelei* is one of Liszt's finest conceptions, but it is only by considering it on its own terms, not by comparing it to Wagner, that we will learn to appreciate its quality and its depth.

The Sonata: the distraction of respectability

The Sonata for Piano in B Minor is perhaps the only work of Liszt to win almost unchallenged critical admiration, and it has seemed to the majority of critics to provide the touchstone for an evaluation of Liszt's genius. I hesitate to disturb this near-unanimity, but the work—while an undoubted master-piece—is neither flawless nor a truly representative achievement. Written in 1852, the Sonata in B Minor is a pivotal work between Liszt's early and late style. With the first "Mephisto" Waltz, it is the only piece to be conceived entirely after 1850 to remain a basic part of the piano repertory (although at least two beautiful late works merit equal respect: the Variations on Bach's "Weinen, Klagen," and the "Jeux d'eaux à la Villa d'Este"). Because of its seriousness and originality of form the Sonata is often considered Liszt's greatest achievement; in both respects it seems to me slightly overvalued. It contains a certain amount of bombast and sentimental posturing mixed with its finest passages. Both the formal structure (four movements—allegro, adagio, scherzo, and finale—compressed into a single sonata movement with exposition, development, and recapitulation) and the technique of thematic transformation that holds it together were worked out with equal elegance some years before by Schumann in the Fantasy for Piano and Orchestra (later to become, with very little alteration, the first movement of his Piano Concerto). In fact, the transformation of themes to create successive movements of different emotional character was used by many composers between 1825 and 1850, including very minor figures like Moscheles.

The variation finale of Beethoven's Symphony no. 9 was a model for both Schumann and Liszt, as Beethoven here combined four-movement and single-movement sonata forms: an allegro exposition, a scherzo as a second theme with fugal development, an adagio slow movement, and a finale as recapitulation or return to the opening key and tempo. An equally influential model was Schubert's *Wanderer* Fantasy, in which the four connected movements make no pretense to a single form, although the final fugue returns both to the tonality of the opening pages and to a similar rhythm and character: the themes of Schubert's initial Allegro reappear transformed as slow movement, scherzo, and final fugue. The B Minor Sonata clearly pays homage to Schubert's Fantasy, but the example of Beethoven enabled Liszt to create a form tighter and more coherent than Schubert's.

The art by which Liszt and Schubert were able to transform a melody from its allegro character into the main theme of a slow movement and then of a scherzo has been much admired. A dramatic phrase towards the beginning of the B Minor Sonata

turns up later with an entirely different character as a lyrical theme of a "second group":

It does not, in fact, take much imagination to use a theme this way—essentially it is a less rigorous version of the traditional variation technique in which the main theme reappears with the same contour and even the same pitches, but with a different rhythm and a much altered expressive character. The skill does not lie in the transformation but in the dramatic effectiveness of the change of character. It is not a very subtle technique and must be distinguished both from the sophistication with which Schumann can at once hide and reveal the opening motto of the *Davidsbündlertänze* throughout all eighteen pieces, and from the profound working out of a motif that enables Beethoven to make all of the movements of a long work appear as if they were developed from the same material—for example, to permute the opening of the Quartet in C sharp Minor, op. 131

into the beginning of the finale:

In Liszt, we hear a melody played two different ways: in Beethoven, the generative energy of tonal material is revealed and exploited. The greatness of Liszt's achievement lies in the dramatic transformation of character.

Other aspects of the thematic structure of the sonata are, however, more remarkable and original: the admiration for Liszt's thematic transformations may be misplaced, but it is not unmerited. The combination of themes is extraordinarily subtle. The opening of the Allegro, for example,

is intricately entwined a page later with the dramatic phrase quoted earlier:

Even more profound is the tendency of all of the themes of the sonata to turn into one another. This fluidity of thematic identity is perhaps the greatest sign of Liszt's mastery. The dramatic phrase, for example,

is hidden—deformed and truncated—within the melody of the slow movement which acts as a development section:

At the end of the slow movement Liszt makes the relation manifest, and then reveals the kinship of this phrase with still another theme of the work, the descending scale of the opening bars:

Three different themes are shown here as springing clearly from a common source: one motif slips easily into the others.

This fluidity suggests a radical difference between a work of Beethoven and even the most formally structured work of Liszt like the B Minor Sonata, or between motivic development and thematic transformation. In Beethoven's technique of development, a motif is made stable or unstable by exploiting its harmonic and rhythmic functions according to its place within the large-scale form. Liszt's thematic transformations, on the other hand, are most often radically different ways of playing the same theme, changes of performance style that impose dramatic changes of character. In Beethoven's Quartet in A Minor, op. 132, for example, the first appearance of this motif of the main theme

firmly defines the tonality of A minor; the second appearance

destabilizes the harmony to suggest a movement towards F, which is confirmed seventeen bars later by an expansion of the original motif and an augmentation of its rhythm:

This is less unstable than the second version, but without the simple firmness of the first. The changes enforce the large harmonic form and the traditional ideals of a sonata movement.

In the various appearances of the main theme of the Liszt sonata, however, the heroic Allegro opening quoted above is transformed into the sweetly expressive:

the scherzando, marked *non legato* to achieve the light tone color:

the dramatic:

and the triumphant:

The functions of the large structure, while present, are not as significant as the changes of character and style; and the themes are transformed less in response to the demands of harmonic form than as a way of following a dramatic scenario, requiring dramatic contrasts of style.

The Sonata in B Minor is not program music, but by its manipulation of clearly defined early nineteenth-century genres, it constructs something like a narrative (the fluid relations among the themes display their effectiveness here). The mysterious and sinister opening and the satanic statement of the main theme quoted above lead, after a powerful stretto, to the hero as Lucifer; the satanic theme then turns into a brilliant demonstration of virtuosity:

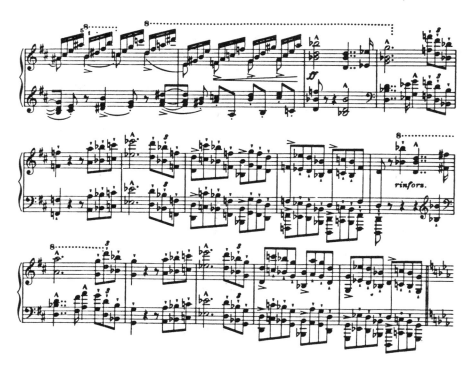

and the section is concluded with a climax of religious exaltation:

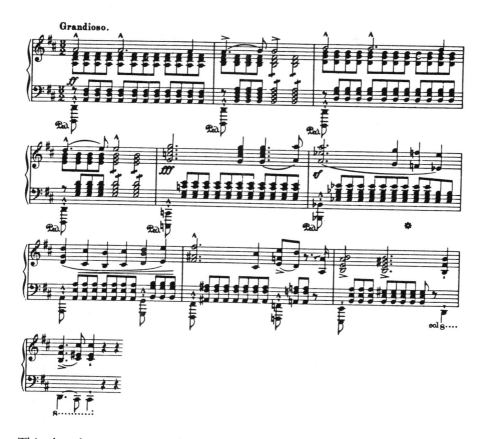

This chorale may appear to be a totally new theme, but in a later development its second half is identified with the opening bars of the Allegro:

In this transformation, the religious security of the original chorale is endowed with a sense of despair. Liszt was always a deeply and sincerely religious man, but the religion of the mid-nineteenth century was less that of the Gothic cathedral than of the Gothic novel.

The first appearance of the religious mode is followed by a deeply felt recitative, and then given a sentimental turn derived from Italian opera, and even a somewhat erotic cast that was by no means foreign to the religious yearnings of the time:

The repeated notes are an operatic trait imported from Italy, but the alternation of the harmonies of E minor and B flat major (a diabolical tritone apart) is a pure invention of Liszt's. He uses it for its exotic color (the B flat major chord is clearly a substitute for the more obvious B minor), and for this reason can only repeat it. The motif here

recalls the main theme,

and is another example of Liszt's ability to deform a sharply defined motif into a less determinate contour, so that each theme can suggest earlier and later ones.

The combination of brimstone and incense is a heady perfume, and, as we have seen, there is more than a whiff of it in the exposition of the B Minor Sonata. The different characters of the diabolical, the heroic, the religious, and the erotic are as necessary to an understanding of this work without a program as they are to Berlioz's *Symphonie fantastique*. The fugue—part scherzo, part opening of a recapitulation and finale—turns the main theme into an exercise in the macabre:

The sonata was originally intended to end with a statement of triumph. In a magnificent revision Liszt returned to the religious mode with its erotic overtones. The most remarkable inspiration is a surprise cadential movement into a mournful gray despair with no brilliance:

This is a parallel to the end of Nicholas Lenau's *Don Juan*, the inspiration for Richard Strauss's tone poem, which has a similar effect at the end. Liszt, however, follows it with an effect of religious absolution and a brief glimpse of heaven:

The last statements of the theme, a final effort at life, are resolved by the celestial harmonies and then the single octave in the deepest register, a laconic sign of death.

A literal and naive interpretation is inescapable. The source of Liszt's Sonata is not only Beethoven and Schubert but Byron (above all the Byron of *Manfred* and *Childe Harold*), the popular Gothic novel, and the sentimental religious poetry of Lamartine. Even the saccharine religious art of the style known as Sainte-Sulpice plays a role in some of the most remarkable pages of the Sonata. If the musical content is sometimes undistinguished, reflecting a poetic content either inflated or all too commonplace, the treatment is always masterly and deeply imaginative. Liszt could not avoid an occasional vulgarity of style, and he was unable to exploit this by irony as Schumann did; he succumbed to its attractions partly because he understood and appreciated them, but it is clear that he was trying in the Sonata to avoid the flashier elements of vulgarity, to attain the sublime. Unfortunately we are, like Liszt, still saddled with an aesthetic that admits works in sonata form as sublime, but not etudes or "characteristic" pieces—short, idiosyncratic works like the fragments in Schumann's *Carnaval* or the landscape pieces which are among Liszt's most distinctive creations.

The invention of Romantic piano sound: the Etudes

It was with the etude and the characteristic piece that Liszt in the 1830s achieved one of the greatest revolutions of keyboard style in history. Most of Liszt's compositions for piano during that time were collected in five great sets, which changed considerably in format and character over the years in various editions: the Transcendental Etudes, the Paganini Etudes, and the three parts of the *Album d'un voyageur*—Switzerland, Italy, and Hungary. The Hungarian section later became the Hungarian Rhapsodies, and the first two parts of *Album d'un voyageur* became the two books of the *Années de pèlerinage* (Years of Pilgrimage); the Italian section acquired an appendix, called *Venice and Naples,* and many years later a third book (mostly Roman) was added.

The least respectable side of Liszt is to be found in the Hungarian Rhapsodies: even more than the opera fantasies, this is what has given him a bad reputation, and it is from the fame of these works that his most earnest admirers feel that he must be rescued. Let us choose a passage from the central part of the tenth Rhapsody in which one cannot speak of thematic mastery or of daring harmonic innovation. The harmonics are banal, the melodies almost nonexistent:

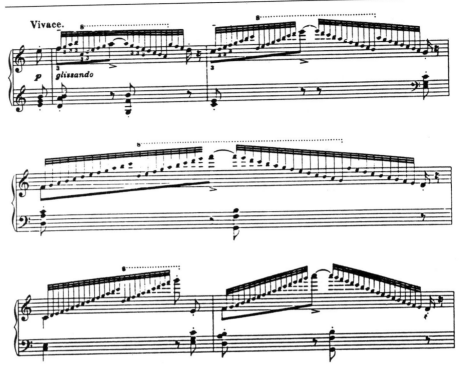

This is, I imagine, the kind of writing that earned Liszt the contempt of his most distinguished colleagues, Schumann and Chopin. It is the zero degree of musical invention if we insist that invention must consist of melody, rhythm, harmony, and counterpoint. Nevertheless, played with a certain elegance, these pages are both dazzling and enchanting. The real invention concerns texture, density, tone color, and intensity—the various noises that can be made with a piano—and it is startlingly original. The piano was taught to make new sounds. These sounds often did not conform to an ideal of beauty, either Classical or Romantic, but they enlarged the meaning of music, made possible new modes of expression. On a much larger scale, Liszt did for the piano what Paganini had done only a few years previously for the violin. Listeners were impressed not only with the beauty of Paganini's tone quality but also with its occasional ugliness and brutality, with the way he literally attacked his instrument for such dramatic effect.[1] Liszt made a new range of dramatic piano sound possible, and in so doing he thoroughly overhauled the technique of keyboard playing.

1. See the quotation from a contemporary of Paganini's, Ludwig Rellstab, in the article by András Batta, "Les Paraphrases d'opéra" *Silences 3 (Liszt)* (1984).

To see what kind of composer Liszt was, one must start with the two sets of Etudes, the first important works of his to be published. Each exists in three basic stages: the first stage of the Paganini set is the version for violin by Paganini, the Caprices from which Liszt selected six for transcription. The second stage is the first piano version of 1838, dedicated to Clara Schumann; if Liszt had not been so essentially generous in nature, one might suspect malice in the dedication—the music must have been unplayable even on the light-actioned pianos of the time by anybody but Liszt himself. This version is practically never attempted today: what has survived in the concert hall is a third stage, or second piano version, published in 1851. This version has been stripped down, and in some respects brought closer to the original violin Caprices: there is a gain of effectiveness and a loss of pianistic imagination. Liszt at his most extravagant could be very grand.

The first stage of the Transcendental Etude was composed by Liszt himself at the age of fifteen: Studies for the Piano in Twelve Exercises, op. 6. One or two of these studies have a certain charm, particularly the ninth in A flat major; the seventh study, too, has some of the rich sonority of Liszt's mature style. The others have little musical interest, not even so much as most of Czerny's studies, and they are not even particularly difficult. I doubt whether anyone since the adolescent Liszt has ever found it worthwhile to play them in public. As a child prodigy Liszt must have been a remarkable pianist, but in composition he was considerably inferior to other fifteen-year-olds like Clara Wieck or Chopin, to say nothing of Mendelssohn.

In 1837, however, when he was twenty-six, he published the Twelve Great Studies for the Piano (actually called Twenty-Four, but nothing further came out of this plan); eleven of these are rewritings of the early exercises, and the remaining Etude is based on the Impromptu, op. 3, composed many years before. Rewriting is too mild a term: in this second stage the early exercises are completely transformed. Only two or three of them would be recognizable at first hearing in their new guise. Like the Paganini Etudes published a year later, they skirt the edge of the impossible in piano technique, the limits to what the human hand can be made to do. Once again, like the Paganini set, they were revised by the composer in 1851, pruned of their Romantic excesses, thinned out—classicized, in short. Even in the easier final form they remain among the most difficult works in the piano repertory.

A study of the relation of the first and second versions of the Transcendental Etudes reveals a wonderful paradox: the version of 1826 rarely rises above the mediocre, and it has, in itself, neither interest nor distinction; the version of 1837 is fascinating, stupefyingly brilliant, and magisterial. Yet the second version is often identical with the first in many respects—and these respects are normally considered fundamental to the composition of music: the basic melodic line, the underlying harmonic structure, the rhythmic organization. Liszt was often able to leave these almost untouched and yet transform an

uninteresting student's effort into a radical work of great originality. He re-
works what is sometimes considered only the surface of music: that is, he keeps
the earlier structure—its melodic profile and the succession of harmonies—and
changes the sonority. It is the imaginative reconception of the sound that makes
the later version a masterpiece.

Between 1826 and 1837 the Etudes of Chopin had made their appearance.
The original version of Liszt's F Minor Etude began with groups of three notes:

Liszt did not fail to notice Chopin's Etude in F Minor, op. 10, no. 9:

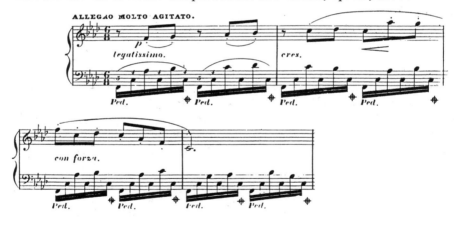

In his second version, he appropriated Chopin's phrase:

altered it slightly to

making it more dissonant and, indeed, more dramatic. Then he imposed it as a rhythmic syncopation of six against four on his own structure:

He polished it in a final version, smoother and more easily playable:

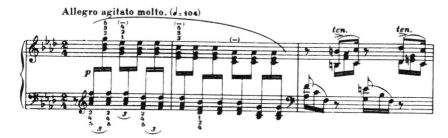

The originality of Liszt's combination is considerably more striking than the fact that he has laid hands on someone else's property: the Chopinesque motif covers the join between Liszt's first and second phrases, and magnifies both the continuity and the agitation. All this, however, obscures the most important source of the newly increased power of the agitation, which has little to do with Chopin; it comes above all from Liszt's discovery of a new way of playing parallel sixths with one hand over the other. The technique may have been suggested by certain pages of Czerny, but they have nothing like the force that Liszt creates; the arrangement of triplets in this new form imposes a kind of syncopation as the execution always proceeds in groups of two and foreshadows the syncopation of bar 4. I do not wish to imply that Liszt's innovation is a purely technical one of fingering: it means that Liszt was the first composer in history to understand fully the musical significance—dramatic and emotional as well as aural—of new techniques of execution.

We can see the new dramatic power with an almost comic clarity in the transformation of the early D Minor Etude into "Mazeppa." The original is almost absurdly uninteresting, and makes pages of Clementi's *Gradus ad Parnassum* seem richly complex by comparison:

The transformation proceeded in several stages. First Liszt discovered that

could most effectively be hammered out with just two fingers: $\frac{2}{4}\frac{2}{4}\frac{2}{4}$. He also added an obbligato melody to the figure:

The new *obbligato* melody helps to make this version considerably more interesting than the first one, but the character of the piece, and, probably, of the added melody, was defined chiefly by the new fingering, which created a radically new keyboard sound. This double-note *martellato* must have been suggested by the way that Paganini occasionally used to chop at his instrument with startling effect, and it does indeed suggest string playing: in any case, nothing like it had been heard on a keyboard before (even if it distantly recalls Scarlatti's delight in hammering away at dissonant clusters).

The next step may appear more purely musical, but it is essentially as much an invention of sonority as the new fingering was—the change from diatonic to chromatic harmony:

The latest improvement makes the new *martellato* fingering more effective, and gives greater richness to what has become an accompaniment figure—although basically as important a figure as it was in the initial work of the fifteen-year-old composer. I do not wish to underestimate all the other elements of Liszt's rewriting: the introductory cadenzas, the *obbligato* melody, the new rhythmic energy. Nevertheless, all of these novelties seem to me to derive from his reconception of the means of execution which creates an unprecedented dramatic force. It should be clear that any attempt to play the *martellato* figure with four fingers, ₄²₃¹ instead of only ₄²₄² (as pianists often do to avoid strain on wrist and arm), is an inexcusable betrayal of Liszt's intentions.

Fingering has particular weight in this Etude, as Liszt, towards the end of the piece, reconceives the sound yet again.

and here at last the fingering, ₄²₃¹ in the left hand, and ₁³₂⁴ or ₂³₁⁴ in the right, is the only one that will produce the new snap that this passage requires. Throughout this third version Liszt invents different sonorities for his original material; the final one transforms the hammered texture of the inner notes to a smear:

In spite of the imaginative brilliance, the final version of "Mazeppa" is not one of Liszt's most satisfying works, but it is among the most important and most influential. Above all, it clearly reveals the extravagance of his imagination, which enabled him to develop a childish and insignificant trifle into one of the most famous warhorses of the Romantic repertoire, one which amply justifies the Byronic title of "Mazeppa," the rebellious hero who aspired to a love beyond his lowly station and, tied naked to a horse, was sent off into the wilderness. The music does indeed seem to depict the sound of a galloping horse, but a study of the gradual elaboration of this Etude would indicate that it was the music that suggested the title: the programmatic significance of some of Liszt's works, like many of Schumann's, are afterthoughts intended to add poetic resonance and stimulate the listener's appreciation. In any case, the distance travelled from the easy finger exercise of 1826 to the final "Mazeppa" of 1851 can help us comprehend the idiosyncratic nature of Liszt's mind and see what gave him his supreme distinction.

The existence of the early version is fundamental to our understanding. In his excellent biography of Liszt, Alan Walker seems puzzled by the relationship; he writes, "It is not clear why he chose to revise his 'prentice pieces, rather than to compose a completely fresh set of works."[2] One can detect a trace of that impatience so often found with admirers of Liszt, the echo of a regret that their hero was not more often original, that he wasted so much of his time making paraphrases of his own or other composer's works. Here there is a critical failure to recognize an extraordinary form of originality. The new versions of the Transcendental Etudes are not revisions but concert paraphrases of the old, and their art lies in the technique of transformation. The Paganini Etudes are piano transcriptions of violin etudes, and the Transcendental Etudes are piano transcriptions of piano etudes. The principles are the same.

For Liszt, paraphrase was basic to the process of composition. We can see how this worked with the Etude in B flat Major, later called "Feux Follets" (Will-o'-the-Wisp). The pretranscendental original has once again little to recommend it as music or even as a finger exercise:

---

2. Alan Walker, *Franz Liszt, the Virtuoso Years* (New York, 1983), p. 305.

The revision of 1837 is one of Liszt's most brilliant inspirations:

He keeps the earlier structure—its melodic profile and the succession of harmonies—and changes the sonority. What is added in the later versions of 1837
and 1851 is the supremely difficult chromatic finger exercise in double notes
that gives a wonderful flickering effect. Liszt took the work of a child and
reconceived the sound.

This naturally provoked a thorough alteration of the basic structure seen as
a whole. The new chromaticism of the opening would have made the simple,
largely diatonic course of the original piece insipid and even embarrassing, and
it stimulated a series of modulations, the most remarkable to A major, which
entails a new version of the principal theme. Liszt exploits the ambiguity of
the modulation by writing out the trill alternately on E♯ and F♮, as it can resolve
upward to F♯ or downward to E♮.

Donald Francis Tovey has remarked that when a figuration in one of Liszt's
Etudes becomes awkward for the performer by modulation and transposition,
the composer rewrites it in a more comfortable form, while Chopin, when
faced with the same problem, ruthlessly forces the pianist's hand into whatever
contorted positions are demanded by the new harmony. The double notes,
difficult in the key of B flat, are so awkward in the new key of A major as to
make it almost impossible to play with any grace. Liszt provides a different
sound and new, but more reasonable, difficulties.

The revision of the early Etudes did not always make them spectacularly
difficult. The beginning of the third Etude in F Major is, if anything, easier in
the later version, although now intended for larger, more adult hands. Here is
the first version:

and the second:

The early version is not even distinguished enough to be banal, but a decade later it has been turned into poetry and entitled "Landscape." The new poetic feeling, however, is bound up with the technical aspect. Reconceiving the first four bars as a solo for the left hand inspired a different character, and made it possible to add an *obbligato* melody in the right hand. The effort to encompass all the notes in one hand is the most important source of the new expressivity. This caused radical changes in the course of the whole work, giving it an altogether original form; extensive alterations took place in the third version of 1851 and brought a greater unity of sentiment, an even more refined poetic feeling.

In short, the paraphrase of the opening bars of an early etude involved Liszt in a complete rethinking of the whole piece. The basic structure of the opening bars remains unaltered beneath the elaborate rewriting of the later version, but the rest of the piece now takes off in different directions, although the presence of the early form never entirely disappears. In this respect, speaking of two "versions" hides the fact that these are two very different works, related by genealogy but by little else. Paraphrase has shaded off into composition. At what point Liszt ceases to paraphrase and starts to compose is a question that often makes very little sense, even when applied to many of the Liszt transcriptions of operas by Mozart, Wagner, and others. Composition and paraphrase were not identical for him, but they were so closely interwoven that separation is impossible.

A final example from the Transcendental Etudes shows how profound was the interrelationship. The original C Minor Etude is sadly commonplace:

From this, Liszt isolated two elements: first, a simple scale outlining a fifth in the bass:

and second, an equally simple arpeggio in the treble:

Certainly Beethoven worked often enough with motifs no more complex or promising than these, and developed them into something magnificent. Liszt's way is not Beethoven's, however. He does not develop these motifs but rather finds fascinating ways of realizing them in sound. The third and final version of 1851 realizes the short scale passage with thunderous octaves in the bass:

This is the version played today with great effect, and the gap between it and the original Etude is astonishing. The second version was even more astonishing: closer to the original and less effective, at once extraordinarily imaginative and almost impossible to execute decently and clearly today with the necessary velocity (it was more practicable on the lighter action of the pianos of the 1830s):

This was, at the time, a truly original sonority, a kind of low growl or blur from which the fingers had to pick out the notes of the descending scale and set them rapidly in relief one after the other. If the final version is more grateful to play, this second version is a superb finger exercise, developing both strength and tone control.

The second motif, the descending C minor arpeggio, is recomposed with a dramatic and asymmetrical rhythm in a series of chords:

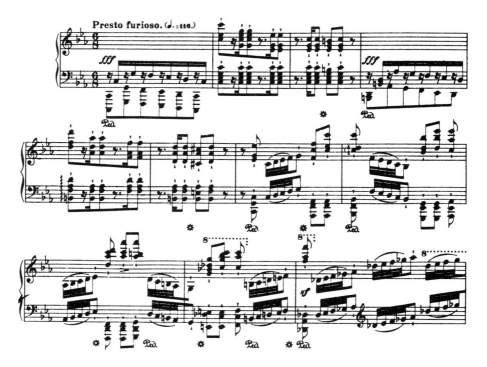

The irregular rhythm inspired a more unexpected irregularity. The harmony of the succeeding bars—a relatively simple sequence—is reconceived in groups of five: in spite of the opening indication of 6/8, the real time signature in bars 7 to 11 is 5/8, and the notation disregards the bar lines.

This experiment in rhythm is not unique in the work of Liszt before the age of thirty. Even more radical is the passage from the first publication of *Harmonies poétiques et réligieuses*:

or the extraordinary moment in the early paraphrase of a Schubert waltz in *Apparitions,* where the rhythm seems to dissolve completely:

This is an almost purely coloristic use of rhythm, and the groups of five in the Transcendental Etude in C Minor are employed in the same way: they act to accelerate the structure of 6/8, which has already been undermined by the asymmetrical rhythm of the first six bars.

Conception and realization

A tiny scale section and a short arpeggio are motifs so basic to tonal music that the reworking of the early Etude may be considered simply as a form of composition like any other. The original, however, must have provided a simple framework for years of improvisation out of which came the extravagance of the publication of 1837 and finally the more sedate but effective decisions of 1851. Liszt's habit of paraphrasing earlier work, his own or those by other composers, is closely related to the use of specific earlier works as models by so many nineteenth-century composers—by Mendelssohn, Schubert, Clara Wieck, and, most systematically, Brahms. This was, no doubt, a practice that had always had a certain attraction, above all for very young composers, but it increased notably after 1820. There is, however, an important difference between the method of Brahms and that of Liszt: Brahms often closely follows the phrase structure and the texture of his models (generally chosen from Beethoven, Haydn, and Schubert), substituting new melodies—changing the pitches in short; Liszt retains the pitches, and plays with the texture and the sonorities—working essentially with tone color.

In his concentration on tone color Liszt may be seen as the most radical musician of his generation. His example attacked some of the basic assumptions of Western music, in which pitch and rhythm were the essential determinants of form, and spacing and tone color were subordinate, only a means to the realization in sound. How shaky this hierarchy had become by the early nineteenth century can be seen from the role of dynamic accent in Beethoven (both the violent *fortes* and the sudden *pianos*) which now played a basic structural role, an essential part of the motifs and of the general rhythmic movement.

The supremacy of pitch and rhythm over dynamics and color was turned upside down by Liszt. Realization now took precedence over the underlying compositional structure. There were many composers before Liszt who wrote with a specific sound in mind, but none for whom this realization in sound is more important than the text behind it. Beautifully sensitive to the character of his musical material, and deeply indifferent to its quality, all Liszt's genius was directed toward the realization in sound. The 1837 version of his youthful etudes must have been the result of hundreds of performances, thousands of hours of improvisation. Why should he have written new etudes? The invention of material was never his strong point; one suspects that as he developed new effects of realization, he created material to fit and show them off. Liszt is perhaps the first composer of instrumental music whose music is, for the most part, conceived absolutely for public performance. That is why there are so many different versions of the same piece: each successive version is itself a new performance.

In one of the variations from the Paganini Etude no. 6 in A Minor, Liszt takes from the original a simple succession of notes: C, A, E, C, A, E, C, A. The 1838 edition is very different from that of 1851:

In the 1838 version this variation represents violin *spiccato,* the bow bouncing
from string to string, the hand bouncing all over the piano. In 1851, the same
succession of notes stays within a small range, and it now represents a *pizzicato*
effect. The 1838 version commands admiration for its imaginative extravagance, and part of the delight comes from the fact that it is almost unplayable.
By 1851 it has become more faithful to Paganini, but it is still the new effect,
the new color that counts. The succession of pitches remains the same, although transposed to different registers. In any case, who cares for Paganini's
original notes when faced with such an imagination?

The only forms of music in which composition and realization are absolutely
identical are improvisation and electronic music; sound and conception coincide absolutely here. In jazz improvisation, however, as in Liszt's Paganini
Etudes, there is a text behind the sound, a tune given in advance; but in
listening to one of Art Tatum's recorded performances, it makes almost no
difference who wrote the musical text behind the realization—Cole Porter, Fats
Waller, Rube Bloom. What counts is the "paraphrase." In bringing composition and realization closer together, Liszt made it possible to give qualities of
sound—resonance, texture, contrasts of register—an importance they had
never had before in composition. Tone color is even more important in his
music than in that of Berlioz, and his combinations of invented sound are often
as astonishing as those in electronic music.

Liszt's feeling for sound was the greatest of any keyboard composer's between Scarlatti and Debussy, and he surpassed them in boldness. Critics often
write as if Liszt's innovations in piano technique were merely ways of playing
lots of notes in a short space of time, instead of inventions of sound. His
mastery of different ways of fingering scales is a case in point: he sometimes
played scales with five fingers, sometimes with four, or with just three. Only
the first is Liszt's invention; the others were mentioned by Beethoven in a letter
to Czerny (the most distinguished of Liszt's piano teachers), where he explained
how he wanted his nephew to study the piano. The three-fingered scale was
the best for achieving a light, detached, "pearly" touch, the most fashionable
technique when Beethoven was very young—during Mozart's lifetime, in fact.
The use of four fingers aided a controlled, singing legato. Liszt's playing a scale
with all five fingers in succession—12345, 12345—enabled him to reach extraordinary velocity, a smear like a glissando: the trick consists of a rapid shift
of the hand at the end of each group of five between the fifth finger and the
thumb on the next note. It was the variety of touch that Liszt extended.

What Liszt's technical innovations enabled him to achieve were not only new kinds of piano sound but layers of contrasting sound. His arrangement of Schubert's "Der Lindenbaum," for example, in the last stanza presents the theme in the right hand in octaves simultaneously above and below a steady, delicate trill, which gives a continuously vibrant sonority, while the left hand imitates a *pizzicato* bass and, at the same time, realizes Schubert's simple flowing accompaniment as if it were performed by a trio of French horns:

This is, one must confess, rather an awful thing to do to a Schubert song, but it would be churlish to refuse one's admiration for the grandeur and richness of the conception—or for the pianist who can play it and make it sound as vulgarly beautiful as it was intended—particularly the spectacular passage where the trill is transferred to the fourth and fifth fingers and the accompanying triplets must be played with the thumb and the melody by the left hand. To comprehend Liszt's greatness one needs a suspension of distaste, a momentary renunciation of musical scruples.

This renunciation is not easy today, nor was it ever. Liszt was the great philistine musician. Right-thinking music lovers looked with horror on what they considered his charlatanry. He was indeed a charlatan, and he knew it, and sometimes laughed at it. He was also a composer and pianist of the utmost refinement and originality. It is, unfortunately, useless to try to separate the great musician from the charlatan: each one needed the other in order to exist.

In 1844, at the height of Liszt's career as a pianist, a lover of Bach in Montpellier, Jules Laurens, reproached him with his charlatanry, and then asked him to play his famous arrangement for the piano of Bach's Prelude and Fugue in A Minor for organ:

"How do you want me to play it?"

"How? But . . . the way it ought to be played."

"Here it is, to start with, as the author must have understood it, played it himself, or intended it to be played."

And Liszt played. And it was admirable, the perfection itself of the classical style exactly in conformity with the original.

"Here it is a second time, as I feel it, with a slightly more picturesque movement, a more modern style and the effects demanded by an improved instrument." And it was, with these nuances, different . . . but no less admirable.

"Finally, a third time, here it is the way I would play it for the public—to astonish, as a charlatan." And, lighting a cigar which passed at moments from between his lips to his fingers, executing with his ten fingers the part written for the organ pedals, and indulging in other *tours de force* and prestidigitation, he was prodigious, incredible, fabulous, and received gratefully with enthusiasm.[3]

(I hope that it was only during the Prelude that the cigar went from lips to fingers, as there would be little chance to accomplish this gracefully in the Fugue.)

The variety of styles with which Liszt could perform a single work is given eloquent witness by Laurens here; it corresponds absolutely with the variety of styles he had at his command as a composer, the different ways in which he could realize or paraphrase a work by another composer or by himself. Laurens is also a witness to Liszt's ability early in his career to perform a work with the utmost fidelity: it is sometimes claimed that Liszt's faithful renditions date from late in life, and that earlier he was more than cavalier in his high-handed treatment of other composers' creations. Berlioz too, however, testified to the total fidelity with which the young Liszt performed Beethoven's *Hammerklavier* Sonata—not a note changed, not a single dynamic altered. Perhaps it was a question of how great the challenge was: it was a difficult feat to perform the *Hammerklavier* and the Chopin Etudes as written, and Liszt's interpretation of these pieces treated them with respect. Other works were too simple, or else something about them caught his fancy and he took possession of them as if they were his personal property. He treated his own compositions in the same ruthless manner.

The masks of Liszt

I do not think that it serves any useful purpose to classify Liszt's versions of other composers' works into the two categories of faithful transcriptions and free paraphrases, as many critics do—and, indeed, as the new edition now coming out of Hungary does—with the assumption that the free paraphrases are more interesting and that the transcriptions are mere hackwork. The piano version of Berlioz's *Symphonie fantastique* is a simple transcription, bar by bar, but it is also one of the most imaginative conceptions of keyboard writing of the entire nineteenth century: it was often publicly performed by Liszt, at least in part, and it recreates orchestral sound on the piano as no one had ever dreamed before that it could be done. The Six Organ Preludes and Fugues of Bach for piano are ostentatiously austere: not a note added, and the engraving without any indication of tempo, dynamics, or phrasing. Yet the first, in A minor, the most famous, is immediately recognizable as Liszt, paradoxical as this may seem (it suggests that an important aspect of Liszt's sound was inspired by his early experience of playing the *Well-Tempered Keyboard* on the piano). In a later transcription of the great G Minor Organ Prelude and Fugue

---

3. Quoted by Jean-Jacques Eigeldinger in "L'Interprète de Bach," in *Silences 3 (Liszt)* (1984).

of Bach, on the other hand, Liszt unscrupulously enriched Bach's original with
his own ideas. It is absurd to pretend that many of the arrangements, like those
of the Schubert songs, were done only to make the originals more available to
the public and to popularize them: there must have been very few of Liszt's
contemporaries who could even have attempted the transcription of Schubert's
"Der Lindenbaum."

Some of Liszt's most extravagantly free paraphrases have, in fact, an unsuspected fidelity, a genuine and often successful attempt to enter into the original
composer's skin, to intensify his work in a new medium as if Liszt had done
it himself. The arrangement of Chopin's songs is, for example, a considerable
improvement on the vocal versions. Chopin wrote his songs at different times,
and charming as some of them are, he clearly did not waste any time over
them. Liszt's transcription welds a group of these songs into a cycle, in which
one song even goes without pause into the next. By making a single work of
these separate songs, Liszt was concerned to give them a musical weight and
even a depth of feeling they had not before had—a truly Chopinesque feeling,
however. This is the original opening of *My Joys:*

Liszt transforms this amiable mazurka into a nocturne,

and it is quite evidently a nocturne by Chopin. Liszt has taken Chopin's Nocturne in D flat Major, op. 27, no. 2, and combined it with the song:

Later in the song Chopin perpetrates a passage of a rare banality and even awkwardness, perhaps the only such passage that he composed after the age of twenty:

With considerable tact, Liszt takes pains to conceal Chopin's astonishing miscalculation. He covers it up by breaking into the phrase with two fermatas, a cadenza, and a modulation to the dominant,

and turns an unconvincing moment into a complex lyric conception which can be executed with great charm.

The last song of the cycle has a folklike simplicity which Liszt understandably did not find adequate:

The introductory bars, however, gave him the hint of an idea, as they faintly resemble the so-called "Revolutionary" Etude in C Minor, op. 10, no. 12, of Chopin. Liszt rewrote the song in the style of the famous Etude, using the opening bars as a model, particularly bars 7 to 12:

Liszt's version of the song follows this closely and makes a splendidly effective conclusion to the cycle.

In short, from these songs Liszt created something very closely resembling an original Chopin work. It is not so much the stylistic mimicry which is noteworthy as the real sympathy and understanding of another composer's idiosyncrasy, and it enabled Liszt to write an entirely original climax to *My Joys* which remains entirely convincing.

The cycle of Chopin songs for the piano stands midway between transcription and original composition, but the best way to understand the success is to note the analogy with Liszt's ability to vary the style of his performances. These transcriptions are, in fact, written performances—above all, performances of great originality and freedom. A mazurka is performed as a nocturne: the fundamental structure is, for the most part, unchanged until the final climax, but the style of performance has been transformed until it takes over aspects of composition. To a great extent, a composition was a performance for Liszt.

The functions of the large structure, while present, are not as significant as the changes of character and style. The themes are transformed less in response to the demands of an abstract harmonic form than as a means of following a dramatic scenario, requiring dramatic contrasts of style.

Recomposing: Sonnet no. 104

Each of the multiple versions of so many works by Liszt, like the multiple versions of the main theme of the sonata, is a new creation in its own right—essentially a different performance of basic material which rises to the level of a radically original reconception. The revisions are neither clarifications of the fundamental idea in order to make it more effective, as in Beethoven,[4] nor, as in Schumann, the simple excision of details that had come to seem Romantically excessive in a sober and classically minded decade. Liszt's revisions are generally newly improvised forms.

In the great set of landscape pieces and characteristic music that finally became the *Années de pèlerinage*, many of the works went through years of elaboration. The Petrarch Sonnet no. 104, rightly admired and often performed, has a long history. Since the first published version is a transcription for piano, we must assume a lost vocal form that preceded it. That gives us five different forms that were at least temporarily fixed:

1. The original vocal setting of 1838–39 (there is no way of proving that this resembled the second version rather than the third, but there is reason to believe that this was the case).

2. A piano transcription published in 1846.

---

4. I am not considering here Beethoven's process of sketching (although the generalization would, in fact, apply pretty well to much of that), but the revisions of completed works—that is, the changes made between fair copy and publication, or between publication and second edition. Even the most extensive of these revisions, that which transformed *Leonora* into *Fidelio*, consisted in large part of tightening the phrase structure by eliminating repetitions.

3. A song for tenor and piano also published in 1846.

4. A new piano transcription published in 1858 in the *Années de pèler-inage,* largely reflecting the third version for tenor, published twelve years before.

5. A song for baritone and piano published in 1861.

The openings of the two versions for piano are very different. The introduction of 1846 is considerably longer, with a pedal point in the bass that started, in fact, one note lower than the range of most keyboards at that time:

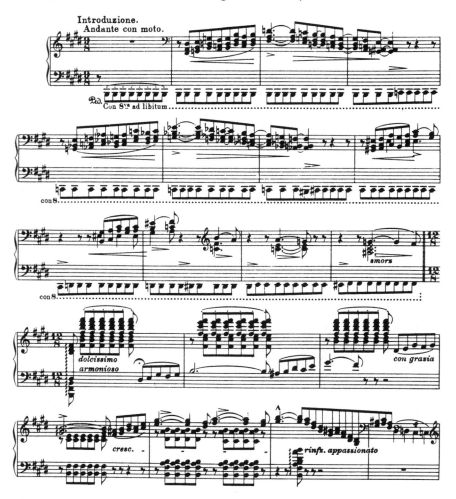

This, although rarely played, is one of Liszt's most extraordinary and exquisite pages, and exploits different kinds of keyboard sonority. The phrase structure is remarkably original in its fluidity: the bass avoids any emphasis at the bar lines, and it is out of phase with the upper line, giving an impression of great freedom. The sonority starts with a kind of thick mist and only gradually clarifies itself.

The introduction in the later piano transcription is more laconic and more dramatic:

This interestingly resembles the original introduction to *La Vallée d'Obermann*, first published in 1840 in *Impressions et poésies* (which became volume 1 of *L'Album d'un voyageur*):

La Vallée d'Obermann, the greatest of Liszt's landscapes, was revised for volume 1 of the *Années de pèlerinage, première année, Suisse,* and published in 1855. The introduction was cut, and the piece now began with the slow meditative melody (quoted on p. 193). The revision of the Swiss landscapes began in the late 1840s, just after the publication of the first versions of the Petrarch sonnets; the tenor and piano song of 1846–47 seems to have appropriated some aspects of the original recitative-like introduction to *La Vallée d'Obermann.*

In the first published vocal version of the sonnet, the introduction in the piano now leads not to the melody but to a recitative set to the words of the first stanza, and which acts as a further introductory form:

e vo.lo so.pra'l cie.lo,e giac.cio in ter.ra;

The principal melody does not appear until the second stanza. Nothing that could correspond to a full recitative setting of the opening stanza appears in either of the piano transcriptions, and in the final vocal setting for baritone the singer starts directly with the principal melody. It seems most likely that the original song, now lost, also started the setting of Petrarch's text with this melody, which fits the opening words too well and too effectively, and that Liszt did not substitute the recitative until he decided to publish a vocal form for the first time.

In the piano transcription of 1846, the principal melody is played as a solo for the left hand alone:

This has a wonderfully idiosyncratic effect, forcing the pianist to play with the phrasing of a cellist, a kind of expressive virtuosity that Liszt must later have found outlandish, as he rewrote it for the 1855 publication in a less ostentatious form:

The musical style of the melody is Italian opera with no interference from any other tradition. Deciding between the two keyboard versions would be pointless: from the earlier to the later one, there is a clear loss of poetry and adventure and a decided gain in drama, economy, and effectiveness. The tenor version of 1846 is even more brilliant than the piano transcriptions, as the singer is asked to produce a soft falsetto on a high D♭:

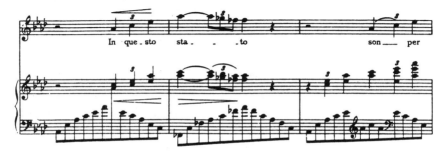

All the luxuriant virtuosity, however, disappears in the 1850s; the baritone version is emphatically, almost willfully austere, with a new rhythmic freedom and a repressed intensity. The melody has been reshaped, although it is recognizably the same melody, but the expression has been made more inward, the rhythm closer to spoken prose:

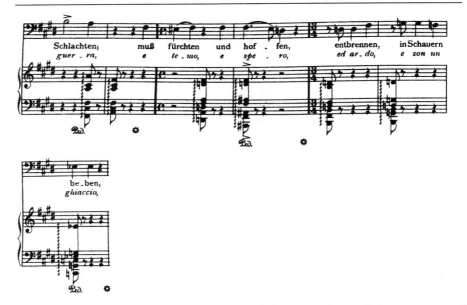

The final revision is a beautiful example of the originality and the economy of Liszt's late style, all the more remarkable as he is still dealing with a musical idea he produced in his late twenties. The end of the final version, indeed, develops the words "In this condition have you brought me, lady" ("In questo stato son, Donna, per voi") as a deeply moving stammer, completely unresolved:

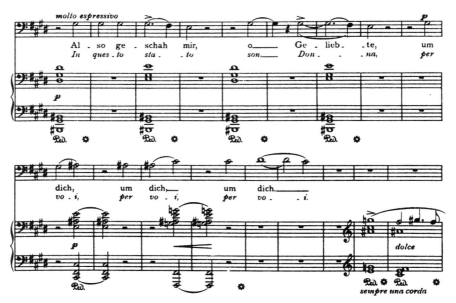

This is a memory of the Romantic fragment of the 1830s ending on only a half cadence, half implied, after Liszt's beloved diminished seventh chord. We can see how Liszt—perhaps unique in this respect—remained faithful to the early Romantic aesthetic, and was only partially influenced by the new conservative ambiance after 1850.

How far his style had changed, however, can be seen by comparing the setting of the words "Pascomi di dolor" (I nourish myself with pain) in tenor and baritone versions:

The transformation is now so complete that, although we may recognize that the later version is derived from the earlier, the relationship has come to seem irrelevant, even far-fetched. Other considerations provide Liszt with inspiration for this final version: the old melody is nothing but a convenient substructure on which to hang his new sense of the words, his development of a new characteristic emotion.

The presence of the same melody in all four versions ought not to obscure the fact that each one has a form radically different from the others. A schematic summary of these forms may show how different they are in function in spite of all they have in common. The song for tenor is organized:

1. a. Introduction, in the piano, 5 bars.

    b. Recitative, voice, 22 bars.

    c. Return of introduction, 5 bars.

2. a. First half of melody in piano, A, 8 bars.

    b. Melody in voice, $A + B$, ending on minor mediant, 16 bars.

    c. Melody repeated, $A + B^2$, ending on flattened mediant major, 16 bars.

3. a. New motif, 4 bars.

    b. Principal motif A on dominant interior pedal.

    c. Cadenza.

4. Return of recitative (see 1b), 4 bars.

5. Coda based on A (interior tonic pedal).

The first piano transcription may be described:

1. Introduction, 21 bars.

2. Threefold presentation of melody.

    a. $A + B$, 14 bars, half cadence on V.

    b. $A + B'$, 16 bars, cadence on iii mediant minor (G sharp).

    c. $A + B^2$, 16 bars, half cadence on III^b flatted mediant major (G).

3. a. New motif, 4 bars.

    b. Principal motif A on dominant, 4 bars.

4. Recitative, 4 bars.

5. Coda based on A (interior tonic pedal).

The second piano transcription follows the tenor version but eliminates the twenty-two bars of recitative (1b) and the repeat of the introduction (1c), and this alters the significance of the form, now much more straightforward.

In the tenor version the recitative is the basic frame, returning at the end before the coda; and it is itself framed by the five bars of introduction which return twenty-two bars later. The recitative here is not exactly an introduction as normally understood, but an initial operatic *scena:* it is a complete setting of the first stanza of Petrarch's sonnet. The return of the recitative before the coda emphasizes its structural importance. In the first piano transcription, however, the concentration is mainly on the triple presentation of the principal melody, and everything is subordinate to that.

The song for baritone uses the elements of the earlier forms in an essentially new arrangement:

1. a. Introduction, 6 bars.

   b. Recitative in piano, 7 bars.

2. a. Principal melody in voice, E major, 11 bars.

   b. Development of melody with modulation to mediant major (D flat) (12 bars).

   c. Development of melody over rising diminished seventh chords to mediant major (G natural) (18 bars).

   d. Further development over rising bass, 18 bars.

3. New motif in unaccompanied voice, then continued with spare accompaniment (10 bars).

4. Return of melody, mutilated, and now harmonized in submediant minor, vi (C sharp minor) (16 bars).

5. Return of piano, recitative (number 1b) ending on an implied dominant ninth chord of C sharp minor (9 bars).

Here the recitative is in the piano alone and is a purely instrumental framing device, while the vocal part witnesses a gradual disintegration of the melody, presented in *arioso* style, as if half spoken, half sung. The form imposes a new conception of both text and melody. We might almost call this an antisonnet, written against the symmetrical extravagance and paradoxes of the words, and above all against the rich lyricism and romantic passion of the original melody.

The form of each composition is defined neither by the melodic or thematic material nor by the structure of the Petrarch sonnet, not even by an abstract, traditional pattern imposed on the material. In each of the four versions there is some kind of return, but of a very different nature: in both piano transcriptions, it is not a formal return but a distant echo or distorted reminiscence of the principal melody; in the song for tenor, the initial recitative returns explicitly; only the baritone version has a true return of the main theme, but truncated, compressed, and unresolved. What dictates the shape of Liszt's structures is the character of his treatment of the material, the style of realization—dramatic, lyric, or epic. This gives the most interesting of his forms a looseness of organization that can seem either a crippling fault or an incomparable virtue. From a classical point of view, his structures, even the Piano Sonata, betray a lack of cohesion, an imperfectly persuasive formal logic. Nonetheless, the brilliantly conceived first movement of his E flat Concerto has been underrated because it is basically a series of fanfares that break up a set of half recitatives, structured by the progression from heroic through lyrical to intense passion and resolution. His forms achieve effects of narrative and freely developing expression unknown before.[5] The most original aspect of Liszt's procedure revealed in Sonnet 104 is the disjunction between material and the stylistic treatment, which is most dramatic in the tenor version, more purely lyrical in the piano transcriptions, meditative and elegiac in the song for baritone. For Liszt, the musical material—invented by himself, or taken from somewhere else—was essentially malleable, and could be given a different dramatic order.

Self-portrait as Don Juan

This ability to reformulate a musical idea in terms of new styles of performance, and to reorder material according to various dramatic scenarios made Liszt the only true master of the opera fantasy. There has been a revival of interest in the old-fashioned—indeed, obsolete—form of the opera fantasy; the interest, however, is largely due either to a certain kind of "camp" aesthetic or to a sociological interest in the history of nineteenth-century taste. Except by a few scholars and critics, the opera fantasy is considered a bastard genre—as it indeed mostly was: the majority of opera fantasies were only strings of popular tunes arranged for virtuoso display. Some of the Liszt opera transcriptions are, in fact, not much more than that: the quartet from *Rigoletto*, for example. The finest of the opera fantasies, however—*Norma, Les Huguenots,* and *Don Giovanni*—are much more than that: they juxtapose different parts of the opera in ways that bring out a new significance, while the original dramatic sense of the individual number and its place within the opera is never out of sight. Chopin's youthful arrangement of "Là ci darem la mano" from *Don Giovanni* conveys no awareness that this was a duet:

---

5. Martia Grabócz, in her thesis "Morphologie des oeuvres pour piano de Liszt: influence du programme sur l'evolution des formes instrumentales," has stressed the variety of Liszt's forms, their novelty, and their relation to literary genres.

Liszt, on the other hand, faithfully renders the contrast between the amorous and importunate Don and the coquettish but only half-willing Zerlina:

It is not simply the melodies of *Don Giovanni* that Liszt transcribed but the dramatic situations and the sense of the whole opera.

The title, *Réminiscences de Don Juan,* must be taken not as a series of isolated memories but as a synoptic view of the opera, in which the different moments of the drama exist simultaneously: what Liszt reveals is the way they are interrelated. He combines material from different parts of the opera freely. The work begins with the sinister phrases of the statue in the cemetery, act 2, scene 11, and follows these immediately with the statue's terrifying appearance two scenes later (act 2 finale, bars 433–436):

The two phrases of the statue's warning in the cemetery reappear, now played over the pathetic figuration of the overture (which also appears in the finale, bars 445ff.), and this leads once more to the statue's entrance in the finale, but with a scale figuration that comes slightly later (bars 462ff.):

An astonishing shift to the harmony of B major (made doubly surprising by the dynamics, suddenly soft) leads yet again to the diminished seventh of the statute's entrance, rescored in a brilliant climax:

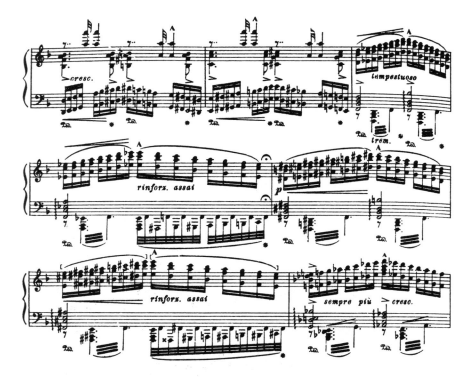

This brings us to bars 454 to 461 of the finale, where the statue refuses the invitation to eat mortal food, and the rising scales are rescored with the flashiest virtuoso chromatic thirds, intended to strike terror in the heart of the performer as well as of the public:

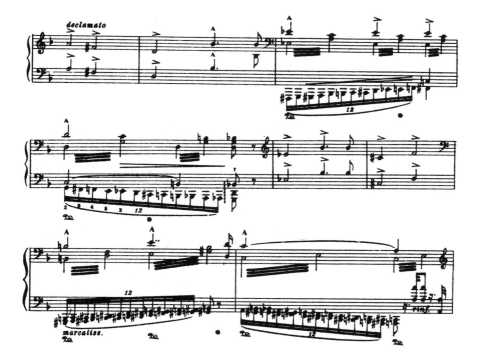

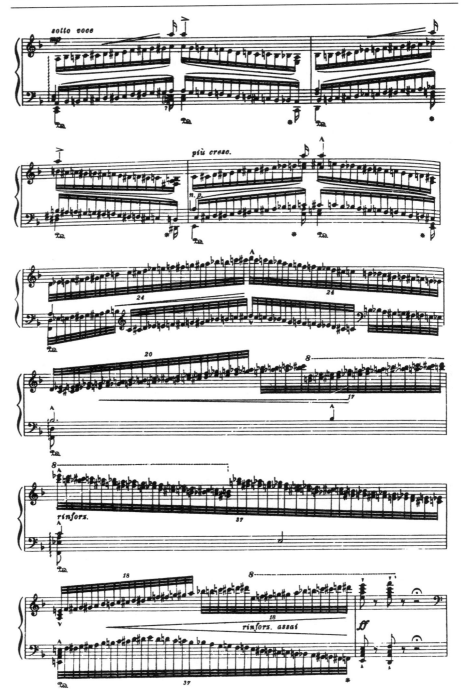

Then Liszt uses bars 474 to 477 of the finale with the pathetic figuration once again as a counterpoint to introduce the first suggestion of the love duet, "Là ci darem la mano" (Give me your hand); a later arrangement for two pianos made this passage more like the Prelude to Wagner's *Tristan und Isolde*:

Bernard Shaw called the variations on the duet conventional, but they contain passages harmonically in advance of their time and which predict the Richard Strauss of *Der Rosenkavalier*:

The delicate suggestion of the harmonies of G major and B flat major laid over A major is purely coloristic.

The second variation of the love duet is interrupted by the statue's invitation that will take Don Giovanni to hell (bars 487ff. of the finale):

This leads to a spectacular chromatic cascade of octaves alternating with single notes which must have dazzled the audiences on Liszt's tours throughout Europe:

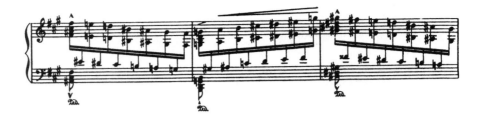

This way of playing chromatic octaves is, I believe, Liszt's invention, and enables the performer to stupefy the audience with the sudden crescendo and a speed like a glissando. These passages make explicit a Victorian condemnation of Don Juan's morals and amount to an assertion that his erotic misbehavior will lead to eternal damnation—an assertion which does not betray the eighteenth-century libretto. Liszt, however, ends with the triumph of Don Juan. In a long dramatic cadenza which is one of the most original pages of the fantasy, the pathetic figuration of the overture and the statue's warning combine with the theme of the so-called Champagne aria, the celebration of hedonism, as the figuration now becomes a thunderous virtuoso display:

The "Champagne" aria is perhaps Liszt's most extravagant and effective transcription, and the end is invaded more and more by the music of the statue:

The last pages are exhilarating. Every phrase of the *Réminiscences de Don Juan* is derived from Mozart, and yet, at the same time, every note testifies to Liszt's profound originality.

The *Réminiscences,* written in 1841 as Liszt was setting out on the most spectacular triumphs of his career as a virtuoso, the tours of Germany and Russia, has won, as Busoni observed in the preface to his edition, "an almost symbolic significance as the highest point of pianism." In it, Liszt displayed almost every facet of his invention as a composer for the piano. That the tunes are by Mozart is largely irrelevant; the work is one of Liszt's most personal achievements. With his international reputation for erotic conquest already set, Liszt must have known that the public would take his fantasy as a self-portrait in sound, just as everyone had assumed that Byron's *Don Juan* was an autobiography. It does not, in fact, matter much whether or how often Liszt went to bed with the women who threw themselves at him: he did almost nothing to discourage his international reputation as a Don Juan. Every performance of his fantasy must have been understood by his audience as an ironic image of the composer-performer. As Mozart had used coloratura brilliance in *The Magic Flute* as a metaphor for rage and power, so Liszt uses virtuosity here as a representation of sexual domination. Bernard Shaw, one of the rare critics to understand both Mozart's *Don Giovanni* and Liszt's *Réminiscences de Don Juan,* wrote that "the riotous ecstasy of *Finch'han dal vino* is translated from song into symphony, from the individual to the abstract, with undeniable insight and power." Shaw further remarked that "when you hear the terrible progression of the statue's invitation suddenly echoing through the harmonies accompanying Juan's seductive *Andiam, andiam, mio bene,* you cannot help accepting it as a stroke of genius—that is, if you know your *Don Giovanni au fond.*"[6] If you know your *Don Giovanni*—that has always been the principal barrier to an appreciation of Liszt's fantasy. One must know the Mozart opera by heart, and then forget it. Humphrey Searle (in the *New Grove*) praises the fantasies on operas by Donizetti, Bellini, and Auber, and then adds that "the fantasia on *Don Giovanni* is more open to question," although he finds it "a satisfying piece."

If it is satisfying, why is it more open to question? Evidently because it is one thing to appropriate the work of an Italian or French composer and another to lay sacrilegious hands on a German classic. Even Busoni, in the preface to his edition of the fantasy, wrote defensively: "We readily admit to the strict purists that the Don Juan Fantasy treats of holy matters in an all-too-worldly manner." Mozart's themes, in short, are too good for Liszt. The Gypsy melodies of the Hungarian Rhapsodies, on the other hand, are not, in this view, good enough; they are not even rustic folk songs, it is often alleged, but cheap, urban popular music. In fact, nothing was ever too bad or too good to serve as material for Liszt's compositions. He had little feeling for the *quality* of his musical material, although he showed an extraordinary perception of its nature and of what could be done with it.

It was this indifference to the quality of his material that earned Liszt the contempt of his most distinguished contemporaries and of many of the most respectable critics and historians of posterity. It was, nevertheless, his greatest strength. It made it possible for him to manipulate the material ruthlessly, to concentrate on effects of realization with unprecedented intensity, and to integrate styles and techniques of performance into composition in a new way. His invention of novel keyboard effects and his mastery of musical gesture have always been undervalued, especially by pianists of the German school who prefer the kind of music that can be executed while soulfully regarding the ceiling. On the whole, the most genuine understanding of his music has been displayed by musicians of eastern Europe, and he may almost be considered as the founder of Russian pianism.

6. Review of Paderewski's recital in *The World,* November 19, 1890.

He was a master not so much of sound as of the transformation of sound into gesture: that is why he controlled only the sonority of the piano. His orchestration is, in most cases, dreadful. For this reason I have not discussed as important and remarkable a work as the *Faust* Symphony, which contains a treatment of motif even more sophisticated than that of the Sonata for Piano. He made us realize how misleading questions of taste can become when dealing with the nineteenth century, and he taught the composers who followed him how aspects of music like texture and intensity of sound, violence and delicacy of gesture could replace pitch and rhythm as organizing principles in the development of new forms.

Berlioz: Liberation from the Central European Tradition

Blind idolaters and perfidious critics

Perhaps the cruelest remark ever made about Berlioz came from Mendelssohn, who said that what was so philistine about Berlioz was that "with all his efforts to go stark mad he never once succeeds." Donald Francis Tovey, who quotes this in his essay on Berlioz's *Harold in Italy,* comments that "from its own standpoint the criticism was neither unfriendly nor untrue."[1] (I feel sure that Berlioz would have found it unfriendly.) Mendelssohn, in fact, liked Berlioz personally. He considered the music "indifferent drivel, mere grunting, shouting and screaming back and forth," but he thought the composer himself a "friendly, quiet, meditative person" with an acute critical sense for everything except his own work, and he was depressed by the contrast.[2]

Mendelssohn was writing in 1831. Years of the kind of misunderstanding revealed in his comments must have eroded Berlioz's friendly good nature. More than fifty years later Verdi wrote: "Berlioz was a poor, sick man who raged at everyone. He was greatly and subtly gifted. He had a real feeling for instrumentation, anticipated Wagner in many instrumental effects. (The Wagnerians won't admit it, but it is true.) He had no moderation. He lacked the calm and what I may call the balance that produce complete works of art. He always went to extremes, even when he was doing admirable things."[3] For all his recognition of Berlioz's genius, Verdi is disingenuous and ungracious, particularly in the way he insists on Berlioz's influence on Wagner without acknowledging his own debt, which was enormous and went far beyond simple instrumental effects. The opening of the fugue in the "Libera me" of the

1. Donald Francis Tovey, *Essays in Musical Analysis,* vol. 4 (London, 1936), p. 75.
2. Quoted by Edward T. Cone in his Norton Scores edition of Hector Berlioz, *Fantastic Symphony* (New York, 1971), p. 282.
3. Letter to Opprandino Arrivabene, June 5, 1882, quoted in *Letters of Composers,* ed. Norman and Shrifte (New York, 1946).

Manzoni Requiem, for example, signals the entrance of each new voice by an interjected dominant-tonic cadence, with a wonderfully percussive effect. This clarifying device, which ensures public comprehension of a fugal exposition, came directly from Berlioz's grim "Ronde du Sabbat" in the finale of the *Symphonie fantastique.*

Mendelssohn's gibes show that Berlioz's contemporaries were already aware how much of his Romantic madness was only skin deep, although he fought passionately for the cause of Romanticism. He took up arms for Shakespeare, for Goethe's *Faust,* Oriental exoticism, program music, the Swiss mountains with the lonely sound of shepherd's pipes, the Gothic macabre, the projection of the ego in the work of art, as well as the artist as inspired lunatic—all the commonplace intellectual bric-a-brac of the period, in fact. Berlioz's eccentricities impressed almost everyone, as he hoped and expected, but it has taken more than a century to realize that it is not Berlioz's oddity but his normality, his ordinariness, that makes him great.

In this he differed from a composer like Schumann, whose genius was tied to a profoundly eccentric sense of form and of polyphony and a deep irrationality. In spite of Schumann's obstinate aspiration to aesthetic respectability through his symphonies, quartets, and sonatas, his short, fragmentary piano pieces and songs remain his most enduring achievement. Berlioz's greatest work, some critics now argue, is *The Trojans,* an opera on the most classical of all subjects and the most academic, Vergil's *Aeneid.* Like Delacroix's mural decorations for the National Assembly, Berlioz's finest opera reconciles avant-garde technique with academic ideals. Berlioz was, in fact, as he himself confessed, inspired by the academic history painting of his time. *The Trojans* is the musical equivalent of the *grandes machines* that the so-called *pompiers* displayed at the midcentury salons—a pretentious historical costume drama, life-size and imperturbably earnest. It is the only French grand opera since the works of Cherubini, Berlioz's hated master, to be untouched by cheap melodrama and to attain the genuine seriousness of the high academic style. In order to achieve this more conventional nobility, Berlioz renounced some of his audacity. A comparison of the love music of the earlier *Roméo et Juliette* with the love duet in act 4 of *The Trojans,* "O nuit d'ivresse," shows the later work, beautiful as it is, to be much closer to the music of Gounod (who did, indeed, admire this particular number).

The polished surface of this love duet is a remarkable achievement. In *The Musical Language of Berlioz,* Julian Rushton writes: "Berlioz remarked of the love-duet in Act IV that the music 'settled on this scene like a bird on ripe fruit,' yet it took him sixteen pages of sketches to get it right. If it seemed easy in retrospect it must have been because he enjoyed every moment of rigorous self-criticism."[4] Rushton is too kind. It is more probable that Berlioz was simply lying, as he often did about these matters. He wrote in his memoirs,

---

4. Julian Rushton, *The Musical Language of Berlioz* (New York, 1983), p. 13.

for example, that he composed the fourth movement of the *Fantastic Symphony* in one night—and no doubt he did, as he merely copied it out from a work written a few years before, *Les Francs-juges.*

Criticism of Berlioz generally reveals a perfidy as insidious as the remarks of Mendelssohn. Debussy's few allusions to Berlioz are typical in their ambiguity: "One can even say without irony that Berlioz was always the favorite musician of those who do not know much about music . . . Professionals are still horrified at his harmonic liberties (they even would say his 'clumsiness') and the negligence of his form."[5] "Berlioz is an exception, a monster. He is not at all a musician; he gives the illusion of music with procedures borrowed from literature and painting."[6] It is possible but awkward to reconcile this judgment with Debussy's claim to venerate Berlioz, and his description of the *Fantastic Symphony* as "a feverish masterpiece of romantic ardor . . . moving as a battle of the elements."

These contradictions remain basic to the modern conception of Berlioz. There are, of course, the Berlioz idolaters, still in a minority, who hold passionately that he could do no wrong and that any other view is fed either by malice or by a willful refusal to listen correctly. For other musicians, Berlioz remains a puzzling figure. The belief in the clumsiness of his harmony, the naïveté of his counterpoint, and the negligence of his forms has not been dissipated. Few contest his greatness: what is in question is his competence. This is very odd; it is hard to see how Berlioz can be as great as we all know him to be if he is as incompetent as so many think.

The opposition to Berlioz in our time is a very powerful one and includes Stravinsky ("Berlioz's reputation as an orchestrator has always seemed highly suspect to me") and even champions of his work such as Pierre Boulez ("There are awkward harmonies in Berlioz that make one scream"). They do not deny his importance, but their objections are not simple to deal with. An easy answer is provided by a letter of 1886 from Emmanuel Chabrier, the French composer most openly indebted to Berlioz: "Berlioz, a Frenchman above all (he wasn't old-hat in his time) put variety, color, rhythm into *La Damnation, Roméo,* and *L'Enfance du Christ*—there isn't any unity, people say—and I answer, Shit!"[7] This is a possible approach to the Berlioz problem, and ultimately, I suppose, a practical one. It has the merit of recommending an immediate and workable course of action: the dismissal of all adverse criticism, and an enjoyment of the music for its evident merits, however these are to be defined.

Berlioz had his idolaters from the beginning. In 1841 Richard Wagner wrote (somewhat enviously, I should imagine) that Berlioz had "a party of supporters who will listen to no music in the world but the *Symphonie fantastique.*" This

5. Review in *Gil Blas*, May 8, 1903.

6. Interview in *La Revue bleue*, April 2, 1904.

7. The quotation in this paragraph and the next come from Rushton, *Musical Language of Berlioz.*

does, indeed, suggest the isolation of his admirers, their lack of contact with the mainstream of musical thought. The idolaters reject the absurd image of an incompetent genius and substitute one of an infallible composer who can do no wrong.

Even today there is some difficulty of communication between idolaters and critics. "Much has been said about Berlioz's 'false' basses and his love of root positions, both of which are clear misrepresentations," writes Hugh Macdonald, one of the most distinguished Berlioz scholars, in the *New Grove*. It is hard to see how there can be any misrepresentation, much less a clear one: there is nothing wicked in root positions, and a "false" bass is no more sinful in music than a "degenerate" equation in mathematics; Berlioz does, indeed, use both root positions and false basses. The misrepresentation is in Macdonald's characterization of the reproach. What is claimed is that Berlioz often uses a root position when the harmony or the voice leading demands a second or third inversion.[8] It is not immediately evident that this should be deplored.

Admirers of Berlioz starting with Schumann have had no difficulty demonstrating the weakness of most of the charges against him. Berlioz's alleged inability to write correct counterpoint is the easiest reproach to dispose of. It is clear that, early in his career, he was a master of what is not after all a very difficult craft. Julian Rushton perceptively observes that the strictness of the fugue in the last movement of the *Fantastic Symphony* is ironic: it must have appealed to the composer's grim humor to portray a witches' Sabbath by an absolutely correct academic fugue. Much of Berlioz's polyphony, however, escapes from classical standards through his imaginative use of rhythm. His exploration of what he called intermittent sounds is an example. These are individual "sounds independent of the principal melody and of the accompanimental rhythm and separated from each other at expanding or contracting distances in proportions impossible to predict" (Berlioz's own description).[9] This technique of intermittent sounds not only cannot be subjected to laws of classical counterpoint but is clearly developed against them. It also demands a basic classical texture on which the intermittent sounds are superimposed in order to realize their full effect. It is this double requirement of a classical system and an anticlassical subversion of it that makes it so hard to generalize about Berlioz's achievement.

8. Macdonald's defense in the *New Grove* of Berlioz's use of root positions is brief: "A root position is sometimes disturbing when it anticipates a cadence on to the same root, but Berlioz preferred a smooth, often stepwise, movement to the striding pattern of a functional bass." As we shall see, however, Berlioz's most eccentric and effective uses of root position often entail not stepwise movement but a leap into the chord unjustified by traditional contrapuntal motion.

9. Quoted from Rushton (*Musical Language of Berlioz*, p. 128), who gives a beautiful example in the septet from *The Trojans*.

Tradition and eccentricity: the idée fixe

One of Berlioz's most famous pages, the first presentation of the idée fixe in the *Symphonie fantastique,* reveals both his originality and his violation of classical tradition (I use the transcription of Franz Liszt):

Here it is the accompaniment itself that has an intermittent rhythm, the space between its appearances expanding and contracting in ways impossible to predict. Although Berlioz defined his "intermittent sounds" as independent of accompaniment as well as of melody, we may accept this as an example: the melody is intended to be heard as if essentially unharmonized, with no accompaniment; the cellos and basses are interruptions, at first a mimesis of the agitation in the poet's or musician's heart, an image of the passion that mounts as the melody proceeds. This irregular growth of passion provides the basis for a regular measurement of the melody's rhythm, which seems otherwise to float freely in space as if to justify Schumann's suggestion that Berlioz was the composer who would free music from the tyranny of the bar line.

In reality, the impression of freedom is achieved by a beautifully hidden manipulation of the most traditional procedures. About the idée fixe, Edward T. Cone remarks[10] that an opening phrase of eight bars is succeeded by one of seven, and that this is the kind of irregularity that upset a contemporary critic like Fétis, one of Berlioz's bitterest enemies. This is, of course, correct as far as it goes, but the irregularity of phrase is all on the surface. The forty bars of the theme are governed by a regular underlying rhythm of four bars: the change in phrase length is only the sign of a more important shift of accent applied to the unchanging four-bar group. It is by using this shift of accent that Berlioz gives the melody its dramatic character, the increase of excitement and tension towards the center, and the broad, singing resolution of the final bars.

The seemingly irregular phrase structure conceals a simple symmetry that helps to impose the dramatic unfolding of the melody. It may help to outline the scheme briefly:

10. In his 1971 edition of the *Symphonie fantastique* for the Norton Scores, p. 236.

Bars

$\begin{cases} 1-8 \\ 9-15 \end{cases}$	8-bars 7 bars	Presentation, strong-bar accent	Tonic → dominant
$\begin{cases} 16-19 \\ 20-23 \\ 24-17 \end{cases}$	4 bars 4 bars 4 bars	Intensification, multiplication of accents and emphasis on weak bars	Sequences and acceleration of harmonic motion
$\begin{cases} 28-32 \\ 33-40 \end{cases}$	5 bars 8 bars	Resolution and return to strong-bar emphasis	Return to tonic with subdominant color and broad harmonic movement. Cadence

This is a basic classical plan, and its relation to eighteenth-century forms, even to sonata form, will not escape us. The symmetrical placing of the seven-bar and five-bar phrases shows that the metrical irregularity is only a surface phenomenon. What Berlioz is doing here is changing the accent of the four-bar grouping (which is, as we have seen, partially independent of phrase lengths). For the first fifteen bars the accent lies on the first and third of each four-bar group: that is, when we consider each bar as a single beat, the downbeat and the third beat are emphasized, and this is the most stable metric. Suddenly, with bar 16, the phrases start on the fourth bar of each four-bar group, as if giving an importance to the upbeat. With the increased harmonic motion as well as the use of harmonies other than simple tonic and dominant, this heightens the agitation, shapes the melody by breaking it into smaller units.

The five-bar phrase (bars 28 to 32) starts with an accent on a weak upbeat bar (the fourth of a module of four), but restores the stability of the opening of the melody by giving an even stronger emphasis to the next bar, 29, which functions as a downbeat. This phrase works as a transition between the two forms of accent. It is also the true climax of the melody and is marked by a *ritenuto*. Its outline resembles the preceding phrases,

but with a more intense movement and something like a fermata on bar 29, which has a sudden long note identical to those at the beginning of the first two phrases (bars 1 and 9), and which reestablishes the supremacy of the downbeat, or first bar of a group of four.

Although the five-bar phrase begins clearly in bar 28, the following four bars, 29–32, are rhythmically a return to the opening four bars.

The motivic symmetry is regulated not by the phrase length but by the four-bar grid. In this respect Berlioz's technique, in its combination of flexibility and systematic rhythm, is similar to that of his most astute contemporaries, above all to that of Chopin. Where Berlioz differs, however, is in the surprising harmonization of bar 13 with a tonic chord.

Surprising, indeed, from Berlioz's own point of view. The phrase demands a harmonization by a dominant, and in fact defines a dominant by the four bars that precede. It is by a dominant that Berlioz harmonizes the passage at a later appearance:

In the sketch for the first appearance, as Cone points out, the harmony was a variant of this, with a 6/4 tonic chord resolved into a dominant. The definitive printed version of this phrase is the most radical, as it partially undercuts the

6/4 chord with an initial root position, and omits the dominant chord (which is nevertheless clearly understood, as Cone remarks, through the F♮ of bar 14). In spite of the fact that the bass is the dominant G, the emphasis on the root position of the tonic chord provides a shock here that Berlioz must have considered indispensable to the first playing of the theme. One might say that the "wrong" tonic harmonization is possible without loss of meaning above all because the dominant is so clearly implied by the melody itself. In my experience, this tonic does not cease to sound wrong even after repeated hearings, but it also makes the right harmony insipid if one tries to substitute it, and it even makes Berlioz's later harmonizations of the idée fixe in the first movement a little disappointing. The brightness of the root position of the tonic—half affirmed at the opening of the bar, half withdrawn by the 6/4 chord that follows a fraction of a second afterward—gives a flash of brilliance to this moment of the idée fixe that never appears again.

Chord color and counterpoint

In tonal music, each form of the triad has a different function and a different sonority that endow it with a special expressive color: the root position is used for cadences, and has the most stable effect; the first inversion, or sixth chord, is consonant but not final, and can be used for intermediate resolution—without being dissonant it is nevertheless indecisive, and the interval of the sixth which is its outline does not have the bright clang of the fifth that characterizes the root position; the second inversion is a dissonance, a 6/4 chord, and the harsh sonority of the fourth requires resolution, and consequently gives the greatest sense of tension.

One of Berlioz's most individual characteristics, only remotely derived from Gluck, is his choice of chord inversions and root positions for expressive accent. We have no technical word for this device—perhaps coloristic accent would do. Berlioz chose which form of the chord to use for its color, and many of the root positions that sound so awkward and that have no contrapuntal rationalization in his work can be justified expressively. The opening of "L'Absence" from Les Nuits d'été creates a shock, and not only to a pedant:

The chord in the fourth bar is decidedly wrong: Berlioz resolves a dissonance with an ungainly leap by the bass into a root position. He needs both the poignancy of the austerely dissonant third bar and the brightness of the fourth bar, the vibrance that the root position has and that the more correct and mellifluous sixth chord would not. He could not allow the fourth bar to be less brilliant in sonority than the first, which it repeats. One cannot correct Berlioz, as everyone from Schumann on has seen.

A similar and even more effective shock is found in the harmonic setting of the opening melody of "The Specter of a Rose," one of the finest of Berlioz's songs. By itself the melody implies a dissonance resolved into a consonance at the second bar with the word "close":

But Berlioz, with great originality, reverses this into a consonance leading to a dissonance:

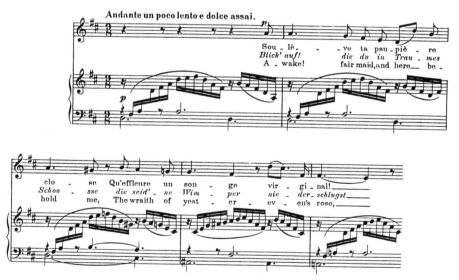

This means that the harmony enforced by the bass is battling the harmony embodied in the melody; it also battles the prosody, giving a more intense expression to the unaccented *e* of "close" than to the more open vowel *o* of the first syllable. It is not clear to me that Berlioz's harmony is either better or worse than a more conventional one—which would be either

or

Putting a dissonance on the second syllable makes the cadence both more mysterious and more awkward, but it does intensify the movement into the next beat. Two bars later the D major tonic chord in 6/4 position on the last syllable of "virginal" is equally eccentric, but only because it blocks any expected resolution of the chromatic A sharp in the bass. We might say that the A sharp does not resolve but only descends—and into a 6/4 tonic chord, at once dissonant and commonplace. Berlioz's tonics can be more unorthodox than other composers' most complex chromatic chords. They work by first sounding wrong; then what follows half or fully convinces us of their necessity.

A page like this suggests that the only criticism of Berlioz that cannot be washed away with complete success is the one made by Chopin, and copied by Delacroix into his diary for April 7, 1849:

> [In Mozart] each of the parts has its own movement, which, while still according with the others, keeps on with its own melody and follows it perfectly; *there* is your counterpoint . . . He [Chopin] told me that the custom now is to learn the harmonies before coming to counterpoint, that is to say, the succession of notes which lead to the harmonies. The harmonies of Berlioz are overlaid like a veneer; he fills in the intervals as best he can.

Throughout most of the eighteenth century, only counterpoint was taught to young composers, and any knowledge of harmony was informally picked up by experience or by reading the few theorists who tried to deal innovatively with the subject. Counterpoint was absolutely fundamental. Beginning with harmony was an early nineteenth-century novelty, introduced, I think, by the Paris Conservatoire. Chopin attributes what he thinks of as Berlioz's clumsiness to the newfangled system of music instruction. He himself, having grown up in a backwater like Warsaw, had studied the old-fashioned way. He insists that counterpoint must precede the study of harmony, or else the harmonic movement will have no inner life—it will be laid on from the outside, as he says, like a veneer.

As we see from Chopin's remarks, the idea of putting part writing (counterpoint) before chords (harmony) is not a surprisingly modern idea—it is the old traditional way, and Chopin deplored its disappearance. It was the late eighteenth-century development of large harmonic areas, of modulation, in fact, that made the teaching of harmony independent of counterpoint. The same stylistic development also gave Rameau's theory of classifying chords by their roots an importance it did not have when it appeared in the early eighteenth century: his theory became of central importance to musical education in early nineteenth-century France. Berlioz seemed to think naturally in Rameau's terms. He chose the harmonies often because of the roots and then employed the inversion which sounded most expressive.

It seems to me that Chopin's claim of a failure on Berlioz's part is partly true—and nevertheless that this failure accounts for much that is powerful and original in Berlioz's music. Until the nineteenth century, music education began with what is called species counterpoint. In this exercise the student is given a simple phrase of long, even notes like part of a Gregorian chant, called a *cantus firmus,* and is asked to write another phrase of long, even notes that could be played or sung with it. The first species is one note of the countermelody for one note of the *cantus firmus;* the different species then advance in rhythmic complexity, the last being a free rhythm against the original *cantus firmus.* The student advances from two voices to three-, four-, and five-part counterpoint.

The rules of species counterpoint are exceedingly simple: the countermelody must not make parallel octaves or fifths with the *cantus,* since that would be too much like a simple doubling of the original line; the countermelody must not often leap into a dissonance and never out of it, but the dissonance must be approached and, above all, resolved in stepwise motion, directly and simply, to the nearest consonance—this last is a recipe for making dissonant movement seem graceful and beautiful, and is central to all tonal music.

Nevertheless, the role of counterpoint in tonal music has a double and conflicting aspect that is not always clearly understood. The rules of counterpoint apply not only to several voices but also, paradoxically, to simple unaccompanied melodies: the successive notes of a melody are conceived as dissonant or consonant to one another. A tune in C major itself defines the C major triad, implies its own harmony as it goes along, and must end on one of the notes of its central triad. This is what enabled Bach to write music for solo violin or cello, using for long stretches only a single unaccompanied line: the harmony is implicit in the melodic line. Everyone unconsciously imagines some of the notes as lasting, as being valid beyond the moment of sound, and providing the basic harmony. The other notes are heard as dissonances resolving into the basic harmonic movement according to the rules of species counterpoint. The subjection of even the most unpretentious unaccompanied melody to the laws of species counterpoint is one reason why Chopin felt that study starts with counterpoint and only afterward considers harmony.

In classical terms—but not always for Berlioz—counterpoint has priority over harmony because the relations of consonance and dissonance that govern harmony and melody are derived, as we have seen, from counterpoint. The harmony of every phrase of tonal music is therefore determined by more than one factor—overdetermined, in fact, to use a term of psychoanalysis, since each one of these factors alone is conceived as a sufficient determination. The two principal factors are the melody itself, which implies a specific harmonization, and the movement of each independent voice, which must approach and resolve its dissonances with ease and grace. As Chopin said to Delacroix, "Each of the parts has its own movement, which, while still according with the others, keeps on with its own melody and follows it perfectly." Every chord, every note of the harmony, therefore, is the result of conflicting forces: the demands of the melody (the harmony it implies when it is played by itself) and the similar demands of the individual subordinate voices which make up the harmony, all subject to the same conventions.

Berlioz, as we have seen, was a master of academic counterpoint when the occasion suited him—that is, when he felt like it. In addition, he understood the harmonic implications of melody as well as anyone, and he worked them out with an imagination that equalled that of his greatest contemporaries, although only at rare moments was he as radical in harmony as Chopin or Wagner. Tonality is not simply a harmonic system but a rhythmic one as well, as many theorists now realize—resolution of dissonance depends as much on rhythm as on anything else (this is how Schönberg was able to reconstruct the effect of dissonance and consonance rhythmically within a nontonal system). The originality of phrase structure in Berlioz is the basis for the astonishing idiosyncrasy of some of his harmonic progressions. Rushton remarks that "most of Berlioz's melodies have clear tonal and harmonic implications: some of these are fulfilled, others denied. But they are difficult to harmonize in an 'ordinary' way, for rhythmic reasons. Classic and romantic melody usually implies harmonic motion of some consistency and smoothness; Berlioz's aspiration to musical prose tends to resist such consistency."[11] In this respect, Berlioz is more modern than Chopin or Wagner and clearly anticipates Debussy. But no one can deny both the sensitivity of Berlioz's harmonizations and his mastery of academic counterpoint.

This, however, does not answer Chopin's reproach. It is evident that Berlioz was not able instinctively to do both at once, to carry out the full implications of his melody through a contrapuntal web in which each inner strand has its own life. There are places in his music where the significance of the melody takes total precedence over contrapuntal decorum. At some but by no means all of these moments, an expressive aspect of the melody is realized with such intelligence that initial professional outrage is generally succeeded by admiration.

How did some composers escape the bad effects of the degenerate educational system deplored by Chopin? Berlioz did not have, in his training, the necessary corrective that almost every other contemporary composer had from childhood: the *Well-Tempered Keyboard* of Johann Sebastian Bach. This was the basis of instruction at the piano. Through this work, Beethoven, Schumann,

---

11. Rushton, *Musical Language of Berlioz*, p. 145.

Mendelssohn, Chopin, Liszt, and more or less everybody else learned to play the piano. Even if their training in composition was theoretically defective (as Chopin claimed, and as most theorists today would agree), they learned the contrapuntal realization of harmony in a purely practical way—by playing Bach. For Chopin and many others, the *Well-Tempered Keyboard* was the foundation of all composition. It is impossible to overestimate the educational value of this work for the early nineteenth century. Berlioz, however, could not play the piano, and he thought Bach was a bore. He played the guitar, the flageolet, and the kettledrums; and he loved Gluck.

It is interesting that Gluck was reproached, and still is, with the same inadequacies in counterpoint as Berlioz. What Berlioz learned from Gluck was a harmonization of melody for expressive purposes that violates the contrapuntal movement of the individual voices. (It is, as a practical matter, easier to explain Gluck by means of Berlioz than to understand Berlioz's individuality as a derivation from his idol.) All composers have at times exploited the ambiguous and surprising effect of a "wrong" harmonization but none with greater genius than Berlioz. As we have seen, Berlioz often sets the climax of his melodies in relief with the most emphatic chord—a triad in root position, and often a tonic where the melody implies a dominant, giving a brightness to the climactic note that would make the "right" harmonization in its place seem impossibly bland. This effect, which sounds like a simple mistake when it does not come off, has often been ascribed to Berlioz's guitar playing. All that can be admitted, however, is that the guitar encourages thinking of harmony in blocks, while every pianist is physically aware through the muscles of the hand and arm of the movement of independent voices.

There is one instrumental effect that appears throughout orchestral music from 1770 to 1820 in which the wrong harmony—or wrong bass—is implied: that is, the use of the kettledrums. Only two timpani were generally available, and when Mozart and Beethoven needed a dramatic accent, they had to choose one or two notes for the timpanist to hit. This was very often not the bass note of the chord. The trouble is, a kettledrum always sounds like a bass, even when it is playing higher than the cellos. Normally we eliminate from our listening the fact that the kettledrum is playing the wrong bass, just as we disregard wrong notes, coughs, and unnecessary acoustical phenomena—all this is partially filtered out of our consciousness, although a vague sense of it remains. Beethoven was the first composer to exploit the "wrong note" effect of the timpani, and Berlioz was the first critic to appreciate what he was up to, in a brilliant remark about the bridge to the last movement of Beethoven's Symphony no. 5 in C Minor: "The A-flat chord . . . seems to introduce a new key; on the other hand, isolated hammering of the timpani on C tends to preserve the ambiance of the original tonic. The ear hesitates . . . one cannot see the outcome of this harmonic mystery."[12] I do not want to duplicate the

12. Quoted in Rushton, ibid., p. 221.

nonsense of Berlioz's enemies who said that he composed as a guitarist by claiming that he harmonized as a timpanist—although when he played the timpani he quite evidently relished a "wrong" note that gave emphasis to the climax.

The history of progress in music runs from the composer who thinks wrong notes are funny, as in the polytonal cadences and the whole-tone scale in Mozart's *Musical Joke,* to composers like Debussy who employ them seriously. That does not mean that Berlioz always sounds right—at least not at first hearing. In spite of offering an alternative to the classical German system, he remains too close to it, and deviates from it too unpredictably, for the music to satisfy at once. The first stanza of Marguerite's romance from *La Damnation de Faust* sounds beautiful but a little awkward; the reappearance of the melody in the second stanza seems much less odd; and the third has become convincing, beautiful without any reservation, completely normal. I have found this to happen at each performance, and it reminds one of the Bellman in *The Hunting of the Snark:* anything said three times is true. The substitution of repetition for logic is more than persuasive. It carries complete conviction for one's experience of Berlioz. It seems to me absolutely valid, but disquieting.

Long-range harmony and contrapuntal rhythm: the "Scène d'amour"

There is nothing more natural for a composer who writes for public effect than to try for surprise, to frustrate the expectations of the listener, and to break with convention. In general, however, the fulfillment is only postponed, the expectations eventually satisfied, the conventions respected. In the case of Berlioz this is true often enough, as we have seen with the presentation of the idée fixe of the *Symphonie fantastique;* but, significantly, in some of the pages we have been considering, the violation is of such a nature that no ultimate resolution can be imagined. The tradition has been not so much attacked as ignored. No satisfying resolution is possible because the terms of resolution have been basically denied, or treated as nonexistent.

It is not only at the level of detail that Berlioz's imaginative evasion of some of the fundamental demands of the central tradition of Western music operated successfully, but on a much larger scale as well. The "Scène d'amour" from *Roméo et Juliette* is one of Berlioz's two or three finest achievements—and so the composer himself thought: here ordinary expectations are frustrated and new ones created on the largest scale in ways analogous to the small-scale surprises we have been considering. It is through his long-range vision that Berlioz achieved both the intensity and the sweep of passion that were his greatest pride and his most convincing claim to originality.

In the great orchestral section of the "Scène d'amour," the dichotomy between melodic and harmonic structure that Berlioz exploited with such effect plays a much grander role. The fundamental key is A major, established firmly

in a long opening section, and the harmony implied by the principal theme
when it finally arrives is also clearly the tonic A major:

but that is not how Berlioz harmonizes it. He opens the theme, a wonderfully
long arch of ten bars, with the harmony of C sharp minor, and, moreover
previously establishes the key of C sharp minor in the simplest and most
decisive way with the most ordinary IV–V–I cadence:

This principal theme ends decisively here in the tonic A major, but the opening
in what is evidently an unstable harmony at odds with the melody has an
unexpected intensity that comes from the insistence in bars 144 to 146 on the
chord of C sharp minor, and from the "enharmonic" clash of this chord with
the F♮ and D♮ of the following bar, 147.

The sense of unfulfilled desire, of half-repressed longing, comes in part from
this harmonic play. In the simplest terms, the first bars of Berlioz's melody
outline

and he substitutes the more powerful and dissonant form

But this does not completely obliterate the simpler and more basic harmony implied by the melody itself. A greater power is given in this way to the clash between the dissonant F♮ in bars 147 and 149 and the F♯ that appears in the accompaniment in bar 150 (violas, violins, and fourth horn) and four times in the melody in bars 151 and 152. The reappearance of the F♮ in bar 153 is a stroke of genius, an extraordinarily expressive inspiration—the melody reaches down, outside its original range, for this dissonance, and must descend again in the following bar to resolve into the low E with a cadence that reaffirms the tonic A major in the simplest way.

Strictly speaking, the harmony has, in fact, never left A major: the C sharp minor harmony is a deception, and the previous cadence that apparently establishes it is part of Berlioz's sleight of hand. In short, the melody begins in the "right" key with the wrong harmonies. The next stage carries the process further: the main theme is played with the right harmony in the wrong key, C major. This time, however, there is no attempt to establish the new key in any traditional fashion, but it appears dramatically at the end of an ambiguous chromatic ascent:

The first playing had been kept within the range from *ppp* to *p* and was marked *canto espressivo*. With the brightness of the new key, a third higher, the dynamic is now *ff* and marked *canto appassionato assai* (although the violas and cellos are still muted). The major-minor interplay of the original theme, opposing F sharp and F natural, is also removed in favor of a pure major—except in the last bars, where the expressive motif

remains intact. This motif is, in fact, unaltered almost throughout, an invariant, stable element in the structure. In the recitative in the cellos that follows the passionate version of the theme in C major, the opening of the main theme is distantly evoked, but the motif keeps its characteristic shape at the end:

The long final section is subtle in a way that perhaps only Berlioz could have imagined and controlled: enough of the principal melody is retained to make it appear like a return, yet so much of it is transformed that it seems like a novel continuation. The tonic A major is recalled through its relative F sharp minor, and the initial motif of the theme

provides the point of departure:

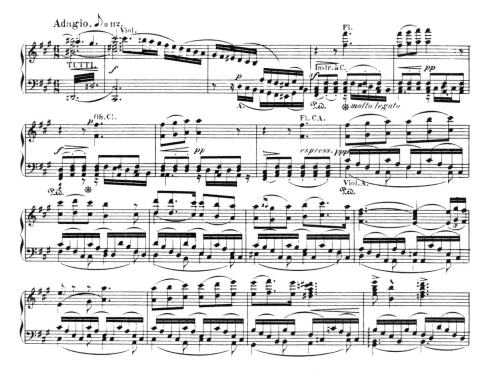

The harmony is F sharp minor, but the chord is a first inversion with A in the bass subtly insisted on by the contrabasses, and this A soon becomes the fundamental harmony. (The lesson of the transition from scherzo to finale of Beethoven's Fifth Symphony had been well learned.)

The first bars of the F sharp minor section treat the beginning of the main theme with great fluidity, although separate elements of the original melody are easily recognizable. When the harmony at last resolves more clearly onto the tonic A major, the main theme is now reduced from twelve to seven bars; the second half is unaltered but the first half retains only the original contour of

and transforms this into

and the theme is played at last with a pedal point on A, the tonic:

This is the most stable form, still deeply expressive, but its effect depends on the instability of its previous appearances, which I summarize:

Introduced	*Played*	
1. C sharp minor cadence	Melody:	A major
	Bass:	C sharp minor → A major
2. No proper cadence	Melody:	C major
	Bass:	C major
3. Cadence on F sharp minor	Melody:	F sharp minor→ A
	Bass:	A
4. Cadence on A major	Melody:	A major
	Bass:	A major

It is significant for Berlioz's sense of long-range form that it takes one hundred and fifty bars, most of them *adagio,* for the main theme to arrive at this point of stability. Until then, any clear feeling of harmonic direction is wonderfully avoided: the harmonic movement is as fluid as the main theme itself. It drifts away from the tonic center and escapes any clear polarization with any other harmony. Even the fourteen bars of muted *fortissimo* in C major are felt as an illusion—it is important to recognize that part of the effect of pathos and excitement comes from playing the melody in a key which has not been properly established and which is immediately dropped once the brief theme is over. The stable form (*poco f ma dolce*) which comes at bar 274 is deeply moving because of the postponement. The central tonality of A major had been clearly established at the outset in the remarkable opening section of twenty bars (124–144), and the main theme was presented immediately after, but we are made to wait for a complete integration.

In the final hundred bars that follow the harmonically stabilized form of the melody, Berlioz can now achieve the first sense of Classical development with its clearly defined pull away from and back to the tonic. The placement of this development is, of course, deeply unclassical:

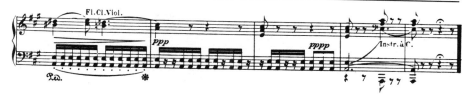

It was, indeed, a Romantic ambition to set the moment of greatest excitement close to the end, but the sequential development with an *accelerando* is almost unprecedented in this place, and the arrival of the main theme at the dominant that follows is even more astonishing. By all Classical standards, the full presentation of the dominant by the theme should be possible only in the first half of a work. In consequence, the resolution at the tonic in the final bars is a series of broken phrases, fragments, exhausted reminiscences. Finally, even the integrity of the one stable motif is attacked:

The coda disintegrates, breaks into pieces, the motifs lose their identities.

The opening section, too, before the entry of the main theme, had resisted all sense of definition. At the beginning of the "Scène d'amour," the key of A major is established almost as pure atmosphere in sixteen bars of *pianissimo* before a crescendo is sketched. The different rhythms float in and out of each other; they are not opposed but blend together like the various pulsations of the night. The orchestra is divided into distinct groups, each with its own large-scale phrase rhythm, its own periodic movement. None of these groups articulates a central phrase system, but each is independent:

1. Violas, cellos, and basses
2. Violin II
3. Violin I
4. Clarinet I, English horn
5. Flute, Clarinet II, then Horns I, II, III; then Bassoons

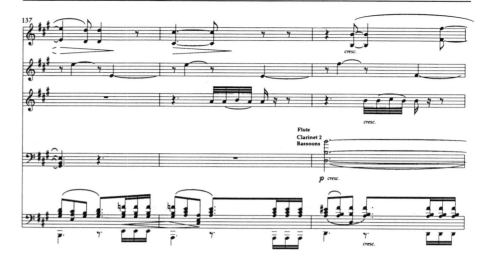

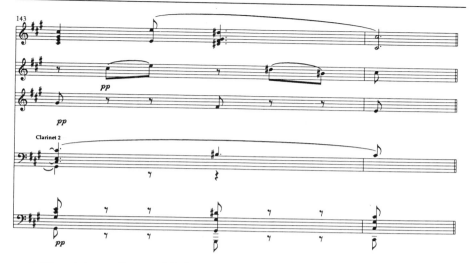

1. The violas, cellos, and basses give the central texture starting at the second bar (bar 125), but their movement is too homogeneous and too continuous to impose a central phrase rhythm on the other groups of instruments: the symmetry of the pattern, however, makes us half aware of a series of 5 bars, 5 bars, 4 bars, and 6 bars.

2. The second violins are more clearly articulated starting at the third bar of the section (bar 126 of the movement); their period begins again every fourth bar, always on the more weakly accented second half of the bar, and the pattern is 3 bars plus 1 of silence, with an increase of density at the end: 4, 4, 4, 7.

3. The first violins start on the eighth bar (131): their phrase lengths are 4, 1, 4, 5—they interrupt their initial pattern after one bar of a second phrase, and start a new pattern at bar 136.

4. First clarinet and English horn start on the fourth bar of the section (bar 127), and the pattern is 4, 6, 2, 6.

5. The last group of instruments relays a pattern over different sets of instruments starting at bar 1 (124), and it is articulated as a series of five-bar sets: flute and clarinet II (bars 124–128); horns I, II, and III (129–133); three bassoons (134–138); at bars 139 to 143 most of these instruments combine with first clarinet and English horn, but bassoons and second and third horns continue a five-bar period, finishing a bar before the others.

The independent rhythmic periods are not cross-rhythms: they overlap and blend with no opposition but without completely fusing. We normally perceive the direction of time through harmonic change, and more than half of the first dozen bars display the tonic harmony in root position. We are aware only that time is suspended, almost motionless; no other composer achieved this kind of stillness. In their interaction the different periods largely cancel one another out, and the irregularly flowing streams do not combine their forces. Only with the rising melody and the crescendo of bars 134–144 is the unified movement of time partially restored, and the complex rhythmic counterpoint creates an unfocused sense of expectation.

These layers of contrapuntal rhythm are as complex as the three orchestras on the stage with three different dance meters in the first-act finale of Mozart's *Don Giovanni*. For the astonishing opening pages of the "Scène d'amour," classical counterpoint is irrelevant to Berlioz's purpose. It is, of course, impossible single-handedly to invent an entirely new musical language, and we can understand Berlioz's frequent failures. Nothing else in *Roméo et Juliette* is on the high level of the "Scène d'amour"—but then very little of the symphonic literature composed by Berlioz's contemporaries reaches that level, either. Nevertheless, much of the rest of *Roméo et Juliette* is ineffective—or, when effective, rather coarse, like the vulgar contrapuntal display of combining themes in the "Bal des Capulets." Of course, no long work remains throughout on the level of its highest poetic inspiration, but what Berlioz often lacked was the kind of organization that gave momentum to the moments of prose. Of all his long works, only the *Symphonie fantastique* is completely effective throughout, even if the last four movements lack the richness, profundity, and refinement of the first. *L'Enfance du Christ*, on the other hand, cannot sustain the power of its first thirty minutes. When uninspired, Berlioz can sink to the commonplace pomposity of Grétry's revolutionary cantatas or sound unconvincingly eccentric like his teacher Lesueur at his most dogmatic. Perhaps most disconcerting of all are the moments when Berlioz has a genuinely original inspiration but does not know what to do with it. The wonderful contrast of soft high flutes and soft low trombones in the "Hostias" of the Requiem is an example: having invented this impressive juxtaposition, Berlioz can think of nothing better than simply repeating it many times—after the third time, it loses its novelty and becomes merely bizarre. This section, however, should not prevent one from appreciating the magnificence of the opening pages of the Requiem, and of the "Lacrymosa." I have finished by dwelling briefly on Berlioz's failures because an uncritical attempt to justify the totality of his work prevents one from appreciating the magnitude and the nature of his successes.

CHAPTER TEN

Mendelssohn and the Invention of Religious Kitsch

Mastering Beethoven

In 1837 Schumann reviewed what he felt were "the two most important compositions of the day": Meyerbeer's opera *Les Huguenots,* and Mendelssohn's oratorio *Saint Paul.* The comparison of the two composers was developed in the most vivid terms, and created a scandal: Meyerbeer's work is common, perverse, unnatural, immoral, unmusical, while Mendelssohn's has total musical mastery, a nobility of song, a marriage of words and music, and a perfectly formed style. Mendelssohn's "road leads to happiness, [Meyerbeer's] to evil." This was Schumann's final affirmation, "and I have never signed anything with such conviction as this," he added. The violence of the contrast is particularly ironic today: no other composers of the early nineteenth century have lost as much of their former prestige as these two. In neither case is the fall from glory inexplicable; for both it is, at least in part, unmerited and unjust.

Mendelssohn was the greatest child prodigy the history of Western music has ever known. Not even Mozart or Chopin before the age of nineteen could equal the mastery that Mendelssohn already possessed when he was only sixteen. Most astonishing is the nature of Mendelssohn's precocious talent: not only a gift for lyrical melodic lines and delicate, transparent textures, but, above all, a control of large-scale structure unsurpassed by any composer of his generation. In the octet, written when Mendelssohn was sixteen years old, the subtle way the return of the scherzo is integrated into the finale is an example of craftsmanship that amounts to genius, similar to the beginning of the recapitulation of the overture to *A Midsummer Night's Dream,*[1] where the flute harmonies of the opening simply reappear, posed delicately over the soft, deep final cadence of the development. The most admirable aspects of these

---

1. See my book, *Sonata Forms,* rev. ed. (New York, 1988), pp. 272–274.

early works is the ease and economy with which Mendelssohn brings off his most original strokes.

Every young composer imitates, as Bach had imitated Buxtehude and Vivaldi, and Mozart had imitated Haydn and Johann Christian Bach. What is most impressive about Mendelssohn's imitations when he was still a teenager, however, was the outrageous ambition and the nature of the success. The model was Beethoven, but not the middle-period Beethoven that most other composers found so useful: it has often been pointed out that what Mendelssohn had before him were the most eccentric and imaginative works of the final years of Beethoven's life, the last sonatas and quartets. It might seem that such a model for a very young composer would lead straight to disaster, but Mendelssohn handled the problem with astonishing ease. The greatest surprise, however, lies in the character of the imitations. Far from being a secondhand reproduction of Beethoven's ideas, they are individual and personal—in short, peculiarly Mendelssohnian.

The most uneven of these imitations is the Sonata for Piano in E Major, written when Mendelssohn was seventeen and modelled on Beethoven's sonatas, opus 90 and, most of all, opus 101. The paradox is that the closer the imitation, the more personal the result. The kinship to Beethoven's opus 101 in A major is easily seen by comparing the opening of the two works:

How distant from, and how near Mendelssohn is to Beethoven becomes clear when we compare Mendelssohn's third and fourth bars with Beethoven's sixth and fifteenth. The essential difference is curiously betrayed by the keys of the two works: Beethoven's is in A major and Mendelssohn's in E major, yet the two opening themes are not only similar but at the same pitch level. That is because Mendelssohn has dispensed with the most original aspect of Beethoven's invention. Beethoven's opus 101 begins not by establishing the tonic key of A, but in the middle of the traditional modulation to the dominant, E major: the tonic is established only by implication. Under the modest lyric surface is a powerful dynamic process. Mendelssohn, however, starts by accepting the central key as E major, and this results in a more conventional and placid form, but the opening seems typical of Mendelssohn's most idiosyncratic manner—in part because Beethoven's opening page already sounds like Mendelssohn. One of the most important steps in the development of a personal style by a young composer is not inventing it but discovering it where it already exists in one's precursors. The next step is to isolate and intensify those stylistic characters that give the greatest promise for one's own work. Mendelssohn recognized himself in Beethoven.

Mendelssohn's opening, however, displays an essential weakness in his style which remained a liability throughout his life, although he managed often enough to exploit it and make it appear a virtue. Mendelssohn rounds off his phrases, his paragraphs, and eventually his sections with a certain comfortable sweetness. Where Beethoven keeps the dynamic process in motion—his feminine half cadence in the fourth bar of opus 101 goes directly into what follows—at the equivalent point Mendelssohn places a full tonic cadence, which he even repeats eight bars later. Beethoven's first emphatic pause, in bar 6, is not static but a confirmation of the ongoing modulation: its asymmetrical placement and the chromaticism give it a dramatic force to which Mendelssohn's relaxed grace does not and cannot aspire.

It has often been said that Mendelssohn's melodies begin well but end feebly. The most famous of his melodies shows this fatal dropping off—the beginning of the Violin Concerto:

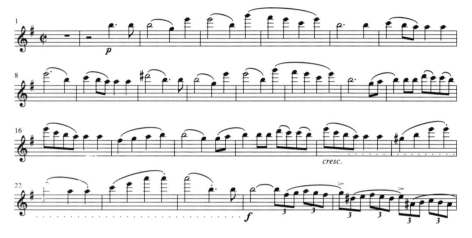

The magnificent sweep of the opening is followed (in bars 14 to 17) by a slightly fussier and even pedestrian formula, which is not made more interesting by being immediately repeated. It is clear that the ideal of Mozartean grace could not be realized in the 1830s with a fully sustained dramatic power, perhaps because the basic elements of musical style were no longer defined with so clear an articulation as in the 1780s. The style by then had become more fluid, and dramatic force now required either a neurotic or even a morbid sense of expression, or else a kind of grit unwelcome or unnatural to Mendelssohn.

A little later in the E Major Sonata

a passage from the finale of Beethoven's opus 90

provides further inspiration. Mendelssohn's version is passive, almost sedate next to Beethoven's, as he remains on a tonic harmony while his model is centered on the more dynamic dominant. Yet in one of the most idiosyncratic works of the older composer, Mendelssohn was able to find a source for his own vein of characteristic lyricism.

Nevertheless, in this opening movement it would appear that Mendelssohn had to minimize or even eliminate the more dramatic or radical aspects of Beethoven's ideas to make them viable in his own more relaxed manner. This is not always the case, however. The last two movements of the E Major Sonata continue to incorporate details from Beethoven's opus 101, but with more startling effect. The slow movement of opus 101 is a rare incursion for Beethoven into Baroque style:

and later there are hints at a knowledge of Bach's *Chromatic* Fantasy and Fugue. The influence of Bach on Beethoven was profound but less openly displayed than in Mendelssohn's work, and Mendelssohn now makes something more daring from the suggestions he took from Beethoven:

The slow introduction to Beethoven's finale has been transformed by Mendelssohn into a Baroque fantasia, elaborate and imaginative, and it will lead, like Beethoven's, directly into a quotation from the opening movement.

The dependence of the young Mendelssohn on Beethoven allows him, as we have remarked, to discover his own originality. This is even more obviously the case with the first two string quartets, written shortly afterward, when Mendelssohn was eighteen and twenty years old. The String Quartet no. 2 in A Minor was written first, and draws principally on Beethoven's opus 132 and opus 95, with some details from opus 130 and opus 135. The borrowings from opus 132 have often been recognized, and are in the first movement so flagrant as to constitute a public homage to Beethoven: in fact, it is remarkable how effectively the character and the passion of the original are reproduced.

Even more significant is the way Mendelssohn transformed and recombined Beethoven's inspirations into a new conception. Among the most important elements borrowed are, first, a slow movement with a central fugal section and an introductory recitative before the finale. Here is the opening of the internal fugue from the slow movement of Beethoven's opus 95:

Mendelssohn's fugue theme has a similar contour, and a similar expressive character and chromatic harmony; it also starts with the viola followed by the second violin:

Like Beethoven, Mendelssohn twice alternates the contrasting fugal section with the opening of the slow movement, but the borderline between the opening page and the fugue is, typically, less clearly marked, and the two sections are combined at the end in a way that obliterates all distinction between them.

In Beethoven's Quartet in A Minor, op. 132, the last bars of the march-scherzo are followed without pause by a recitative that leads directly into the last movement. The fidelity and the length of Mendelssohn's imitation are astounding. Beethoven moves from Scherzo to Allegro through a recitative:

Mendelssohn goes from his scherzo into an introductory recitative that shamelessly imitates Beethoven's; once again the line between sections is not so clearly drawn, and the integration of recitative and finale is more complete than in the model:

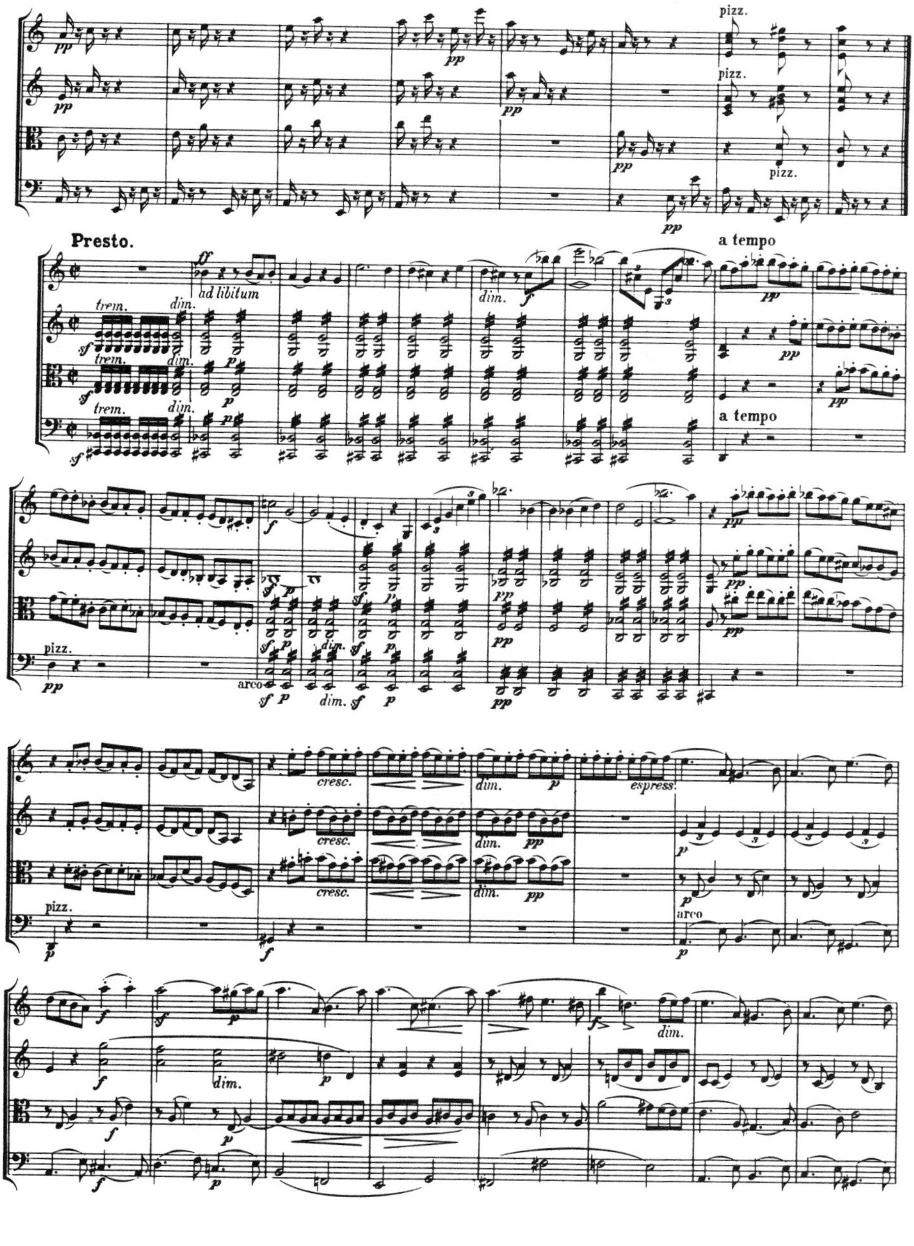
pizz.
Presto.
ad libitum
trem.
dim.
a tempo
arco
cresc.
espress.

Listeners and performers alike were expected to appreciate the young composer's ingenious adaptation of the work of the older master, who had died only a few months before this homage was composed. Most adaptations are a travesty of the original, but Mendelssohn had a genuine understanding of what Beethoven was up to in his last years.

So profound was his comprehension, in fact, that Mendelssohn could turn the structure into something more personal. As the finale proceeds, he transforms the recitative into a reminiscence and return of the central fugue of the slow movement. The subtlety of the young Mendelssohn's procedure is intellectually breathtaking, but it ends up as deeply expressive. The main theme of the recitative interrupts the cadential theme of the exposition of the finale, but the recitative is now laid out in fugal texture:

The cadential theme is taken up again, and the fugal texture reappears, but now with a return of the theme of the slow movement:

This transforms recitative into fugue. In the development that follows, the main theme of the finale is combined with both the recitative motif and the slow-movement fugue melody. Recitative and fugue are radically opposed textures, and Mendelssohn's synthesis is unprecedented.

It remains for the coda to complete the circle of metamorphosis and to transform the slow-movement fugue into a recitative. In turn this dissolves into the adagio introduction to the first movement. The synthesis, in short, combines in one continuous line in the first violin the main theme of the finale, the recitative introduction to the finale, the slow-movement fugue, and the motto of the first movement:

The return of the first movement here is crucial to Mendelssohn's aesthetic, not only because it reinforces the cyclical aspects of the whole work and ties the beginning to the end, but also because it enables us to hear that the contour of the opening motif

has an outline similar to the fugue theme. The construction may indeed appear overingenious when we reflect that the lyrical melody that both opens and closes the quartet is based on an early song of Mendelssohn's and at the same time on the introduction to the finale of Beethoven's Quartet, op. 135; it even includes a three-note motif with the sound of a question that closely resembles Beethoven's "Muss es sein?" (Must it be?), but in a more amiable and Mendelssohnian form. All these intricate thematic relationships are laid out with a kind of precocious virtuosity, a facile display that Beethoven, I think, would have disdained (it has been remarked, for example, that in the slow movement of his Quartet, op. 95, which served as a model for Mendelssohn, the opening theme and the fugue theme could easily be combined contrapuntally, but that Beethoven never bothers to carry out this possibility). Mendelssohn's ingenuity, however, lends an extraordinary fluidity to the musical experience, as recitative blends into fugue, slow movement into finale, and all of them into the opening bars of the quartet.

The use of cyclical form takes an important step beyond the inventions of Beethoven, in which an earlier movement intrudes dramatically into a later one, and it goes even beyond the form shown in Schubert's *Wanderer* Fantasy, in which each movement is based somewhat ostentatiously on the same melody, like a gigantic set of variations. Mendelssohn's conception is closer to those noncyclical forms of Beethoven's like the *Appassionata,* the *Hammerklavier,* or the Quartet in C sharp Minor, op. 131, in which the successive movements use very similar motifs without actually quoting each other, so that they appear to fit together by an identity of musical relationships that make up the underlying material. Mendelssohn's forms, however, push to the surface and display for the common listener relationships which lie half buried in Beethoven and work on us unconsciously. In being made evident, these relationships lose some of the power they had when hidden, as their action is now concentrated within the specific moments so that they become overt instead of being suffused throughout the work; however, they also gain in theatrical effectiveness.

Mendelssohn's second Quartet in E Flat Major, op. 12, shows even greater mastery than the first, although the dependence on Beethoven is equally frank. The opening bars

acknowledge the motifs in bars 1–2 and 11–13 of Beethoven's Quartet, op. 74, also in E flat major. Mendelssohn, in fact, telescopes Beethoven's long phrase into three bars:

Once again it is evident that Mendelssohn was not ashamed to reveal his sources: an allusion of this kind is intended to be noticed, its recognition to produce the satisfied glow that comes from being in on the secret. Yet Mendelssohn in his reworking of Beethoven is no less original than other young—and even older—composers. Mozart and Beethoven, too, borrowed from their predecessors, but they took over techniques and formulas, and rarely attempted to quote or recall one particular work so that it would be immediately brought to the consciousness of the performers or the audience. One exception is Beethoven's Quartet in A Major, op. 18, no. 5, modelled for all to hear on

Mozart's Quartet, K.464, in the same key. This rare case in Beethoven should help us to understand Mendelssohn's procedure. The six quartets of opus 18 were written when Beethoven was thirty years old, and they were his first quartets to be published. In 1801 Mozart had been dead almost a decade, and Haydn was too old and weak to be able to accomplish much more. Several of the six quartets of opus 18 are radically different from any previous works of that genre, but Beethoven needed also to demonstrate that he could produce a work of Mozartean form and character if he liked, and to lay claim to the succession and to his rightful place within the tradition. The quartets of Mozart, particularly the six dedicated to Haydn, had classic status by 1800; they provided a standard by which all future quartets were to be judged, and a composer had to prove that he could start where Mozart had left off.

Transforming Classicism

For Mendelssohn, Beethoven was the new point of departure, and a German composer could not afford to ignore him, as Chopin and Verdi were able to do. Gradually a body of classical work had been assembled from Mozart and Beethoven. That is why composers like Hummel, Schubert, and Mendelssohn not only learned from their forerunners but display that learning proudly: they deliberately quote from the new classical canon just as poets of the eighteenth century displayed quotations from the classical Latin poets for the pleasure of connoisseurs. Later, with Brahms, this was to become a basic principle of composition. It did not, however, prevent the creation of works of great individuality. In his E flat Major Quartet, for example, Mendelssohn imitates the wide spacing he learned from Beethoven to achieve new and deeply personal effects. The way the recapitulation of the opening theme is prepared is in many essential respects like nothing in Beethoven or anybody else. At the beginning of the Allegro, the main theme is scored with the tonic harmony in root position only in the fourth bar:

The end of the development brings back the first theme with the tonic now in the bass, exploits the space between the first violin and viola, and slows down the tempo:

This is an exemplary lesson in how to make a traditional device into a radically original effect. From 1750 on, the most commonplace way of rounding off a development section is a cadence on the relative minor (or vi) followed by a retransition to the tonic—so commonplace in fact that composers often preferred a more dramatic form of an interrupted cadence or half cadence on the dominant of the relative minor (V of vi), followed either by a leap directly into the tonic or by a more elaborate transition. This is what Mendelssohn uses here transformed by the dynamics and the extraordinary pacing.

The music, violent and expressive, breaks off at the climax with the harmony of the dominant seventh of C minor (V^7 of vi) and a crescendo to *fortissimo*. Then the first violin, three octaves above all the other instruments (and with the cello playing its lowest open string), descends slowly; the harmony moves with equal slowness not to the tonic but to a half cadence on the D major dominant of G minor (V of iii), and the dynamics descend to *pianissimo*. Even the tempo descends with the long slow notes and the final *ritardando*. Harmony, rhythm, and texture conspire to produce an effect of extreme exhaustion after an access of passion, and it is with the sense of exhaustion, of wasted energy, that Mendelssohn reintroduces his main theme and the tonic harmony.

Mendelssohn here manipulates the most traditional elements of Classical form to achieve a deeply unclassical effect. The cadence on V of vi is traditional, and so is the device of surrounding a tonic (E flat) by the mediants (C and G) balancing each other, and a clearly marked articulation of the return of the main theme—all this was taken from the music that Mendelssohn had grown up with. Ending with a half cadence drained of all force on the leading tone, D, and then raising the pitch gently and unobtrusively a modest half step to E flat is Mendelssohn's own contribution and resembles nothing he could have heard. He reinforces the originality of his conception: there is no suggestion of a dominant in the six bars marked *pianissimo* preceding the theme so that the harmonic movement is as gentle as the sonority marked *dolce* that sets the reappearance of E flat major in relief. Since the theme is harmonized for the first time here with the tonic in the bass, it gains a quiet stability that it never had until this moment. Most remarkably, the main theme starts slowly, under tempo, moving only little by little back into the full *allegro* of its first appearance (the *poco a poco* applies to the *a tempo* and not to the *ritardando*). These violations of the Classical tradition only serve to attach Mendelssohn all the more tightly to it: replacing the traditional climax at the end of the development with an extraordinary effect of tranquillity is like a negative image of the expected event, and ends by creating the same powerful tension, just as a sudden soft chord works as an accent (Beethoven had demonstrated this when he used a *subito piano* the way other composers used a *sforzando*).

The E flat Quartet is, like so many early works of Mendelssohn, a cyclical form. A new theme which derives from the opening theme enters in the development of the first movement. The derivation is laid out for all to hear. Mendelssohn begins the development with the main theme at the tonic (as in Beethoven's Sonatas, op. 31, no. 1, and op. 31, no. 3) and then presents the "new" theme fourteen bars later so we can hear it arise from the main theme:

Mendelssohn makes the derivation evident in the coda when he plays both themes, one after the other.

The motif reappears in the finale, where it is prepared by the main theme:

This relationship makes a grand effect as the first movement theme leads back to the main theme of the finale:

The coda of the finale seems almost inevitable when it arrives, as it simply returns to the coda of the first movement, coming out of the same motifs and ending in the same way, as the opening theme dies into silence.

Classical form and modern sensibility

In Mendelssohn's hands, the cyclical form breaks down the sense of separate movements to an extent that surpasses almost all previous examples, and the cyclical works are Mendelssohn's most radical experiments with form. It is significant that the unconventional cyclical experiments largely disappear from his work after the age of twenty-one, as if, after sowing his youthful wild oats, he had decided to settle down to a more acceptable and conservative style. If the early works of Mendelssohn, from the age of fifteen to twenty-one, remain more satisfying and impressive than the products of his later years, it is not that he lost any of his craft or even his genius. What he renounced was his daring.

One important and influential innovation was left to him. The Violin Concerto in E Minor, written when Mendelssohn had reached the advanced age of thirty-five, is the most successful synthesis of the Classical concerto tradition with the Romantic virtuoso form. The displacement of the cadenza from the end of the first movement to the transition between development and recapitulation was unprecedented. It was made possible by the most idiosyncratic trait of Mendelssohn's sense of structure, the frequent draining away of energy at the end of his developments, that preference for a lyrical moment of stasis that inspired some of his most original effects. A cadenza is basically a relaxing of structural tension, a mimesis of improvisation which loosens both phrase structure and tempo. Mendelssohn's innovation places the purest display of virtuosity and the most individual expression at the heart of the form, at its center—and it has the result of making the balanced recapitulation that follows more like a gesture of obedience than of conviction.

The recapitulation of sonata form (a form that had become an academic tradition by the 1820s) was the stumbling block for many Romantic composers: the balanced working out of the tensions at length was felt less as a necessity than as a duty. Mendelssohn's delight in placing a moment of relaxed grace at the end of the development provided some of his most exquisite details, but it undermined the logic of the academic model, which Mendelssohn would never abandon. Only once did he solve the problem with complete satisfaction, in the magnificent and exhilarating opening movement of the Italian Symphony, written when he was twenty-three years old. Here the recapitulation freely combines a new fugal theme presented in the development with the main themes of the exposition: this gave a rare complexity to the final pages of the movement and sustained the interest to the end.

How poorly adapted the Romantic sensibility was to the continuation of Classical techniques may be shown in concentrated form by the first of the Seven Characteristic Pieces, op. 7, one of Mendelssohn's earliest and finest achievements, where we can see how much he could learn from a study of Bach, and yet how different was his sensibility:

The first section is nine bars long, and seems to be moving by the eighth bar from E minor to the traditional cadence in the relative major, G, but then suddenly swerves to a surprising cadence on a B minor chord. The eighteen-year-old composer could have learned the trick from Haydn, but the return to the opening theme is an invention that belongs to him alone. After a second phrase of eight bars, traditional in form if beautifully expressive, Mendelssohn reveals his most personal side. The opening bars seem to return, but the literal return is pushed off: repeating the first four notes of the piece, the music hovers on the edge of recapitulation with a rising sequence that would, in any other hands, move to a dynamic climax, but here dies away *calando*. As the bass gets heavier, the texture thicker, the harmony and melody more expressive and more dramatic, the dynamics paradoxically become softer, the tempo slower—this is Mendelssohn's craft at its most subtle and idiosyncratic. The recapitulation of the opening phrase finally begins in bar 22, abridged to half its original length. The climax of the short piece is reserved for the coda, and even there it is postponed until after what might have been the final cadence three bars before the end. The structure may be the adaptation of a simple eight-eenth-century binary form, but the sensibility is entirely modern.

The decline of Mendelssohn's reputation may appear inexplicable when we consider these achievements, particularly when we add to them the wonderful tone painting of pseudo-Celtic character in the overture called "The Hebrides" or "Fingal's Cave," as well as the invention of that type of scherzo that became almost the trademark of the composer. It is true that too many of these scherzos are very similar: a light staccato continuous movement most often in duple time, concentrated in the highest registers and largely *pianissimo*. He created his type of scherzo for the Octet in 1825 at the age of sixteen, partly on the model of Beethoven's scherzo in the Sonata for Piano in E flat Major, op. 31, no. 3:

But he repeated it, perhaps too often, in the String Quintet in A Major, op. 18, the last of the Seven Characteristic Pieces, op. 7, the second of the Three Caprices for Piano, op. 16 (the whole set is one of his most beautiful works), and in the Piano Trio in C Minor, op. 66. A variant, very similar but in 6/8 time, was elaborated for *A Midsummer Night's Dream,* and another version is found in the Piano Trio in D Minor, op. 49.

The decline in Mendelssohn's prestige may prove more comprehensible if we reflect that in the late nineteenth century the foundation of his fame rested principally on the oratorios and the Songs without Words. Attempts to revive both genres are always attended by a basic lack of success, combined with expressions of surprise at how much beautiful music they contain.

The Songs Without Words have a Mozartean grace without Mozart's dramatic power, a Schubertean lyricism without Schubert's intensity. If we could be satisfied today with a simple beauty that raises no questions and does not attempt to puzzle us, the short pieces would resume their old place in the concert repertoire. They charm, but they neither provoke nor astonish. It is not true that they are insipid, but they might as well be.

The two oratorios, *Saint Paul* and *Elijah,* present a different problem. They are not works like the Schubert operas, products of a genius fundamentally ill equipped to handle a particular form (Schubert's operas have wonderful pages of music—how could there not be such moments?—but Schubert had no instinct for dramatic rhythm). Mendelssohn's craft easily surmounted most of the demands of the oratorio, and they are the most impressive examples of that form in the nineteenth century. It is tempting to say that the difficulty is religious rather than musical, but that would be only a half-truth, and an evasion of the issues. Nevertheless, it is the juncture of religion and music that is at stake, and the subject turns up throughout the nineteenth century from *Saint Paul* to *Parsifal* and takes in the nocturnes of Chopin, the operas of Meyerbeer, Bellini, and Verdi (including not only *Don Carlos* and *La Forza del destino* but also *Aïda* and many others) and even the piano concertos of Brahms.

Religion in the concert hall

Mendelssohn is the inventor of religious kitsch in music. His first essay in this genre is a masterpiece, the Fugue in E Minor, published in 1837 but written ten years earlier, when the composer was eighteen; for publication as opus 35, Mendelssohn added a prelude in the style of an *appassionato* song without words and five other preludes and fugues, none of which has the vitality or the extraordinary character of the earlier fugue. This work is a summation of what Mendelssohn learned from his constant study of Bach, but it is also a remarkable prediction of what the later nineteenth and twentieth centuries would make of Bach's style. In addition, conceived principally in terms of a virtuoso drama, it is perhaps the first independent concert fugue.

The quiet opening of the fugue may be the most superb pastiche of Bach ever produced with nineteenth-century means:

A *pianissimo* cadence in bar 24 rounds out the opening exposition with an effect of hushed piety. The addition of nineteenth-century dynamics to early eighteenth-century fugal texture is not simply a modern way of articulating old forms: it implies an emotional agitation which was not audible or present in the original style. A commonplace cadence on the relative major, beautifully worked out in detail, is given a new meaning by Mendelssohn's gradual dying fall. It evokes the quiet folding of hands in prayer. I do not know about the practice in the Middle Ages or during the Baroque, but it is obvious from Mendelssohn's fugue that in the early nineteenth century a reverent whisper was the proper tone to adopt in church. Mendelssohn's concert fugue is a character piece.

It is also intended as a practical work for a virtuoso to take on tour. After the ostentatiously humble opening, there is a slow buildup of brilliance and drama. With this goes a continuous acceleration of the tempo until it reaches a furious Allegro. Nothing farther from the Baroque fugue can be imagined in texture, form, and general affective character. Much of the contrapuntal texture is lost as the music develops into a Classical Allegro style with a commanding melodic line and an *obbligato* accompaniment:

As it reaches its climax, the ongoing acceleration transforms this Classical character in turn into a Romantic display of octaves for the left hand alone, a flashy device if there ever was one:

It is, however, a device directly based on J. S. Bach's virtuoso cadenzas for pedal keyboard alone in some of the great organ toccatas and fugues. Virtuosity, for Bach, was not out of place in a church: for Mendelssohn, religion was not out of place in the concert hall. The left-hand cadenza moves directly into the climax of the fugue: a chorale tune accompanied by the still continuing left-hand octaves, which gradually descend from *fortissimo* to *pianissimo* with an effect of undiminished brilliance. The inflated use of Baroque style is very close here to the later achievements of Ferruccio Busoni and Leopold Stokowski: the creation of awe through bombast. The coda combines fugal texture and chorale together in a soft atmosphere of devout reverence, a beautiful expression of sincere repentance and genuine submission to divine will:

The final bars evoke, as well as or better than anyone had ever done before, a sense of religion and piety which dispenses with the unnecessary and inconvenient trappings of dogma and ritual. It does not represent, like Bach's music, either some point of dogma or some aspect of the drama of religious experience: it conveys, rather, the emotional satisfaction that religion can give, the pleasure that is the aftermath of participating in a religious rite, of making a confession, of contemplating the traditional Sunday service.

"I do not care how much harm the Catholic Church has done, provided I can use its symbols in my poetry," Goethe once stated. Mendelssohn, much more genuinely devout than his great elder contemporary (whom he knew, and to whom he dedicated his first important chamber work), aestheticizes religion in a similar way. Earlier composers, notably Haydn in the Symphony in F Minor, no. 26 *(Lamentations),* had used sacred tunes in profane works, but none before Mendelssohn had attempted to evoke an ecclesiastical atmosphere with such sensuous immediacy. The sole exception is, of course, opera, but a comparison with operatic tradition reveals Mendelssohn's radical originality. In the religious scenes in opera, from Gluck's *Orfeo* to Verdi's *Don Carlo,* we watch others present at a rite; with Mendelssohn's fugue it is we who are coerced into becoming the worshippers. In opera, religious music is either a form of the picturesque as exotic as the yodel themes in *Guillaume Tell,* or it has an objective dramatic function. The chorale-prelude in Mozart's *Zauberflöte,* as well as the choruses and the airs of Sarastro, are not only dramatically relevant but are musical representations of important points of Masonic doctrine. Mendelssohn's evocation of religion is both more general and more concentrated: it represents no doctrine, and no particular issues are touched, but it is designed to make us feel that the concert hall has been transformed into a church. The music expresses not religion but piety.

This is kitsch insofar as it substitutes for religion itself the emotional shell of religion. It evades all aspects of controversy, of dramatic conflict. It does not comfort, but only makes us comfortable. Virtuosity and religion have a reciprocal relation in Mendelssohn's fugue: the religious atmosphere makes the virtuoso display seem less trivial, more deeply serious, while the virtuosity makes the feeling of being in church more effective, passionate, and interesting. Religion is drained of all its content and has become powerfully sensuous, a purely aesthetic form of the sublime.

The E Minor Fugue is, as I have said, unequivocally a masterpiece. Any moral disapproval that it may stimulate today implies a disapproval of nineteenth-century religion, for which the traditional faith and even the old sense of sin had become less important than a feeling of belonging to a community and an assurance of social respectability. It is fashionable to jeer at nineteenth-century religion, but we must remember that the fashion did not begin in the twentieth century with Lytton Strachey but was already an acceptable intellectual position during the nineteenth century itself. It is easier today to see the importance for that time of popular religious movements like Methodism, but these did not have their chief support among the people who financed and supported what we think of as high art, and consequently their musical expression belongs within a different tradition. On the other hand, the development of official Catholic doctrine in the nineteenth century is not taken seriously by theologians today (the two new dogmas proclaimed—the Immaculate Conception and the infallibility of the pope—are an exploitation of popular Mariolatry and a consolidation of centralized administrative power), and official Protestant thought attempted largely to accommodate an already established theology with a social conscience. None of the important composers from 1820 to 1850 were inspired by recent religious ideas, as Mozart had been moved by Freemasonry. (Whatever sympathy Liszt may have found for radical figures like Lamennais, his religious music largely reflects the most orthodox, traditional Catholic positions.) It is for this reason that Mendelssohn's invention of religious kitsch was so influential throughout the century. It neither expressed nor represented anything, but only stimulated in the listener the illusion of being present at a religious service. It created a feeling of pious devotion in the audience without making any awkward demands. This is clear, after the E Minor Fugue, in such works as the *Reformation* Symphony and the Trio for Piano and Strings in C Minor; it even affects the picturesque slow movement, apparently a Pilgrim's Chorus, of the Italian Symphony. It vitiates the drama of the two oratorios, *Elijah* and *Saint Paul*, with a respectably conservative piety.

The finale of the C Minor Trio shows how religion for Mendelssohn had dwindled into a simple feeling of awe that could serve as an impressive climax to a profane work. The opening excitement shows all of Mendelssohn's habitual craftsmanship:

The course of the movement is interrupted by a chorale. The exhausted rhythm and the fragmentation of the first theme beautifully prepare the new melody, but there is no obvious reason for the display of piety:

Beethoven had used a chorale texture to give weight to a movement (for example, the F major theme in the finale of the Sonata for Piano in C Major, op. 2, no. 3), but he was never as shameless as Mendelssohn, who later in the work even employs a simulated drumroll to make his climax exciting and credible:

The relation between the furious opening and the triumphant chorale suggests a program, but it does not seem as if the appreciation of the work would be enhanced by our discovering one. The chorale gives a sense of a spiritual community to the listener, and a spiritual purpose to what might otherwise appear simple entertainment.

This pseudo-religious—or, better, hyper-religious—genre remained important for the rest of the century, as late as the Prelude, Chorale, and Fugue of César Franck, and the Organ Symphony of Camille Saint-Saëns. Mendelssohn's new blend of the religious and the profane had a fantastic success in Victorian England: many composers, most of them happily forgotten, were indebted to it. The genre remained essentially different from the picturesque appearances of religious music on the operatic stage, although, at the end of his life, Wagner turned to the Mendelssohnian style with *Parsifal:* the debt to the *Reformation*

Symphony of Mendelssohn is evident enough, and not merely in the use of the theme of the "Dresden" Amen in both. In *Parsifal*, Wagner aimed at creating the illusion for his audience of participating as communicants in the presentation of the Holy Grail. This, his last opera, was meant to transform Bayreuth into a shrine (its performance at any other theater was forbidden), and Mendelssohn's technique of turning his listeners into devout worshippers lay conveniently to hand. Wagner was also undoubtedly influenced here by the music of Liszt on religious themes. Although Liszt started from the operatic picturesque, he gave it an original subjective form. Like Mendelssohn, Liszt aimed at inducing a glow of piety in the listener, but his religious subjects have an exotic air which betrays their picturesque origin, in contrast to Mendelssohn's more homely Lutheran sources that rendered both his bombast and his sentimentality more effective than Liszt's.

Most of the oratorios and masses of the nineteenth century after the deaths of Beethoven and Schubert are not only dead today, but embalmed: resuscitation would be quixotic. It is true that Rossini produced two fine works of sacred music in an old-fashioned style that made it seem as if nothing had happened in music since his retirement from opera in 1830. The ostentatious modesty reflected in the title of the *Petite Messe solonnelle* is proclaimed by its humble instrumentation for harmonium and piano: it attains greatness while appearing to shy away from it. With the younger composers, in spite of occasional fine pages and interesting dramatic conceptions in the sacred music of Mendelssohn, Liszt, Schumann, Gounod, and others, most of it remains pastiche—of Handel, Bach, or Palestrina—brought up to date at odd moments, generally by references to contemporary opera. Religious style is properly conservative and even archaic, and has been so through most of history, but nineteenth-century religious forms tended to induce timidity in composers from Liszt to Sir Arthur Sullivan, as if the nobility of the enterprise made their most obvious talents unworthy. What causes, for example, Liszt's oratorio *Saint Elizabeth* to be so exasperating is that the music contains so little of the composer's fundamental vitality: for the most part, he represses even his genius for a play of sonorities.

One oasis appeared in the desert of religious inspiration during this period: the requiem. It is as if only death had enough human significance in a religious context to inspire composers as different as Cherubini, Berlioz, Brahms, Verdi, and Fauré. There are also rare exceptional successes with shorter works like the *Te Deum* of Bruckner, of Berlioz, and of Verdi, but otherwise religion in music for the nineteenth century remained anchored in the representation of death. Perhaps the terror of dying was the only part of religion that easily captured the imagination. At any rate, the representation of death needed none of the exotic picturesque on which Berlioz had to draw for *L'Enfance du Christ*, and the terrors and the consolations that the music could express in a requiem were not as factitious as the piety, however sincere, in the work of Mendelssohn, Wagner, and Liszt. The concert requiem was neither an inexpensive substitute for opera, like most of the oratorios of the time, nor a musical exercise in devotion without content. It was the one chance for the Romantic composer to feel as if he had been able to appropriate some part of the great tradition of religious music from Palestrina to Bach and reconceive it in his own language.

CHAPTER ELEVEN

Romantic Opera: Politics, Trash, and High Art

Politics and melodrama

The most important of Meyerbeer's operas deal directly with religion, starting in 1824 with *The Crusader in Egypt,* which was his first great international success. *Robert le Diable* (1831) treats of popular medieval religious mythology and diabolism, and its most spectacular moment is the ballet in which the ghosts of dead debauched nuns rise from their graves; *Les Huguenots* (1836) puts the religious conflict of the Massacre of Saint Bartholomew on the stage; the hero of *Le Prophète* (1849) is the fifteenth-century religious leader John of Leyden; and *L'Africaine* (1865) dramatizes the clash of Christian and pagan worlds in the Portuguese exploration of Africa. The popularity of religious themes in opera is already found in the Napoleonic era with the Ossianic operas of Le Sueur and Méhul, and *La Vestale* (1807) of Spontini, but it becomes more intense after 1830, with Bellini's *Norma* (1831), Wagner's *Tannhäuser* (1845) and *Lohengrin* (1850), Halévy's *La Juive,* and the work of Meyerbeer. It is possible that Meyerbeer's loyalty to his Jewish faith may have inspired him to the choice of such themes, just as the ambiguity of Mendelssohn's situation may have driven him to compose one Christian and one Jewish oratorio. (His father, son to Moses Mendelssohn, the most famous Jewish figure of the eighteenth century, converted to Christianity and changed his family name to Bartholdy. Felix, to his father's consternation, took back the name of Mendelssohn, although he never returned to the Jewish faith.) In opera, however, religion was largely another word for politics.

Les Huguenots of 1838 was Meyerbeer's most successful and representative work, and its political message was clearly tied to the still controversial Revolution of 1789. The sixteenth-century Catholics and Protestants symbolize, respectively, the corrupt aristocracy and the stiff-necked, dogmatic proletarian Jacobin party. The sympathy lies—as almost always in these operas—largely with the downtrodden proletariat, who are nevertheless represented as barbarous, unwilling to compromise, and easily misled. The middle class, trapped between the two extremist parties, is almost invisible, reduced to a pair of lovers, one from each side, like Romeo and Juliet, who form an illicit liaison that is doomed. This simple-minded conception of sixteenth-century history is not that of Meyerbeer and his librettist, Eugène Scribe, alone. Three years before the premiere of *Les Huguenots,* the most illustrious French historian of the time, Jules Michelet, published a book on Luther, in which he proclaimed the Protestant movement as the origin of the French Revolution: "What do I see in the sixteenth century?" he wrote. "That protestantism alone gives us the Republic . . . I say it gives us the Republic—the idea, and the thing, and the word."

The change of serious opera from an aristocratic art that dealt largely with court intrigue and dynastic marriage, sometimes disguised as classical mythology, into a popular form that expressed the political ideals of republicanism and patriotism was a long development that started slowly in the last decades of the eighteenth century, before the French Revolution.

At the end the changes were rapid, and confirmed by the Revolution of 1830, after which the Paris Opera was rented out for commercial exploitation. Serious opera is almost always political in nature, and a political interpretation of the stylistic changes is not a modern critical luxury; it was explicitly made at the time. Doctor Véron, a rich amateur who leased the Paris Opera in the early 1830s and quickly made a fortune running it, wrote that since the Revolution of 1830 had brought the bourgeoisie to power, he decided to make the Paris Opera the Versailles of the bourgeoisie, the symbolic manifestation of its new status.

One must not imagine, however, that by becoming representative of the new middle-class taste, serious opera became commercially profitable in any real sense. Véron was frank: when asked how he had been able to make a fortune from the Paris Opera in a few years, he always replied that he got out just in time before the government subsidy was reduced. The subsidy was all-important. Véron also redesigned the interior of the opera house, substituting a larger number of smaller loges for the few large ones that were generally sold by subscription to aristocratic families, and making it possible for more of the upper-middle class to have a box of their own. Véron also tried to reduce expenses. It was impossible, he said, to economize on the lavish scenic effects, the ballet, and the décor, all of which were felt to be essential to the Paris stage. Nor could one refuse to pay the outlandish sums demanded, then as now, by singers with an international reputation. That left only the musicians of the orchestra, who were helpless, as Véron remarked cynically but with a certain air of being ashamed of himself, and he cut their salaries to the bone. All this, of course, would have been useless without the traditional subsidy.

Serious opera from its inception has almost always been subsidized by the state. Aristocratic support for the opera continued throughout Europe, indirectly as well as by government grant—it was a status symbol to have a ballerina as a mistress. Aristocratic patronage should not fool us into thinking that the music necessarily reflected aristocratic taste. There was no aristocratic taste in France and Italy after Napoleon. Just as the paintings of Paul Delaroche appealed to a wide range of middle-class taste, although they were acquired largely by those aristocrats who were rich enough to pay the high prices they brought at the time, grand opera after 1830 embodied the artistic and political ideals of the middle class, and a government subsidy then as now made it possible for the bourgeois music lover to afford a ticket.

The simple political message of many of these operas is similar to the pattern set by *Les Huguenots:* the hero and heroine—rarely seen as tied to their class but characterized only as individuals or else as rising above narrow class interest—are caught between the immoral corruption of the aristocracy and the doctrinaire rigidity or the secret greed of the leaders of the proletariat. In *Le Prophète* by Meyerbeer, the local seigneur rapes a peasant girl, while the hero, who becomes the religious leader of a popular revolt, is coerced by his wicked Anabaptist henchman into denying his own mother publicly at his coronation; in the end, his love for his mother wins out and he redeems himself by blowing up the palace with himself and everyone else in it.

This naive and pleasing depiction of the class struggle is sometimes varied, above all in an Italy still suffering from foreign domination, by turning the vicious aristocrats into a foreign army of occupation. The native revolutionary party, in this case, becomes more idealized, while generally remaining no less doctrinaire or bent on merciless revenge (in Verdi's *Sicilian Vespers* of 1854, the Sicilian leaders encourage the occupying French troops to rape Sicilian women in order to set off a spirit of revolt among the local peasantry); the hero or heroine, as in Bellini's *Norma,* is still trapped between the two forces. *Norma,* in fact, is a fine example of the scheme, in its intimate combination of religion and politics: the captain of the occupying Roman army is corrupt and immoral (he is about to go off with another priestess after fathering Norma's two children), and Norma's father, the native high priest Oroveso, reluctantly applies Druid law in its full harshness by condemning his daughter to death.

For personal reasons, Verdi preferred a variation in which the corrupt aristocracy is replaced or complemented by an evil priesthood, as in *Don Carlos* or *Aida.* The downtrodden proletariat are offstage in *Don Carlos,* back in their native Flanders, but they are represented by their champion, the Marquess of Posa, whose liberal ideals stir up the hatred of the Grand Inquisitor and so cause his own death and the doom of Don Carlos. *Aida* combines all these elements: the evil priests; the army of oppressors; the slaves with their unscrupulous leader whose intransigence seals the fate of his daughter; and the hero and heroine who stand outside their class, to betray it and themselves.

I have insisted on this simpleminded political background of the plots since it provides us with a nonmusical source for some of the most powerful moments in grand opera, pages of extraordinary rhythmic energy and vitality. This essential element in nineteenth-century opera should be given its true name, one that any contemporary would have understood: rabble-rousing. The chorus *"Guerra, guerra!"* (War! War!) in *Norma* was intended to fire the blood of Bellini's audience with patriotism. There are scenes and arias in Verdi that sound like a call to arms, and were clearly understood as such when they were first performed: "Di quella pira" from Verdi's *Il Trovatore* is the most famous of these today—it is, indeed, a call to arms, and gives an explicit political tone to an opera in which the political significance is carefully repressed. The opposition of the freedom-loving Gypsies and the autocratic count must have been evident enough at the time; the magnificent musical representation of the imprisoned Gypsy's homesickness must also have spoken as a metaphor to the emotions of a public whose native land was occupied by an Austrian army.

It was the French Revolution that invented jingoism as a musical style, and Schumann observed that the "Marseillaise" stood as a model behind some of the most effective moments in Meyerbeer. Nineteenth-century opera owes a heavy debt to the French revolutionary cantatas, with their massed choruses and their martial rhythms. By 1810 Spontini had created an explicitly Napoleonic grandeur on the operatic stage with these means. It was, however, Auber who really perfected the jingoistic technique and wrote music that made every member of the public feel as if he should rush out and seize a musket. *La Muette de Portici,* performed in Brussels in 1830, is said to have set off the Belgian revolution. It was Auber who took from military band music the vulgar Meyerbeerian trademark that horrified Schumann, the crash on the last beat of the second or fourth bar in a piece in 4/4 time; this can still be heard in Verdi as late as *Aida.*

Popular art

Opera as a whole has a shabby reputation (it is also the most prestigious of music genres, but that is the other side of the coin). It has been, and is, viewed with suspicion by most lovers of drama and of music—like the movies, it appears sometimes not to be art at all but only a pretentious variety of low entertainment. This is particularly true of Italian opera (German opera has partially escaped the stigma, perhaps because, as Lady Bracknell once remarked, German is an eminently respectable language). Philip Gossett has amusingly attempted to caricature this common view: "Melodramatic plots, banal tunes over oom-pah-pah accompaniments, sopranos warbling in thirds with a flute, tenors bellowing high C's . . ."[1] The catch is that this is not a

1. Philip Gossett, review of *Donizetti and His Operas* by William Ashbrook, *New York Review of Books,* March 31, 1983, p. 30.

caricature—most of the time nineteenth-century Italian opera is really like that, down to the parallel thirds in the flute—although the mad scene in *Lucia di Lammermoor* must have sounded considerably more entertaining and eerie at the first performance when the accompanying instrument was not a flute but a glass harmonica. The melodramatic plots remained in force throughout the nineteenth century, as did the vocalizing sopranos, the bellowing tenors, and even the oom-pah-pah accompaniments.

The banality of the tunes is the heaviest charge, and this might seem to be a relative, even a subjective, matter—the banal is the overfamiliar, the too-often-heard. But that was exactly what was wanted—or, rather, the initial success of an opera demanded at least one original melody that seemed long familiar at first hearing, and could be whistled by the audience on leaving the opera house. Both Donizetti and Verdi needed such tunes, at once original and instantly banal, for their dramatic structures to work: neither the sextet from *Lucia di Lammermoor* nor "La donna è mobile" from *Rigoletto,* to take only two examples, would have the right effect if they did not sound immediately as if one had known them all one's life.

Nineteenth-century music lovers understood this well enough. One critic described the effect of "La donna è mobile" at the premiere of *Rigoletto,* the first sustained masterpiece by Verdi: "Hardly had the first verse finished before there arose a great cry from every part of the theater, and the tenor failed to find his cue to begin the second verse. Verdi must have realized that the melody had always existed: he wished to shock the imagination with the commonplace fact that he had rediscovered it for himself." This is quoted by Roger Parker in his excellent and interesting essay on the music of *Rigoletto,*[2] with the odd comment that "far from having 'rediscovered' the melody, Verdi obviously spent some time in honing it to his precise needs." Parker quotes the sketch for "La donna è mobile," which he calls "much simpler and more predictable." The sketch is, in fact, less symmetrical than the final version, and the end of the first phrase, far from being predictable, is sadly unconvincing. Of course, Verdi worked hard to "rediscover" a melody that had existed since all eternity. He knew how well he had succeeded when he kept the tune secret—even the tenor was not allowed to see it until the dress rehearsal. Parker remarks that "Verdi was perfectly aware of the potential popularity of this melody; and also that its tunefulness could conceivably undermine its dramatic effect." This is again wide of the mark, and suggests absurdly that the dramatic effect is undermined once the tune is known, and therefore ceases to work after the premiere. On the contrary, the dramatic effect depends on the tunefulness at this point.

The genius of Verdi and of Donizetti lay as much in the dramatic use they made of such tunes as in their creation, but neither had the ability to write the

2. *Rigoletto,* Opera Guide Series, ed. Nicholas John (Cambridge).

long aristocratic melodies of Bellini. These melodies were the object of Verdi's admiration and envy, but he would have had no use for them in his own operas. Serious opera had changed radically in Italy and France during the 1830s and 1840s, as Verdi reached his maturity as a composer; it lost what little was left of its aristocratic elegance and became a form of popular art. (In his later years, indeed, Verdi was to achieve a new kind of refinement with *Don Carlos,* the second version of *Simone Boccanegra,* and above all the third act of *Aida.* But that is another story.)

"Popular art" is a loaded term: it has different meanings, impossible to define with any precision, that range from folklore to junk. The two poles are clear enough, but the meanings tend to blur. The Hollywood Western of the 1930s and 1940s, for example, has elements of folklore but is better understood as popular trash: this did not, of course, prevent masterpieces from being produced in that genre. Like the Western—and the Elizabethan revenge tragedy of Kyd, Marlowe, Tourneur, and Shakespeare—nineteenth-century opera in France and Italy is closer to junk than to high art or folk art. We cannot escape the normative connotation of these terms, but it should be evident from these examples that there can be great trash, just as there is bad high art (and, of course, the special category of trash pretending to the status of high art, for which the only existing term is the German *edel Kitsch,* or "noble trash": the movies of Ken Russell, the plays of Maxwell Anderson, the operas of Erich Wolfgang Korngold—everyone can make up his own tendentious list).

The relation of high art to popular art is always complex—partly because, as we have seen, the concept of "popular art" is ambiguous and slippery. The operettas of Jacques Offenbach, the musicals of George Gershwin and of Harold Arlen, the waltzes of Johann Strauss, Jr., are great popular art; none of them claims to be high art. Schubert and Brahms, however, often used popular Hungarian Gypsy themes as material for works which are clearly intended to be sublime: the slow movements of Schubert's last symphony and of his Piano Trio in E flat Major; the finale of Brahms's Piano Quartet in G Minor. In a similar fashion, Berlioz composed a ballroom waltz in the *Symphonie fantastique.*

The case of nineteenth-century serious opera is a very different one: here we are dealing with a popular genre for which the composer tried to give an adequate musical expression and, intermittently, to transmute it into high art. We need a term like "trash" for this genre, nevertheless, as the plots and the librettos of the operas of Donizetti, Verdi, Mercadante, Halévy, and Meyerbeer are, with almost no exceptions, as coarse and as absurd as the scripts for the films of Greta Garbo and the epics of Cecil B. DeMille—and the music largely reflects that coarseness without embarrassment. I take it for granted that the drama of the nineteenth century must also be considered with some sympathy, a suspension of disapproval as well as disbelief, and that few music lovers today have any difficulty in surrendering to the finest moments in Donizetti or even in Meyerbeer (on the rare occasions when the latter is performed with some musical intelligence). Nevertheless until the essential trashiness of the genre is faced, the extraordinary musical achievement will remain incomprehensible.

I have not used terms like "junk," "trash," and "cheap melodrama" to imply that serious nineteenth-century Italian and French opera is worse than the eighteenth-century variety. On the contrary, the change seems to me in almost every way an improvement, even politically. Eighteenth-century *opera seria* is above all an explicit apology for absolutism. The chief librettist was Pietro Metastasio, a poet idolized by his contemporaries but who has permanently lost the luster which once seemed to grant him immortality. In spite of an evident mastery of his craft, he no longer fires our imagination, yet his works were set over and over again by dozens of composers, including Handel and Mozart. Most of these operas were designed to celebrate absolute royal power, and they were always an artificial form: *opera seria* in England, Germany, and Austria was, for the most part, written in Italian by German composers or by imported Italians. It was an embodiment of the most superficial aspects of eighteenth-century politics: court scandal, ritual, and dynastic marriage.

The psychology, if that is the word for it, is equally simplistic, even primitive: there were rarely any characters at all in *opera seria,* only a succession of dramatic situations which allowed the singers to express a series of emotional states. The attempt to find psychological consistency in the operas of Alessandro Scarlatti, Vivaldi, Handel, and Jommelli is misplaced ingenuity, even if the individual numbers are of magnificent quality. The only consistency was the singer's vocal technique: when the cast changed, new arias were almost always substituted, generally adapted from other operas. The change from Metastasio's stiff, artificial dramas to the clever and sensational melodramas of Eugène Scribe, the leading nineteenth-century librettist, is nothing to deplore.

The snobbish distinction between high art and popular trash is not one that we ought to accept willingly today at its face value. Most of the respectable tragedies of the eighteenth and nineteenth centuries are even less defensible than the cheap melodramas of the period. Yet the distinction is essential to nineteenth-century thought, and above all to an understanding of the serious opera of the age. The aspiration to the sublime is responsible for almost all of the absurdity and the hollow, pretentious pomposity of grand opera. It is also, however, responsible for scenes of great power and for the rare masterpiece. The equivalent of nineteenth-century grand opera is in the visual arts; academic history painting is still, in spite of scholarly efforts at revival, a form of period bric-a-brac appealing only to camp aesthetics; the large historical novels of the time remain outmoded curiosities. Grand opera has its camp followers, too, and the more absurd it is, the better they like it. Nevertheless, most amateurs and critics would agree that several works of the time, from Bellini's *Norma* to Verdi's *Otello,* transcend the inescapable vulgarity of nineteenth-century "high" art, and make all considerations of good and bad taste momentarily irrelevant. The success may be due to the fact that the Italian operatic tradition was more openly and comfortably vulgar than the historical novel or the more grandiose form of salon paintings: in any case, only the tension between the vulgarity of the genre and the consistent high aspiration of the composers can enable us to understand the frequent disparagement of Bellini's music by French and German critics and the unqualified defense of it offered by Richard Wagner.

A musical style able to deal with the greatest drama has been the intermittent ideal of opera since its initial conception in the late sixteenth century as a resurrection of the classical Greek stage. This ideal has almost never been realized. Most operas based on a play of any real merit are travesties of the original, much like Hollywood versions of *Anna Karenina* or *War and Peace,* and for many of the same reasons: the exigencies of the star performers; the demands of the producers; the belief that everyone except the composer knows best how to give the public what it wants. As a result, an opera is not only generally inferior to the play from which it is derived but almost always disastrously so. No one thinks that Gounod's *Faust* or Ambroise Thomas's *Hamlet* are adequate musical representations of the plays from which they came, whatever their musical merits. Mussorgsky's *Boris Gudonov* is a rare success: to achieve it the composer had to invent a new and more realistic musical declamation that could render prose without becoming recitative. It remained a model for the great twentieth-century achievements of *Pelléas et Mélisande* and *Wozzeck.*

The failure of nineteenth-century opera with contemporary drama is even more striking. In the eighteenth century, not until Mozart took on Beaumarchais's *Marriage of Figaro* was there any adequate setting of an interesting contemporary play, and with this work both Mozart and his librettist, da Ponte, understood that they had done something radically new, as da Ponte specifically claimed. The greatest German playwrights of the early nineteenth century, Heinrich von Kleist and Georg Büchner, were not even attempted by composers until almost a century later. In the twentieth century, Maurice Maeterlinck, Hugo von Hofmannsthal, and Franz Wedekind inspired Debussy, Richard Strauss, and Berg. The second quarter of the nineteenth century, however, had reached an impasse. For most critics today, the finest theatrical work after 1830 is cheap, vulgar farce, the magnificent farces of Nestroy in Vienna and of Labiche in Paris. This was, indeed, the tradition in which much of Bernard Shaw's style was formed. The tradition of boulevard farce, however, was not one open to a composer with high ambitions.

The absurdity of much of the serious drama of the nineteenth century is a stumbling block to modern sensibility. It is hard for a modern reader to swallow the scene in Victor Hugo's *Lucrezia Borgia* where Lucrezia tells the young Gennaro, who hopes to avenge the poisoning of his friends, that he must not kill her for he, too, is a Borgia, the son of Cesare. The following exchange then occurs:

Gennaro: Then you are my aunt!
Lucrezia (aside): His aunt!

in which the actress must convey to the audience that she is his mother, and that he is born of an incestuous union. I quote this to show to what extent some of the serious drama of the time can only be enjoyed as some kind of high camp. Donizetti's *Lucrezia Borgia* follows much of the Hugo original fairly closely, and it is a pity that this particular fragment of dialogue was eliminated.

Grand opera demanded cheap melodrama dressed up as aristocratic tragedy. The only real seriousness came from the simple and direct rendering of powerful emotions, the only complexity from the partially suppressed embodiment of political aspirations. All composers of opera from Rossini to Verdi lived in fear of the censors, who would unhesitatingly condemn any suspicion of liberal thought when they could detect it, and most of the operas give the new political philosophy only indirect expression, although it is generally at the heart of the drama.

Republican ideology on the operatic stage may have started in comic opera—the most distinguished example is Cherubini's *Les Deux Journées* (The Two Days)—but it reached its greatest power after 1825 with Rossini's *Guillaume Tell* and the works of Donizetti, Meyerbeer, and Auber. The subtlest music is perhaps that of *Guillaume Tell*, Rossini's last work for the stage; it has never been a real success, and the fault has generally been ascribed to an awkward and ineffective libretto. The true reason for the failure was perhaps Rossini's refined and aristocratic sensibility. To many of his contemporaries he seemed a popular figure who pandered to common taste, but he belonged to an older generation than Auber and Donizetti, and he was unable to muster the full-scale vulgarity that the new grand opera demanded. The gathering of the clans in *Guillaume Tell* has an impressive grandeur, but it also has a nobility and elevation of tone which must have seemed its greatest drawback in terms of the hypnotic driving rhythms of the next generation.

The eighteenth century demanded happy endings. A tragic end to an *opera seria* was largely unacceptable, and is rarely found. Even on the nonmusical stage, a play like *King Lear* was rewritten in order to save Cordelia's life. The advent of serious Romantic opera may be conveniently dated from Rossini's *Otello* of 1816, where the tragic ending is retained, although Desdemona is not smothered, as in the original play, but stabbed. The premiere was held in Naples, and it is said that the end created such a shock that on the second night, members of the audience called out to Desdemona as Otello appeared, "Watch out, he has a knife." Even if this anecdote is apocryphal, its currency reflects the historic change. The good manners, the decorum of eighteenth-century *opera seria* had disappeared. The violence now acceptable in serious opera was responsible for the new coarseness of musical style, but also for the immediacy and power with which the music could be used to express sentiment. Within a few years Rossini would represent both incest and matricide and Donizetti's operas would portray royal executions, suicides, and the wholesale poisoning of almost an entire cast of characters.

Bellini

The musical forms of all the Italian operas for more than half a century were set in the mold imposed largely by Rossini, although his own music never lost the Classical decorum that began to seem inappropriate for the new subject matter. If he did not create the conventions, his prestige made them universal. The basis of these conventions was the two-part aria or ensemble, with a slow lyrical first section called the *cantabile* (or *adagio*) and a more brilliant second part, or *cabaletta,* in which a melody was sung twice; the cabaletta tune was generally squarely articulated, and the repeat was ornamented with virtuoso figuration most often left to the improvisation of the singer. (In the cabalettas of duets we frequently find that each singer has the complete melody once, and then they sing it together.) Placed between the cantabile and the cabaletta, both in strict verse forms, we almost always find a *tempo di mezzo,* most often in a less formal verse pattern which allowed a more dramatic action to unfold. In the case of duets or ensembles, an opening section, *tempo d'attacco,* also in unrhymed verse, set the stage for the whole form and prepared the cantabile. The recitatives and *ariosos* (half recitative and half aria) needed to introduce this elaborate series were called the *scena.* The conventions may sometimes have seemed rigid, but the scheme was serviceable and could even be adapted to the action, and in unpredictable ways. The essential contrast was between the closed forms of the slow section (cantabile or adagio) and the final cabaletta, and the open textures that introduced and held them together.[3] This five-part structure (*scena, tempo d'attacco, cantabile, tempo di mezzo,* and *cabaletta*) had reached the stage of "ossification by 1825," as Philip Gossett has written,[4] but they remained in force even until the end of the nineteenth century. The cantabile allowed the expression of pathos which was at the heart of the Italian style, and the cabaletta provided a brilliant close. The *tempo d'attacco* and the *tempo di mezzo* made room for action.

3. Most of the details of this paragraph have been drawn from two essays by Philip Gossett, "Giachino Rossini and the Conventions of Composition," *Acta Musicologica* 42 (1970), and "Verdi, Ghislanzoni, and *Aida*: The Uses of Convention," *Critical Inquiry,* 1, no. 2 (December, 1974), as well as from Harold Powers, "La solita forma and the Uses of Convention," *Acta Musicologica* 59 (1987).

4. Philip Gossett, review of "Vincenzo Bellini und die italienische Opera Seria seiner zeit" by Friedrich Lippmann, *Journal of the American Musicological Society* 24 (1971).

The partition between expression of sentiment and rendering of action was a step backward into a late Baroque conception of opera, in which all the action took place in recitative and the arias were tableaux of emotion. This should not be surprising, as the musical style of the 1820s and 30s was in so many other respects a return to the Baroque: the reappearance of homogeneous rhythmic texture, the rejection of the clear-cut Classical articulation, the attempt to achieve a more fluid transition between phrases. At first sight, the abandon of Mozart's ideal of finding strict forms that were adequate for the movement of his drama may seem like a loss. Rarely with Rossini and never with Bellini do we find arias or ensembles in which complex action is taking place, like the aria in which Susanna is dressing Cherubino as a girl, the duet when the Countess dictates a letter, or the trio in which the Count discovers Cherubino hiding in a chair under a dress. Action and sentiment are now kept apart as they were in eighteenth-century *opera seria*. To insist on the reactionary character of Romantic opera, however, would be to miss the greater concentration of the new, closed forms in the rendering of sentiment. Gossett is justified in calling the cantabile and the cabaletta static, but they play a dynamic role in the opera as a whole that was denied to the more formally structured eighteenth-century aria, which moved listener and spectator by its portrayal of sentiment. The Romantic aria works more directly on the nerves: it does not so much portray, or even express, but induces and even coerces. At least in part, this is due to the new simplicity of forms, in which most often there is no modulation, no contrast of key, and little opposition of harmonies. The formal tonic/dominant structural symmetry of the early and late eighteenth century is replaced with a focus on repetitive rhythm, sometimes almost hypnotic, and on a single, uninterrupted melodic line with a climax pushed close to the end. Compared to this ostentatious simplicity, even the most moving of the arias in an opera by Handel or Gluck may seem like a mediated reflection of the dramatic sentiment. In Romantic opera, the two-part pattern of recitative and aria was replaced by the complex five-part structure outlined above: within this larger sequence, the individual sections could benefit from the immediacy and directness of an exaggeratedly simple form.

The danger of the conventions was the way they divided the music into separate compartments. Most of the serious composers objected at some time to the constraints, above all to the rigidity of the cabaletta form; but, as Gossett has shown,[5] they continued to be drawn to them. The obligatory repetition of the main theme of the cabaletta was particularly onerous to both critics and composers, but the structural cliché was unfortunately too effective to renounce: ending a scene with a rousing good tune was essential to the success of the opera, and the repetitions of the cabaletta form only served to set the tune into relief, make it memorable. Even if the composers' protests generally

5. Gossett, "Verdi, Ghislanzoni, and *Aida*," and in his study of the manuscript of *Anna Bolena: Anna Bolena and the Artistic Maturity of Gaetano Donizetti* (Oxford, 1985).

came to nothing, however, they are as significant as the final conformity; they reveal the dramatic ideals with which the conventions would be used. From the beginning there was an effort to make these forms less artificial, more continuous, more responsive to the dramatic action. Late in his career Verdi asked his publisher to print the third act of *Aida* without the usual indication of the separate numbers: aria, duet, trio. The publisher paid no attention to the composer's request.[6]

It was with the hardening of these conventions that Vincenzo Bellini came on the scene. He acknowledged the supremacy of Rossini; he accepted the forms set by the old master and imposed by the librettists. Yet in important respects his style was anti-Rossinian, a reaction against the mechanical brilliance that dominated the Italian vocal scene. He hoped, he wrote, to give his name to an era, and that "the public would see in me an innovative genius, and not a plagiary of the dominating genius of Rossini."[7] Bellini became the supreme master of an elegiac style, a lyricism which transforms even the scenes of action.

Gossett has remarked that Rossini was also capable of achieving an elegiac effect, and points to the beautiful duet from *Zelmira* as a rare example:

The flourish at the end of the phrase, however, still has some of the typical Rossinian brilliance. It was this kind of *fioritura,* often moving suddenly from

6. Philip Gossett informs me that Verdi's manuscript divides the act into separate numbers, and that his request is an idealizing afterthought. (It does, however, reflect a genuine concern for unity that can be heard in the structure of the act.)

7. Letter of February 16, 1829, to V. Ferlito, quoted by Maria Rosaria Adama in *Vincenzo Bellini* (Turin, 1981).

an eighth-note motion to a nervous thirty-second-note quadrupling, that Bellini began to eliminate from his style with his first success. It should be remarked that the sudden increase of speed at the end of the phrase would have been executed by Rossini's singers with a slight expressive slowing down; nevertheless, the simpler and more intense ornaments of Bellini would also have been sung with a certain rhythmic freedom. Although a few examples of Rossinian melodic flourishes may be found even in Bellini's later operas, they are no longer pervasive. In the works of Donizetti, on the other hand, a coloratura in Rossini's style is always present, often at odds with the dramatic meaning and even with the new melodic energy that so wonderfully characterizes Donizetti's art. The Rossinian flourish appears throughout *Anna Bolena* of 1830, for example, from the beginning in Anna's cavatina (or entrance aria):

and in the duet that follows between the King and Giovanna Seymour:

In the impressively pathetic terzetto of the second act

King Henry VIII suddenly appears to recall the first-act finale of Rossini's *Cenerentola* (Cinderella):

Bellini largely purified his style of these figures. For brilliance he substituted intensity. The technique may be seen in his early triumph *Il Pirata* (The Pirate): Imogene's final aria begins with a flute solo, *andante sostenuto,* in which the third and fourth bars of the melody display the traditional brilliant contemporary ornaments:

In the vocal part these bars are rewritten. The ornamentation of bars 3 and 4 is simpler and incomparably more expressive, although echoing the end of the flute melody. Then the return of the first bars is also transformed. Here, too, pathos takes priority over brilliance:

Instead of descending simply from C to F, the line moves for a moment in bar
5 expressively to D, expanding the range by one note. At the return of this
melody, the line, even leaner and more pathetic, now moves up one note further
to an E:

This is, employed in a new way, the simplest form of expressive ornament, the
appoggiatura, sometimes used traditionally like a sigh. The original melody is
made up of this appoggiatura:

In the final form these grace notes become arabesques. The first, has the simplest expansion:

Much more elaborate is the transformation of

which the soprano has first brought up to a D and now renders even more graceful. With

the curve makes us wait for the resolution of the D until the C in the middle of the next beat, and the momentary suspense of resolution reinforces the expressive value of the appoggiatura

just as the resolution of the A to the G is suspended by the last beat. The short leaps of the melody, its graceful curves, add delicate dissonance to delicate dissonance; the B♭ is an appoggiatura to the A and must be resolved into it, the C must be resolved into the B♭, the D into the C, and the leap into the E makes this note hover above the phrase. In short, Bellini has arranged his arabesque so that the expressive potential of every note is brought forward with the utmost simplicity. A Rossinian *fioritura* still intervenes elsewhere in this aria, but expanding the first two bars in this fashion is both simple and powerful. The appoggiatura becomes more than a local effect; the two expansions

increase the intensity each time of the entire phrase, not merely of the individual notes decorated.

The economy of the technique is striking. It complements the simplicity of Bellini's orchestration, which the composer himself justified: "*La natura piena e corsiva delle cantilene . . . non amettono altra natura d'istrumentazione* [The full-bodied and flowing nature of the sung melodies do not support any other kind of orchestration]." The combination of simplicity and intensity that leaves Bellini's art untouched by the vulgarity of the nineteenth-century melodramatic form, a vulgarity that Verdi himself would escape in his finest works only by his extraordinary dramatic power.

It may be thought that the simplicity of Bellini's style would have been adulterated in contemporary performance by the singers' insistence on adding the kind of decoration that displayed their vocal capacities, and it is certain that this was often the case. The new style, however, had its effect on performance practice. *Il Pirata* was given its premiere on the twenty-seventh of October, 1827, at La Scala in Milan. Two months later a critic wrote about a performance with the famous tenor Rubini, for whom the title role had been written:

> Rubini, who sometimes exaggerated his studied ornamentation, gave a fine example of taste when, according to the observation of some amateurs, he removed some elaborate decoration from his wonderfully beautiful aria in *Il Pirata,* and gave the aria as sweetly and passionately as it had issued from the inspiration of the poet and the composer.[8]

We see that Bellini's innovations had an influence on the style of performance: it is said that when Bellini heard Rubini sing Rossini, he predicted that in his own opera *Il Pirata* Rubini would be heard to sing in a manner so different that listeners would not recognize him. It is probable that the composer was consciously trying to revolutionize the contemporary style of singing. In any case, it is clear that attempting to perform the works of the 1820s today in the style of the time is not a straightforward, simple affair: it requires an attempt to decide which contemporary practices were suitable, and which had been left behind by changes in musical style. In particular, we must distinguish between the repetition of cabaletta melodies, where the literal reprinting of the original, unchanged, calls for the addition of ornamentation by the singer, and the execution of the new ornaments by Bellini, for which the style requires a performance that sticks much more closely to the text.

Bellini's innovations were, in fact, felt as reactionary, a welcome return to an older style of ornamentation which demanded an older style of singing. But no one before Bellini had used these simple ornaments with such focussed intensity; in his work they became not simple expressive dissonances but ways of prolonging dissonance, and they play a central role in his capacity to write the astonishingly long melodies envied by Verdi (*melodie lunghe, lunghe, lunghe* as Verdi said). The same old-fashioned simple ornaments quoted earlier serve to postpone the cadence in Tebaldeo's cavatina from *I Capuletti ed i Montecchi:*

---

8. Cited in Friedrich Lippmann, *Vincenzo Bellini* (1981), p. 457.

These ornaments must be sung slowly and with a subtly nuanced expression: they replace the agility of Rossinian coloratura with a *spianato* style, the free, evenly sustained, soft floating of the vocal line. It is this *spianato* technique which is the basic vehicle of Italian lyricism. For Mozart, the *spianato* was the opposite of *parlando,* the latter being a style of singing which suggests speech, and which, as Mozart remarked, is basic to ensemble numbers. The radical nature of Bellini's approach was to apply the lyrical style even to ensemble and to recitative. The radical approach was recognized at once by Rossini, who admired *Il Pirata,* but added that it was "so philosophical as sometimes to lack brilliance."[9]

---

9. Bellini's greatest appreciation of Rossini's work was largely reserved for *Guillaume Tell,* in which the old master, in deference to the French manner, had renounced most of his brilliant Italian coloratura.

La Straniera, Bellini's next opera after *Il Pirata*, was to be even more "philosophical," more dogmatic in his quest to "make a new kind of music which strictly expresses the words, to form a single object of both song and drama."[10] These are the explicit ideals of almost every original composer of opera, but Bellini tried now to introduce a purely declamatory style into aria and ensemble. What should be the cantabile of the quartet "Che far vuoi tu?" (What do you want to do?) in the last act has no melody in the strict sense, but it works only if sung not *parlando* but as if it were melody:

10. Remarks attributed to Bellini in Francesco Florimo, *Bellini: memorie e lettere* (1882), pp. 16–17.

This is not even *arioso*, but intensely lyrical recitative, and it allows Bellini a new harmonic freedom as the music appears to move toward B flat minor and suddenly switches at the last minute to G minor. (Structurally the quartet is very experimental. The long declamatory section is followed by a genuine cantabile *(Larghetto),* but then, after a brief new and faster tempo, lyrical declamation returns to conclude before a purely instrumental *Presto.*)

Even more astonishing is the terzettino in the finale of the first act:

ALAIDE

98 Ah! non par _ tir:......... già sten _ de o _ scu_ra notte il

ve _ lo: fo _ sco, neb _ bio _ so è il cie _ lo, nes_

AL. _su _ na stel_la ap _ par. VAL. Fin _ chè un sol rag _ gio

V. splende, e gli e_le_menti han po _ sa, per la fo _ resta om_

The vocal parts are measured, lyrical recitative. What is unprecedented is the expressive urgency concentrated in the monophonic orchestral accompaniment. The shock of the harmonic shift down a half step to E flat major introduces a single phrase of *arioso* with beautiful effect, but the elegiac intensity is dependent on the opening motif of the orchestra, so impressive that Bellini brings it back as a motto at the opening of the duet in the second act (an effect more characteristic at that time of French opera than of Italian).

The aria-finale of *La Straniera* demonstrates how Bellini's preference for expressive decoration over brilliance enabled him to lengthen his melodic lines:

The cadenza must be slow and expressive, and to be effective requires that the previous phrases be executed almost entirely without added ornaments. The means by which the cadenza withholds the final resolution is essentially no different from the way Bellini will delay resolution in the most famous melodies of *Norma* and *I Puritani*.

The experiment with pure lyrical declamation and bare monophonic lines in *La Straniera* was never repeated so dogmatically by Bellini, but it gave him the technique which produced the simple lyric intensity of the operas that followed, above all the final scene of *I Capuleti ed i Montecchi*. The recitative that opens the final duet of Romeo and Juliet, both dying, is at first stripped bare of almost all accompaniment:

It would be a mistake to think that here everything has been left to the singers. Bellini has done most of their work for them: the expression is built in to the bare lines, and the singers must only call upon the production of a beautiful sound and the simplest, most traditional conventions of phrasing.

The declamatory style is introduced even into the last concerted section. Romeo begins a cabaletta-like theme, but Giulietta's interjection *(ciel crudel)* is astonishingly simple. The expressive weight given here to such a phrase had not been heard on the operatic stage since Mozart's works, and it was rare even there:

Gradually the concerted form gives way again to declamation, and then to a rising sequence which achieves the climax:

The climax is, typically for Bellini, marked *con abbandono:* the power of this extraordinary moment does, indeed, depend upon the singers. The actual death of Romeo is once again declamation, interrupted in the middle of his singing Juliet's name. The passage displays a pattern, probably derived from the Rossini stretto, which Bellini was to make personal for the second half of a melody: a rising sequence with an agitated *accelerando* and a *ritenuto* at the climax. The greatest employment of this form is certainly the final pages of *Norma.*

We may sum up the ways in which Bellini imposes a lyrical intensity on every kind of texture and transforms the traditional Rossinian aria and ensemble structures into a more personal form. He introduces pure instrumental cantabiles into the initial *scena* of an aria or an ensemble following some remarkable precedents by Rossini, but Bellini's have a density lacking in the work of the older master. The *scena* before the first-act duet in *Il Pirata* ("Tu sciagurato") has an extraordinary flowing movement:

and there are even complete formal arias for instruments alone, as in the opening *scena* of the finale of *Il Pirata,* a melody which predicts Donizetti's "Una furtiva lagrima." The lyricism here surpasses the examples that Bellini had learned from Rossini's instrumental "arias," even the impressive horn solo in *Otello* before the duet of Desdemona and Emilia. Above all, Bellini's instrumental solo has an astonishing dramatic function:

Here, this aria without words accompanies the signs of the heroine's madness; it is less an illustration of her delirium than a mournful commentary on it. To these devices for giving lyric intensity to the sections of action and recitative must be added the many *ariosos*—fragments of vocal melody that informally break down the passages of dialogue, lyric interruptions of the drama.

Going from the other direction, Bellini introduces recitative-like passages into the closed forms of aria and ensemble. We have seen this most radically in *La Straniera,* and, earlier, Imogene's cavatina (entrance aria) in *Il Pirata* already has a semi-recitative or declamatory texture for its principal slow section *(Andante assai mosso).* The innovation here is its place in the formal structure, which demands that this declamatory line be sung *cantabile:*

The penultimate opera of Bellini, *Beatrice di Tenda,* is an unsatisfactory masterpiece that was a disaster at its premiere and is rarely produced. Both heroine and hero are unattractive, but the work contains some of the composer's most impressive music. Here we have two of the finest examples of Bellini's ideal of integrating the lyrical and the dramatic. The duet that opens the first-act finale presents a wonderfully balanced single melody as a dialogue between the duchess, Beatrice, and Orombello, the courtier who loves her:

The technique is not original with Bellini, but the lyrical sweep of the melody gains extraordinary tension when broken up in this antiphonal dialogue.

More impressive still, and more innovative, is the use, in the middle of a *scena,* of an instrumental *arioso* that is interrupted and finished by the singer. The aria of the Duke of Milan, Filippo, in the second act, begins with a *scena* of great richness and variety. Filippo meditates on the death sentence he is about to pass on his wife. His recitative becomes a lyrical *arioso,* and then turns into a pure instrumental solo on which the Duke first comments and then takes over and finishes, instrumental and vocal line becoming one:

Much of the emotional power of Bellini's music derives from the tension generated by the long, sustained arabesques described by his melodies and by the way the expressive dissonances in the melodies are set in relief with the utmost simplicity. In the famous mad scene from *I Puritani*, we first hear Elvira's voice from behind the scenes with a phrase that was the composer's most powerful invention:

The C♭ in bar 3 is resolved into the B♭ only after a leap upward to the F, and its expressive force is magnified by the postponement. In turn, the F is never resolved at all, and this refusal sets off Bellini from his predecessors—the dissonance (an appoggiatura to an E♭ that never appears) belongs to the chord with the C♭, and it lets this resonance linger as the phrase moves into new harmonies.

The principal melody of the mad scene reveals Bellini's art of postponing the inevitable resolution and cadence:

The melody is atypical in that some of its notes (as in bar 3) are present only in the orchestra, but the apparent inability of the singer to realize the entire melodic line is a symbol of the distress and anguish of the now crazed heroine. The way Bellini refuses to let the melody pause even on a half cadence is beautifully evident in bar 5. The brief vocal pause two bars later is a moment of chromatic dissonance on a diminished seventh chord that drives forward to the cadence, and this is realized as a long, slow descent that suddenly rises expressively upward once again just before the end. We may today rejoice in the simple, even primitive quality of Bellini's accompaniment, which has often been deplored: anything else, as he claimed, would detract from the intensity of listening demanded by his melodies.

Part of this intensity is created not only by length but also by the way the melody pulls beyond the expected range. In the most celebrated of Bellini's arias, "Casta Diva" (Chaste Goddess) from *Norma,* the second part of the opening period rises with extraordinary effect from the limited range of the beginning, and also opposes the conventional ornamentation of the first bars with a more slowly moving, larger, and more urgent contour:

NORMA

Ca - - sta Di - - va, ca - sta Di - va, che i - nar -

N

- gen - ti que - - - ste sa - - cre, que - ste

N

sa - cre, queste sacre an - tiche pian - te, a noi vol - gi il bel sem -

N

- bian - te, a — noi vol - gi, a noi vol gi il bel sem bian . . . . . .

sempre cresc. sino al.....

sempre cresc. sino al.........

The increase of tension is subtle and depends on the simplest details, above all the way bars 5 to 8 almost repeat 1 to 4, but with the pitch and the harmony raised from tonic major to supertonic minor. Typical of Bellini's economy is the way that the cadential turn in bar 2

is beautifully altered in bar 6 to:

This may seem minimal, but it is exactly enough to increase the pathos. The contrast between the static first half of the melody and the more dynamic second half is already found, on a lower scale, between the first two bars and the two succeeding. Bellini's art lies, above all, in the way that from bar 9 onward, the increase in range and passion is not sudden and unprepared but gradual and, above all, unremitting. There is no leap at a high note but a steady movement relentlessly propelled by the harmony towards the high B♭ with a sudden acceleration at the end of bar 11 that is breathtaking. No loss of intensity appears after this climax; rather, there is a controlled slow descent. Every beat in the final bars starts with a melodic dissonance, and the expressive power is sustained up to the final tonic note.

Bellini's supreme achievement is the final scene of *Norma*, where his ability to sustain a long line is now applied to the entire stretto:

Wagner, listening to these pages is said to have exclaimed admiringly, "This, Richard Wagner could not have done!" It was, in fact, the only part of Bellini's art that Wagner ever learned to master, and the final scene of *Norma* remained the model for much of his music as late as *Tristan und Isolde*.

One of the major problems in opera from its inception almost ceases to exist in the finest works of Bellini: the problem of action in music. He does not solve the problem, but ignores or evades it. The music of *Norma*, for example, even the choruses like the procession of the Druids and the call to war *("Guerra, guerra!")* are a succession of arrested states of feeling, lyric and intense. They exist in musical time, but seem to have little to do with dramatic time, or time of action. To a certain extent, this is necessarily true of all opera, where action momentarily ceases to exist as musical form fulfills itself, but rarely does the realization of dramatic incident in music descend so close to zero as it does in Bellini. This is not because his prose is incompetent, but because the poetic moments are rendered with a passion so much greater that it makes the dramatic frame that surrounds them unimportant. Even in a passage of such ferocity as Norma's announcement of vengeance, *"In mia man alfin tu sei"* (At last you are in my hands), the lyricism overpowers any sense of dramatic development:

This is why so little seems to happen in *Norma,* and almost all of that in the final act. It is like a play by Racine, *Bérénice* above all, in which the action is implicit in the expression of feeling and passion. This is, in a sense, the ideal operatic style of the early nineteenth century, but it is not the one the rest of the century wanted, and Bellini's elegiac melody could not be reproduced—except, of course, by Chopin. Both Wagner and Verdi were profoundly influenced by him, but they achieved a fusion of lyric expression and drama on very different terms from those laid down by Bellini. His work was not a dead end but an isolated monument.

Meyerbeer

Meyerbeer had nothing of Bellini's exquisite sensibility or his art of creating a sense of passion through melody alone, and he had little of Donizetti's passion or ability to invent tunes that seemed a direct and natural expression of the text: but he had a feeling for long-range operatic rhythm that was unsurpassed in his time until the works of Wagner and Verdi of the late 1840s, and an understanding of the musical construction of large units—scenes, acts, and entire operas—that set the pattern for Wagner's early and late works and for the operas that Verdi wrote for the French stage. It was not simply that Meyerbeer knew how to make things work, but that he had a wonderful instinct for sustained dramatic power. His grasp of the relation of music to scenic action almost never faltered: he always seemed to realize that the effectiveness of a musical number depends as much on the way it is placed as on its content.

The most famous composer of his time, Meyerbeer will never recapture anything more than an insignificant fraction of his former glory. It is not so much that he has fallen too low ever to be able to recover as that any revaluation is too expensive. *Les Huguenots,* for example, requires at least six singers with the kind of authority that comes from international experience, including three sopranos capable of executing the most difficult and brilliant passage-work: frequent changes of scene, elaborate decor, a huge orchestra, and the necessity for numerous rehearsals of large crowd scenes complete the requirements. Even Richard Strauss's *Woman without a Shadow* makes fewer demands on the budget. In addition, Meyerbeer is no longer taken seriously. To my knowledge, the rare recent revivals have been either a signal for the stage directors to let loose all the most absurd effects that they had so far been prevented from carrying out, or else a perfunctory showcase for a single star to show off her talents, accompanied by a mediocre cast and an indifferently rehearsed orchestra.

The charges against Meyerbeer are heavy: his melodies are undistinguished, his harmony commonplace, the rhythm repetitive. None of these assertions is false, although many honorable exceptions can be found to each, but it makes one wonder how such despicable means enabled him to construct such long sequences of extraordinary effectiveness in the operas from 1830 onward. There remains the orchestration, often much admired—and justly, since Meyerbeer was sometimes capable of reaching Berlioz's level of craftsmanship and invention. In his major works, however, he was in a position to profit from Berlioz's previous achievements—and Berlioz, too, came from a vital French tradition, mostly underestimated, which experimented with new instrumental sonorities, a tradition which included Méhul and Lesueur, and which Rossini exploited in his French stage works. There are, however, moments in Meyerbeer that combine a sensibility to instrumental sound with wonderful originality. The air of Raoul in act 1 of *Les Huguenots* has an accompaniment realized at first only by a solo viola that traces its lines above and below the voice:

Here one cannot distinguish between orchestration and musical conception. It is noteworthy that this obbligato, novel both in sonority and in contrapuntal invention, sets in relief one of Meyerbeer's finest melodies.

What gave Meyerbeer his supremacy, however, was not orchestration but dramatic impact: he knew how to adapt music to action—above all, how to fit music to the complicated twists of plot of the French historical melodrama. The melodies of his airs are often no better than serviceable; the harmony is relatively uninventive until his last work, *L'Africaine,* where he was able to assimilate some of the lessons of Wagner; but the suiting of music to dramatic action is impeccable—lucid, economical, effective, and deeply original. Following Auber, but with much greater logic, he adapted the swift-moving procedures of comic opera to the tragic stage. In one sense, he degraded and vulgarized serious French opera, which had become unbearably dignified and slow-moving with Cherubini and Spontini. Meyerbeer destroyed the dignity and retained the grandeur and the pretensions to the sublime. The incidents move rapidly in his music, just exactly as fast as one needs for understanding without awkwardness, incoherence, or ambiguity.

The fourth act of *Les Huguenots* remained unsurpassed, and even unequalled, in French grand opera before the fourth act of Verdi's *Don Carlos,* also written for Paris. In this act the noble Catholic conspirators meet to have the daggers with which they will massacre the Protestants that night blessed by two monks. The Protestant hero, Raoul, hidden by the Catholic heroine, Valentine, Countess of Nevers, overhears the plot and is about to rush off to warn and join the victims but is delayed by Valentine's involuntary declaration of love for him. The delay will be fatal.

Even Meyerbeer's most implacable detractors, even Schumann, admired this act, one of the most splendidly constructed and moving creations of the Romantic scene. The chorus of conspirators, modelled on the "Marseillaise" (as Schumann observed), is wonderfully invigorating, without, however, much quality or refinement. Any Bellinian refinement would be out of place: Meyerbeer is depicting the aristocrats as a mob. With the next number, the benediction of the poignards, refinement would be equally absurd. It is a chorale, with a dotted accompaniment in the Baroque style, then considered proper for religious music, with an effect unprecedented in its savagery:

The harsh string passage at the end of each phrase of the chorale has a sarcastic edge to it, and this is confirmed by the rescoring at its reappearance with the amazing squeals added in the woodwind:

This does not depict or represent the action or even the emotion: it induces the emotional response of the listener by irritating his sensibility. The music is less a mirror than a stimulus. It may be compared to the *style artiste* a few years later of the Goncourt brothers, which was meant not so much to describe but almost, so to speak, to hammer what was represented physically into the reader's head. The music arouses sentiment by grating on the ear, as in this case, or by caressing it in others. It points towards the style of Richard Strauss.

After the conspiracy, the love duet treats a simple motif with what would become, a few years later, a Verdian pathos:

The climax of the duet, Raoul's understanding of the significance of Valentine's involuntary confession of love, is an invention of Meyerbeer that became one of the most important conceptions for later operatic composers, the model for most of the moving cries from the heart with which Verdi, Puccini, and others would close their passionate scenes:

This passage was remembered for decades to come: the string tremolo, the cello melody, the drive toward a high register, and above all the expressive curve of the melody which combines a wonderful sweetness with a dissonant outline of a ninth and an emphasized tritone—one of Meyerbeer's finest inspirations. It is curious to reflect that it is supposed to have been a last-minute addition: the tenor felt he had not enough to sing at the end of the scene, and brought Meyerbeer a few new lines to set. The passage puts into unforgettable lyric form a moment of action which would otherwise have been left to accompanied recitative. This moment is the ancestor of Violetta's wonderful cry *"Amami Alfredo"* from *La Traviata,* and also the model for the scene in *Il Ballo in maschera,* where the situation from *Les Huguenots* is almost literally repeated: Amelia involuntarily confesses her love for Riccardo and causes him to delay his departure, with fatal results—once again, the tremelo in the strings, the cello melody, and the impassioned tenor cry reappear as if on cue.

Meyerbeer's approach to opera may seem cynical. His music is not, like Donizetti's, an immediate expression of the sentiments of his characters but a calculated manipulation of the audience. It must be admitted that there is indeed something cynical about placing an ice-skating ballet (performed, however, on the newly invented roller-skates) in an opera about fifteenth-century religious and social problems. The cynicism, however, reflects the dramaturgy of the preeminent librettist Eugène Scribe, for whom major historical changes depended upon trivial but picturesque accidents—whether someone at the court brought a glass of water; whether the leader of the Sicilian rebels discovered he was the bastard son of the general of the French occupying forces. Valentine's unconscious betrayal of her love and Raoul's hesitation represent just such a trivial incident, and the implication that the fate of French Protestantism hangs in the balance emphasizes the personal element present in all historical action, but runs the risk of transforming history into material for cheap melodrama. Meyerbeer knew how to make the most of such a *coup de théâtre,* and how to make it the center of an elaborate musical form. He gave extraordinary musical vitality to historical melodrama. More clearly than Rossini and Auber, he produced a model of Romantic grand opera from which other composers could learn. He did not ennoble the form as Bellini had done with the Italian model. It remained in his hands a debased but effective form with moments of great power.

CHAPTER TWELVE

Schumann: Triumph and Failure
of the Romantic Ideal

The irrational

In the early nineteenth century, madness had its attractions as well as its terrors. On June 9, 1796, the young Charles Lamb wrote to his equally youthful friend Samuel Taylor Coleridge about a brief period when he had been in an insane asylum:

> I look back upon it at times with a gloomy kind of Envy. For while it lasted I had many hours of pure happiness. Dream not Coleridge, of having tasted all the grandeur and wildness of Fancy, till you have gone mad. All now seems to me vapid; comparatively so.

Some years later, in 1819, William Blake, fascinated by a passage on religious mania in a book called *Observations on the Deranged Manifestations of the Mind, or Insanity*, wrote on the flyleaf an account of a vision of the poet William Cowper, recently dead after many years of bitter religious melancholia:

> Methodism etc. p. 144. Cowper came to me and said: "O that I were insane always I will never rest. Can you not make me truly insane? I will never rest till I am so. O that in the bosom of God I was hid. You retain health and yet are as mad as any of us all—over us all—mad as a refuge from unbelief—from Bacon, Newton and Locke."

"Mad as a refuge from unbelief," from what was felt as the monotonous and unsatisfying rationality of the modern scientific and philosophic movement. It is significant, however, that religion alone did not seem to provide an adequate refuge—neither the conservative established churches on the continent and in England nor even the new popular sects were able to fill an intellectual and emotional void. The terrifying religious thought of Joseph de Maistre, in which any religious institution depended upon blind obedience to an absolutely arbitrary divine will, just as all civilization and culture rested upon the continuous practice of capital punishment, was like a form of religious melancholia hardened into dogma—and this, indeed, explains its curious fascination for nineteenth-century intellectuals.

Like Blake, Gerard de Nerval in 1855 insisted upon the essential health of the insane; on the first page of his most impressive work, *Aurélia,* which purports to be a description of his sensations and visions during a period of mental illness, he writes: "I do not know why they call it illness—I never felt better." By the beginning of the nineteenth century, madness—for writers, painters, and musicians—was not simply a withdrawal from the distress of everyday life, a protest against intolerable social conditions or against a debilitating philosophy. It had gained a new ideological charge: madness was a source of creative energy.

It would be cruel to say that madness had then become fashionable, as it was always the subject of profound anguish, but there is a grain of truth. There were precedents from the classical and medieval worlds for the almost religious awe that madness could inspire, but the idea gained new force. Several of the finest German writers of the generation born around 1780 would be considered clinically insane by most standards: Friedrich Hölderlin passed the last decades of his life in an almost total schizophrenia, Heinrich von Kleist ended his with a suicide pact, and Clemens Brentano was afflicted with a religious melancholia and depression as great as Cowper's. In these cases and others, the most remarkable creative work was accomplished before the onset of mental illness (unlike the case of the great mad English poets Christopher Smart and John Clare, who did some of their most memorable writing within the walls of an insane asylum). Nevertheless, for all these writers—and for many of their contemporaries—madness was an ideal as well as an anti-ideal, a state that transcended consciousness and escaped the mechanical and blind workings of rationalism, but also a state that could not be controlled and could end with the destruction of the individual mind.

Madness, for the Romantic artist, was more than the breakdown of rational thought; it was an alternative which promised not only different insights but also a different logic. As Hölderlin wrote in 1801:[1]

So! and exultant madness may well mock mockery
When it suddenly seizes the singers in holy night.

Drum! und spotten des Spotts mag gern frohlockender Wahnsinn,
Wenn er in heiliger Nacht plötzlich die Sänger ergreift.

Madness was an unpredictable form of inspiration. It had its own ritual of demonstration and its own methods of persuasion, a logic of the night and of

---

1. Friedrich Hölderlin, "Bread and Wine," lines 47–48.

dreams, in some ways as powerful and as convincing as the logic of the day. Nowhere is this clearer than in the work of E. T. A. Hoffmann, who exerted the most profound influence on Robert Schumann. In his stories, the world of everyday reality coexists with a hallucinatory world of delusion which gives significance to the former: the "real" world has priority but is unintelligible without the irrational and often absurd world of shadows, magic, and paranoia that is always present.

Schumann was haunted from the age of seventeen by the fear of going mad. Only at the end of his short life were these fears realized. In 1854, aged forty-four, two years before his death, Schumann voluntarily incarcerated himself in an insane asylum. In his greatest creative years, from the age of twenty to thirty, he played with the idea of insanity, incorporating elements of madness into his work—his criticism as well as his music—inventing wonderful effects of logical incoherence and schizophrenia. Whatever Schumann's personal disposition, these elements are clearly stylistic rather than autobiographical. We have no warrant for taking them even as superficial reflections of Schumann's private life. In the rare case that we find an interesting correspondence between Schumann's art and his life, we must remember that the desire of the Romantic artist to express his personality through his work is no stronger than the effort to make his private character conform visibly to the stylistic personality of the work itself. The Romantic ideal of the unity of life and work is not one which made the work subsidiary to, and dependent on, the artists' private affairs. The most interesting composers have arranged their lives and even their personalities in order to realize their projects and their conceptions most effectively and convincingly. Even the common assumption that a composer's private life—his loves, his success, his despairs—provide him with the precise emotional experiences which he then somehow renders into music is not tenable; for many composers a purely musical experience is as powerful a sensation as anything outside music. I suspect, indeed, that in some cases—that of Beethoven, in particular—a composer has tried to find experiences in his life outside music as powerful and as concentrated as those that came to him from music itself.

Whether the source was personal or stylistic, Schumann was both drawn irresistibly to madness and repelled by it, fascinated and terrified at the same time. He is, in fact, the composer who achieved the most powerful musical representations of pathological states of feeling before Wagner, and some of his music has, because of its modest scale, a concentration denied to the necessarily more diffuse form of large-scale stage works. Indeed, the small scale was sometimes essential to Schumann's technique: the moments of greatest power often arrive almost unprepared, and they take the listener by surprise. A work of larger dimensions cannot astonish in this way: in a symphony or opera even a surprising dramatic reversal must be led up to carefully, and a climax which is purely psychological needs an even more prudent construction. Schumann can effect a kind of shock denied to Wagner and Verdi.

The third song of the Heine *Liederkreis* is one of Schumann's most extraordinary achievements. Heine's poem is elegantly moving, at once nostalgic and bitter. Music will always make verse of this kind more directly affecting, but no one would have suspected the intensity of Schumann's setting and the way he transforms Heine's charming central conceit into a kind of hallucination:

> I wandered under the trees
> Alone with my sorrow:
> The old dreaming came
> And slipped into my heart.
>
> Who taught you this little word
> You birds in the airy heights?
> Be still! if my heart hears it
> It brings once again such pain.
>
> There came a young girl
> Who sang it over and over:
> There have we birds taken
> That beautiful golden word.
>
> You should not have told me
> You wonderfully sly birds.
> You want to rob me of my grief.
> But I trust no one.

14
hat euch dies Wört_lein ge_ _ _leh_ret, ihr Vög_lein in luf_ _ti_ger Höh? Schweigt
18
ritard.
Langsamer.
still, wenn mein Herz es hö_ret, dann thut es noch ein_mal so weh. Es
Ped.
23
rit.
kam ein Jung_fräu_lein ge_ _ _gan_gen, die sang es im_ _ _mer fort, da
27
rit.
ha_ben wir Vög_lein ge_ _ _fan_gen das hüb_sche gold_ _ne Wort. Das
31
sollt ihr mir nicht er_ _ _zäh_len, ihr Vög_lein wun_ _ _der_ _schlau; ihr
35
ri_tar_dan_do.
wollt mei_nen Kum_mer mir steh_len, ich a_ber Niemanden trau, ich a_ber Niemanden

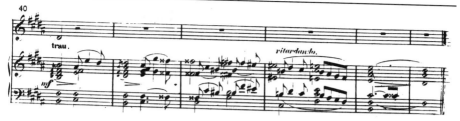

The introduction is a masterpiece of fake counterpoint—and I do not use "fake" pejoratively but to indicate the illusion of polyphony where little true polyphony is to be found. It is a great art of illusion. There seems to be four-voice polyphony in this introduction, but the three upper voices are all devoted to tracing the same line, mostly in parallel but with an occasional appearance of independence. The line is basic to the song, a partial synthesis of what is to come:

The line is here unfinished and unresolved, and will remain so until the end of the fourth and last stanza. The passionately expressive character comes from the obsessive use of tritones that define the melodic contour:

The song proper begins inexpressively; it is unassuming, neutral, and with no sense of movement for the first four bars, which only repeat the same few notes and employ the simplest tonic and dominant seventh harmonies. The next four bars—"The old dreaming came and slipped into my heart"—are among the most powerful in all of Romantic music: the phrase starts to move and expand, the range doubles; and harmony and polyphony become suddenly more complex. As in the introduction, the apex is G♯, and there is, in fact, a triple move to G♯. This emphasis is crucial for the whole song. First the tenor in bar 9 rises chromatically:

Then the vocal line doubled by the upper line in the piano moves down to G♯, and then leaps up to the G♯ above, both notes emphasized by a grace note that gives an expressive sense of effort:

This beautiful motif is repeated in descending sequence by the alto, and then by the tenor, which rises once again to G♯ and ends the stanza on the crucial dissonance of a ninth chord:

The beauty of the second half of the stanza is due only in part to a contrast with the inexpressive, neutral opening of the melody. What is characteristic of Schumann's inspiration is the way that everything changes at once: the new harmonic richness, the sudden rhythmic acceleration of bar 11 and the leap into a high register, the new polyphonic complexity with the series of imitations—a genuine contrapuntal structure here. It is the swiftness with which all this happens that makes the emotion so overpowering. What is most extraordinary, however, and accounts for the intensity of expression is that while the polyphony is "real," the cadence is "false"; that is, the melody at the end of the stanza mimics the form and structure of a perfect cadence (with the right harmony, in fact, it would be a full cadence), but fails to resolve and ends on a dissonant chord. The phrase is at once complete and suspended in midflight. It is the combination of a satisfactory full close and a frustration arrived at by a simple and logical sequence that gives this passage its ambiguous reflection of the poet's resignation and impossible desire. The contradiction implicit in the poetry is made sensuously immediate by the music.

The second stanza differs only in two respects from the first: the opening phrase is no longer an unassuming *piano* but is marked *mezzo forte*, which calls for a more emphatic performance, although the wonderful second phrase returns to the soft dynamics of the first appearance; and, most important, the last note of the stanza is no longer a G♯ but a startling G♮. This descent from G♯ to G♮ not only repeats the climax of the basic melodic line of the introduction but also prepares the birds' song of the third stanza.

At first sight, this third stanza (bars 23 to 30), building on the G♮, is in the key of G major. When is a key not a key? When it is nothing more than a simple chord; when the relation of tonic and dominant does not function within it; when the tonic note is not the center or the basis of resolution. All these negatives are true of the third stanza, which is indeed not in G major; but it is not in any other key either.

The sense of unreality is promoted first by the transparent airy sonority and the new slower tempo. The sonority, however, depends to some extent on the ambiguous harmony—or, rather, the ambiguity is enforced by the sound and the tone color. The piano part is now an undifferentiated *pianissimo*, and it lies mostly above the vocal line (sung properly by a tenor), which actually provides a bass to the ethereal accompaniment. Since, as so often in Schumann and other composers of *Lieder*, the upper line in the piano largely doubles the vocal melody, the effect here is disquieting and strange, as the bass (in the vocal part) and the melody two octaves above in the piano are almost consistently parallel: the exceptions in fact only reinforce the parallelism of bass and soprano. Four times the piano suddenly provides a new bass slightly below the voice, but this added bass closely echoes the vocal melody (bars 23–24 and elsewhere):

The tied grace notes mean that the bass must be set into relief by slightly preceding the melody (grace notes in Schumann must be played before the beat, those in Chopin with the beat). We must remember that the tenor is sung an octave below the notation, and that the singer's notes are therefore identical with those in the piano bass.

These added bass notes are important not only as an echo of the motif in the voice but also because they impose the harmonic ambiguity. The third stanza starts as if G♮ were the bass, as if the chord were in fundamental or root position, but the bass is suddenly taken over by the rising motif B–D, giving only the first and second inversions of the G major chord, and nothing more is heard of the elusive root position. The third stanza, in short, consists essentially of the obsessive repetition of a G major chord (twenty times in fact), while the third and seventh bars of the stanza do nothing beyond a soft decoration of this chord. Twenty repetitions of a G major chord will still not give us the key of G, and no preceding modulation has established a new tonality. The suggestion of the key of G major is as unreal as the song of the birds that it so exquisitely represents. Nor is there any transition from G back to B major: the fourth stanza returns to the reality of B major as if the third had never existed—which in one sense is true.

The note G♮ never appears in the melody of the third stanza; the melodic center is still B. In fact, the melodic contour is a twisted variation of the first two bars of the vocal melody:

Almost all movement has been removed from the original form. The third stanza is immobile: it does not develop, it has no direction, it is a static aural image. The presence of a G♮ in every chord of this stanza may not succeed in imposing the tonality of G major, but it does impose the sense that all action has been brought to a halt. The immobility works, of course, directly on the emotions. Time seems to stop: the music hovers indecisively in an undefined tonal region that has no solid foundation.

The last stanza begins by reproducing the neutral opening phrase, simple as a folk song. Then the second phrase moves again to G♯, and brings the melodic line gradually down, recalling not the expressive motif of the first stanza but the contour of the introduction; this time the line resolves to D♯:

Even the left hand of the pianist echoes part of this descent:

After the voice concludes, the postlude repeats the introduction, but now *mezzo forte* instead of *piano,* and the line is resolved into the D♯ in both upper line and inner voice:

The clash between G♯ and G♮ is the central element of both small-scale expressive detail and large-scale structure. Stanza 1 uses the G♯ for its climax in a sublimely inspired moment; stanza 2 lowers the G♯ to G♮ in a last-minute shock; stanza 3 magnifies the G♮ as an unreal vision; stanza 4 resolves the opposition. The end of the final stanza in the piano shows that this detail still preoccupies the composer:

As the upper line reasserts the G♯ immediately after the G♮ in the lower voice, the passion ebbs out of the music with this resolution. The end is resigned but bitter.

The lightness of Heine's verse is destroyed by the music, which emphasizes the implicit bitterness; the return of the old dreaming is more powerful and more anguished in the song. The poet's neurotic nursing of his grief ceases to be witty and becomes painful; the song of the birds is no longer a charming

literary trope but an uncanny vision of the irrational. A single chord obsessively
repeated to create the momentary but unpersuasive illusion of a new central
tonality, a sudden increase of density, texture, range, melodic and harmonic
motion, and chromaticism combine with the quiet dynamics to create a cadence
which turns out to be a suspended dissonance—these musical devices endow
the poetry with an unsuspected power. The form of the song, basically a
semistrophic type derived from Schubert, a slightly altered *AABA,* is given an
idiosyncratic twist by refusing any resolution to the first two appearances of
A and by giving *B* a harmonic character difficult to classify. As the final chord
arrives, the tonic note in the bass is removed, leaving the B major chord
suspended in a 6/4 inversion. Schumann used the same end to his Self-portrait
as Introvert, "Eusebius," in *Carnaval.* It makes a closure at once complete and
incomplete, leaving the harmony of a final tonic chord but taking away the
bass root, as if only the overtones of the tonic note were sustained. The
resolution is not questioned, but only left open to question. Throughout his
short musical life, Schumann produced his most striking works not by developing and extending Classical procedures and forms but by subverting them,
sometimes undermining their functions and even making them momentarily
unintelligible.

The suspension of traditional musical logic is perhaps most perceptible with
Schumann's occasional attempts to destroy the listener's sense of the bar line.
This is rarely done by Schumann in order to give the impression of freedom,
as in a cadenza as Mendelssohn had done (in the introduction to the last
movement of his Piano Sonata in E Major, for example), but rather for shock
value, as if a competing system of rhythm had suddenly invalidated one already
established in the piece, but without being able to replace it completely. The
most famous of these moments is found near the end of the Toccata:

At first the contrast between the two notes played *fortissimo* and the rest of
the bar *pianissimo* is outrageous only on the surface, but it provides the basis
for a shift of bar accent as the sixteenth-note upbeat begins to sound like the

downbeat with a more lyrical line.[2] The anticipation of the bar line proceeds for some time, but at the climax the former system begins to reassert itself in the left hand and the two compete on equal terms for four bars until the left hand at 256 finally conforms to the bar line with a jolt:

2. It is clear that the dynamics are to continue for sixteen bars even though Schumann stops indicating them and leaves it to the good sense of the pianist.

A similar and even more disruptive effect occurs in the *Humoresk*, with the right hand marked *mezzo forte* "As if out of tempo," and the left *pianissimo* "In tempo":

Wie ausser Tempo ("As if out of tempo") does not mean played freely; the direction means that the right hand is to sound as if it were notated as follows:

in a beat that conflicts with the left hand and with the bar line. (The indication *senza tempo* in the introduction to the finale of Mendelssohn's Sonata in E Major (quoted above, page 574) must be interpreted in the same way.) Similarly, in the introduction to the final fugue of Beethoven's *Hammerklavier,* the rhythm is not free (the composer even gives a metronome mark), but there is to be no feeling of a bar line, and in fact the bar lines are omitted by Beethoven. In Schumann's *Humoresk,* however, the left hand continues to enforce the written bar line, while the right hand displaces it, a combination fairly tricky to execute. This rhythmic effect must be distinguished from the elaborate cross-rhythms that previous composers, Mozart in particular, had conceived (a rhythm of eight against three in the finale of Mozart's Oboe Quartet, for example). The opposition in Schumann is both simpler and far more disconcerting: both hands are in a simple 2/4, but out of phase. What this sets up is a self-contradictory rhythmic framework.

This is an extreme point of Schumann's style—although it is a hidden constant, a latent possibility in much of his work, in which so many details of harmony and rhythm are so often momentarily out of phase that the danger of spilling over into a genuinely systematic contradiction is a menace, never far from the surface. This page of the *Humoresk* is certainly intended as both serious and humorous; above all, it is capricious and fantastic.

The *Humoresk* is the last of the great piano works that Schumann wrote between the age of twenty and twenty-nine; it is one of the most sophisticated of his creations, perhaps the subtlest and most personal, although the large-scale structure is no longer controlled with the full power and the energy that Schumann had shown a year or two previously with the *Davidsbündlertänze* and the C Major Phantasie. The dislocation of Classical rhythm and syntax began, however, many years before that with his first published works. In one sense Schumann's style was parasitic: it often depended upon calling up the expectations of the works of previous composers, Beethoven in particular. This dependence paradoxically brought out his originality: the imitation was rarely servile. Beethoven's forms were twisted to meet Schumann's very different musical intentions.

The inspiration of Beethoven and Clara Wieck

The early *Impromptus on a Theme of Clara Wieck,* op. 5, based on Beethoven's "Eroica" Variations for Piano, reveal both the dependence and the radical originality. The theme was by the thirteen-year-old Clara, but the harmonization was Robert's. The melody has been called awkward, but this very ungainliness gives it an extremely personal character, which provided Schumann with some of his most personal inspirations. Clara Wieck was undoubtedly a great talent, perhaps the chief disaster of the nineteenth century's prejudice against female composers, which has lasted, indeed, until today. It is true that her least academic works were all composed before she was eighteen, but that is also true of Mendelssohn. Her ambitions as a composer were repressed by Robert Schumann after marriage, although before that she herself had already decided that she would have to abandon the effort to continue, and she renounced all hope of a full career as a composer. Her individual melodic ideas are often original and idiosyncratic, but the large forms are almost always derivative. Her Scherzo in D Minor, op. 10, for example,

is evidently a simplification of Chopin's Scherzo no. 1 in B Minor:

Her most beautiful inspiration is the Notturno from the *Soirées musicales,*
op. 6, an amazing achievement for a sixteen-year-old:

This shows a mastery of a long melodic line that compares favorably with the
work of any of her contemporaries. It was incorporated, as a kind of homage,
by Robert Schumann into the last of his *Novelettes,* and he gave it an extraordinary effectiveness in the large form that she could never attain: it appears
like a memory, called "a voice from afar." However, there is no way to evaluate
her work properly: she was offered no proper encouragement, not even, later,
by Brahms.

Schumann's *Impromptus* on her theme are a relatively strict set of variations;
the model of Beethoven's "Eroica" Variations is acknowledged openly at once.
Beethoven began mysteriously and humorously with the bass alone:

Schumann keeps the mystery but abandons the humor. He also abandons the opening chord that defines Beethoven's tonic: he does not need so decisive a clarity. (It is interesting that Beethoven started *An die ferne Geliebte* with the identical chord, and that when Liszt transcribed the song cycle for piano, he omitted just this opening chord. The generation of composers born in 1810 evidently wanted less definition.) In consequence, Schumann's bass becomes more ambiguous, more overtly poetic, and makes a lyrical introduction to Clara's Romance:

In this form, the theme seems to rise out of the bass as a kind of obbligato to it, and in the second variation Schumann writes a new melody over the bass, and then plays both Clara's and his own melodies together in counterpoint. It is the first variation, however, that reveals Schumann at his most personal:

The accents in the middle of the sustained chords are an example of Schumann's mysterious humor, similar to the effect toward the end of the "Abegg" Variations (see Chapter 1). They indicate that the chord must continue to resonate as it turns into a dissonance, but the paradoxical impossibility of execution must have intrigued the composer. With pages like this Schumann permanently enlarged musical experience. The treatment of dissonance is revolutionary: turning each chord into a dissonance by making it a suspension as the bass changes immediately after the chord is a traditional technique; resolving each dissonance only after a rest, however, is an open challenge to tradition. Every short pause separates a dissonance from its resolution, which becomes—in a rhythm consistently out of phase with the bass—a new attack rather than a release. This subverts the relation between consonance and dissonance which is the foundation of Western tonality.

In bar 4, by the time the resolution is reached at last, the bass changes, and what would have been a momentary consonance is now already another dissonance. The rests are the principal source of the poetic mood of this variation: they impose an impression of human breathing upon a keyboard instrument. The dissonances left floating during the momentary silences are the source of its continuously expressive sound, yet paradoxically the right hand gives no sense of a melodic line—it is all nothing but accompanying harmonies. The effect of melody suddenly appears in the upper voice for a brief moment at the climax on a G♯ in bars 11 and 12, when the line is not broken. The most beautiful and, indeed, most expressive detail is found at the end: the lowest note, A♭, of the next-to-last chord is sustained until its resolution at the end of the bar. This makes the final chord not an attack but, for the first time, a release. The sustained note calls attention to the chromatic descent in the alto,

and the A♭ is no doubt a reflection of the melodic climax on a G♯ three bars before. Its sudden isolation, however, as the rest of the chord disappears, and the way it is allowed to sing forth as a single note act as the composer's signature.

The original effect of sustaining a single note of a chord was removed by Schumann in the second edition, published some twenty years after the original composition. This presents us with the problem of Schumann's late revisions of his youthful works. It is understandable that a composer in his forties should have lost sympathy with the work he had written one or two decades earlier. In addition, Schumann's fears of insanity had increased, and the republication of the early works preceded only by a short time his voluntary entrance into a lunatic asylum. In some cases it would seem as if Schumann had gone through the early works to remove anything which might have seemed insance or even odd. His refusal to allow the A♭ to be sustained as the chord disappears in this first variation of the *Impromptus* is paralleled by his refusal to allow the B at the end of the first phrase of the *Davidsbündlertänze* to continue to sound and to become the first note of the new melody. In both cases what is most idiosyncratic in his musical invention is erased by Schumann in an apparent attempt to make his work sound like everybody else's. There is no more Schumannesque effect than the single note that detaches itself from a cloud of sonority.

It is perhaps wrong, however, to give a purely personal explanation for what was a much larger phenomenon. In the early 1850s, when Schumann's second versions appeared, there had been a change in the artistic climate, and a return to a more academic classicism was in the air, with Brahms as its greatest representative. Even more important was the difficulty experienced in all the arts of sustaining the original revolutionary energy of what we still think of as Romantic style. Ingres repainted many of his early pictures to give them what he must have considered a more classical look, and the revisions of their great early works by Wordsworth, Coleridge, Goethe, Sénancour, and Chateaubriand are often as disastrous as Schumann's, and for much the same reason: what was most radical and characteristic of each author was either expunged or smoothed out. All these artists had lost much of the faith that had inspired those years when they first found an individual voice.

The third variation of the *Impromptus* was excised in the later edition. It is a typical study in playing melody and accompaniment in systematically opposed rhythmic frames:

In its place we find a new variation in Mendelssohnian style:

This is charming, and it demonstrates that the revisions did not necessarily result in something worse, although always in something less characteristic.

The finale of the *Impromptus* returns to the model of Beethoven, although now inflected by the influence of Bach. The "Eroica" Variations had ended with a brilliant fugue followed by a return of the principal theme. Beethoven was synthesizing three traditions: a finale in fugal form, a finale as a brilliant Allegro fantasia, and a return of the theme at the original slower tempo. To this Schumann adds a fourth tradition derived from the Bach suites: the finale as fugal gigue. Oddly, Schumann writes a plain, nonfugal gigue as a full variation, and then follows it with the fugue.

Beethoven had used the bass of his original theme as a fugue theme:

Schumann's imitation is so uncharacteristically servile that we must assume he expected us to notice the model and appreciate his new handling:

In the nineteenth century, the fugue had become a demonstration of conventional mastery, a proof of craftsmanship. Besides competing with Beethoven, Schumann conforms to the standard pattern of fugue laid down by Cherubini.

At one point, however, he essays a complexity of rhythmic structure that is very personal, and has little precedent in its self-contradictory opposition of various rhythmic periods:

The basic time signature is 6/8, and the gigue rhythm maintains this steadily with a pattern that repeats in every bar:

The harmonic sequence, however, a simple circle of fifths, moves with a period of 9/8, or every one-and-a-half bars. The harmony descends a second every nine beats:

The melodic line is double: descending thirds in groups of four every nine beats, at which point the pattern repeats a second lower in a descending scale. A syncopated upper voice rearranges the descending scale against the groups of nine in alternating sets of twelve and six, by sustaining some of the notes:

The descending scale moves only on weak beats, which makes the pattern of the *sforzandi* more remarkable, as they occur on the downbeat of every second bar, cutting across both the melodic and harmonic patterns. The bass has a complex acceleration, entering late in this passage to drive towards the half cadence on the dominant:

A diagram of the various rhythmic patterns will clarify this (see next page).

These independent shapes, although difficult to keep clear and separate in performance, do not give an impression of an overzealous pedantry. The basic harmony is too simple for that, but all these cross-rhythms give it a density, and cast a continuously changing light on different parts of the descending harmonic sequence. The entrance of the bass, out of phase with everything else, sets the move to the cadence dramatically into relief. The influence of Bach is apparent here: more than any of his contemporaries, Bach tended to vary the carrying out of the simpler harmonic sequences, but he never attained the dynamic complexity of this page of Schumann.

A later passage of the fugue combines a most unpianistic texture with a remarkable pianistic effect:

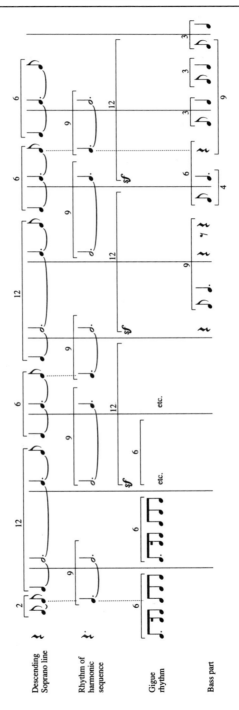

The passage demonstrates a particular aspect of the influence of Bach on the early nineteenth-century musician: the attempt to play the organ works on the piano. This page appears to require a pedal keyboard, as it is strictly impossible for two hands to encompass all those notes. That is, however, precisely what makes it so grand. The feeling of effort, of overcoming obstacles, of making it seem as if all those notes were really supposed to be struck together gives this climax much of its dramatic tension and accounts for its power. It certainly testifies to the fact that Schumann, like so many other musicians of his time and later, had been trying out the organ works of Bach on the piano. (It must have been this practice, rather than any stimulus of nineteenth-century organ music, that accounts for the invention a decade later of a piano with a pedal keyboard, for which Schumann wrote six beautiful canons.) The contrast with Chopin's experience of Bach is striking: as we have seen, Chopin reproduces in his own music the aural effect of playing Bach on the piano; Schumann, on the other hand, here reproduces the physical, muscular experience of playing Bach.

The fugue of the *Impromptus* ends with a complete reprise of the gigue, which in turn leads directly into a return of the first bars of the work, the bass of the theme, now played *fortissimo* in unison octaves, gradually diminishing as fragments of Clara's theme reappear. The last few seconds are the most astonishing closure that Schumann was ever to write. The theme disappears in the middle of a phrase. The bass continues softly until the end, but the harmonies simply disappear as well—the dissonances are left hanging in the air, unresolved, in a striking example of the aesthetics of the fragment:

In the last four bars, the dissonant interval of the major second C/D in the right hand does not resolve: the D is removed, leaving the C suspended, a

dissonance as well over the G in the bass. The final tonic note is left unharmonized. With this extraordinary ending, we touch one of the experimental
limits of Schumann's style, but one which illuminates, by its radical treatment
of dissonance, much of the later work.

The last phrase was revised and completely recomposed in the later edition
to provide a proper and more comfortable cadence:

This is certainly lovely, with its Biedermeier charm, but it has none of the
daring and mysterious poetry of the original.

The inspiration of E. T. A. Hoffmann

The experiments of the *Impromptus* were to leave their mark upon later works
with much greater power and more intense passion, above all the violent,
eccentric, and poetic *Kreisleriana,* op. 16, of 1838. The violence is evident on
the opening page, and so is the use of systematically opposed rhythmic periods.
In the first piece, the bass never coincides with a strong beat until the eighth
bar, and the extraordinary passage work, which seems to start in the middle
of a process already initiated before the piece begins, has a raging violence not
often met with:

In the original edition, printed here, the syncopation of the bass is set in relief as the upbeat to every strong beat in the right is intended to be marked: the six notes of each group are beamed as three, two, and one, and the last note has a separate tail. This implies a very slight but audible accent before the first and third beats of each bar, difficult to execute effectively but making it clear that all of the notes of the left hand are on offbeats (bars 1 to 8). In the second edition, the notation was ironed out:

The separate tails for the notes before the first and third beats have disappeared. Was the change made by the composer, or did the engraver, on his own, normalize the notation of all the triplets? It is difficult to say. In any case, if the slight extra emphasis in the right hand to the first and third beats is removed, the second and fourth beats seem to be the strong beats—and this is the way they sound in most performances. This effectively destroys the original rhythmic opposition of treble and bass, only resolved in the last four bars. Here the two hands are in phase, and the bass becomes an obbligato melody. The changes of beaming in bars 9 to 16 indicate very subtle alterations of phrasing and emphasis.

The middle section of this opening piece introduces, by its inner accents, a typical example of eccentric polyphony:

The accents in bars 34 and 38 introduce a new voice unprepared by what precedes, and which contradicts the basic harmony of the bar. This accented inner voice anticipates the harmony of the following bar: in fact, the dissonant A♭ of bar 34 does not appear to be resolved into the G in the second half of the bar but to be prolonged by the A♭ in bar 35. This kind of polyphony has little rational justification within the traditional system of counterpoint, vocal in nature: Schumann's polyphony, however, is essentially pianistic and coloristic. The dissonant A♭ of the unexpected inner voice colors the harmonic structure, and is apparently justified as a preparation, or even a pre-echo, of the harmony that follows. The interior accents reappear in the final bars (46 and 47) of this section:

These accents do not create any true polyphonic line: they emanate as if from a separate, independent voice, and do not cohere to form motif or theme. They give rhythmic emphasis (one must in fact linger almost imperceptibly on each accent to make it work without interrupting the flow) and they color the harmony, adding an inner density to the chords, but have no genuine melodic significance. Schumann's academic training was traditional and his study of Bach profound, but his treatment of polyphony foreshadows some of the developments that did not take place until almost a century later. Even Wagner's polyphony was more orthodox.

The title *Kreisleriana* comes from E. T. A. Hoffmann; the work is based, I think, less on the collection of stories and essays called *Kreisleriana* than on the novel *Kater Murr* (Cat Growl), which has Johannes Kreisler as its hero. In this unfinished novel, the manuscript account of the stormy and passionate life of the young musician is found by his cat, Murr, who proceeds to write his own autobiography on the back of each sheet of paper. The manuscript is sent in this state to the publisher, who prints it as he finds it, alternating pages of Kreisler and Murr. The events are seen from two perspectives, but the cat, although vain of his intelligence and learning (the beast has obviously read German idealist philosophy), regularly misunderstands what happens to the humans in whose company he finds himself—and we are at liberty to conclude that the humans, themselves surrounded by higher spiritual powers, are similarly unable to make perfect sense of their own mysterious lives. The alternation of passion and satire must have seized Schumann's imagination, giving him, as it were, an excuse to yoke together musical ideas that seem incompatible at first sight, to change mood and expression without warning, to go directly from a lyric meditation to a strangely sinister scherzo or an outburst of rage.

Schumann's greatest weakness was the handling of transitions: his larger works either continue the same rhythm almost obsessively for long periods or break down continuously to start new sections (examples of the first solution are the Toccata for Piano in C Major, the first movement of the Piano Sonata in G Minor, and the finale of the *Concerto without Orchestra* (the F Minor Piano Sonata); of the second, the finales of the Piano Sonatas in G Minor and F sharp Minor). The first movement of the Fantasy in C Major owes its supremacy among all the long movements to the idea of using the splintering into fragments as a formal principle, but this work, as Schumann himself knew, is unique, unrepeatable. In compensation, his greatest strength in formal construction was his ability to make a unity out of the most disparate material, to create a single work out of apparently complete single miniatures. Schumann had an uncanny genius for being able to place a tiny, and often almost insignificant, detail into a phrase which would turn it into a fragment, would force the listener into agreeing that something further was needed, that the music must continue beyond the written text. The song cycles, with the *Carnaval* and the *Davidsbündlertänze,* are the great achievements of this kind of genius: the individual elements welded together are very short, on the average about two minutes long. The *Kreisleriana,* however, deals with durations that are more ambitious; it takes as long as the eighteen dances of the *Davidsbündlertänze* but contains only eight pieces. The method of construction was therefore somewhat different, necessarily so if the air of caprice and willful imagination was to be preserved.

The central tonality is defined gradually but persuasively. The successive key centers are:

1. D minor–B flat major–D minor

2. B flat major–G minor–B flat major

3. G minor–B flat major–G minor

4. Ambiguous: B flat major / G minor

5. G minor

6. B flat major

7. C minor–G minor–C minor (coda E flat major)

8. G minor–B flat major–D minor–G minor

By the time we reach the fifth piece, G minor is established as the center, and confirmed with the final piece (we must remember that the relative major B flat is almost interchangeable with the minor mode of G for composers of Schumann's generation).

A summary, however, gives little idea of the subtlety of Schumann's treatment of tonal relations. In *Kreisleriana*, the pivotal moment in which the tonal unity is achieved is the fourth piece. It is also the lyrical center and demands a very slow tempo. (It is one of the rare pieces of Schumann with a genuinely supple, almost improvised handling of the phrase. There are eight beats to the bar, but most of the phrases are twelve beats long.)

The music starts as if in the middle of a phrase: the key is clearly B flat major. The tonal clarity is ruffled, however, as the opening phrase is repeated in E flat major and then in C minor. With the freedom of an improvisation the piece returns through F minor to the original key of B flat, and the first phrase is repeated. At this point Schumann tries the experiment of imposing a radical harmonic ambiguity on the sense of tonality. The opening melody is transferred to the bass, and begins in G minor. It continues in the bass, now completely unharmonized, to cadence *on* a B♭—but *in* what key? Melodically the phrase is rounded off by a conventional B flat major cadence, but the dominant seventh of G minor, which is the last harmony to be sounded, is still to be resolved, and the melody itself descends with an F♯ to the cadence. This would imply that the final B♭ is to be harmonized with a G minor sixth chord, but the conventional melodic form of the cadence will not allow this. Two contradictory harmonizations of the low B♭ are implied, and there is no way of deciding—both are equally incorrect, and the cadence necessarily sounds incomplete. This enables Schumann to dare to demand a very long pause, with a fermata indicated over every beat—no matter how long the pause, however, the cadence is suspicious, and the listener cannot quite believe that it is final.

In the more agitated middle section that follows, the ambiguity of key is artfully sustained: the opening notes suggest a decision in favor of B flat major, but the F♯ quickly turns the music back to G minor. Bars 14 and 15, although hinting at G minor, reinstate B flat major, at which point Schumann pulls off an effect both poetic and sly at the same time: bars 16 and 17 repeat 14 and 15 with the melody an octave higher, and change the last chord to a dominant seventh of G minor, emphasized by a *ritardando*.

Schumann's *ritardandi* are highly personal: they are mostly intended to be very brief, and, above all, they must be unprepared, catch the listener by surprise. In this central section all of the phrases are equal in length, and the various indications of *ritardando* imply a free rubato that molds the phrases and removes their rigidity. They do not always occur at the ends of phrases. The *ritardando* in bar 21 is intended much more for the opening of the final phrase of this section, to allow the listener to perceive the wonderful overlapping of voices as the bass anticipates the C minor harmony of the next bar while all the other voices continue to sound a G major seventh chord—and Schumann insists on a pedal which will sustain all these voices even through the next chord, an exquisite effect if the indication *pianissimo* is followed. In the concluding bars of the central section the main theme is played in canon between soprano and bass. The ending is a half cadence on the dominant of G minor—but the F♯ is immediately altered to a G♭ and the chord to a diminished seventh as the oscillation between G minor and B flat major is carried further.

The G♭ is then unobtrusively lowered to an F♮, and the first three bars return with a thickening of the harmony at the end. For the cadence, marked *adagio,* the first edition produced a wonderfully strange new version of the cadence at the end of the *Impromptus.* It is a half cadence on the dominant of G, but the F♯ in the final chord is withheld, and the E♮ from the A major chord is sustained intrusively into the chord of D. (The accent is intended for the E♮; the pianist must pick it out of the harmony and allow it to sing into the next sonority.)

The most surprising detail is that the D immediately under the E♮, and which should resolve it, is played, but only briefly, and then withdrawn, and this allows the still sustained E a new prominence. The E is finally removed and the D very softly put back at the last moment—too late, one might say, as the sense of unresolved dissonance has lasted too long to be satisfactorily dissipated by such a timid measure which leaves not even a full triad but only the bare fifths still sounding.

Schumann spoiled this inspiration by supplying the full perfect triad in the second edition. No work, not even the *Davidsbündlertänze* or the *Concerto without Orchestra,* suffered as much from Schumann's misguided rewriting as *Kreisleriana.* The most deplorable of the revisions was the addition of repeat signs to the first two pieces (similar additions were made throughout the *Davidsbündlertänze*). It is true that many of Schumann's phrases slip by like fleeting visions, giving the music its sense of caprice, and even at times a fragility which rivals the delicacy of Chopin. In later years Schumann seems to have been concerned to endow the music with the healthy, rational solidity it lacked. He may have made the early works easier to listen to, but he removed some of their poetry and much of their vitality. Attempting to erase the eccentricity, he made his conceptions more commonplace.

The end of the fifth piece of *Kreisleriana* demonstrates how the suppression of the odd detail made the later edition not only less imaginative but also less effective. In the original version this satirical, even sardonic scherzo—evidently more the image of the cat rather than of the young Kapellmeister—ended with only a half cadence which led directly into the following piece:

In the second edition a more traditional ending was substituted, with a reassuring final tonic chord:

It is the opening of the sixth piece that loses its effect: it is even, in my experience, difficult to begin it persuasively after the revised ending. With the original half cadence, however, the sixth piece seems to arise naturally out of the sonority of the final chord. The original edition makes for a greater unity between the satirical and lyric pieces, and more closely realizes the ideals of E. T. A. Hoffmann.

In no part of *Kreisleriana* is the influence of Hoffmann more important than in the final pieces, numbers 7 and 8. In the first of these a turbulent violence moves with continuous energy and a final acceleration, only to be succeeded by a coda with which it has nothing in common—a distant chorale, like a wind band playing outdoors in a park:

Several passages of this number exhibit one of Schumann's favorite harmonic procedures, a movement through the diatonic circle of fifths

or

Pages like this are sometimes the occasion of a serious reproach to the composer: such commonplaces should have been beneath him. The progression does indeed occur with incredible frequency throughout Western music from the seventeenth to the twentieth centuries. Arnold Schoenberg, and many others, mocked the practice and objected to it wherever they found it. It is true that it becomes monotonous in Vivaldi, that J. S. Bach often varied the voice leading in the sequences to make it more interesting while preserving the harmonic progression, and that Mozart frequently employed the diatonic circle in transitions to give the impression of the inevitable arrival at a theme. The sequence creates a sense of forward drive without effort: it was essential to the contemporary idea of harmonic rhythm. Schumann obviously loved the progression, luxuriated in it, and almost, one might say, wallowed in it. If we wish to maintain that it is a vice, then we must logically admit that it is a pleasure, a genuine temptation. It is, nevertheless, used with great effectiveness here: it imparts an irresistible impetus that propels the music onward. The sequence has a physical effect, a force of motion, as composer and listener abandon themselves to it and allow themselves to be carried along by the energy.

The final cadence of the seventh piece is very slightly troubled, partially opened up by turning the last resolving chord into a 6/4 inversion. The last piece follows directly: "Fast and playful," in a relentless, unceasing dotted 6/8 rhythm, a difficult rhythm for most pianists to maintain at such length, as the

threatens to spill over into a duple form (as in the majority of performances of the opening movement of Beethoven's Seventh Symphony):

This *scherzando* character piece is unique in its treatment of the bass. The indication *Die Bässe durchaus leicht und frei* ("The bass light and free throughout") is misleading: the bass is not free, it only sounds free. In order for it to sound free, however, it must be played absolutely strictly. Schumann has placed many of the bass notes on the wrong beat: coming too late or too early for the harmony, emphasizing the weakest beats with no justification from the melody, at odds in fact with the rest of the texture. (The bass is delicately but clearly wrong in bars 5, 10, 13, 14, and 21.)

The melody is played, all twenty-eight bars of it, three times in a simple *ABACA* rondo form; the first of the subsidiary sections is a long lyrical melody played in the left hand in a duple time against the right hand's continuous dotted triple time, while the second is an outburst of power marked *Mit aller Kraft* ("With all force") in the dotted rhythm, both sections in striking contrast with each other as well as with the playful opening strain. The range of sentiment is remarkable. Each time the opening section comes back, the bass returns in a different, more and more unexpected way (this makes the piece difficult to memorize, and it is rare to hear an absolutely accurate performance):

In these last thirty-three bars (certainly intended to be interpreted with no final slackening of tempo), the music simply disappears. The free movement of the bass that contradicts almost irrationally the dancing rhythm of the melody has an analogue in a letter of the poet Clemens Brentano:

> When writing verse, I let language itself take over and do its own work leaping like a melody, while my consciousness interrupts from time to time like a bass. (To Luise Hensel, December 1819)

Schumann's technique enlivens the strict four-bar phrase structure, as the bass attacks the authority of the bar line with its unexpected emphases, above all it gives the impression of an unconstrained improvisation that refuses to bend to any rigid form. Like the Romantic poets, Schumann both opposed and combined rational and irrational, conscious and unconscious, but here the unpredictable bass against the regular pattern of the melody is less a result of this than an image of the process, a metaphor for the interaction of the logic of day and night.

The accents in the right hand in bars 10 to 12 work similarly:

A surprising accent on the A♭, on the weakest place in the bar, is followed by an unaccented G in the same position, then both notes are given an accent. These are like the accents in the opening piece: they may suggest the counterpoint of an inner voice, but they do not set up a true polyphonic texture. In terms of voice leading, they come from nowhere, and they lead to nothing. They disturb the regular surface of the melody; they hint at forces that will not discover themselves, an ironic interference with the course of the music.

Out of phase

Schumann's rhythm is obsessional: once he has started a pattern he often seems unable to alter it without a considerable effort of will. Equally obsessional, naturally, are the attempts to counter the main pattern by accents that have little contrapuntal justification and act as slight shocks. Most of the middle section of the second movement of the Fantasy in C Major, op. 17, seems to blur the listener's perception of the bar line; the reaffirmation of the bar line at the end of the first phrase, for example, is deliberately willful:

The fourth bar interrupts the scheme, with apparent irrationality, and returns momentarily to an accent on the beat. Later the bar line is reasserted by simple accent in the middle of phrases whose shape literally resists the accent (bars 6 and 12 of the following example). Few pianists, indeed, carry out the unexpected indication:

This is surely intended to sound awkward, almost unprovoked, until the return to the opening section allows us to hear that the superimposed accents indicated the correct beat all along, and that the beats we thought were the right ones were in fact an illusion.

The opening of the overture to *Manfred* is famous, or, better, notorious for its notation: what sounds like chords on the beat are all actually syncopated—on paper! (See facing page.)

It is sometimes claimed that the notation gives a different quality to the attack than a simple downbeat. I think that this is an attempt to make audible sense of what cannot be heard. The notation does, indeed, express an anxiety already audible in the harmony, and it may make the orchestral players nervous, but it changes nothing in the sound. It satisfied Schumann's wonderfully idiosyncratic pleasure in hidden contradiction, revealed here to the eye and not to the ear, another example of inaudible music.

Setting bass and melody out of phase with each other is omnipresent in Schumann's early work, although it is rarely exploited with the dramatic effect we find in the last piece of *Kreisleriana*. One of the songs of the Eichendorff *Liederkreis,* "Zwielicht" (Twilight), makes a more expressive use of the device, starting with the first stanza:

> Evening strives to spread its wings,
> The trees stir frighteningly,
> Clouds move like leaden dreams,
> What does this dread signify?

Rasch. ♩ = 132.
Flöten.
Hoboen.
Clarinetten in B.
Fagotte.
Ventilhörner in Es.
Waldhörner in Es.
a 2.
3 Ventiltrompeten in Es.
Alt. Tenor.
Pousaunen.
Bass.
Pauken in Es. B.
Rasch. ♩ = 132.
Violine I.
Violine II.
Bratsche.
Violoncell.
Contrabass.
f

lieb vor an=dern, lass es nicht al = lei = ne gra=sen, Jä = ger zieh'n im
Wald und blasen, Stimmen hin und wieder wan=dern. Hast du ei = nen
Freund hienie=den, trau ihm nicht zu die = ser Stun=de, freundlich wohl mit

Aug' und Mun = de, sinnt er Krieg im tück'schen Frie=den.

In bar 9, the bass is late in reaching the dominant, and the alto has already moved on to anticipate the next harmony and creates a dissonance with the delayed bass. Even more curiously effective is the way the bass abandons the note immediately before the dissonance can be resolved: the resulting void is uncanny. In the next stanza, through bars 16 to 19, the bass is always late, but now sustained until bar 19, when a similar void occurs. The expressive value of Schumann's play with rhythm and counterpoint, however, is best revealed with the last bar of the first stanza, bar 15. The right hand of the piano refuses to follow the singer and delays the release of the G into an F♯, and the resulting clash is profoundly moving, even anguished.

In the penultimate stanza, the out-of-phase relationship intensifies as the bass accelerates in bar 25 and the harmonic sequence no longer falls but rises:

> Do you have a friend here on earth?
> Do not trust him in this hour.

This dislocation of melody and harmony was essential to Schumann's representation of anxiety. It is paralleled on a larger scale by the frequent disruptions of form, the violent contrasts of mood which characterize his longer works before 1840. It is these disruptions that are often attenuated and weakened in the later editions, particularly in the case of *Kreisleriana,* the *Concerto without Orchestra,* and the *Davidsbündlertänze.*

Lyric intensity

The attempt to weaken the energy of the earlier works was accompanied by a loss of vigor in the style of the new ones. Recent attempts to reevaluate the late works and the more orthodox judgment that there was a falling off in the last decade seem to me both correct. The difficulty that Schumann had in sustaining movement in the chamber works and symphonies which occupied his late years is made more evident by his effort to avoid the quirky, irrational details which were so often the inspiration of the piano music and songs. The obsessional rhythms are now unenlivened and unrelieved. Nevertheless, there is an intense, inward, reflective beauty about the later works, and a few rare undeniable masterly successes: the slow movement of the C Major Symphony, many pages of *Faust,* the first of the *Gesänge der Frühe.* It is true that when Schumann abandons a repetitive rhythmic pattern, he has nothing coherent on a large scale to replace it with. The lack of a strongly felt long-range rhythmic plan is disturbing only if one insists unreasonably on looking for it. That is not the way to listen to the later works of Schumann. The late Cello Concerto has nothing to compare with the dramatic structure of the earlier Piano Concerto: in its place there is a continuously developing lyricism, largely meditative in the first two movements; even the scherzo-like finale is relatively undramatic. If the energy had gone out of his style, Schumann knew how to make this loss deeply affecting.

One might say that he burned himself out, similar in this to so many of the other Romantic musicians, and to poets like Wordsworth, Coleridge, Hölderlin, Brentano, and many others. Most fascinating in Schumann's case, however, is that the burnout was successive. Until the age of twenty-eight, he published almost nothing but piano music, and created all the works that are still in the general concert repertoire. Then came his long-hoped-for marriage to Clara Wieck, and with his new happiness for two years he wrote songs. From this short period came every song of his found today in the general repertory: all of the famous sets belong here—the Heine, Körner, and Eichendorff sets, as well as *Dichterliebe* and *Frauenliebe und Leben.* For months on end he produced nearly a song a day. This pattern—an initial enthusiasm and a subsequent tapering off—continued for the next decade. Both Violin Sonatas are fine works, but the first is more immediately attractive and considerably more poetic than the second. Except for *Waldscenen,* the piano music for two hands was of secondary importance in the 1840s, but a new source of energy came from the pedal piano, a piano with the addition of a pedal keyboard like that of an organ. Fired by this novelty, Schumann composed two sets of pieces for the instrument: six canons called Studies for the Pedal Piano, and Sketches for the Pedal Piano. The instrument quickly lost whatever vogue it had once had, and these works are never heard except in transcriptions, and rarely even in that form. The first set, the six canonic studies, is among Schumann's most inspired and original works, greatly admired by Debussy, who arranged the canons for two pianos. The Sketches for Pedal Piano, on the other hand, are a much stodgier collection, with little of the intensity of the canons. Schumann's interest in piano music seems to have been briefly revived by the novel instrument, but it was a short awakening—the duration of one brief opus.

What is most impressive about the canonic Studies is the combination of energetic passion and simple lyricism; they have a sweep and brilliance missing in much of the later music, and appear to be a return to the songs of 1839:

With the exception of the first study, basically a two-part invention with an added bass, these canons show little influence of Bach. The counterpoint is Schumann's own; they are *Lieder* in canonic form.

It would be false to consider that Schumann's uneasiness about his most radical creations was confined to the last decade of his short life. The same uneasiness and self-doubt are already detectable earlier. The poetic original ending of the Fantaisie in C Major was already expunged in the first edition— perhaps because the composer held back the initial publication for more than a year, enough time to doubt the original inspiration. With the first edition of *Dichterliebe,* four of the songs were cut—and they are among the most striking. Some critics feel that it was Schumann's concern for the large-scale structure of the cycle that is responsible for their disappearance, but I do not think that the work gained by the cutting, and I believe that it was a lack of confidence on Schumann's part that caused the excision. They were not published until after his death. If it was merely the interest of the large structure that was Schumann's concern, he could have included the banished songs in the subsequent volumes of *Lieder* that he continued to publish.

The technical difficulty of the accompaniment of one of the songs, "Es leuchtet meine Liebe" (My Love Shone), which calls for a virtuosity greater than for any other of the cycle, may have been the case for its excision. One passage goes:

The tempo *Phantastisch, markirt* is certainly intended to be quick. Another song, "Lehn' deine Wang'" (Lean Your Cheek), has an inconclusive ending on the dominant, of the kind that Schumann was later to disapprove. "Dein Angesicht" (Your Visage) was to become a much admired part of the singers' regular repertory, and Schumann's rejection is harder to comprehend. Perhaps the harmony, the most daring and even most radical of the cycle, and perhaps of Schumann's entire output, may have been the reason:

The move from E flat major to G minor, while exquisitely worked, is not unusual, but the subsequent drop (in bars 10 to 14) from G major to G flat major is a shock. The extraordinary modulation is justified by the text, with its prediction of death:

> And only her lips are red
> Soon, however, Death kisses her pale,
> The light of heaven will be put out.

The return to E flat major is not at all radical, but the contrapuntal handling is a tour de force: the voice appears to move to a cadence in G flat major in bar 17, but the bass in a thematic imitation of the melody has already started to modulate and turns the B♭ in the treble into the dominant of E flat major.

The fourth song to be removed, "Mein Wagen rollet langsam" (My Wagon Rolls Slowly), is in some ways the most interesting. What is innovative here is neither harmony nor melody but the persistence of repetition. The opening represents the slowly turning wagon wheels:

The movement is relentless: Schumann succumbed to the temptation to write a continuous pattern of descending thirds (or rising sixths), and he made no attempt to dress, disguise, or ornament them. The real moment of courage for the composer, however, was the postlude:

Here the simple repetition of the pattern is exploited literally for its monotony, which becomes poetic and fascinating in its creation of tension. It gradually accelerates only to end on an F repeated over and over for ten bars, when the movement of the wheels begins again. It is a beautiful page, obsessive, extreme, and implacable. No contemporary of Schumann, not even Chopin, had dared to go so far. This postlude is an attack on previous musical aesthetics: it arouses interest by a relentless and monotonous exploitation of the commonplace in a dreamlike atmosphere.

The extremes to which Schumann would go in exploiting obsessive detail gave him his power. It deprives most of his work of breadth except for a very few wonderfully successful large works, but in compensation much of his music gains a hypnotic intensity. Even those pieces in a jolly, old German, beer-drinking college-student style take on a neurotic concentration as Schumann pushes the rhythms too far, too long.

At his finest, Schumann uses this power to transform the simplest structures, and to portray the most complex states of feeling with absurdly simple forms. The erotic vision of landscape that Eichendorff wrote in "Mondnacht" (Moonlit Night) is evoked almost austerely:

Zart, heimlich.

Singstimme.

Pianoforte.

Ped: ✻   ritard:

Es war als hätt' der Him = mel die Er = de

still ___ ge = küsst, Dass sie im Blü = = then =

schim = mer von ihm nur träu = men müsst' ___ .

ritard:

I do not think even educated listeners often realize how little there is in this simple form because of how much Schumann succeeds in conveying. The structure is only too easy to summarize:

Introduction	6 bars
A	8 bars
A	8 bars
Introduction	6 bars
A	8 bars
A	8 bars
B combined with Introduction	8 bars
A	8 bars
Coda based on Introduction	8 bars

Almost two thirds of the song consists of only one phrase *(A)* sung five times, the fifth time with the last bars altered (without adding any new notes to the melody) to make a cadence. The single large-scale formal complexity is the combination of the introduction with the opening of the third stanza, which has the only other vocal phrase *(B)* in the work—a combination that Schumann learned from Schubert, "Der Lindenbaum" in particular.

The unprecedented repetition helps to create the sense of stillness demanded by the poem. "It was as if the heaven had quietly kissed the earth." The necessary variety is concentrated within a single phrase, and all the dissonance and all harmonic movement are contained within the first half of the phrase. Most poignant is the clash of E♯ in the voice with E♮ in the bass each time in the second bar of the phrase (bar 8 of the song). Even softened by the dynamics, it is striking each time it comes back: it combines extreme dissonance with extreme delicacy. The second half of the phrase then appears as pure consonance, simple tonic and dominant with the bass descending in exaggerated purity only on the fundamental tonic and dominant roots.

The introduction starts as if in the middle of an already initiated arpeggio on a ninth chord. When it reappears in the third stanza, transposed to the subdominant and combined with a new vocal phrase (bar 47), it provides the only development and dynamic movement in the song. This departure alters the sense of the repeated initial vocal phrase *(A)* when it returns in bar 53: for the first time it is an answer, a consequent to the preceding phrase. The new significance is confirmed by the slight alteration at the end, which makes a full tonic cadence. It is typical of Schumann, however, that the full cadence in the voice is refused by the piano, which deforms the last chords by the sudden addition of a D♮ and produces an unexpected V^7 of IV. This makes the transition between the end of the vocal line and the short postlude wonderfully fluid.

"Mondnacht" shows us that Schumann's obsessive repetition need not lead to expressions of anguish, despair, and melancholy as it so often does, but can be used almost austerely to produce an atmosphere of simple lyricism. Nevertheless, even here the repetitions work obscurely to create emotions harder to define than the musical surface seems to be willing to admit. The feelings aroused by Schumann's craft are rarely as direct or as immediate as those created by the lyrics of Beethoven and Schubert. The repetitions, the out-of-phase rhythms, the sudden appearance of voices that are inexplicable in the polyphonic structure—these characteristics of Schumann's style not only work together but also against each other. They reflect upon one another; they draw attention. The emotions implied by Schumann's art can never seem entirely innocent. Like the other composers of his generation, but more than any of them, Schumann brought a new complexity and a new uneasiness to the art of music, and they are still with us.

Failure and triumph

Schumann is the most representative musical figure of central European Romanticism as much because of his limitations as because of his genius: in his finest works, indeed, he exploited these limitations in such a way that they gave a force to his genius that no other contemporary could attain. The limitations may be summed up simply: a difficulty in dealing with the Classical forms of the previous generation, or what Schumann and his contemporaries conceived to be those forms. Unlike Chopin, Schumann had little appreciation or understanding of Mozart, and by the 1830s any understanding of Haydn had practically disappeared from the world of music. Haydn had come to be only an admirable but primitive forerunner of modern music: a revival of genuine sympathy for his work had to wait for Brahms.

Contemplating the achievement of Beethoven, however, Schumann clearly felt a sense of shame. By comparison with the monumental output of Beethoven, his own works and those of his colleagues seemed to him trivial. There were, he wrote, too many composers of nocturnes, bagatelles, dances, characteristic pieces; what was needed was symphonies, sonatas, quartets—the sublime, in short. No one, least of all Schumann, was able at the time to acknowledge that the fundamental task and achievement of his age was to attain the sublime through the trivial. The old aesthetic of the hierarchy of genres still ruled almost unchallenged, although Schumann's own work, along with that of Chopin and Liszt, had already shaken it to its foundations. For a time in the following decades, Brahms and Wagner were to be able to shore up the classical hierarchy, but the final destruction came with the early years of the twentieth century. This is certainly one of the reasons why the work of Schumann and Chopin has more affinity with the style of Debussy and the early twentieth century than it does with the music of the last half of the nineteenth.

The chief manifestation of the period's awkwardness in handling the great Classical forms was the inability to vary the pulse: the art of moving back and forth with ease between one strong accent to the bar to two accents and even four seems to have died out with Beethoven. This art is essential for the successive combination of different rhythmic textures, and it made the dramatic contrast of the larger forms of the late eighteenth century possible: it was managed by Schumann and his contemporaries only occasionally, and then with difficulty. The change from one texture to another was generally possible for them only by closing one section and opening another. This is the principal reason why their music seems so often to be derived from the unified textures of Baroque style. No doubt the study of Bach was an influence, but there must have been more compelling forces at work: Beethoven's familiarity with the *Well-Tempered Keyboard* from childhood was at least as great as Schumann's, but it never gave him a taste for the unrelieved, homogeneous textures that we find so often in Schumann. On the rare occasions when Beethoven writes a *perpetuum mobile,* he varies the interior accents of the phrase, not from section to section as Schumann would do, but within the opening bars. At the very beginning of the finale of his Sonata for Piano, op. 54, the accents suddenly force the weight without warning to the second sixteenth note of the beat, and then to the third:

and these accents give a momentary shock to the sense of pulse, even when, as here, the original pulsation continues to govern the form.

Schumann was unable—or unwilling, it comes to the same thing—to indulge in such a subtle manipulation of emphasis (although, as we have seen, he was a master of the irrational disruption of the listener's sense of the beat). His music has a forward-moving energy that is unyielding when compared to Beethoven's, even to those works which, like the finale of the Seventh Symphony, seem so close to the style of the next generations. At the opening of the finale of opus 54, Beethoven's accents shape the uniform flow and give it a distinctive character. Schumann's disconcerting play of accents, which we have observed in the *Kreisleriana* and the Toccata, are attempts to stem an onward-rushing movement, to exert, if only for a moment, a transitory control, or to alter the character of the rhythmic structure slightly without changing its nature.

The difficulty experienced by composers of the period immediately after the death of Beethoven with integrating some kind of rhythmic variety into their large-scale structures is mirrored on the level of small detail. The themes of contrasting character that we sometimes find in Mozart and Beethoven (more rarely in Haydn) disappear from music almost completely in the 1830s. These themes had enabled earlier composers to elaborate a subtle play of different character throughout the work. The opening of Mozart's Sonata for Piano in D Major, K.576, contrasts a hunting-horn call with a graceful, *galant* answer. The contrast is followed by a synthesis, as both parts of the theme are drawn together under an *obbligato* counterpoint that shares in both characters:

Beethoven, at the opening of the Sonata for Piano in E flat Major, op. 31, no. 3, combines an oddly unconventional and passionate phrase of slowly increasing expressive force with a conventional although graceful cadence:

This contrast, too, is overridden almost immediately, with the opening phrase and cadence united:

A new synthesis appears, even more laconically, at the end of the exposition:

This complex yoking together of eccentric passion and conventional charm runs throughout the movement, and derives clearly from the opening bars.

Such complexity of character within one phrase was no longer welcome to Romantic composers. They felt, no doubt, that it was only a static complexity in which two opposing elements coexist and balance each other. For the contrast within a single phrase the later composers, Schumann above all, substituted a developing and dynamic complexity of the listener's successive experience of a theme—not a formal development in the light of Beethoven's practice, which gradually and logically revealed latent possibilities of the theme, but one in which the theme would assume different sentimental and picturesque characters through reharmonization, rhythmic distortion, and sometimes simple insistent reiteration. The kaleidescopic persona taken on by Clara's motto in the *Davidsbündlertänze* or the Sphinxes in *Carnaval* are only the most remarkable examples of such development. The individual pieces of both these collections are less a set of portraits than a series of masks—and underneath the mask we find not (as the titles would indicate) the identities of Schumann's friends and lovers but the faces of "Florestan" and "Eusebius," the divided personality that he created for himself.[3]

The malaise experienced with large, unified Classical forms by the generation of composers born around 1810 testifies to a loss of faith and even of interest in the calculated balances and clear articulations that these old structures implied. It corresponds to a general loss of faith in purely rational systems, a mistrust of the eighteenth-century Enlightenment and the Kantian certainties.

---

3. Schumann himself, however, in a letter to Clara of March 17, 1838, said that the *Davidsbündlertänze* are related to *Carnaval* as faces to masks.

Perhaps it also accounts for the fascination with insanity and the irrational. In music, the most original minds of the 1830s were ill at ease with those Classical procedures conceived as valid for a large variety of forms, and which can therefore be projected in advance. In the large Classical forms, it is true, the unpredictable can happen, as it happens throughout the music of Haydn and Beethoven, and even, for all his conventionality, in the work of Mozart—perhaps, indeed, most startlingly in Mozart because of the more ostentatiously conventional framework: we can predict some aspects of the form, and the composer can then surprise us, frustrate us and eventually satisfy and delight us. In the Ballades of Chopin or the *Kreisleriana* and *Davidsbündlertänze* of Schumann, however, prediction and surprise are downgraded to the level of detail rather than the whole structure. The aspects of their large forms which are conventional tend to be perfunctory—we can have few expectations of what direction the more original inventions in the large form will take because we have almost no precedents on which we can rely. It is true that the Romantic composer had models with which he worked, but he often tried successfully to make it seem as if the music had been created sui generis. Above all, these works appear to deal from moment to moment with the matter at hand as it comes along, with no calculation of the balances and elegant proportions necessary for the late eighteenth-century forms.

For this reason, Schumann is more representative of the new aesthetic than Chopin, who mastered the late Classical sonata style of Hummel and created something more powerful and original with it; and more representative, too, than Liszt, who largely evaded the Classical sonata except for two magnificent attempts, the *Faust* Symphony and the Sonata for Piano in B Minor (in both of which, instead of using sonata technique to unfold a dramatic form as Beethoven had done, he used a dramatic scenario to embody certain Classical conventions fundamentally reshaped by the cyclical experiments of Schubert and Beethoven). Schumann persisted in trying to adapt to the Classical models, to twist his own style to fit the mold, perhaps never realizing that the faith that Beethoven still held in harmonic balance and in an equilibrium of large-scale proportions was no longer tenable.

Schumann could not grasp that any form of Classical sonata demanded the kind of clearly articulated oppositions which were antipathetic to him or which his technique could not encompass: oppositions of large-scale harmonic regions, of themes, or of rhythmic textures. Schumann's great harmonic strength was in the blending or merging of tonalities; his melodic genius lay in the picturesque transformation of a motif into different characters; his weakness was his inability to move convincingly from one rhythmic texture to another. The openings of some of his most successful works, like the Novelette in F sharp Minor, have a rhythmic drive that cannot be reshaped, but that must move on unrelieved until it is exhausted:

The exposition of the finest and most personal of his sonatas, no. 1 for piano in F sharp minor, is structured in separate sections like one of his Novelettes: the first theme drives to a fermata; a second theme expends all its energy; a lyric version of the main theme and a shorter *giocoso* version of it provide a simple and brief transition to an exhausted closing theme. There is, of course, nothing reprehensible about this pattern, nor anything wrong with calling it a sonata. It gives the development that follows, however, no articulated tension to work with, and Schumann is obliged to induce excitement with a series of sequential movements that come to a triumphal end on a tonic cadence—only this is not yet the end, the Classical tradition demanded a recapitulation, and Schumann cannot find the courage, inspiration, or sense to abridge one jot of the conventional repeat. All of it is beautiful, but it lacks the compactness and the compelling logic that the Classical models provided. Particularly awkward is the opening of the recapitulation after what seems like a splendid final cadence.

In the last decade of his life, Schumann was unable to resist the demands of what he and his age judged to be the conventions of the past. Chopin's compression of the entire final return into a few bars (as we saw in the Third Ballade, the Polonaise-Fantaisie, and other works) or his omission of the whole first section of the recapitulation of a sonata must have seemed to Schumann an eccentric, non-German refusal to accept the responsibilities of large-scale form. In the final years of Schumann's life these responsibilities are only too relentlessly carried out. Above all, the addition of repeat signs to many phrases and passages of his youthful works is a witness to his obsession for underlining any detail that might not be obvious, similar to his insistence on doubling all important lines in orchestrating his symphonies, as if the listener could not be trusted to understand.

A comparison with Schubert, the idol of Schumann's youth, is illuminating. In the works of Schubert modelled upon the Classical tradition, impromptu as well as sonata, there is a similarly literal and almost naive insistence upon recapitulating every element of the exposition, and a mapping out of large areas as very elaborate and repetitive sequences: fifty-two bars going from B major through F major to F sharp in the first movement of the Trio for Piano and Strings in E flat Major are immediately transposed to modulate from F sharp through C to C sharp, but this piece is laid out in a leisurely manner for a small public of twenty or thirty friends (an equal tolerance and pleasure in the repetition is perhaps harder to come by in the grander concert halls of today). In Schumann's imitation of Schubert's and Beethoven's large patterns, the easygoing expansiveness has been replaced by a relentless rhythmic tension. This is particularly true of the finales of the *Concerto without Orchestra* (the Sonata in F Minor for Piano) and of the Quartet for Piano and Strings in E flat Major, op. 47, in which the continuous use of short four-bar sequential patterns within larger sequential structures—piling sequence on sequence, so to speak—impels the music forward without varying the pattern.

Schumann's genius was as destructive as it was creative: we might say that he destroyed as he created. No one did more to make the Classical forms untenable, the forms that he himself revered and tried to imitate. Even the simple *ABA* structure lost its coherence in his hands: sectional works like the *Humoresk* and the Novelette in F sharp Minor have trios within trios, and earlier pages return unpredictably, making unexpected outer frames. As we have seen, what sounds like a middle section in the *Davidsbündlertänze* leads not to a return of the opening frame but to something new. The sonata forms that had such prestige were the greatest challenge to Schumann, and it was here that his intransigence made their inadequacy for the new developments in the musical language so manifest. The obsessional nature of Schumann's style resulted in a continual disparity between traditional form and musical idea. Even when Schumann creates wonderfully powerful effects out of this disparity, the awkward moments are almost everywhere to be found, transitions where the music simply seems to stop, as in the last movement of the G minor piano sonata, and to start again as if in response to some formal requirement. Only with the first movement of the Phantasie, originally entitled "Ruins," was Schumann able to rival Beethoven with complete success. Chopin accommodated himself to a loose version of the sonata principle largely derived from Hummel, and created something original and deeply satisfying but more diffuse than Schubert's work in the Classical style. Liszt largely ignored the Classical sonata except for the eccentric and splendid experiments of the Piano Sonata, the "Dante" Sonata, and the "Faust" Symphony. Schumann was both less accommodating and more obstinate: he would not, or could not, change his style nor renounce the attempt to meet the challenge set by Beethoven. The influence of Schumann is therefore paradoxical. The most immediate effect of his work was on Brahms, who did achieve Schumann's ambition and succeeded in restoring a small part of the Classical tradition. It seems to me, however, that the most profound influence was on Debussy, who loved the music of Schumann and understood its capricious imagination: he was able to adapt some of the unresolved sonorities and the fleeting phrases that Schumann himself distrusted into a new musical style, one almost totally liberated from the academic requirements of the past—to realize, in short, both the destructive and creative elements of Schumann's art in his own way.

In the end, the inability to reproduce the full dramatic articulation of the Classical forms that Schumann admired and revered was tragic, but it had compensations and rewards. The obsessive rhythms have a passion that a more controlled structure could not provide in movements like the opening Allegro of the *Rhenish* Symphony, and there are works of resigned meditation like the Cello Concerto (where any classical tension would only adulterate the lyricism) or the Romances for Oboe that could never have come from a composer with the Classical technique to which Schumann aspired.

There is also an extraordinary originality in Schumann's ability to move from one theme to the next and from one tonality to another without preparation and without contrast, spinning out both melodies and tonal movement in one unbroken continuity. This is where Schumann exploited his limitations to achieve effects that were inimitable. It is not clear if he recognized his own originality or if he was able to measure it, but one work, the sixth Novelette in A Major, suggests that he had some consciousness of it. In this work the spinning out of themes and tonalities moves in a continuous acceleration. The tonal changes are at first all mediants (going from A major to F and then to D flat), and they are exemplary for their time in the way they take place with no warning and no preparation:

The principal theme is not the opening one but a lyrical eight-bar phrase played over and over unaltered in different keys, as if its identity were enough to guarantee pleasure (we should remember that Schumann liked to play one of the themes from the last movement of the C Major Fantasy for hours on end). The succession of different tonalities whirls by without establishing any key firmly.[4] Combined with the steady acceleration, the effect is hypnotic:

4. From bar 85 to 174 the succession of lightly established key centers is G♭, D♭, f♯, A, E, C, a, d, and then the whole section is literally repeated from bars 175 to 264 a half step lower, beginning in F and ending in c♯ minor.

Finally, the acceleration increases drastically with a fast stretto, and the opening tempo (but not the opening theme) returns triumphantly:

The end of this Novelette conceals an example of Schumann's humor, comparable to Tieck's witty opening of a play with its epilogue. Poetic, paradoxical, and secret, the final cadence may be taken as symbolic of Schumann's age and of his place in it. Hidden within these bars is a violin that tunes up:

This almost fails to serve as a final cadence; it lacks firmness, decision, conviction. The music does not end, but dies away, and in its fall is wittily concealed a new beginning.

Index of Names and Works